Orkney

the Bradt Travel Guide

Mark Rowe

edition
I

www.bradtguides.com

Bradt Travel Guides Ltd, UK
The Globe Pequot Press Inc, USA

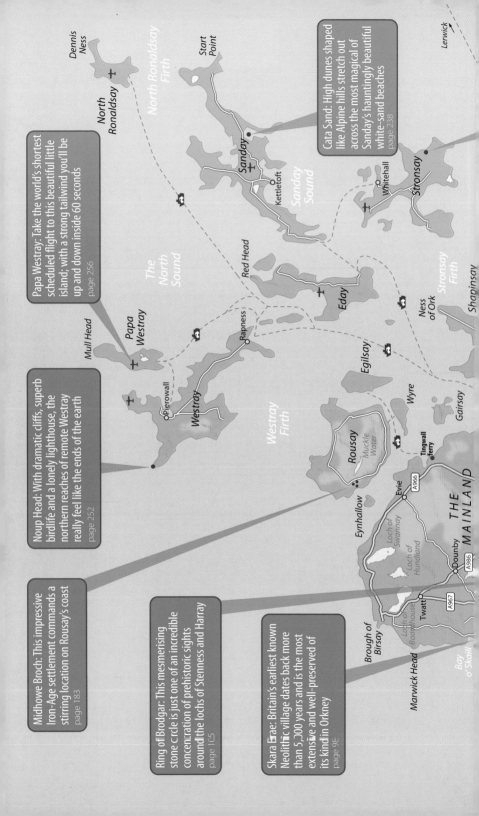

Midhowe Broch: This impressive Iron-Age settlement commands a stirring location on Rousay's coast page 183

Noup Head: With dramatic cliffs, superb birdlife and a lonely lighthouse, the northern reaches of remote Westray really feel like the ends of the earth page 252

Papa Westray: Take the world's shortest scheduled flight to this beautiful little island; with a strong tailwind you'll be up and down inside 60 seconds page 256

Cata Sand: High dunes shaped like Alpine hills stretch out across the most magical of Sanday's hauntingly beautiful white-sand beaches page 238

Ring of Brodgar: This mesmerising stone circle is just one of an incredible concentration of prehistoric sights around the lochs of Stenness and Harray page 165

Skara Brae: Britain's earliest known Neolithic village dates back more than 5,000 years and is the most extensive and well-preserved of its kind in Orkney page 98

Dennis Ness

North Ronaldsay

North Ronaldsay Firth

Start Point

Sanday

Kettletoft

Sanday Sound

Whitehall

Stronsay

Lerwick

The North Sound

Red Head

Eday

Stronsay Firth

Ness of Ork

Shapinsay

Mull Head

Papa Westray

Pierowall

Rapness

Westray

Egilsay

Wyre

Gairsay

Westray Firth

Rousay

Muckle Water

Tingwall Terry

Eynhallow

Evie

A966

Loch of Swannay

THE MAINLAND

Brough of Birsay

Dounby

Loch of Hundland

A966

A967

Twatt

Loch of Boardhouse

Marwick Head

Bay o'Skaill

A967

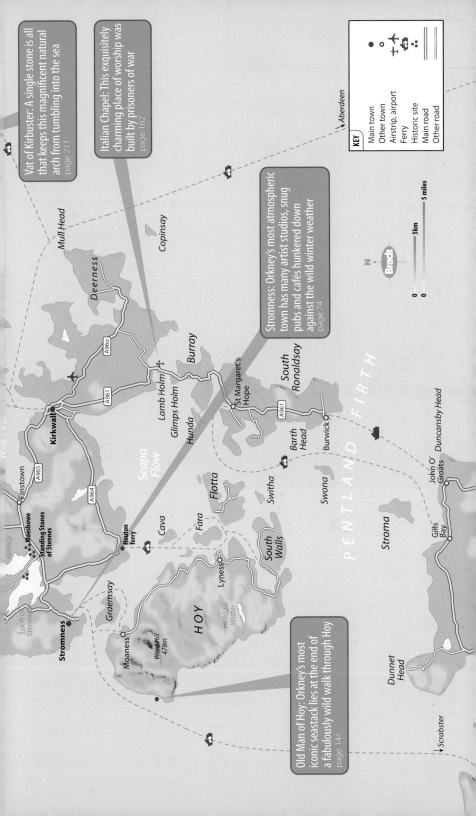

Vat of Kirbuster: A single stone is all that keeps this magnificent natural arch from tumbling into the sea page 211

Italian Chapel: This exquisitely charming place of worship was built by prisoners of war page 162

Stromness: Orkney's most atmospheric town has many artist studios, snug pubs and cafés hunkered down against the wild winter weather page 74

Old Man of Hoy: Orkney's most iconic seastack lies at the end of a fabulously wild walk through Hoy page 142

→ Aberdeen

N

Bradt

0   5km
0   5 miles

Mull Head

Copinsay

Deerness

A960

Burray

Lamb Holm

Glimps Holm

Hunda

St Margaret's Hope

South Ronaldsay

A961

Barth Head

Burwick

Kirkwall

A961

A965

Finstown

A964

Houton ferry

Scapa Flow

Cava

Fara

Flotta

Switha

Swona

South Walls

Lyness

Maeshowe

Standing Stones of Stennes

Loch of Stenness

Graemsay

Moaness

Ward Hill 479m

HOY

Heldale Water

Stromness

PENTLAND FIRTH

Stroma

Duncansby Head

John O'Groats

Gills Bay

Dunnet Head

→ Scrabster

Orkney
Don't
miss...

Wildlife
Otters, seals, diving
gannets (pictured) and the
fearless bonxie — or great
skua — are just a few of
Orkney's natural highlights
(O) page 8

Archaeology
From Neolithic 'blockbusters' such as
Skara Brae (pictured) to little-visited
Iron Age tombs and brochs, Orkney
runs an archaeological timeline
spanning more than 5,000 years
(VS/KL) page 98

Scapa Flow
A huge natural harbour, Scapa Flow forms the backdrop to many journeys around Orkney and is a stirring mixture of stunning coastal landscapes, wildlife and important wartime history (O)
page 6

The islands beyond the Mainland
From wild and lonely Hoy (pictured) in the south to the beautiful North Isles, Orkney's smaller islands will enchant you with their dramatic landscapes
(VS/CK)

Food and drink
Orkney has long been a pioneer of mouth-watering seafood and farm produce, and is home to the world's most northerly distilleries (SS) page 57

Orkney in colour

above   The islands boast countless pristine beaches; pictured here, the vast crescent of Whitemill Bay on Sanday (CC/S) page 234

left   Located on Stronsay, the Vat of Kirbuster sea arch is one of Orkney's premier geological attractions (O) page 211

below   The highest point on Orkney, Ward Hill looks and feels much more like a mountain (aw/A) page 142

above   The UK's tallest land-based lighthouse at Dennis Ness is a true beacon of North Ronaldsay (O) page 275

right   At 450ft high, the Old Man of Hoy is the tallest sea stack in Europe (SS) page 144

below   Separated from the Mainland by a causeway, the Brough of Birsay is a supremely elemental defensive headland teeming with history and wildlife (ID/A) page 95

above left   Thought to be modelled on Jerusalem's Church of the Holy Sepulchre, the ruined church at Orphir is Orkney's only surviving medieval round church (VS/KL) page 112

above right   Dating to the 12th century, St Magnus Kirk on Egilsay is close to where the eponymous saint was murdered (CH/D) page 188

left   The interior of the tiny Italian Chapel on Lamb Holm is exquisitely ornate, with magnificent wrought-iron framework and elaborate frescoes (PF/D) page 162

below   St Magnus Cathedral is the historical heart of Kirkwall, and arguably the most important church on the islands (VS/KL) page 121

AUTHOR

Mark Rowe is a qualified journalist with more than 25 years' experience of writing for national newspapers and magazines and, nowadays, online. His first published article, on the etiquette of slurping noodles, was published in *The Independent* in 1991 after a solo six-month backpacking trip around China. He cut his journalistic teeth at the *Grimsby Evening Telegraph*, reporting on haddock smuggling and dancing-pet competitions. He then became a staff writer at *The Independent* and *The Independent on Sunday*, where

he is the long-standing author of the Walk of the Month column. He is author of the Behind the Headlines column for *BBC Countryfile* magazine, contributes to *BBC Wildlife* and writes regularly for *Geographical*, the magazine of the Royal Geographical Society and *Nat Geo Traveller*, from the National Geographic stable. Mark lives in Bristol but is optimistic that he will one day finally persuade his wife and three children to relocate to a Scottish island. He is the author of *Outer Hebrides, The Western Isles of Scotland from Lewis to Barra*, also published by Bradt.

You can follow Mark on Twitter ➤ @wanderingrowe or via his website **w** markrowe.eu.

AUTHOR'S STORY

My first visit to Orkney back in 1988 was probably similar to that of many people who come to these islands. I stayed in Stromness for a couple of days and visited Skara Brae and the Ring of Brodgar. Then I went home. The main research for this guide took place over nine months in 2018 but this built upon more than 20 visits in the intervening years during which time I quickly realised there was a land to be explored beyond Orkney's Neolithic epicentre.

Towards the end of researching this book, I was waiting with my son at North Ronaldsay airfield for the tiny eight-seater aircraft to whisk us back to Kirkwall. Out of sight, along the coast, we could hear seals 'groaning'. Oscar opened the door to the airfield 'terminal' – which had the dimensions of a large garden shed – and a wren fluttered out. Then we were off. As the aircraft flew in an arc south I looked out and realised that I could now identify not just the islands but every beach and township and even pinpoint some of the less heralded of the islands' countless burial mounds. I'd also walked across just about every edge of coastline and island lanes.

My strongest impressions certainly include the archaeological sites but they range further: walking through a sea mist on Sanday to emerge on dunes at Cata Sands, watching gannets fly past at arm's length on Westray, astonishing sunsets on Stronsay and wondering if 10.00 is too early to eat a chocolate brownie from Argo's bakery in Kirkwall (it isn't).

As much as anything, I cherish Orkney for being somewhere that shows us all that human beings can live on a developed 21st-century island and still have time for others and work with the environment rather than against it. In this respect they sit comfortably within the remit of Bradt's emphasis on places that have stepped back from the madding crowd. I'd like to extend my thanks to them and Rachel Fielding for having the vision to commission this book.

PUBLISHER'S FOREWORD *Adrian Phillips, Managing Director*

When we published Mark Rowe's *Outer Hebrides* guide in 2017, it quickly gained a reputation not only for the quality of the information but of the writing. Mark has knowledge and passion, and the means to communicate it in a way that gives pleasure to the reader. And so we were thrilled when he said he'd like to write a guide to Orkney because this is an archipelago deserving of some lyricism in its treatment. It's a place of mysterious ancient sites, of groaning seals and of islands that seem to shimmer and vanish as you watch them across the water (a phenomenon locals call the 'heather-blether', which tells you much about this wonderful spot).

First edition published May 2019
Bradt Travel Guides Ltd
31a High Street, Chesham, Bucks HP5 1BW, England
www.bradtguides.com
Print edition published in the USA by The Globe Pequot Press Inc,
PO Box 480, Guilford, Connecticut 06437-0480

Text copyright © 2019 Mark Rowe
Maps copyright © 2019 Bradt Travel Guides Ltd; includes map data © OpenStreetMap contributors; contains Ordnance Survey data © Crown copyright and database right 2019
Photographs copyright © 2019 Individual photographers (see below)
Project manager: Laura Pidgley
Cover research: Marta Bescos
Cover designer: Fiona Cox

ISBN: 978 1 78477 630 5

British Library Cataloguing in Publication Data
A catalogue record for this book is available from the British Library

Photographs Alamy Stock Images: Ian Dagnall (ID/A), Iain Sarjeant (IS/A); allan wright (aw/A); Dreamstime.com: Paula Fisher (PF/D), CreativeHearts (CH/D); Orkney.com (O); Mark Rowe (MR); Shutterstock.com: Catriona Crawford (CC/S), Ian Cooper Images (ICI/S), Claudine Van Massenhove (CVM/S), Michel Masik (MM/S), The Perfect (TP/S); SuperStock (SS); VisitScotland: Colin Keldie (VS/CK), Kenny Lamb (VS/KL), Paul Tomkins (VS/PT)
Front cover Noup Head lighthouse (IS/A)
Back cover Standing Stones of Stenness (VS/KL); Walking on Hoy (VS/CK)
Title page Italian Chapel, Lambs Holm (VS/KL); Puffins (O); Hundland Loch (ICI/S)

Maps David McCutcheon FBCart.S

Typeset by D & N Publishing, Baydon, Wiltshire and Ian Spick, Bradt Travel Guides
Production managed by Jellyfish Print Solutions; printed in India
Digital conversion by www.dataworks.co.in

Acknowledgements

A huge thank you to Dave Flanagan of Orkney Tourism who has been selfless and incredibly supportive of this project. To say I owe him a pint is an understatement – more like a whole pub. Several others have also been generous with their knowledge and always offered advice with good humour. These include Destination Orkney (w orkney.com), the Digital Media Orkney Project, archaeologist Caroline Wickham-Jones, Dr Simon Hall for his expertise in island culture and Orcadian, and Loganair pilot Colin McAllister. Also: Julie and Mike Rickards at Straigona on the Mainland, Karen Crichton at the Ferry Inn and Jeanne Bouza Rose in Stromness, Jennifer Foley at the Papay Hostel, Papay Ranger Jonathan Ford, Mick Fraser at Bankburn House, Jane Taylor and Geoff Betts at Backaskaill on Sanday, Paul Hollinrake of RSPB Shapinsay, Lynne Collinson and Sheila Garson on Shapinsay, Alan Leitch at RSPB Orkney, Jerry Wood at No 1 Broughton and Lizza Hume on Westray, Ann Cant of Roadside B&B and Maggie Brown (for baking tips) on Eday, Andrew Blake of Orkney Ferries, Emily Smith of Wild Heather Crafts on Hoy, Alison Duncan and Alex Wright at the North Ronaldsay Bird Observatory and, for showing me how table tennis can be made into a hit film, Mark Jenkins of Westside Cinema. Thanks also go for support and general helpfulness to the folk at NorthLink Ferries, Loganair, FlyBMI and Caledonian Sleeper.

DEDICATION

To the bonxies of Hoy, who don't miss much.

Contents

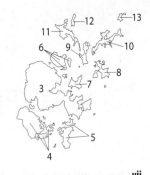

LIST OF MAPS

FOLLOW US

Tag us in your posts to share your adventures using this guide with us – we'd love to hear from you.

- ◼ BradtTravelGuides
- ◼ @BradtGuides & @wanderingrowe
- ◼ @bradtguides
- ◼ bradtquides
- ◼ bradtquides

Introduction

There's an ancient ring to the name 'Orkney'. In the mind's eye it can conjure up a timeless landscape, where, for more than 5,000 years, people have settled and then moved on. In their wake, they left their still-visible imprints, from Neolithic villages and chambered cairns to Bronze Age burial mounds, Iron Age brochs, Viking graves and medieval churches.

Yet Orkney is about so much more than its astonishing archaeological heritage. True enough, visiting the islands and not seeing the prehistoric village of Skara Brae or the burial chamber of Maeshowe would be like skipping the Pyramids of Giza in Egypt or the Great Wall in China (the Orkney structures are, incidentally, older than both those famous sites). And you should indeed explore the Mainland, as, logically enough, the main island of Orkney is called, where you will find the other key Neolithic sites of Maeshowe, the Ring and Ness of Brodgar and the Standing Stones of Stenness.

Yet in many respects these are simply a gateway into an extraordinary island chain. Stand on Ward Hill on Hoy, Orkney's highest summit, and you can see all but one of the archipelago's 70 or so islands laid out around you. Look north and, beyond the Mainland, the skyline blurs then sharpens into the solid lump that is Rousay, behind which the headland of Noup Hill on Westray pokes out westwards. Turning to the northeast, Sanday's long, spindly backbone appears as a curtain draped behind the neighbouring island of Stronsay. Everywhere, there is water: most substantially right in front of you lies the natural harbour of Scapa Flow, graveyard to many wartime ships yet nevertheless bulging with wildlife. Across this water, far to the east, more islands drill south – Burray, South Ronaldsay – tapering sharply into the ski-jump contours of Barth Head.

Each island is distinctive, often markedly, sometimes subtly, in terms of its scenery, history and way of life. Explore these and you will discover that Westray has cliffs as thrilling as any on the Orkney Mainland; that Rousay has equally ancient and impressive – but little-visited – prehistoric sites; that Papa Westray has the oldest Neolithic house of all; that Sanday boasts the greatest number of glorious beaches; and that Stronsay hosts these islands' most extraordinary natural arch. Not only does Hoy have the highest hills but also, in the Old Man of Hoy, the most iconic sea stack of them all. Not all of Orkney's appeal is either natural or beautiful, for the paraphernalia of the world wars is among the most complete you will find anywhere.

Getting around these islands is likely to be a memorable part of your journey. Take the world's shortest flight, from Westray to Papa Westray, and you may be up and down in less than a minute. Yet hop on an inter-island ferry and you can take two hours or more to reach lonely North Ronaldsay, during which you may spot the heather-blether, a beautiful Orcadian term for a mirage where islands vanish as you sail between the North Isles in summer.

You may strike lucky with the weather and visit during a spell of summer warmth, when the sun barely sets and creates an unearthly twilight where dusk metamorphises into dawn. Or you may find yourself tramping along the magical dunes of Cata Sand during a thick *haar* or North Sea mist.

Your enduring image of Orkney may well turn out to be a cloth-of-gold dawn sky seen from Papa Westray; a gull atop a wobbling sea stack; walking in Stromness in broad daylight at 22.30 with fiddle music ringing out from three different directions; or the waters of Scapa Flow, which will form a ubiquitous backdrop to your holiday. Visitors are also constantly surprised at just how good Orkney food and drink is: the emphasis on local produce is impressive, from shellfish to North Ronaldsay lamb – reared on seaweed – and whisky from the world's most northerly distilleries. Orcadians too will form part of your memories, from gentle but sharp-witted accommodation hosts to those who will altruistically go the extra mile for you.

Stare at a map of Orkney for long enough and, rather like a magic eye puzzle, the image of a stag can slowly emerge (the rump is the Mainland, Hoy forms the hind legs, Eday the nose and Westray and North Ronaldsay represent the antlers). The same applies to a visit to these islands. Much of their appeal is ancient and obvious; but just as much is timeless and will only slowly reveal itself.

HOW TO USE THIS GUIDE

AUTHOR'S FAVOURITES Finding genuinely characterful accommodation or that unmissable off-the-beaten-track café can be difficult, so the author has chosen a few of his favourite places throughout the country to point you in the right direction. These 'author's favourites' are marked with a ✳.

MAPS

Keys and symbols Maps include alphabetical keys covering the locations of those places to stay, eat or drink that are featured in the book. Note that regional maps may not show all hotels and restaurants in the area: other establishments may be located in towns shown on the map.

Grids and grid references Several maps use gridlines to allow easy location of sites. Map grid references are listed in square brackets after the name of the place or site of interest in the text, with page number followed by grid number, eg: [103 C3].

FEEDBACK REQUEST AND UPDATES WEBSITE

At Bradt Travel Guides we're aware that guidebooks start to go out of date on the day they're published – and that you, our readers, are out there in the field doing research of your own. You'll find out before us when a fine new family-run hotel opens or a favourite restaurant changes hands and goes downhill. So why not write and tell us about your experiences? Contact us on ☎ 01753 893444 or e info@bradtguides.com. We will forward emails to the author who may post updates on the Bradt website at w bradtupdates.com/orkney. Alternatively, you can add a review of the book to w bradtguides.com or Amazon.

Part One

GENERAL INFORMATION

Location Eight miles north of Caithness in northern Scotland ⊕ 58.98°N 2.96°W

Size Land and sea cover an area 49 miles north–south by 38 miles east–west.

Land area 381.8 square miles

Islands 70 officially named, 19 inhabited

Heights Sea level to 1,570ft (479m)

Climate January 6°C; summer 15°C

Population 21,670

Density 56.76 people per square mile

Capital Kirkwall

Status Unitary authority answering to both the Scottish Parliament and Westminster, part of both Scotland and the United Kingdom

Language English, Orcadian

Religion Predominantly Church of Scotland; very small proportion of Roman Catholic (1–8% depending on island)

Currency Pound sterling

Exchange rate £1= US$1.32, £1= € 1.17 (April 2019)

International telephone code +44

Time GMT (winter); GMT+1 (summer)

Electrical voltage 230V

Weights and measures Road signs in miles; elsewhere both metric and imperial widely used

Public holidays Same as mainland Scotland: 1 Jan; 2 Jan; Good Friday; early May Bank Holiday (1st Monday of month); Spring Bank Holiday (last Monday of month); Summer Bank Holiday (1st Monday of August); St Andrew's Day (30 Nov); Christmas Day; Boxing Day

1

Background Information

GEOGRAPHY

Once at the northern coast of the UK mainland, keep going for another 8 miles across the waters of the Pentland Firth and you will reach Orkney. While the name may initially suggest there is just the one island to be found here, their alternative moniker, the Orkney Islands, gives the game away. In total – no-one has ever settled on a precise number – Orkney comprises around 70 islands and skerries, of which 19 are permanently inhabited. They are spread out across an area of land and sea reaching for 38 miles from west to east and 49 miles north to south, similar in extent to Trinidad and Tobago.

The Orkney Islands stand between the Atlantic Ocean and North Sea. Head due east and you will hit Norway; meanwhile, the waves that crash into Orkney's west coast have travelled unimpeded for 2,100 miles from Newfoundland and Labrador. Rora Head on Hoy is the most westerly limit of Orkney while the most southerly inhabited point lies at the tip of South Ronaldsay. The most northerly and westerly reaches are both to be found around Dennis Ness on North Ronaldsay. In total, Orkney boasts more than 600 miles of coastline.

The islands are generally bracketed into one of three groups: the Mainland, the North Isles and the South Isles. The Mainland forms the heart of Orkney and, at 202 square miles, is comfortably the largest island. With 17,000 people, it is also by some distance the most populated. The only towns on the islands, Kirkwall and Stromness, are both found here. The Mainland is divided, along an invisible line that runs from Kirkwall south to Scapa Bay, into the West Mainland – where you will find the most popular 'blockbuster' sights such as Skara Brae, the Ring of Brodgar and Maeshowe – and the East Mainland.

To the south of Stromness, logically enough, lie the South Isles, whose cast chiefly includes Hoy, South Walls, Flotta and Graemsay. Hoy is by far the second-largest island, 6 miles wide and more than 20 miles in length but with just 400 inhabitants. To the southeast of Kirkwall lie further southern isles, connected by causeways, including Lamb Holm (where you will find the exquisite Italian Chapel), Burray and South Ronaldsay.

Stretching in an arc to the north of the Mainland, rather like pieces of a jigsaw floating in the sea, are the North Isles, which include Rousay, Egilsay, Wyre, Shapinsay, Stronsay, Eday, Sanday, Westray, Papa Westray and, all of 28 miles from Kirkwall, North Ronaldsay. If you make it to the last of these, you are more than a third of the way to the neighbouring archipelago of Shetland. When dealing with ferry timetables you may also find the North Isles further subdivided, into 'inner' and 'outer' groups. The Outer North Isles comprise Westray, Papa Westray, North Ronaldsay, Stronsay, Sanday and Eday; everything else is considered an Inner North Isle.

In between the islands lies an ensemble of sounds, firths (sea lochs) and strong currents known as strings – watery highways navigated first by the Neolithic peoples and later by the Picts, Vikings and Norse earls. The most significant and indeed unmissable of these waterways is Scapa Flow, the vast natural harbour created by the coasts of the South Isles and the southern limits of the Mainland.

The most southerly limits of Orkney are marked by a series of islands and skerries strung across the fringes of Pentland Firth; these include Swona and Muckle Skerry. (Stroma, the first island you may see when travelling to Orkney from the UK mainland is actually part of Caithness.) Other historically important islands include the isolated Auskerry, 15 miles north of Kirkwall and Eynhallow, squeezed between Rousay and the Mainland, and Switha, southeast of Hoy. Beyond these, Orkney fragments further into islands off islands, such as the Calf of Eday, the Holm of Papay, and Papa Stronsay.

While relatively adjacent to one another, every island of Orkney is distinctive (often markedly, sometimes subtly) from the next in terms of its scenery, history and way of life. Only a few, such as Wyre, Egilsay, Lamb Holm and Flotta are predominantly flat. The highest hills are to be found on Hoy, where the glaciated valleys and corries can recall the Scottish Highlands. Almost all the islands have deeply indented coasts demarcated by thrilling cliffs. Most are superbly varied, and offer an extraordinary combination of rocky beaches, dunes, sand and sea, wetlands, lochs and heather-clad moors, meadows and low-lying maritime heath, with the mosaic often additionally characterised by old stone dykes and crofts.

The islands of Orkney described in this book range from Hoy in the southwest to North Ronaldsay in the northeast. Pedants, however, always enjoy pointing out that the Orkney Islands Council area extends considerably further west – 36 miles due west to be precise – to include the isolated islets of Sule Skerry and Sule Stack. Inaccessible to all but the most determined sailors and conservationists, Sule Skerry is low-lying and vegetated, whereas Sule Stack is a higher stack of bare rock. Both are of international importance for the vast numbers of seabirds they support. The peaty soil of Sule Skerry provides ideal burrowing conditions for nesting puffins (58,000 pairs at the latest estimate), while Sule Stack supports a colony of around 6,000 pairs of gannets.

ISLAND NAMES Every Orkney island name has a meaning. Flotta comes from the Old Norse for 'flat island', Westray means 'west island', Sanday means 'sandy island' and so on. While visiting Orkney, you will soon discover that pronunciation of the familiar island names and locations is not always straightforward. The rule of thumb is to stress the first syllable and throw away the last. In practice this means that if an island ends in '-ay' this syllable is turned into an 'ee' sound: Sanday is pronounced 'SANdy' rather than 'san-day', Westray is 'WEST-tree', Birsay is pronounced to rhyme with 'Percy' ... you get the picture. The rule also applies to townships such as 'Harray', which becomes 'harry'; and to landscape features such as the brough, a defensive headland, which should rhyme with the Scottish 'loch' (and is easily confused with the Iron Age towers known as brochs). Perhaps most importantly, you should never refer to these islands as 'the Orkneys'; always use 'Orkney' or 'the Orkney Islands'.

In a similar vein, the largest island of Orkney must always be referred to as 'the Mainland' and never simply 'Mainland'. The same rule applies to 'the East Mainland' and 'the West Mainland'. Orcadians, meanwhile, always refer to the Scottish part of the British mainland simply as Scotland. For clarity, this book generally refers to Orkney's main island as 'the Mainland' but occasionally uses 'the Orkney Mainland' where 'the Mainland' might be ambiguous. The other

One of the earliest records of a name resembling 'Orkney' appears in the 1st century BC, when Greek historian Diodorus Siculus referred to the islands as 'Orchades'. The Roman geographer Pliny subsequently called them the 'Orcades' and described a headland across the Pentland Firth as 'Cape Orcas', which may refer to Duncansby Head.

As for the etymology of the present-day name, there is a strong case for it hailing from a later period, around the 5th century, specifically the age of the Picts. The old Gaelic word 'orc' means 'young pig' – probably referring to wild boar – and the animal may have been a totem of a Pictish tribe on the islands; alternatively, the 'young pig' may refer to 'sea pig', meaning seal. Irish historians wrote of the Insi Orc, or Ork Islands, which, when translated into Latin, became Orcadea or Orcadia. (This would be hugely ironic, as there is barely a shred of Gaelic anywhere to be found in Orkney place names.)

When the Norse settled in Orkney, they interpreted the Pictish 'orc' element as 'orkn', their word for seal (which in turn may have come fromm the 'bark' or 'groan' that seals make). For good measure they added the suffix '-eyjar', meaning islands, and the islands became known as 'Orkneyjar' – the Seal Islands.

'mainlands' of the British Isles referred to in this guide are always described as 'the Scottish mainland' or the 'UK mainland'.

GEOLOGY Orkney's geology is spectacular and, thanks to the unrelenting pressures of weather and sea, is widely exposed for fascinating perusal. Vast slabs of flagstones poke out of high ground and coasts in often rhythmic sequences while in other places dramatically folded rocks, crushed and contoured this way and that, hint at the enormous processes and pressures that have been applied over millions of years.

Around 400 million years ago – 150 million years before dinosaurs emerged – what was to become the Orkney of today was located south of the Equator (somewhere around the present-day location of the Kalahari Desert), in and around a 900-mile-long freshwater lake that geologists call Lake Orcadie. Much of embryonic Scotland at that time was made up of arid mountains and what is now the North Sea was partly desert. During its lifetime the lake fluctuated greatly in area and depth before eventually drying out.

The driver of this process was a subtropical climate characterised by evaporation and variable rainfall, which led to the formation of sedimentary layers comprising sand, silt and mud, together with a finely laminated dark grey to black sandstone. Other features include outcrops of some of the oldest rocks on the planet, granite gneiss and metamorphic schists.

The present landscape has been carved out – in geological terms – relatively recently: vast ice sheets got to grips with Orkney between 70,000 and 10,000 years ago, a time known as the Devensian Glaciation. At this time, the sandstone lowlands of Orkney were moulded by the huge pressure of advancing and retreating ice sheets, although there is no evidence that the structure known as the Great Scandinavian Ice Sheet ever extended west to engulf Orkney. Instead, striations – scratches – found on bedrock suggest that the ice from subsequent glaciations generally moved back and forwards in a northwest–southeast direction, something that explains the presence of metamorphic erratics from northern Scotland and chalk and flint that would have come from the North Sea.

Glacial erosion smoothed and rounded both hills and ridges while gouging out the major firths of Hoy Sound, Eynhallow Sound and Westray Firth. This left the higher ground and more resistant rocks to establish the archipelago we see today. Boulder clay deposited as the ice subsequently melted can be seen in sections of cliff above coastal bays, particularly in the west of the Mainland. On Rousay and parts of Westray the glaciers got to work on this boulder clay and striated sandstone pavements to create distinctive ledges and elongated hills.

The rocks you see today have been mainly formed from mud and sand deposited in that ancient freshwater lake during the Old Red Sandstone period of the Devonian age (about 355–415 million years ago). The whole bedrock of Orkney is formed by the local sandstone, Caithness Flagstone and sedimentary rocks. Where the soil has peeled away, vast slabs of these stones jut out of the land and around coasts. Within this basic structure, there are many variations. The Middle Old Red Sandstone comprises Stromness and Rousay flags, made up of grey and black carbonite-rich siltstones and mudstones mixed with sandstones. Elsewhere, Eday flags contain yellow and red sandstone interlaid with thin lava flows. Volcanic activity is known to have played a role, mainly across the southerly part of Orkney, with small volcanic vents identified in Hoy, South Ronaldsay and the East Mainland.

Perhaps the most dramatic evidence of these processes that visitors will see is the Old Man of Hoy, the towering sea stack that stands apart from cliffs composed of the alternating red, pinks and yellows of Upper Old Red Sandstone.

SCAPA FLOW

Probably best known for its role in both World Wars, Scapa Flow has a natural beauty that can easily be overlooked. This is an immense expanse of deep water whose area of 125 square miles makes it the largest natural harbour in the northern hemisphere. The harbour is ringed by the Mainland to the north and a semicircle of smaller islands: Hoy and Flotta to the west and southwest; Lamb Holm, Glims Holm, Burray and South Ronaldsay to the east. Thanks to the construction of the Churchill Barriers during World War II, Scapa Flow has just three main entrances: Hoy Sound to the west, and Switha and Hoxa sounds to the south.

Life in Orkney has been shaped by this harbour since prehistory; more recently Vikings (who provided the Old Norse name Skalpeid Floi, which translates as 'Ship Isthmus Bay'), Arctic whalers, herring fishermen, the oil industry and now renewable-energy companies have depended on its shelter and natural resources.

The body of water we see today emerged from glacial action on Orkney's Old Sandstone rocks. Layers of sand, mud and silt have, over millions of years, coalesced into the layered mudstones and sandstones. In turn these rocks have been scoured out by successive ice ages to form a deep basin and natural harbour. Wind and sea have further shaped the landscape, cutting geos and sheltered bays out of the coast in some places but leaving behind towering cliffs elsewhere. The deepest part of the water is to be found at Bring Deeps, off Hoy, where the seabed lies at a depth of almost 200ft.

Much of Scapa Flow has a bed of fine sand and mud with areas of gravel. Collectively, these provide habitat for sea creatures such as scallops, whelks, brittlestars and starfish. The geography of Scapa Flow also provides a perfect domain for birds: many gulls and terns feed and nest here, as do guillemots and razorbills. In winter, the waters are relatively sheltered for their latitude and are an

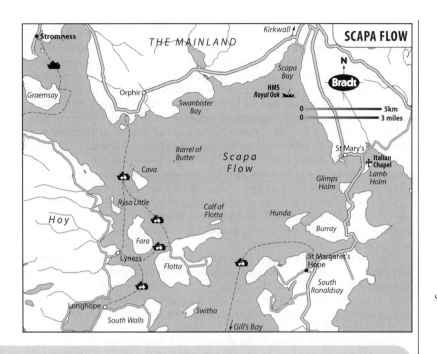

internationally important overwintering area for great northern diver, Slavonian grebe and long-tailed duck, while red-throated diver nests in lochans close to its shores. Up to 2,000 harbour seals breed in the waters and 19 species of cetacean have been recorded. Orcas sometimes manoeuvre their way into the harbour and, in 1993, six sperm whales became trapped for five weeks before finally being escorted to safety by a flotilla of local boats in a rescue effort known as Operation Gentle Shepherd. Among fish, the rarest inhabitant is the critically endangered huge flapper skate, 6ft in length. The waters are also rich in sand eels, which in turn form a crucial part of many seabirds' diet, including that of everyone's favourite clockwork toy, the puffin.

This wildlife has been augmented by the large number of naval wrecks that lie on the seabed. Eleven of the 74 ships scuttled here in 1919 (see box, page 70) remain and provide a haven for marine creatures such as crabs, lobsters, starfish and urchins as well as pollock and saithe. Algae blooms are triggered in Scapa Flow by the warming waters of late spring that attract comb and moon jellies.

Mearl beds in Scapa Flow are important: these are 'corallines', or red algae with branching twig-like calcium rich skeletons. The waters also support many seaweeds and molluscs along with 'meadows' of dense eelgrass that Orcadians traditionally used to deploy as thatch for croft houses.

Many wildflowers make use of the salt-laden soils around the fringe of Scapa Flow, including sea pink, spring squill and dwarf willow. At Waulkmill Bay, seawater merges into saltmarsh to provide a haven for sea milkwort and sea arrowgrass. The northern coast of Scapa Flow has a smattering of moorland that is patrolled by hen harriers and dotted with flowers such as tormentil. All this wildlife lives cheek by jowl with – and seemingly unimpeded by – the Flotta oil terminal.

CLIMATE

Orkney enjoys a hyper-oceanic climate, which means that it is cool and wet all year around, with temperatures averaging 5°C in winter (but sometimes as low as –5°C) and 15°C in summer (with occasional highs in the mid-20s°C). This is largely due to the Gulf Stream, the current of equatorial warm water that travels northeast across the Atlantic Ocean then around the British Isles. North Ronaldsay for example is a good 5°C warmer than anywhere else on the same latitude, such as Newfoundland or Kamchatka in the far east of Russia. Good and bad weather can happen at any time of year. You may get a 60mph gale fly through in June; as a counterpoint, winter is frequently alleviated by a week here or there of glorious weather. The period from October to January sees the most rain and, for somewhere so far north, Orkney can produce solid tropical downpours that ping off your waterproofs like buckshot.

That Orkney ferries run their winter timetable from the end of September to the start of May tells you much of what you need to know about prevailing weather trends. From November through to end February nights are long. The shortest day sees the sun rise at 09.04 and set at 15.15.

March and April often bring the North Sea *haar*, a chilly sea mist, to the northern isles. This can sit all day or suddenly evaporate to reveal bright blue skies. May is historically the sunniest month. The pay-off for the long winter is the extended hours of summer light, with the sun rising on 21 June well before 04.00 and setting at 22.30 – though a half-light persists beyond midnight, particularly on the most northerly islands of Westray and North Ronaldsay.

Orkney has plenty of wind: the average wind speed across the islands is a remarkable 38mph; the highest recorded speed was 125mph on 31 January 1953. As with the rest of the UK, the first storms tend to arrive in late September. Unlike the rest of the country, Orkney generally just takes them in its stride.

CLIMATE CHANGE Sea levels in Orkney are rising and storminess is widely recognised to be increasing. This has implications for shoreline communities and wildlife habitats everywhere but particularly on the more low-lying islands such as Sanday and North Ronaldsay. Archaeologists say impacts are already being seen on important coastal sites, including the Knowe of Swandro on Rousay and the Links of Noltland on Westray, where a race against time is conducted every summer to excavate and protect these settlements. In 2018, Historic Environment Scotland issued a report that combined climatic data from the Scottish Environment Protection Agency with geological information from the British Geological Survey to warn of the effects of heavier erosion caused by greater storms, rising sea levels and wetter weather.

Orkney graziers are reporting a change in climate and say with some certainty that winters are becoming wetter. Consequently, they are only able to put their livestock out to graze for a limited period, often only from mid-May to early October. As this coincides with the season for breeding among ground-nesting birds, it means that climate change has indirect impacts on wildlife: farmers must produce more sileage to feed their cattle indoors, so they place more fertiliser on the grass and cut it sooner, which in turn conflicts with the needs of many birds such as the corncrake.

NATURAL HISTORY

Wildlife is justifiably one of the main reasons people visit Orkney. Between April and July it can seem as though every ledge of every sea cliff in Orkney is occupied by nesting seabirds, the sky whitened with the confetti of birds flying back and forth to their nests. Yet this avian treat is just one of many highlights that make Orkney such a superlative destination for wildlife lovers. The nutrient-rich waters of Scapa Flow and the firths and sounds that connect the Outer Isles are home to an abundance of marine life. Furthermore, for such a northerly location, Orkney boasts several eye-catching wildflowers, along with butterflies and dragonflies, while lichens thrive in the islands' clean air.

The volume of wildlife means that Orkney boasts a large number of nationally and internationally protected areas. These include 13 Special Protection Areas (w tinyurl.com/y97vuurr) that cover the majority of the moorland of the West Mainland, Rousay, Hoy, and parts of Sanday, Westray and Papa Westray. In addition, six Special Areas of Conservation (w tinyurl.com/yckvd3zw) include Hoy, Sanday, lochs on the Mainland, and the heaths around Stromness. Meanwhile, there are three Marine Protected Areas around Wyre and Rousay Sounds, Papa Westray, and the seas to the northwest of Orkney (this last being designed to protect sand eel populations). A Ramsar site for wetlands protection covers the east coast of Sanday (w tinyurl.com/yd5q8pf5).

Furthermore, the islands boast 36 Sites of Special Scientific Interest (w tinyurl.com/ybzx4v2v) including Waulkmill Bay and Marwick Head on the Mainland, the Holm of Papay, Westray and Rousay. Orkney also has one National Scenic Area (NSA) covering 16,000ha of the West Mainland and Hoy. NSAs represent Scotland's finest landscapes, and are equivalent to the Areas of Outstanding Beauty (AONBs) found in the rest of the UK. The RSPB (w rspb.org.uk; select 'reserves and events' and enter 'Orkney') has 13 reserves across the islands: the largest, on Hoy, covers nearly 10,000 acres. A number of reserves have boardwalks and provide a good deal of public interaction in the form of guided walks or rangers/volunteers on hand in bird hides. The Scottish Wildlife Trust (w scottishwildlifetrust.org.uk) also has a presence in places such as the unfertilised and never-ploughed farmland of South Walls (page 153).

Whatever time of year you come, there will be something to see, from the autumn migration to winter flocks of wildfowl and seals pupping. Most of the outer islands employ rangers who lead tours from spring until autumn (and occasionally in winter) across their particular patch. These are well worth looking out for: they cover wildlife but also history, archaeology, heritage and landscape. Details are given in the relevant island chapter.

BIRDS AND INSECTS The abundance of birds is all down to the habitat and food that is available. These drivers – coast, raised bogs, hills, wet corners of fields, sileage fields – are abundant on Orkney. Consequently seabirds, waders, moorland birds and raptors are all common. 'People will get that "wow" factor when they come here,' says Alan Leitch, RSPB Orkney sites manager.

Seabirds Orkney is home to 21 breeding species of seabird, most notably marine birds. Some reports suggest that one in six of all seabirds breeding in Britain nest in Orkney. The charismatic puffins breed here from May to early July (they total around 60,000 pairs, though the vast majority of these are on the inaccessible Sule Skerry, 36 miles west in the Atlantic). The best place to see them is around Castle o' Burrian and Noup Head on Westray and on the southeast coast of Papa Westray; less substantial numbers nest around the Brough of Birsay and Marwick Head on the Mainland. Other seabirds include guillemots and shags, and vast numbers of fulmars and razorbills, black-headed and great black-backed gulls. Smaller numbers of the rarer black guillemot (or 'tystie') can also be seen on lower cliff edges. High above them kittiwakes are a sure bet in spring and summer on the

1

9

upper ledges, their wings distinctively looking as though they have been dipped in black ink. Arctic terns, dipping and ducking for prey in the shallows, add a dainty touch to the maritime heath landscape.

Omnipresent on any coastal heath during the breeding season is the great skua, also known by its Norse name, bonxie, an appropriate onomatopoeia that chimes with its aggressive habits. Bonxies mercilessly chase down smaller seabirds carrying fish to make them drop their catch, whereupon the bonxie swoops underneath and catches the prey item in a tactic known as kleptoparasitism. It's not just seabirds who need to be wary of bonxies: adults are intensely protective of their chicks and will skim low overhead if they judge you to have encroached too close to their progeny. A hat or a flag on a stick is usually enough to keep them at bay. The bonxie's slightly smaller cousin, the Arctic skua, is no less feisty; the coastal heaths of Rousay and Hoy are good places to see this graceful bird.

Gannets are doing well in Orkney and you will see them anywhere off the coast, in the sounds and inter-island waters, plunging in trademark arrow-like fashion for fish before returning to their nests around Noup Head on Westray.

Many of these birds also breed on the uninhabited islands and skerries that are marooned in Orkney's waters. The Pentland Firth islands, Swona and Muckle Skerry are home to internationally important breeding colonies of Arctic tern.

Little auks usually appear in winter below the Holm Cliffs on the northeastern edges of Scapa Flow and the Churchill Barriers.

Birds of prey You can be as confident as anywhere in the UK of seeing birds of prey on Orkney. Heather-covered moorlands and marshy grasslands such as Hobbister and Cottascarth on the Mainland are home to hen harriers; some 65 pairs are here, making Orkney one of the UK's most important locations for the bird. (The hen harrier's rude health on Orkney is due to the absence of driven grouse-shooting on the islands; this is in stark contrast to the situation in England, where the bird is relentlessly persecuted on such estates.) In spring you can catch the graceful 'sky dance' performed by the male as it climbs, plunges and rolls in thin air to attract a mate; after the birds have paired up there is more drama as the male passes prey in mid-air to its mate.

Meanwhile, the merlin, the UK's smallest bird of prey, can often be seen chasing a meadow pipit to exhaustion. Another raptor, perhaps spotted hovering over an oat stack in search of mice, is the kestrel; sparrowhawks are best sighted darting in and out of the rare slivers of Orkney woodland while sea cliffs across the islands are the domain of peregrines. Ravens honk their way around the islands and occasionally you may catch them nesting on ledges adjacent to fulmars, this juxtaposition of black and white bringing to mind the vague impression of a piano keyboard.

The short-eared owl is Orkney's only breeding owl. Fields around Kirkwall airport and the Yesnaby coast on the west of the Mainland are good places to see it. In all, there are round 50 breeding pairs with sightings possible on Hoy, Rousay, Stronsay, Sanday and North Ronaldsay.

Historically, Orkney has been home to both white-tailed and golden eagles, the latter breeding in the 1980s. At the time of writing there are no goldens: it's hard to pin down a single reason for this but it's thought that fulmars have played a part, mobbing the adult eagles and projectile-vomiting on their chicks such that they cannot fledge. Young golden eagles are occasionally spotted wandering across on thermals from the UK mainland. In 2018 a pair of white-tailed eagles successfully reared the first chick hatched in Orkney for 145 years. The hope is that this may well presage the long-term return of this magnificent bird to the islands.

Other birds Loch shores and marshland attract curlew (one of Orkney's guaranteed spectacles is a curlew gliding in an arc over a field), redshank and snipe. In summer listen out for the truly haunting 'drumming' sound of the snipe's courtship display. Inland, areas of maritime heath are favoured by waders such as oystercatcher and ringed plover who keep a wary eye out for the nesting Arctic skuas that patrol the skies. The nationally embattled corncrake holds on in Orkney – just 13 calling males at the last count – thanks to sympathetic farming practices that leave uncultivated arable land and hayfields uncut for longer into the year. With luck, you may well hear it on Westray, Sanday and, if your luck's in, on North Ronaldsay. *Seeing* this skulking bird is another matter, however. Tiny fluffballs such as wrens and goldcrests are also often spotted – as, with luck, are firecrests – along drystone walls, field edges and even among cliff-edge gorse.

The high moors are a good place to see whimbrels, a relative of the curlew. The lochans on the moors, meanwhile offer sporting chances of seeing breeding red-throated divers, while the other two members of the loon family, great northern and black-throated divers, can be seen around the coasts in winter. A true bird of the 'high north', snow bunting, can be seen in flocks in deep midwinter. Eider ducks can be seen year-round, the photogenic male sporting its white-green plumage. In spring, females are usually seen paddling frantically along the shoreline with a raft of chicks in hot pursuit. Along these shorelines you can also expect to see turnstones and flocks of knot and sanderling. Dunlin can be spotted on Orkney's isolated fragments of saltmarsh.

More than a dozen species of duck can be seen on the islands, including some that are uncommon on the UK mainland. Up to 100 pairs of shoveler reside here (20% of the UK population), and 115 breeding pairs of red-breasted merganser. Tufted ducks are common and mallard, known locally as the stock duck, is everywhere. In addition, you can expect to see gadwall, teal and pintail (an extremely rare breeding duck elsewhere in the UK). Orkney is home to 15% of UK breeding wigeon; in winter, thousands more come to Orkney from Iceland. You will see them marching in tight flocks to graze the lochside fields. Lowland lochs are also good places to see breeding mute swans and most of the inhabited islands have at least one resident pair. Although UK mute swans are technically owned by the Crown, Udal Law (see box, page 19) means that Orkney birds are the property of the people of Orkney. You will see several pairs on the lochs of Harray and Stenness. If you see a swan in a field, however, it will most likely be a whooper swan, either overwintering or enjoying a pit stop before heading south. Winter also sees the arrival of squadrons of greylag geese. This is to the chagrin of farmers, as the geese eat everything in sight, from grass to grain. They number almost 70,000, with more than half in the West Mainland. Goldeneye and the fetching Slavonian grebe are other attractive waterbirds that overwinter.

The islands also serve as a vital resting post for African migrants, which means spring and autumn are the times when birds are most abundant. Some stay to breed. Even small birds such as chiffchaff, pied flycatcher and willow and grasshopper warblers make it here. Willow warblers can usually be seen and heard in woodland such as Binscarth, Trumland (on Rousay) and Balfour (Shapinsay). Orkney is the UK's northernmost outpost for the sedge warbler. Marsh and icterine warblers occasionally make landfall in strong easterly winds and a pair of the latter nested on Stronsay in 2002. Cuckoos seem to be increasing year on year, and you have a good chance of hearing them on higher moorland, such as the RSPB reserves at Trumland (Rousay) and Hobbister and Cottarscarth (the Mainland). Two islands in particular, Stronsay (see box, page 209) and North Ronaldsay (see box, page 268) are renowned for the sheer number of rare migrants that check in. Some 'mega-rarities', such as

For such a northerly location, Orkney has some hardy insects. In one respect, this is not surprising: given that there are so many wildflowers, pollinators such as bees must exist here. Nevertheless, given the well-documented hardships that many species of bee face across the UK, it is particularly welcome that one particular species, great yellow bumblebee, is holding its own here. Distinguished by a clear band of black splitting a yellow back, the bee is one of the rarest of the UK's 24 remaining species. It used to be widespread across the UK but has lost 80% of its range and is now only found in north Scotland, Orkney and the Outer Hebrides. If you want to see it, visit between June and August. The bee benefits from less intensive, more sympathetic and traditional farming that encourages wildflowers favoured by the bee, such as red clover.

Cretzschmar's bunting, trigger major alerts among the twitching community; a 'flock' of hardcore birders, fresh off an eight-seater aircraft, stampeding across fields and bogs, determined to 'clock' the arrival, is a spectacle in its own right.

Insects Seven species of butterfly are found on the islands. South Walls is one of the best places to see common blue and meadow brown. Dragonflies can be spotted as far north as the lochs of Westray and North Ronaldsay and include common hawker, black darter and the magnificent golden-ringed dragonfly. Damselflies include the large red and common blue.

MARINE LIFE Orkney's marine life is just as exceptional as its winged wanderers. You will certainly see harbour (aka common) and grey **seals**. While harbour seals are identified by their dog-like faces, grey seals have more horse-like heads and are heavier. Both species tend to haul out of the water – 'loaf' is the technical term – on isolated sites. Up until the 19th century grey seals were comparatively rare on Orkney but the colonies here now make up more than 20% of the UK population. Autumn is the time to see grey seals breeding while harbour seals generally pup in June and July. Despite this, numbers of the harbour seals have nosedived by 78% since 2000, from 8,500, one of the largest in the UK, to just 1,800. At Widewall Bay in South Ronaldsay, the population has dropped from 500 to 100 in barely two decades. Work led by the Sea Mammal Research Unit at the University of St Andrews is trying to establish the causes, and three possible reasons are cited: a lack of food, attacks by larger grey seals and toxins ingested from harmful algae blooms. Some scientists think a combination of all three may be behind the decline.

A larger relative, the **walrus**, appeared on North Ronaldsay in 2018, then travelled on to Sanday, the second such sighting in five years.

Orkney is also a good place to see **octopus** – from ferries on calm days or in shallow coastal waters – as the seas are full of lobsters, its favourite food.

While taking those inter-island ferries or walking around the coast, look out for **dolphins** and **porpoises**. Many species of **whales** are spotted offshore, including minke, long-finned pilot and (occasionally) sperm whales. One of the best places to see whales is from Cantick Head on Hoy. Orcas are increasingly seen. One pod regularly patrols the Pentland Firth, and individuals or groups have showed up in Eynhallow Sound between the Mainland and Rousay as well as off Eday. Due to the abundance of marine life, it is sadly not uncommon to encounter cetaceans washed up on beaches, particularly in winter and early spring. While many of these will be natural deaths, entanglement in fishing gear, ingestion of plastics and other causes are also responsible. If you find a stranded or dead cetacean contact the UK Cetacean Strandings Investigation Programme (📞 0800 6520333; w ukstrandings.org).

Rock pools, meanwhile, teem with life, including groatie buckies (cowrie shells), starfish, anemones, winkles, limpets, sea urchins and hermit crabs. The best rock pools are revealed at low tide between the Brough of Birsay and the West Mainland.

MAMMALS Orkney has plenty of land mammals ('including humans', as a wildlife guide pointed out to me). Before the first settlers arrived around 4000BC, only seabirds and fish were native. Sheep, cattle, pigs and red deer were all introduced, but the deer have since died out. Foxes and badgers are now extinct and pine martens have never made it here. The best-known sheep is the eponymous North Ronaldsay breed, where they are famed for enjoying a diet based on seaweed washed up on the island's shores.

You have a fighting chance of seeing Eurasian **otters** along much of the coastline of Scapa Flow as well as the shores of all the Outer Isles. They are best seen at dawn and dusk, though you may catch them scuttling across a field to a freshwater loch in broad daylight in order to wash themselves and hunt.

There are smaller mammals to look out for too, if you are lucky. Most interesting is the **Orkney vole**, which is a subspecies of common vole and known locally as the 'cuttick'. The Orkney vole is absent from the UK mainland, larger than its counterparts there and, intriguingly, its nearest relative is believed to have originated in Hungary. It is found only in rough grasslands, wetlands and heaths on Orkney Mainland, Rousay, Burray, Westray and Eday, and it's possible to tell which island each animal originates from by the colour of its coat: those from the southerly islands are said to have a deep brown coat while those from the north are paler in colour. It's thought that the vole was introduced by early settlers, and there is evidence from Skara Brae that they were kept and reared for food. Look for their narrow runs in coastal grasses.

TYSTIES, CATABELLIES AND WATERY PEEPS

The Orcadian language (page 32) has come up with some colourful names for its native wildlife, which often, to non-Orcadian speakers, resonate quite magically with the birds' characteristics. These include 'watery peeps' for redshank and 'tee-ich' for lapwing, both of which capture these birds' distinctive sounds. The local name for the oystercatcher is a 'chalder'; a wheatear is a 'chackie' and eider ducks are 'dunters'; black guillemots are known as 'tysties' and shags as 'scarfies'. Arctic terns are called 'tirricks', the Arctic skua is a 'skooty-allan', a storm petrel is an 'alamotti', gannets are known as 'solan geese' and a 'baakie' is a great black-backed gull. The snipe is known locally as the 'heather bleater', or 'horsegowk', on account of the drumming noise it makes during its courtship display, which can sound like a whinnying horse. The hen harrier is known as the 'catabelly', the short-eared owl as the 'cattie-face', the curlew as the 'whaup' and a red-throated diver in summer is a 'loon' or 'loom'. The fulmar, meanwhile, holds close its Old Norse name, 'foul maar', meaning 'foul gull', on account of its habit of spitting a thick oily and fishy liquid to defend its nests.

Orkney has repelled or assimilated invaders for millennia; but the most recent is decidedly unwelcome. Stoats were first spotted in Orkney in July 2010 and now number several thousand. How they arrived is a matter of conjecture: they may have been deliberately introduced; arrived among straw imported from Aberdeenshire; or possibly even have swum from Caithness (stoats can swim 3 miles, so Hoy is within range from the mainland and it is plausible they could traverse the Pentland Firth to the Orkney Mainland with the aid of flotsam). One stoat was spotted on Hoy in 2017 but none has been spotted since, raising hopes that it was a single individual.

The problem is that stoats hunt everything from ground-nesting birds to Orkney voles; by eating the latter the mammal also deprives hen harriers and short-eared owls of their prey. Stoats are now subject to an eradication programme, and lethal traps have been placed at key access points such as the headlands between the Orkney Mainland and Hoy and Rousay. Visitors are encouraged to report any sightings of stoats – dead or alive – to Scottish Natural Heritage (↑ 01856 886163; e north@snh.gov.uk). In the interest of balance, stoats are not the only animal in the frame: the large number of feral cats on the Mainland – you may well spot them in geos and the moors of Birsay – is also thought to contribute to the loss of eggs from ground nests. Hedgehogs, meanwhile, do take some eggs, but are not widely considered to be a major driver of the decline of bird species.

Mice (both wood and house), pygmy shrews, rabbits and hedgehogs also reside here but squirrels are wholly absent. Brown hares are commonly spotted in fields – although they are extremely twitchy and generally turn tail almost the instant you see them – while Hoy is the place to see mountain hares. They were introduced in the 18th century and their coats turn white in winter, providing a spectral element even as late as May to Hoy's bone-hard whaleback hills and empty moors.

FLORA Orkney is home to more than 500 species of native plants, thriving in habitats that range from the shoreline, heathlands and wetlands to the sub-Arctic glacial environment found on Hoy. They include a rarity on the tick-list of plant hunters across the planet, Scottish primrose (*Primula scotica*), which is found only on Orkney and in Caithness and north Sutherland. A beautiful flower, it is easily identified thanks to its bluish-purple petals with delicate yellow centre. The moors close to the Yesnaby cliffs on the Mainland are just about the best place to find it, though it also grows on Rousay, Westray and Papa Westray. An added bonus is that the flower gives visitors two chances to see it as it blooms both in May and July.

Orkney's sea-sprayed soils nurture a range of plants such as eyebright (which thrives on sand dunes and dune pasture), speedwell and milkwort. The red campion and wild angelica found on clifftops tend to be larger than their counterparts on the British mainland. Sea aster thrives on the saltmarshes and Orkney is considered a key European habitat for this delightful plant with its radiating lilac petals. A wander through shoreside vegetation can release a pleasant aroma as the stems of water mint are crushed by your boots. Along the cliffs, rosy rafts of thrift are often interspersed with the purple and pink of various marsh orchids.

In spring, loch shores and fields are carpeted in wildflowers, from lady's smock to meadow buttercup, the dark pink of ragged robin, yellow flag-iris and northern marsh orchid. Other flowers that dominate include the honey-scented white blooms of grass-of-Parnassus (distinguished by heart-shaped leaves and a single delicate vein) on marshland. Such landscapes, as well as damp moorland, are home to carnivorous sundews along with marsh marigold and primrose. Heather and ling emerge in late summer on these moorlands, where you may also find Alpine cloudberry. Along or close to roadside verges you may well find Oriental, poppy-like plants. Papa Westray and Sanday are home to Orkney's small slices of machair – coastal meadows of sand overlain with grass that are extremely rich in plants. For much of the year machair resembles a snooker table and is kept short by nibbling sheep. In summer, it is transformed into a collage of colour as wildflowers emerge, including the showy purple petals of felwort and the wan yellow of cowslip.

Curiosities include white thistles found on Stronsay. Not all Orkney plants are so welcome: invasive species cause some headaches, including Magellan ragwort, which can quickly overwhelm the sides of burns, and salmonberry, a favourite of gardeners, whose fetching pink flowers belie a swift-spreading predilection for smothering any ground flora and young trees it comes across.

Around 5,000 years ago, a change in climate to cooler, wetter weather created waterlogged soils that were ideal for the formation of peat and a landscape where trees struggled to maintain a presence. Yet contrary to popular perception, Orkney has native trees that defy, and are adapted to, salt-laden winds, extremes of day length and short growing seasons: downy birch, hazel, rowan, aspen, roses, honeysuckle, juniper and willow. These tend to thrive in modest woodlands that are either sheltered in valleys from the elements or actively supported by community tree-planting projects. Pollen studies in Berriedale Wood in a valley in northwest Hoy indicate that native woodland of birch and hazel was widespread in Orkney around 5000BC, before the arrival of Neolithic man and a changing climate. One theory is that felling the trees on the periphery of woodlands made the core vulnerable to the effects of the unrelenting and cooler weather. This has been suggested as a reason for the collapse of the community at Skara Brae (page 98). Other woodlands worth exploring include Happy Valley (page 109) and Binscarth Wood on the Mainland, the grounds of Trumland House on Rousay (page 180) and Olav's Wood on South Ronaldsay (page 171). On all islands, the rare slivers of woodland, from Rackwick Valley on Hoy to strains of sycamore hanging on by a ruined farm, are bombarded by avian life.

HISTORY

Simply put, history goes way back on Orkney. Farming communities were settled here before the Pyramids were built in Egypt. Over millennia, a mesmerising mixture of Mesolithic, Neolithic, Bronze Age, Iron Age, Pictish and Norse influences has ultimately evolved into modern-day Orkney.

Given Orkney's rich and ancient history, it can come as a surprise to learn that there are an awful lot of gaps where we simply know very little. Several periods are well documented, eg: 3000–2200BC, 1000BC–AD200, and from the Viking era to the 20th century. For the times in between, however, including much of the Bronze Age, historians mostly operate in the realm of informed conjecture.

THE FIRST COLONISTS Discoveries of three or four spear points, dated to 15,000 years ago, suggest that groups of hunters passed through Orkney at that time. There is no evidence that these people hung around; instead they may have been moving eastward, following herds of reindeer, working their way around the coast hunting seals, or just simply climbing the next hill to see what was there.

The first hunter-gatherers to arrive and settle were Mesolithic people who moved into Orkney after the last glaciations around 8,000 years ago. It's thought they may have hailed from the northern plains of Doggerland, the area that connected Britain to continental Europe. As Doggerland shrank and became submerged by rising sea levels to form the bed of the southern North Sea, these voyagers may have been displaced to the west and north. They were highly specialised coastal people. Given similarities between them, they may have shared a common ancestor with a group from Scandinavia.

Around 5,000 years ago farming communities began to move in from what is now France, bringing with them seeds and animals, and breaking the ground with horses and ploughs. What had happened to the hunter-gatherers is unclear but genetic evidence suggests there was a significant change in the origin of these peoples. As Orkney archaeologist Caroline Wickham-Jones puts it: 'these people brought new crops and animals that were alien to Orkney, so someone was coming in by boat.' At this time, small trees such as birch and alder were common, which meant there were no great forests to replenish stocks when wood was depleted. There were no native cereals so bere, a primitive form of barley, was introduced and became the main crop.

These first settlers turned to the beaches, which yielded water-worn pebbles and nodules of flint for tools, plus seaweed and sand for fertilisers. Axe heads were made from igneous stones such as camptonite and monchiquite. Settlers used clay to make pots, dug peat for fuel and turned to the moors to gather heather for bedding, thatch and ropes. Baskets were woven from grasses and straw. Steatite, a type of soapstone, was imported from Shetland to make into dishes, bowls and urns.

In such an environment the great surviving archaeological sites began to emerge. Construction started on Skara Brae around 3100BC. The Knap of Howar (page 260), a farmhouse on Papa Westray, preceded this by up to 500 years. Groups of standing stones such as Stenness were built around the same time, but the Ring of Brodgar a little later, perhaps 2500–2000BC. Neolithic people blended natural pigments to paint walls, carved zigzags and spirals into stone and decorated pottery with similar patterns. This distinctive style gave rise to what became known as Unstan and grooved ware pottery.

After 2200BC evidence is scant for any settlements at all. The climate deteriorated, becoming wetter and windier. This accelerated the accumulation of blanket peat, which became established around 1500BC. Towards the end of the Bronze Age, around 650BC, peace and planting seems to have been replaced by discord and famine. Too many animals were kept on good pasture, crops failed and farms were abandoned. People began migrating to better lands.

THE IRON AGE (500BC TO AD800) People settled in low-lying areas and it seems that the early Iron Age was a time of some conflict in Orkney, as tribes fought over the best available farmland. Order seems to have slowly established itself as communities coalesced around a ruling class and fortifications and dwellings, such as the broch and roundhouse. Iron Age Orkney is generally considered to have been a wealthy and organised society in which powerful overlords kept social order and commissioned draughtsmen for their houses. Orcadians of this time were more able to trade with people from the south. They enjoyed only slight contact with Roman Britain but there is evidence that they imported metals and stones, along with Roman jewellery, glassware and pottery. There were also extensive sea-trading links with Shetland. The good lands were mainly around the coasts, where roundhouses were built, complete with byres and sheds, and defended by ditches.

They built with stone, including flagstone, quarried from cliffs. Driftwood was used for roofing and doors. The most distinctive Iron Age settlement was the broch, which emerged during the last centuries BC.

By the 6th century, the Picts had seen off the Romans and proceeded to establish the Kingdom of the Picts across Scotland. At its height, this kingdom stretched from the Firth of Forth (near present-day Edinburgh) right up to Shetland. By the early 7th century Orkney was fully in the Picts' embrace, although there was no invasion as such. It was less the case that the Picts moved in physically, rather that contemporaneous Orcadians were assimilated into Pictish culture. Orkney had its own ruler during this period, subject to the authority of the higher Pictish king.

Pictish society on Orkney appears to have been comparatively stable: fortified villages were replaced in the 7th and 8th centuries by substantial family farmsteads made of stone and turf. The Picts farmed deer for meat and skins, and used antlers for pull-rings (to function as handles for lifting items such as baskets) and combs. Power, meanwhile, was held by a handful of noblemen and centred in places such as the Brough of Birsay on the Mainland and Pool in Sanday.

Orkney's involvement with the Pictish kingdom brought it into the wider world of early medieval Europe, and the islands began to hold an important role in Celtic culture. By the 7th century the Picts had converted to Christianity and the religion subsequently expanded slowly in Orkney. While the earliest Orcadian church dates to the 10th century, earlier ruins may well be awaiting discovery.

ENTER THE VIKINGS Orkney's Norse period runs from the 9th to 13th centuries. During this time Orkney was part of Norway, not Scotland, and ruled over by Viking earls (Jarls). The Vikings settled around 850 and their era oversees the transition from prehistory – before written records were made – to a documented history of Orkney. Norway was only 2–3 days' sailing from Orkney and the Vikings' arrival was part of a wider Scandinavian migration that took place across much of Europe. This period sees Orkney's history intertwined with the fortunes of Shetland, Norway, Iceland, Scotland and the Faroes.

The arrival of the Vikings is typically associated with fearsome tales of sacking but the truth may be a little more complex. By and large, while it is possible that the Vikings enslaved parts of the local population, there is no evidence from Orkney of burning and pillaging. Some historians argue that the Pictish presence had dwindled such that, to some extent, the Vikings stepped into a vacuum. What is clear is that the Vikings were efficient and able farmers, their settlements built around family farms where bere oats and barley were cultivated. Orkney moved from pagan to Christian worship in 995 with the conversion of the Earl of Orkney Sigurd Hlodvisson (see box, page 154). Genetic studies show that many Orcadians are derived from the Norse people who settled on the islands from the 8th century.

By the 11th century, Birsay was again an important centre. Now ruled by powerful Norse earls, the Brough of Birsay was clearly of great strategic value. From 1014 to 1064 Thorfinn Sigurdsson, known as Thorfinn The Mighty, ruled from Birsay as Earl of Orkney. He also commanded the Hebrides, Caithness, several other Scottish earldoms and much of Ireland. In his later years Thorfinn ceased raiding and instead guarded his subjects. Accordingly, Orkney became more settled. Thorfinn appointed Orkney's first bishop and is said to have built a cathedral at Birsay, though its location is unclear. The Norse earls oversaw a sophisticated society and this period is now characterised as Orkney's 'golden age', where the islands reached their height of power and influence. A local language, the Norn, even evolved from Old Norse (page 33).

The Norse earls dominated Orkney for more than 300 years and considered the islands an ideal base from which to extend and bolster their empire. While they appear to have quickly discarded or assimilated the Celtic Pictish culture that confronted them, they were not immune to being influenced themselves, exchanging Viking runes for the Western alphabet and rejecting their Norse gods for Christianity. The dynasty can supposedly be traced to one man, Eystein 'Rattle', who was followed by some creatively named descendants, including Rognvald the Mighty and Wise, Eric Bloodaxe, Thorfinn Skull-Splitter, Havard 'Harvest Happy' and Einer 'Wry Mouth'. The earls also happened to be distantly related to the English (Norman) royal family. William the Conqueror was related to Rolf 'The Walker', who married the granddaughter of Eystein 'Rattle'. Thorfinn the Mighty, meanwhile, was the grandson of Malcolm II, King of the Scots.

THE BATTLES OF THE NORSE EARLS By the end of the 12th century, the Orkney earldom had effectively become a job share between the earls Paul and Erlend. In 1098, the Norwegian king, the superbly named Magnus Barelegs, unseated both earls and installed his son Sigurd in their stead. After a brief but active period of pillaging along the shores of western Britain, Barelegs died in 1102 in Ireland. Sigurd, meanwhile, returned to Norway, leaving Haakon, the son of Paul, to assume the title of Earl of Orkney. He shared this position with Magnus, son of Erlend and grandson of Thorfinn the Mighty.

Magnus Erlendsson (see box, page 188) is undoubtedly the best known of Orkney's earls. In one of the most dramatic events of Orkney's history, Erlendsson was murdered on Egilsay in 1117 on the orders of his cousin Haakon. The latter was succeeded by his son, Paul. After Paul was taken captive on Rousay by the pirate Swein Asleifsson, the path was clear for Magnus's nephew, Rognvald Kolsson, to sail from Norway to Orkney and reclaim his uncle's earldom in 1136.

Rognvald reigned as Earl of Orkney and Caithness and shortly afterwards moved the seat of power from Birsay to Kirkwall. Rognvald was careful to cultivate the cult of sanctity that had evolved around Magnus after his death and promised to build a 'great stone minster' in his uncle's honour. Magnus's remains were brought to Kirkwall, a journey followed by the bones of Rognvald when he too was murdered in 1158 and subsequently beatified.

The last of the Norse earls, Earl Jon Haroldsson, a descendant of Thorfinn, was murdered in a dispute in 1231. With no clear Norse heir, Jon's death marked a turning point and the line of the earldom died out. Scottish nobles, with whom the earls had already intermixed for a decade or so, stepped into the vacuum in the form of the Earls of Angus.

THE BATTLE OF LARGS The 150 or so years after Jon's death have been called the Dark Period because the historical records are sparse. Nevertheless, it is known that the future of Orkney was shaped by a battle in 1263 in a small town in Ayrshire, 280 miles south of the islands. Often referred to as 'the last battle of the Vikings', the Battle of Largs was the scene of a face off between Haakon IV of Norway and Alexander III of Scotland. At stake was control of not only the Clyde islands (west of modern-day Glasgow) but of the Hebrides, the Scottish mainland and, by extension, Orkney. While Haakon had control of much of the lands in question, it was all now claimed by Alexander.

The expected cataclysmic battle never quite unfolded. Haakon had 120 ships and up to 20,000 men but the conflict itself left no clear winner, with a ferocious storm throwing the Norse forces into as much disarray as did the advances of the Scots' army. Haakon's forces were driven off and he returned to Orkney, where he died in the Bishop's Palace in Kirkwall in December 1263. His son, Magnus the Lawmender, was (as his name suggests) more amenable to a practical resolution and at the Treaty of Perth in 1266 gave up the Isle of Man, and the Hebrides; in return he gained recognition from the Scots of Norwegian rule over Orkney and Shetland.

The Earls of Angus ruled until 1320 with the earldom subsequently transferred to Earl Malise of Strathcarron. The Earls of St Clair (Sinclair), hailing from Midlothian, took over the dynasty later in the 14th century; their dominance marked the end of the Norse era in Orkney. Increasingly, there were tensions between the earls and the bishops. As language and culture came under increasing Scottish influence, old customs, as well as the Norn language, began to die out.

PART OF SCOTLAND The late Middle Ages saw great upheavals in Orkney. The Black Death (1347–51) devastated the population and caused the grain market to collapse. Norway, a key importer, lost a third of its population to the plague. The islands were also vulnerable to European economic pressures and in the 15th century the Hanseatic League of powerful German merchants gained a monopoly over the grain trade and further squeezed Orkney out of a diminishing market. The last impact of the Battle of Largs was played out with the transfer of Orkney to Scotland. First Orkney was pawned (the technical term is 'impignorated') to Scotland as part of a dowry in 1468 and formally annexed on 20 February 1472. Many Orkney families lost their lands to the incoming Scots, and fierce emotions were stoked over the Norse legal concept Udal Law, which allowed permanent possession after land had been held for six generations. In contrast, Scots feudal

UDAL LAW

Udal Law is an unusual form of tenure found in Orkney and Shetland. It derives from the Norse legal system, which applied in the islands when they were part of the Norwegian kingdom. In essence, it is an old Norse system of inheritance. Although the islands are now part of Scotland, Udal Law has never been formally abolished in Orkney and Shetland and, in principle, still applies, insofar as it has not been superseded by United Kingdom or Scottish law. In practice, however, Udal Law now applies only to certain aspects of land tenure, the most relevant one for the visitor relating to the ownership of the foreshore. Elsewhere in the UK, a landowner's rights only extend to the high-water mark with anything beyond that claimed by the Crown. Under Udal Law, the foreshore is included in coastal titles, meaning that ownership extends right down to the low-tide mark and that the Crown has no prior right to the foreshore.

A convention deployed over the years has been to settle the issue of just where the foreshore starts and stops by how far a stone can be hurled, a salmon net cast or a horse can wade until neck-deep. In theory, the Crown cannot claim any archaeological finds in this area as treasure trove, though in the rare cases this issue has arisen, the courts have found for the Crown.

law assumed ownership of all land. By the mid 16th century Orkney was operating under a form of home rule similar to that of the Isle of Man. Even the landscape was changing, as incoming Scottish lairds built substantial stone dwellings. At least the last battle on Orkney soil had already taken place: in 1529 the Battle of Summerdale saw an uprising by James Sinclair quashed by rival Sinclairs from Caithness under the command of James V of Scotland.

Influences of the earls were not always positive, not least the notoriously cruel Stewart family, who were known for their barbarity. That said, they left more positive architectural legacies in the form of early 17th-century palaces in Kirkwall and Birsay. In order to curb the power of the earls, James VI (James I of England and Ireland) abolished Norse Law in Orkney and Shetland in 1611. However, like every subsequent monarch and lawmaker, he was unable to comprehensively shift Orcadians on the issue of Udal Law. Plague returned in 1629 and famine followed in 1631 and 1633, with bitterly cold winds that destroyed corn before it ripened. Harrowing accounts from this time tell of people simply dying in fields, living off dogs and seaweed or hurling themselves into the sea.

THE JACOBITE REBELLION When the Stuart King James VII (James II of England and Ireland) was deposed in 1688, the smaller Orkney lairds supported the rebellion and also, to a lesser extent, the later attempts to reclaim the Crown by James's grandson, Bonnie Prince Charlie, in 1745. After Charlie was defeated in emphatic fashion at Culloden in 1746, the 18th- and 19th-century clearances formed part of the reprisals, ravaging much of the Highlands and the Hebrides. Orkney escaped the worst of the impacts, mainly because by this time most of the islands had already been parcelled up into individual ownership and no single person held too much land. Where this was not the case, such as on Rousay, clearances did occur and their imprint there is still felt today (page 178), particularly in Quandale and Westness, which now exude the mournful legacy of ruined crofts.

Industry in the 18th century was dominated by kelp production, of which Orkney emerged as the main British centre from around 1720. By the end of the century more than 3,000 people were employed in the industry and the lairds of Orkney enjoyed handsome profits.

At the same time, Orkney supplied the bulk of workers to the emerging trading empire of the Hudson's Bay Company, as well as to the whaling industry. Communities were characterised by small farms and tenants; arable land, in particular, was divided into 'tunships', a local farming area controlled by a main landowner. Turnips and potatoes were introduced in the 18th century. Hills and moorland were generally treated as common grazing land while farms were separated by turf dykes. Access to the markets of the south, however, remained poor so lairds continued to rely on kelp and linen for their income. The kelp industry collapsed around 1830, forcing migration from islands such as North Ronaldsay. During the 19th and early 20th centuries herring fleets filled several harbours to the brim with both catches and boats.

While Orkney and Scapa Flow in particular were to play a key role in the great wars of the 20th century, it is less well known that the British government recognised the islands' strategic importance much earlier. During the Napoleonic Wars between 1803 and 1815, Hoy and Longhope were fortified against the French navy and American privateers (page 135).

THE 20TH CENTURY For Orkney, the impact and importance of the 20th century's two world wars cannot be overstated. During both World War I and World War II, Scapa Flow was the main anchorage and headquarters for the Royal Navy's battle fleet. While the historic home ports of the Royal Navy were in the south of England, a base from which to control the northern entrances to the North Sea was essential to counter the threat from Germany. To this end, there was a need to command and defend an area radiating out into the North Sea, and both the Atlantic and Arctic oceans; Scapa Flow provided a superb natural harbour for the large number of naval vessels and supporting infrastructure. That said, the final decision to make Scapa Flow the main base for the Grand Fleet in the event of war (rather than the Invergordon dockyard in the Firth of Cromarty) was made only on the eve of war.

The arrival of the Grand Fleet at Orkney from 1914 transformed the islands into one of the world's most important strategic locations. Scapa Flow provided natural defences in the form of narrow access channels from the east, west and south, which could be defended against enemy ships and submarines from headlands and the many islands within its waters.

Guns were installed at all entrances, on Graemsay, Hoy and Ness (on the headland at Stromness) in the west, and on South Ronaldsay, Burray and smaller islands in the east. Minefields were laid and submarine nets draped across Scapa Flow. Meanwhile, drifters and trawlers patrolled the approaches. A number of ageing coastal steamers were sunk – becoming known as blockships – to defend the narrow passages between the five islands on the eastern side of Scapa Flow. At its height, the Orkney garrison numbered around 100,000 personnel.

For all the preparations and military presence at Scapa Flow, the British and German fleets clashed just once – though dramatically – at the Battle of Jutland, which, while failing to provide decisive victory, confirmed British naval dominance.

The waters around Scapa Flow have borne witness to several horrific disasters. In 1916, HMS *Hampshire* (see box, page 99) was sunk by a mine off Marwick Head with the loss of 737 personnel and passengers. On 9 July 1917, HMS *Vanguard* blew up at anchors in Scapa Flow, the ship torn apart by unstable cordite in the ship's magazine. The force of the blast was so powerful that a complete 12in gun turret, weighing 400 tons, was found on Flotta, a mile away; 804 men died and just two survived. The ship is a now a war grave.

On 12 January 1918, the destroyers HMS *Narborough* and HMS *Opal* were engulfed in a violent snowstorm and smashed on the rocks of South Ronaldsay; just one man survived out of 180 crew across both ships. At the end of the war, the captured German fleet was interred in Scapa Flow, where, after months of internment, it was dramatically scuttled in on 21 June 1919 (see box, page 70). When hostilities were fully concluded, Scapa Flow's batteries were all dismantled in the 1920s and the guns cut up for scrap.

As World War II approached, there were just two batteries on Orkney: at Stanger Head (Flotta) and at Ness (Stromness). In World War II, Scapa Flow again housed the Home Fleet but its defences had deteriorated: harbour barriers were inadequate, there was little anti-aircraft protection and patrol vessels were in short supply. This was made all too apparent on 14 October 1939 when the German submarine U-47 slipped through Kirk Sound at South Walls and torpedoed the *Royal Oak* (see box, page 161) with the loss of 833 lives.

In response, Churchill ordered the construction of four substantial barriers along the eastern entrances to the Flow (see box, page 6) but in an age where air defences were now also required, the barriers alone would not be sufficient (it would also take four years for them to be completed).

Sea defences, anti-aircraft guns and military were assembled to form the Osdef (Orkney and Shetland Sea defences) garrison. By spring 1940 Scapa Flow had begun to re-establish its defences and the Orkney battery was formed. Boom defences were overhauled and formidable anti-aircraft batteries were built, which together with the ships at anchor, constituted the Orkney Barrage. Eventually six batteries guarded the western entrances to Scapa Flow.

By 1940, within an 8-mile radius of Scapa Flow, there were 88 heavy anti-aircraft guns, 36 light anti-aircraft guns, 88 operational searchlights, 96 Lewis machine guns and 81 barrage balloons. Scapa Flow also became home to 60,000 troops dedicated to guarding the fleet. Aerodromes were established (including several dummy ones across the Outer Isles) and the Navy's patrol service expanded. As it turned out, no German ships ever took on the coastal batteries but several warning shots were fired across the bows of errant merchant ships.

Lyness on Hoy, which had been the headquarters for Scapa Flow in 1919, now became the main shore base for supplying the home fleet. As many as 12,000 military personnel and civilians were stationed at the naval headquarters at Lyness. It wasn't all hard work: to relieve the boredom that sailors called 'Orkneyitis' – most personnel were unused to living on a smattering of remote and small Sottish islands amid such an unforgiving climate – inter-ship rowing regattas and athletics were organised, and cinemas and social centres built. Many of these buildings survive, if now crumbling, to this day (page 146).

The principal military resting ground for those who died in the naval disasters around Scapa Flow is the Naval Cemetery at Lyness but most cemeteries on the island are home to war graves. Just as likely to halt you in your steps are the war memorials on the outer islands, which record the shockingly high casualty rates among what were already small communities: Sanday alone lost 50 men, 48 in World War I.

The events of both world wars have left their mark in the form of a remarkable collection of wartime structures, ranging from observation posts to Martello towers and dummy airfields. The legacy for the islands has also been substantial: the Churchill Barriers (see box, page 160) now serve as causeways that enable visitors to drive from South Ronaldsay to the Mainland in just a few minutes.

More recently, the discovery of oil and gas in the North Sea has pumped money into the economy. Since 1977, crude oil has been transported to the processing terminal on Flotta. The site currently employs more than 170 people and also handles liquid petroleum gas pumped along a 130-mile pipeline from the North Sea. Maintenance of fossil-fuel vessels also takes place in the sheltered waters of Scapa Flow.

ARCHAEOLOGY

Orkney's extraordinary landscape of Neolithic villages, standing stones and burial mounds is one of the major – arguably *the* major – attractions for visitors. In many respects, the landscape is unchanged from the time these structures appeared. It is no exaggeration to say that Orkney is one of the richest archaeological landscapes in Europe.

Most of the sites that have gained global recognition date to 5,200–4,000 years ago – during the Neolithic or New Stone Age. The inevitable focus – rightly so – is on the Heart of the Neolithic Orkney World Heritage Site on the Mainland, which comprises the ensemble of Maeshowe, the Standing Stones of Stenness, the Ring of Brodgar and Skara Brae. Most predate or are contemporaneous with the Egyptian pyramids; all precede Stonehenge. These sites have played an important role in establishing theories and knowledge of prehistory, not just in Orkney but across the world. Yet while they are indeed spectacular and well worth a visit, there are countless less-visited Neolithic tombs, burial cairns, standing stones and green mounds awaiting exploration. More 'recent' sites feature Iron Age brochs, Norse settlements and early

Christian hermitages perched dramatically on rock stacks. Walking around such sites, scrambling on all fours through a chamber barely changed for thousands of years, can prove simultaneously haunting, moving and exhilarating. What is also impressive is that access to the vast majority of sites is free.

Skara Brae was the first Neolithic settlement to be discovered in 1850; since then, the remains of several further Neolithic communities have been identified, starting with a settlement on the island of Rousay in 1930. Significant archaeological ruins turn up all over the place and in unlikely locations, even, in the case of the Grain Earth-House (page 123), on what is now an industrial estate in Kirkwall. Just about every island boasts a solitary, or dominant, sentinel stone, that often carried particular significance either in relation to the sun, moon or legend.

The obvious question is: why do all these treasures turn up in Orkney? 'Archaeological evidence like this does exist elsewhere but we don't always look for it,' says Orkney archaeologist Caroline Wickham-Jones. 'It may be difficult to find, under modern developments, made of different materials, or have suffered from agricultural or urban attrition.'

The soils of Orkney are less acidic than those of mainland Scotland, which has enabled the remarkable preservation of artefacts as well as buildings. Furthermore, for those who arrived some 6,000 years ago, Orkney proved a good place to live: rich fertile soil yielded food and the Gulf Stream moderated the environment. Location mattered then, as it does today: a glance at a contemporary map suggests that Orkney is relatively isolated but to Stone Age peoples the opposite was true. 'Today, political power is in the south and we are generally restricted to inflexible terrestrial transport,' says Wickham-Jones. 'But look at Orkney through the eyes of a boat traveller and it becomes the centre of things.' The natural boundaries of the islands also perhaps encouraged cohesive communities that on the British mainland may simply have moved on in time to new ground. The result is that Orkney represents an early flourishing and sophistication of the culture of these prehistoric farming communities.

The burial mounds you see across the islands tend to date to the early Bronze Age, after 2000BC. Although metals were introduced and bronze tools were common across much of Britain, they were scarce in Orkney. Archaeologists have, however, found considerable evidence of a change in burial and other social practices from this time: bodies were no longer placed in communal tombs but in individual cists made of stone slabs, mounds or pits, in which the body was placed in a crouched position. This shift, combined with a change in settlement patterns, is assumed to indicate a major upheaval in society after 2200BC.

Roundhouses – sturdy stone dwellings, sometimes with defensive outer walls and ditches – emerged around 700BC. They were much more conspicuous (perhaps deliberately so) than the semi-subterranean sites where communities had traditionally settled.

Orkney also has a smattering of important Iron Age brochs – of which roundhouses are regarded as early prototypes – dating from the last years BC through to about AD300. Home to tribal leaders, brochs are enigmatic, their exact purpose uncertain: perhaps they were fortified houses, food stores or simply statements of wealth. Orkney brochs typically stand – or stood, in some cases – 25ft in height. They are scattered across many islands.

The Pictish era left its mark on Orkney's archaeology, primarily in the form of symbols carved on stone monuments. Ten symbol stones have been found on the islands, including an eagle, a mirror and a hippocamp (a horse with piscine hindquarters). The Picts also deployed a writing system known as *ogham*, a script dating to the 1st century AD that was used to write early Irish languages, and to

Here is a summary timeline of key events and periods in Orkney's early history. Note that dates are often approximate; even authoritative historical sources are challenged!

8000 BC	End of last Ice Age
8000–3500BC	Mesolithic
3600–3100BC	Knap of Howar (Papa Westray)
3500–2000BC	Neolithic
3100BC	Skara Brae
3000BC	Maeshowe chambered cairn, Ness of Brodgar, Midhowe Cairn (Rousay), Tofts Ness (Sanday), Pool (Sanday), Links of Noltland (Westray)
2900BC	Standing Stones of Stenness, Elsness-Quoyness chambered cairn (Sanday)
2500BC	Skara Brae abandoned
2500–2000BC	Ring of Brodgar
2100BC	Stonehenge
2000–500BC	Bronze Age
500–200BC	Early Iron Age
200BC–AD300	Middle Iron Age
200BC–AD100	Broch of Gurness (the Mainland)
200BC–AD200	Midhowe Broch (Rousay)
AD300–800	Later Iron Age
AD565	Orkney incorporated into the Pictish kingdom
AD800–1065	Viking era
AD1065–1240	Late Norse Earldom
AD1472	Orkney becomes part of Scotland

inscribe stone slabs and personal objects. (The actual language they used, however, remains unknown: it may have been a relict from the language used by Bronze Age peoples or a Celtic language, perhaps related to Ancient British.)

Early Christian sites account for an important – and often dramatically located – element of Orkney's archaeology. They include the 7th-century church St Boniface Kirk and corbelled chapel on Papa Stronsay. In all, at least half a dozen hermitage sites are to be found across the islands, such as the broch of Burgh Head on Stronsay.

FILLING IN THE GAPS Two striking elements of archaeology in Orkney are its sheer variety and depth. 'You go to Skara Brae and you see where Neolithic people lived but you also see the beautiful jewellery they wore. It's somewhere you can immerse yourself in the ancient past in a way that is not possible elsewhere,' says Wickham-Jones. 'Orkney gives you an intimate view of people who lived 4,000–5,000 years ago and again 1,000 years ago during the Norse period. You just don't get that kind of information about anywhere else. Stonehenge, for example, is amazing but it's just the bare bones of a monument.'

In some cases, archaeologists can be reasonably confident of what happened, why and when. When Skara Brae was in use, single stones and circles of stones were erected in open-air ceremony sites. The Ring of Brodgar, meanwhile, was seen as an important ritual site, a place to bury the dead near but too important to bury them inside.

Yet a striking feature of Orkney is that archaeologists are uncovering primary evidence and revising the history of Orkney on what feel like a continual basis. In 2007, the discovery of a single hazelnut at Tankerness on the East Mainland resulted in the history of human settlement on Orkney being pushed back several hundred years to 6700BC, meaning that humans were rambling around these islands in Mesolithic times. Two years later, a dig on Westray uncovered the Orkney Venus, a 5,000-year-old female figure – by some distance the oldest of its kind identified in Scotland. The huge Ness of Brodgar was revealed to the world (including watching tourists) while a dig was taking place. The Ness, possibly a sophisticated temple complex, is one of Europe's largest ongoing archaeological digs and is regularly throwing up newsworthy finds, some of which are turning conventional history on its head.

Not the least of these is the theory that thousands of years ago Orkney may have been the cultural centre of the British Isles, due to the islands sharing influences with the world beyond the Pentland Firth and North Sea. Pottery fragments found at Skara Brae and the Barnhouse Village near the Standing Stones of Stenness are similar to styles found on the Scottish mainland and across England as far south as Wessex, pointing to contact between cultures, exchange of ideas and trade in materials.

There's little doubt that much more awaits discovery. Geophysical surveys of lands surrounding Skara Brae and Brodgar and on islands such as Rousay, Westray and Sanday have revealed the existence of as-yet unexcavated settlements. Sea levels are much higher today than they were 5,000 years ago and many Neolithic sites and landscapes almost certainly now lie beneath the waves. Just north of Skara Brae are the remains of a prehistoric quarry with several large monoliths still in place, waiting for transportation that never came.

TOMB FEVER

Orkney has the most remarkable density of archaeological sites, enough to fill not just one book but several (something that has been done many times over). Consequently, this guide is not a compendium of all such places; instead it covers the major 'blockbuster' locations as well as many of the less heralded but important or dramatically situated ones. Archaeology can quickly become addictive: it is easy to suffer 'tomb fever' and find yourself running from one site to another, almost irrespective of whether what you are looking at is important or even interesting. When you find yourself rubbing your chin thoughtfully in front of a protruding ankle-high stone in the middle of a moor (in a howling gale), perhaps call 'time out'. The other condition afflicting visitors is that of being 'tombed out', when the thought of visiting yet another cairn makes your eyes water.

Another issue derives from ever-tighter government funding. Because of this, the costs of archaeological digs are increasingly met by crowdfunding. This can mean that any new find has to be promoted and perhaps occasionally sprinkled with hyperbole in order to justify funding and secure further support. An objective view of just how meaningful a site actually is can become skewed: not every site is as important as the next, nor are they all must-sees. Orkney does not have an overlay of Celtic and Gaelic culture to dig up but medieval Orkney has been arguably under-researched and eclipsed by the focus on the Neolithic. Take time to stand back and judge for yourself. Orkney's lumps and bumps have been around for up to 6,000 years and will be around for a little longer yet should you wish to return.

The wonder of Orkney is that there is still so much that we just do not know and may have to accept that we will probably never know. Bayesian radiocarbon dating may have tied down the precise dates when certain sites were active but, while just about every archaeologist worth their salt has combed over the islands, we are still left with a jigsaw with many missing pieces and where informed conjecture plays a significant part in filling in the gaps.

This mystery and the enigmatic purposes of many sites on Orkney arguably adds to their allure. 'I like the idea that archaeology is not a given,' says Wickham-Jones. 'There is always a quest for a precise date. But it can be a dangerous route to go down, especially if you use Bayesian dating to prove patterns you think you know exist. New sites are coming up all the time. People like a bit of mystery and we all like to be given a chance to think for ourselves.'

The Vikings' imprint can be seen primarily in the Norse settlements and burial sites at the Brough of Birsay, the Broch of Gurness and the Earl's Bu at Orphir, all on the Mainland. Discoveries at Gurness included tortoise brooches found at the burial site of a 10th-century woman. Other important Norse sites include Pierowall, Quoygrew and Tuquoy, all on Westray. Meanwhile, distinctive bone pins and combs of the resident Picts have been unearthed in a number of Viking settlements, which suggests that the invaders absorbed rather than exterminated earlier inhabitants.

The mid-12th century saw the emergence of castles at a time when building flourished. Wealthy landowners and chiefs were inspired by St Magnus Cathedral and began to raise substantial structures.

While many of the treasures discovered on Orkney are now housed either in the British Museum or the National Museum in Edinburgh, a significant number of finds have been kept on the islands: everything from burial cists to intricately carved antler combs and Pictish symbol stones can be found in the Orkney Museum in Kirkwall (page 123), the Westray Stone and Westray Wife carvings are in situ

EXPLORING ANCIENT SITES: YOUR RIGHTS

It's entirely plausible that a visitor to the islands may come across a new find. Indeed, this usually happens at least once a year: a polished, carved rock with a weathered swirling pattern you pick up on the beach may have a history. At the same time, if you do go down this route be prepared for a good deal of disappointment. That same stone carving could be an antiquity but it might just be a cast-off from a sculptor who has dumped the contents of their workshop on a shoreline. If you do think you have found something interesting, and you're confident it will not be washed away by tides, take a photograph and contact either the Orkney Museum in Kirkwall (page 123) or the Orkney county archaeologist via Orkney Islands Council (℡ 01856 873535). In the case of a hump or a mound in a field, you can see if anyone else has beaten you to it, or add further details if they have, at w pastmap.org.uk.

One should also be mindful of Scotland's Treasure Trove legislation (w treasuretrovescotland.co.uk), which states that any find belongs to the government of Scotland. You must report any finds directly to Treasure Trove, which is an easy process. The exception to this – and unique to Orkney and Shetland – is the foreshore, where Udal Law (see box, page 19) comes into play. Any skeletal remains suspected of being human should be reported to Police Scotland.

in the island's heritage centre (page 249) and you'll find the Skara Brae Buddo in Stromness Museum (page 84).

Books and online resources abound and you can either tiptoe in the waters of Orkney's prehistory or dive in as deep as you wish. Excellent resources to get you started include the archaeology website **w** www.orkneyjar.com, maintained by local antiquarian Sigurd Towrie; an authoritative book, *Monuments of Orkney*, written by Caroline Wickham-Jones for Historic Environment Scotland; and Canmore (**w** canmore.org.uk), a website of archaeological surveys operated by Historic Environment Scotland, which is impressively surgical in its descriptions and assessments without missing much. Wickham-Jones's own blog (**w** mesolithic. co.uk) is regularly updated with fascinating insights, recent discoveries and shifts in the understanding of the deep past of Orkney.

GOVERNMENT AND POLITICS

The islands are governed by Orkney Islands Council, Britain's smallest council, which was established in 1974. Its political make-up is unusual, in that councillors are generally independent and not tied to a specific party. At local elections in 2017, 20 of the 21 councillors were independent, the exception being a Green Party representative. Before the 2017 election, all 21 candidates had been independent. Councillors are elected under the Single Transferable Vote, whereby voters use numbers instead of a cross and rank candidates in order of preference. A quota and formulae system then decides who is elected, based on the preferences as indicated by the voters. At the last election three councillors were elected unopposed.

Historically, the Mainland of Orkney has been divided into parishes. On the West Mainland, these are: Orphir, Harray, Stenness, Rendall, Birsay, Evie, Firth, Sandwick and Stromness. On the East Mainland the parishes are St Andrews, Deerness and Holm. The parish of St Ola surrounds Kirkwall.

Nationally, at Westminster, the seat of Orkney and Shetland has been held by the Liberal Democrat (or its predecessor, the Liberal) Party since 1950. In the 2017 election, Alistair Carmichael was returned with a majority of 4,563 (49%) on a turnout of 23,277. Orkney has a single seat at the Scottish Parliament and again, the present incumbent is a Liberal Democrat. At the time of writing, Orkney, along with the rest of Scotland, is represented by six members of the European Parliament, elected by a system of proportional representation.

In the Scottish independence referendum of 2015, Orkney voted emphatically by 67:33 on a turnout of 17,806 to remain part of the United Kingdom. In 2016, the islands voted almost as unambiguously (63:37, on a turnout of 68%) to remain in the EU.

While these votes are instructive about the world view that broadly prevails in Orkney, there is an undercurrent that would, if given the chance, take things even further. A common joke is that during the independence referendum, several ballot papers were spoilt by voters adding in the options to be independent of Scotland or even to join with Norway. Sure enough, a preliminary shot in this debate emerged in January 2017, when a majority of Orkney's councillors backed a motion demanding an investigation into what was called 'greater autonomy or self-determination'. The motion demanded the chief executive put together a report considering 'whether the people of Orkney could exercise self-determination if faced with further national or international constitutional changes,' adding pointedly 'or indeed to decide if more autonomy might be beneficial for the well-being of Orkney'.

Close your eyes momentarily to the archaeological sites, the wonderful landscapes, cliffs and birdlife and you realise that, in essence, Orkney is one big farm. Being so close to the sea has brought high levels of calcium and sea minerals to the soil, creating fertile grazing for cattle (beef and dairy) and sheep. Farming is the mainstay of the economy. At least 30,000 head of beef cattle reside on the islands and much is made of the fact the cattle is fed almost entirely on lush grass with only rare recourse to imported soy, silage and grain supplements. Agriculture employs more than 1,200 people, or 10% of the population; construction accounts for 10% and wholesale/retail activities for 13%.

In contrast to Shetland, fishing is a relatively small player, employing around 350 people. Inshore vessels collecting crabs and lobsters is the main activity here, and Orkney boasts the UK's largest crab production facility in Westray. Aquaculture is growing exponentially in the sheltered bays around Scapa Flow and in some of the bays and sounds of the North Isles. These include both salmon farms and the lobster hatchery at Lamb Holm, which releases around 60,000 juvenile lobsters every year. Food and drink are becoming significant employers, with two breweries, two distilleries and three gin producers on the Mainland along with bakeries and cheesemakers on other islands. Marine renewables are being developed, with Lyness on Hoy (plus Shapinsay and Eday) becoming a centre of assembly, storage and servicing of marine renewable-energy devices. Creative industries are also strong, with knitwear and textiles increasingly providing employment.

Oil sprung upon the scene in dramatic fashion in the 1970s; ever since, the island of Flotta has been a major site for processing oil and for tanker-to-tanker transfers (see box, page 157). So far, there has been no pollution spillage in the pristine waters of Scapa Flow. The Islands Council was widely praised in the 1970s for striking a deal with the oil companies that a percentage of all profits was to be given to the council. By and large, the consensus is that this dividend has been invested wisely on infrastructure projects and for rainy days to top up dwindling central government funding. This, though, is unsustainable in the long term (dwindling North Sea oil reserves have been topped up by new gas field discoveries in Shetland waters), which is why renewable energy appears to be such a crucial factor in Orkney's future prosperity. In the 1970s and 1980s, plans were kicked around for a uranium mine on the west coast of the Mainland near Yesnaby. Although the prime minister Margaret Thatcher was keen on the idea, it ultimately came to nought, thanks in part to a local campaign led by the composer Peter Maxwell Davies, who lived on Hoy.

Tourism is now a close second to farming in terms of economic importance. In 2015, 173,200 staying visitors injected an estimated £60.5m into the economy, up from £46m in 2009. So, in general, the statistics suggest the economy is in good health. The employment rate (90.3%) is higher than in both Scotland and the rest of the UK. The unemployment rate among those aged 18–24 dropped by 70% between 2013 and 2018.

In 2013, the Office for National Statistics calculated that Orkney's Gross Disposable Household Income (money left after expenditure associated with income generation, for example, taxes and social contributions, property ownership and provision for future pension income) was £18,579, higher than any other region of Scotland.

Yet the economy operates within the context of a handful of seemingly fixed issues: high transport and shipping costs and a trend of depopulation on the Outer Isles, with a concentration of people on the Mainland and particularly Kirkwall.

One topic guaranteed to divide opinion on Orkney is the islands' burgeoning popularity as a cruise-ship destination. In 2010, Hatston Pier outside Kirkwall welcomed 70 vessels, with a total of 25,440 passengers; by 2016 this had risen to 116, with 95,750 passengers in all. That 2016 figure represented a 20% rise on 2015. Orkney is now the number-one UK destination for the cruise-ship industry and at some times during the season (March to September), there is no denying that the larger ships and the passengers they disgorge can be intrusive.

Talk to some shopkeepers on Kirkwall's high street and they welcome the chance to sell their wares; others are far less keen, not always because the revenue passes them by, but more because of the visual impact on their town. Outside Kirkwall, locals and tourists can find it frustrating to have to reverse or give way to coaches that are ill suited to sweeping along narrow lanes. At times, major sites can be overwhelmed with visitors, dissipating the very atmosphere of solitude and repose that many visitors seek on Orkney. Either way everyone is increasingly mindful of the impact and the need for co-ordinated efforts to bring the issue under control and for cruise ships to be carefully managed.

Fortunately, there is now a dialogue between the public, local authorities and the liners that increasingly regulates when, where, and in what numbers their passengers can go. Meanwhile, guesthouse and hotel staff may have a quiet word with you and suggest you visit the main attractions another day and point you towards other locations unvisited by cruise passengers. One intention of this book is to demonstrate how wrong-headed is the notion that Orkney begins with Skara Brae and the Ring of Brodgar and ends with Kirkwall and the Italian Chapel (just about the only sites visited by cruise passengers).

Fishing is in decline, farming less so, but there is a clear need to train and support new businesses. All the islands have established development trusts, which have remits to reinvigorate the local economy and put in place measures to reverse population decline. In the way of such things, their impact is entirely dependent on the outlook of those who become involved: some trusts are highly dynamic but one or two seem keener to preserve their island as it is and keep the wider world at bay.

Nor is everything perfect. A large number of jobs, as elsewhere in the UK, are part-time and low-wage. Many Orcadians were taken aback when a food bank was opened in Kirkwall in 2013. And, despite the progressive approach to renewable energy, the reality remains that many properties are poorly insulated and rack up high fuel bills. Some islands, such as Stronsay and Westray, have palpably vibrant communities and are good at securing grants to kick-start enterprises. Others can feel as though they are on the edge of depopulation.

REINVIGORATING THE NORTH ISLES The population of the North Isles dropped by 3.85% to 2,122 between the censuses of 2001 and 2011. The primary challenge Orkney faces is common to islands worldwide: how to stop the young generation from moving away and reversing a demographic that is increasingly elderly and has seen traditional industries such as fishing and agriculture decline as people retire without being replaced. In order to help halt these seemingly inexorable trends, the

North Isles Landscape Partnership Scheme (w nilps.co.uk) was founded in 2017 with an aim to inject £4.5m into the communities. The wider aim of the project is simply to raise the profile of the islands and showcase their appeal in terms of viable jobs, whether in agriculture or renewables, and their attractions (peace and quiet; and the chance to part of a meaningful community). Some islands, such as Westray and Papa Westray, appear to be showing the way, creating a cat's cradle of

GREEN ENERGY

Having reaped the benefits of fossil fuels for so many years it is ironic that Orkney, surrounded by strong currents and tidal waters and not short of wind, is now emerging as one of the major players in the UK's renewable energy transition. Orkney produces more than 100% of its energy needs from green energy – renewable energy is seen as a good fit for the islands as it ties in with the ideas of a clean, pristine environment where wildlife thrives and pollution is something that happens elsewhere.

The islands are home to the highest concentration of small and micro-wind turbines in the UK – more than 500 at the last count – and also has single locally owned and commercial wind farms, at Hammars Hill near Tingwall and Burger Hill above Evie, respectively.

Tidal-energy projects are more advanced than wave energy, mainly on account of the fact that tides are predictable. Tidal energy was pioneered in the Fall of War Ness, a narrow channel off Eday where currents reach almost 7.8 knots/sec. The fast-flowing waters of the Pentland Firth have also attracted interest in establishing a tidal array. Average wave height on Orkney is 2–3m, with a maximum of 19m. The islands made the news in 2008 when a project powered by Pelamis became the world's first to use offshore wave energy to generate electricity into a grid system.

Surf 'n' Turf (w surfnturf.org.uk) is a community project that aims to use surplus electricity generated from wind and tidal energy to split water molecules to generate hydrogen gas. Central to this has been the activity of the European Marine Energy Centre on Eday (see box, page 222) which has worked to develop an electrolyser that can use power from tidal turbines to produce hydrogen. The idea is that stored hydrogen will be shipped to Kirkwall where a hydrogen fuel cell will convert the hydrogen back into electricity using oxygen from the air. This energy will initially be used for auxiliary power for ferries in dock and for wider harbour operations.

On Shapinsay, the intention is that such hydrogen be used to power infrastructure such as heating in the island school. These developments will not only reduce carbon emissions but also mitigate chronic electricity-grid issues on the islands.

For now, Orkney has no means of exporting its surplus green energy to the British mainland; negotiations continue to install a highly expensive sub-sea interconnector cable to enable this.

More positively, the growth in renewable-energy technology and production is viewed as a means of halting or even reversing the ever-present threat of island population declines. Increasingly, highly educated young professionals, often motivated by the virtues of green energy, are employed on Orkney. To some extent this helps to reverse the exodus of young people.

employment, whereby many jobs are mutually interdependent: a school will employ a teacher, a classroom assistant, a janitor; the airfield will keep two or three people in employment; and there's always a need for firefighters and a postman or woman plus people to run the village shop. The NHS on such islands is also important. The buildings people live and work in require maintenance, so construction is another useful employer. Remove one thread and the whole thing may unravel. Tourism is part of this, though not the fulcrum: changing bedsheets on a weekend and converting a liveable house to self-catering are not viable in the long-term.

PEOPLE

Orcadians have long asserted their Norse heritage and, in 2015, a DNA study across the British Isles confirmed what islanders already knew – namely that Viking genes are prominent throughout the isles. However, the research also suggested that while Norwegian DNA accounted for 25% of Orcadian DNA, the genetic legacy of Pictish and other pre-Viking communities remained strong.

Whatever their heritage, the National Records of Scotland put Orkney's population at 21,670 in 2015, an increase of 0.4% from 2014 and up from 19,290 in 2000. Orkney's population accounts for 0.4% of Scotland's total. Nearly 15% of the population are aged 16–29 years, lower than in Scotland overall (18.2%). Persons aged 60 and over make up 29.2% of Orkney's population, significantly higher than in Scotland overall (24.2%). Between 2014 and 2015, Orkney experienced a 5.5% increase in the number of births, rising from 181 to 191 – and this against a backdrop of a 2.9% decline in Scotland. Whether this is within the range of natural variation or an indicator of population growth remains unclear, though the National Records of Scotland has predicted that the population of Orkney will increase by 2.4% to 22,098 by 2039. Over the 25-year period from 2014, the trend is towards an increasingly ageing population in Orkney, with the age group 75 and over projected to show the greatest increase. At 78.8 years, male life expectancy is two years longer than the Scottish average; women on average live 1.5 years longer than the Scottish average, to 82.5 years.

Nine-tenths of Orkney's dwellings are occupied, 7% are vacant and 4% are second homes. The total number of households in Orkney is projected to increase by 17% from 2012 (9,859) to 2037 (11,534); the number of single-adult households is projected to increase by 39%.

Island culture can be very distinctive and nowhere more so than Orkney. However short or long your visit you will become aware of just how important Orcadian culture is to local people. Entrepreneurship is key: people are innovative, independent, self-reliant and good at making 'stuff' that works. In the past, those who couldn't do so either starved or had to move on. Many islanders have more than one job, several have half a dozen or more.

This ability to think on one's feet and change direction on a sixpence is evidenced by the way in which local marine and fossil-fuel operators are moving swiftly and seamlessly into renewable energy. 'It's the Orcadian way to look for new things,' says Dave Flanagan, a local journalist and Orcadian. 'Everyone chips in. People are very quietly proud of their heritage. They're not in your face all the time.'

This culture is also evident in family life and in tight communities. A vital component of any wedding, for example, is the Bride's Cog, a wooden drinking vessel filled with spicy punch that bride and groom must lug around the dance floor. The making of a cog is a highly skilled art and all cog-makers have their own prints and styles. It's easy to infer from what you see that there is a sense of Orkney first, Scotland second; and that people don't want to be over-governed, whether by Edinburgh or Westminster.

Another striking facet of Orcadian life is the ubiquity of fundraising. You will rarely attend any event without a raffle of some kind being held, with ticket receipts put to a good cause. People make time in their everyday lives to help others; on outer islands this may manifest itself in drivers offering you lifts when you are walking. Should accommodation be at a premium, no Orcadian will watch you sleep in a bus shelter or in your car.

Finally, it's worth pointing out that is impossible to tell an Orcadian anything they don't already know. No matter how remote the tomb you have just visited, rare the bird you have just spotted, or extreme the storm you have spent watching for 36 hours from your hotel or cottage, your host or new-found friends will nod in recognition and then politely trump you with a story of their own. Their grandfather may have excavated the tomb in question, or an aunt hand-reared the aforementioned species of bird back from the edge of local extinction. Far from this being a case of people being fat-headed, there is a plausible case that something altogether more primordial is at work: a seed planted deep and long ago in the Orcadian gene pool that stirs a curiosity and knowledge of the world, and which was most likely a useful survival tool as far back as the Neolithic era.

GENEALOGY Orkney did not endure the 18th- and 19th-century clearances on the scale that devastated many areas of Scotland's highlands and islands and forced communities to sail across the oceans. Nevertheless, the Orcadian diaspora is substantial; surveys suggest that 18% of Orkney visitors come because they have family connections. Orcadians sailed in search of new ventures in Canada (through the Hudson's Bay Company) and to the United States, New Zealand and Australia. Consequently, third- and even fourth-generation families are increasingly keen to track down their roots. Should you wish to do so, an excellent place to start is the Orkney Family History Society (w orkneyfhs.co.uk/an) which has an office at the Orkney Library and Archive in Kirkwall. The society is run by volunteers and visitors need not be a member to gain their advice. A good website to peruse is w oldscottish.com/orkney.html, which lists rolls of male heads of families, baptismal and marriage registers, kirk sessions and other records. Another website (w janealogy.co.uk) is consistently reliable at unearthing records.

Several islands, such as Rousay, have family-history centres, some running on a more formal basis than others, while w southronaldsay.net has marriage and death records for that island, Burray and the Pentland skerries. Local knowledge should not be underestimated – families and memories, good and bad, go back centuries. Ask at a shop on most islands, or, where it exists, at the office of a development trust, and people will point you in the direction of someone with a store of local history. Records have been kept from the days of the earls and also cover clergy, lairds, tenants, udallers and townspeople – somewhere within all of these, the details you seek may well emerge, whereupon you can use one of the above sources to verify the account.

LANGUAGE

Everyone in Orkney speaks English fluently but as a visitor you will quickly notice that a large number of Orcadians, when talking to one another in shops or pubs or on ferries, seamlessly glide into something quite different. What you're overhearing is Orcadian, which has been described as both a language and, because you can sometimes catch the gist of what is being said, a dialect.

In a nutshell, Orcadian has evolved hand-in-hand with the history of the islands; this is a language that is also a dialect of Scots, the tongue that was introduced to Orkney after the islands became part of Scotland in 1468. The roots of Orcadian, however, go back further than that, to the arrival of the Vikings.

Old Norse was introduced to the islands by the Vikings; this was the same language they took to Shetland, the Faroe Islands and Iceland. Over time, as is the way of languages, it evolved and diverged in each set these islands. Before long, the Old Norse that was spoken in Orkney was different to that spoken elsewhere. This localised version of Old Norse was known as the Norn.

Things changed when Orkney became part of Scotland. The people of Orkney were required to speak Scots as the language of officialdom and commerce, and it slowly supplanted Norn. At home, however, they still spoke the Norn. Over time, however, the Norn began to disappear, as the all-dominating Scots language became more widespread. The last official reference to the Norn on the Orkney mainland came in 1750, although it may still have survived a little longer on North Ronaldsay.

The Norn did not entirely die out, however; instead it was pushed to the periphery, the North Isles and even the fringes of the West Mainland: 'in those days it was quite a journey from Kirkwall on horseback to Birsay,' says Dr Simon Hall, author of *The Orkney Gruffalo* and an expert on the language. In this way, words and fragments of Norn held on; it also benefited from the similarity between Scots and the Norn, which meant that many Norn words remained in use when Scots became widespread.

Today you can find books written in Orcadian and even children's classics, such as *The Gruffalo*, have been translated into it. 'Orcadians will speak it between themselves, at home and with their friends,' says Hall. 'It's really very rich in terms of its vocabulary, being a mixture of English and Scots and a bit of Norn – it is all a grey area because Scots is full of Norse words. This explains why you don't understand it as a visitor: its own sounds and features are unique.'

Some of this is down to the great vowel shift that occurred within English from the 14th to 17th centuries and which also influenced Scots. Originally, words such as house, mouse, out, etc. were pronounced with a short vowel, ie: 'hoose', 'moose', 'oot'. Linguistic fashion changed in southern English, and the short vowel sound gave way to the diphthong sound 'ou'. In much of Scotland, the sound remained (and remains) the same, regardless of southern usage. However, prejudice developed towards the older form, particularly in educational establishments, and people were taught not to use Orcadian. This has contributed to the several historical challenges the language has faced, not least of which is how it, and indeed Scots, has been looked down upon in parts of Scotland. 'People were told Orcadian was inferior, that you had to speak "proper" English to get on. If you said "aye" rather than "yes" or "hoose" rather than "house", you stood out,' says Hall. At one time, 'nornie' – from the Norn – meant old-fashioned, or awkward.

Happily, Orcadian is enjoying something of a resurgence these days, being used in schools and local broadcast media. Hall is encouraged by the range of people who speak Orcadian. 'Orkney is a pretty classless place and you will hear highly educated people speak Orcadian. People are proud of it.' As is the case with Gaelic in the Outer Hebrides, there is a rising interest in speaking Orcadian; offers of night classes are increasingly being taken up.

Support for the language also comes from people digging their heels in. 'There is a sense that some will think "if I don't speak like this then it's just going to go and everyone will speak English." In the same way, people don't want any aspect of their culture to disappear.'

Nevertheless, the language still faces challenges. Cultural snobbery may not apply in Orkney but Hall points out that it is alive and kicking in other parts of Scotland, where Scots is clearly delineated as a language of the lower classes. Moreover, unlike Gaelic, Orcadian does not have its own television channel. 'It's sometimes difficult to persuade people that Orcadian is a "thing",' he says. 'Aspects of Orcadian are in decline because of the demographic. About half of the people living in Orkney weren't born here, so they don't really feel it belongs to them.'

'When you meet someone who does speak Orcadian it can come as a relief. I was born here and introduced to Orcadian at a young age. Most of my life has been spent around farms and country people and I have always engaged with the language.'

Another cause for optimism for Orcadian is how it has withstood the turbulence of the centuries since the Vikings first made landfall. As Margaret Flaws and Gregor Lamb put it in *The Orkney Dictionary* (page 286), the concoction of the Norn and Scots that has become modern-day Orcadian 'must be a very strong plant to have survived as it has done all these centuries … we still have a language of our own, Orcadian.' Dr Hall's website (w brisknortherly.wordpress.com) is well worth dipping into for insights and observations about Orcadian and its place in the scheme of things.

RELIGION

The percentage of Orcadians who say they have a religion ranges from 57% on Rousay to 83% on Westray. Even this latter figure is slightly lower than the Scottish average; certainly, religion is less intensely followed than in the Outer Hebrides. Long gone are the days when Westray elders would greet the ferry as it docked at Pierowall and inform arrivals of what they were – and were not – allowed to do while on the island. Around half of all islanders belong to the Church of Scotland, with Roman Catholics accounting for around 3%, and Hinduism and Islam together forming about 1%. As you explore the islands, the local kirk is often a building of stark appearance located in a place of some beauty: the kirks at Flotta and Old Hoy come to mind. Whatever your faith, or if you have none, a service in St Magnus Cathedral or a Roman Catholic service in the Italian Chapel is a worthwhile experience and a reminder that some of the great Orkney 'sights' remain integral to everyday life.

EDUCATION

As for education, all the outer islands have primary schools and three – Westray, Stronsay and Sanday – have Junior Highs, where children study until they are 16. If they wish to study highers (the Scottish equivalent to A-Levels and required for entry to university), they must board on the Mainland and study at either Stromness Academy or Kirkwall Grammar School (which, despite the name, is not selective). Children on other islands must board on a week-long basis in Kirkwall from the age of 11.

CULTURE

Orcadian culture is extremely rich and finds its expression chiefly through the mediums of music, storytelling and literature. The one curious exception – so far – is film.

ARCHITECTURE Many properties are functional rather than stylish. This reflects Orkney's working landscape: buildings were not built to win architectural awards but to keep people warm and housed in the face of low incomes and tough weather. This approach is most apparent on the North Isles where isolated homesteads dominate and low-slung villages and settlements are strung around the safer harbours.

MUSIC Orcadian music covers a vast repertoire, extending from fiddle to country music and what is best described as 'rebel yell'. Good places to hear it are The Reel in Kirkwall (page 118) and the Ferry Inn in Stromness (page 77), as well as community halls. If you see a flyer, or hear of a gig, do grab the chance to listen. Orcadian music reaches a crescendo during the Orkney Folk Festival (w orkneyfolkfestival.com), usually held during the last week of May. The composer Peter Maxwell Davies fell in love with Orkney to the extent that he spent the latter half of his life here (see boxes, page 143 and page 227).

A host of internationally, nationally and locally well-known, top-notch musicians ply the bars and venues mostly on the Mainland. They include Ivan Drever and his son Kris (a folk artist who won a BBC Radio 2 award) and the twin Wrigley Sisters, Jennifer and Hazel, a fiddle and guitar duo who have performed around the world but can still be heard in their own café, Wrigley and The Reel, in Kirkwall. Local performers to look out for include Bruce Mainland, a vocalist and instrumentalist who has sung about everything from Orcadian life to discounter supermarkets; and duo Jenny Keldie and Brian Cromarty who mix ballads with more energetic beats. Kate Fletcher and Corwen Broch are newcomers to Orkney who mix Nordic influences with British folk traditions. Kirkjuvagr is a five-piece family band that plays traditional songs on fiddles, accordions and keyboards.

Hullion is another popular, long-established group, featuring fiddles, mandolins, vocals and dialect songs interspersed with banter. You may also come across the Driftwood Cowboys, who describe themselves as three parts Orkney, one part Nashville. The future of Orcadian musical traditions would appear to be in safe hands and Haadhirgaan is a rolling group of young musicians who attend

THE *ORKNEYINGA SAGA*

Orkney is extremely rare in that is one of the only island groups in the world where a story has been specifically told about the history and major events of the location in question. Sagas were an Icelandic means of preserving oral poetry and tales of the turmoil of the Viking age. Written in the early 13th century by an anonymous Icelandic author, the *Orkneyinga Saga* offers an intimate view of people who lived during the Norse period 1,000 years ago. It hands down the deeds of the ruling earls (Jarls) through a heroic series of stories. The saga is written in Old Norse (not greatly different from modern-day Icelandic) and, in the best tradition of Icelandic sagas, is designed to entertain its contemporary audience with ample drama. Like all sagas, it mixes realistic and fictionalised accounts but nevertheless tells us a good deal about the personal characters on the islands. It brings to life Orkney sites too: you may learn from the *Orkneyinga Saga* that a woman who once lived there wore a headdress made from horse hair, for example. Or, as Orkney archaeologist Caroline Wickham-Jones points out, 'that Rognvald dried his ship's sails from the top of the cathedral because there was nowhere else high enough on the island'. The story of the *Orkneyinga Saga* is retold thoughtfully at the eponymous Orkneyinga Saga Centre in Orphir (page 112).

Kirkwall Grammar School. This list is far from exclusive, however, as village and island groups regularly play at community halls and the default standard is extremely high.

FOLKLORE 'Frootery' is a wonderful Orcadian word, meaning witchcraft, or something that cannot be explained. An island people can't evolve over thousands of years without developing an extraordinary wealth of tales and superstitions. From islands created from the fangs of ancient monsters, to standing stones that go for a walk in the moonlight and fairy folk who lie within the abundant burial mounds, every landscape feature seems to contain a tale designed to raise the hairs on your neck.

It's also easy to see why the natural phenomena that are so vivid in Orkney would inspire a prehistoric community to turn beyond the mortal world to make sense of it all. A sun that looked set to disappear for good in mid-December might be persuaded to blossom once again if a stone were place in the right direction; perhaps the same would work for the moon on a monthly basis.

Beliefs in natural portents have survived until relatively recently. A halo around a moon, a phenomenon called a broch in Orcadian (like the tower), was a harbinger of bad weather in the 19th century. This superstition went further, for the number of stars visible within the broch corresponded to the number of days of good weather left before the wild winds kicked in. In some cases, ignorance or rigid superstition got the better of people: the 'sea monster' that legend asserts was washed up on Stronsay in 1805 was almost certainly a basking shark.

Such legends made their way into wider literature and gripped their audiences. Sir Walter Scott visited Orkney in 1814 and reported how he visited Bessie Miller, the Stromness witch who resided in a smoke-filled hovel on Brinkie's Brae, the hill above the town. Miller would charge sixpence from sailors to guarantee them a favourable wind by boiling a kettle and uttering her charms. Scott used her as the inspiration for Norna in *The Pirate*, published in 1822.

As Orkney is surrounded by heaving seas, on which islanders had no choice but to venture for food, Orcadian yarns would naturally contain malevolent figures or human victims unable to rest peacefully.

'Selkies' – seals in Orcadian dialect – were said to shed their skins on Midsummer's Eve. At other certain states of the tide, they would become seal-humans who bewitched and enchanted people. Selkie folk lived in the outskerries around Orkney and love between them and humans was – some say still is – common.

Then there were the 'finfolk', mythical sea creatures steeped in sorcery who used boats made of fish skin; the boats had no masts and instead the finfolk used their immense strength to row them. Their winter home was Finfolkaheem at the bottom of the sea but they also resided in underwater townships or on submerged islands that could rise up above the waters; they would kidnap sailors or youths who caroused carelessly on the shore. They resented fishermen intruding on their grounds, so would hold on to fishing lines until they snapped or the poor man was dragged overboard. Although they had supernatural powers, on dry land finfolk were barely distinguishable from humans. Although the fin-man had fins like a fish he could only be distinguished by a gloomy face; the fin-woman, meanwhile, was a mermaid and had the power of enchantment.

Most of the customs, tales and popular beliefs in Orkney originate in Norway. This is perhaps unsurprising, given the influence of Norse culture with its rich history of trolls and giants. *Trows* (trolls) were playful fairy folk; both they and the *hogboon* were keen to indulge in mischief. The latter was the spirit of a hill-farmer who would guard the land jealously in the farmer's afterlife. Each island had a real-life *trowie* doctor to deal with mischievous, sometimes unco-operative or darker fairy folk.

In Orkney, all these mythical creatures and sprites were swiftly adapted to local lore and culture while lowland Scottish elements were also absorbed. Giants have quite an influence in Orkney; the Norse word for them, 'jotun', crops up a good deal. On Papa Westray, a tarn is known as Ettan's Pow, or the jotun's pool. On Rousay, the *Yetna-steen* (jotun stone) still stands proud, waiting patiently for New Year's Eve when it walks to the sea. Other giants, such as Cubbie Roo on Rousay, were more restless and inclined to throw boulders to work anger out of their system. A witch on Eday managed to hurl a huge stone all the way to Sanday. Witches certainly did not have it all their own way and the Scottish Church unsurprisingly came down hard on those it identified as possessing supernatural powers: during the 17th century, witch fires often burned on Gallow Hill in Kirkwall.

Today, the best way to get a flavour of these tales and the atmosphere they engendered is to attend one of the storytelling evenings or tours of spooky sights conducted in Stromness (page 83).

LITERATURE Orkney has contributed considerably to Scotland's canon of literature with several home-grown heavyweights serving to inspire writers on the British

GEORGE MACKAY BROWN

Son of a Stromness postman, George Mackay Brown (1921–96) was one of Scotland's leading 20th-century authors and poets. Having survived tuberculosis, he worked as a journalist and studied English at Edinburgh University, enjoying the tutelage of Edwin Muir. He then returned to Stromness and rarely left Orkney thereafter. Much of his work is informed by Orcadian Norse history and his conversion to Roman Catholicism. He wrote many volumes of short stories and poetry, including *The Storm, Loaves and Fishes* and *The Year of The Whale*. His themes, as he put it in *Contemporary Poets* in 1980, were 'mainly religious (birth, love death, resurrection, ceremonies of fishing and agriculture)'. Keeping his hand in journalism he wrote entertaining and informed pieces for the local media. In 1994 he was nominated for the Booker Prize for his novel *Beside the Ocean of Time*. Later in life he collaborated with composer Sir Peter Maxwell Davies, including the libretto for the music-drama *The Martyrdom of St Magnus*.

mainland. The history of Orkney literary contribution is long: witness the 13th-century *Orkneyinga Sagas* (see box, page 35) and the *Haakoner Saga*, written in the 1260s about the reign of King Haakon of Norway. The literary tradition was maintained by James Russell Lowell, a US-born contemporary of Herman Melville and Nathaniel Hawthorne, who was strongly influenced by his Orcadian mother's ballads, oral tales and sonnets.

Recent poetry has drawn heavily on Orcadian life. Edwin Muir, one of Scotland's great 20th-century poets (see box, page 191), grew up on Wyre, where his experiences informed much of his writing. Muir also acted as a mentor to

ORKNEY INGENUITY

Jackie Miller, who makes Orkney chairs in Kirkwall (page 119), has a theory to explain the islanders' palpable ingenuity and the extraordinary number of crafts people among them (from jewellers to artists, textile makers, producers of high-quality yarn from island sheep and woodworkers): 'Perhaps it's the dark nights in winter, when the sun goes at 3.30pm. We have to have something to do and occupy our minds.'

Along with chairs, jewellery making is another craft that has evolved on Orkney to extremely high standards. The modern-day tradition dates from the 1960s when Ola Gorie set up the first jewellery and silver workshop on Orkney. Today, several jewellers and silversmiths of local, national and international renown either hail from Orkney or now call the islands home. Names to look out for include Burray-based Karen Duncan, who was the first Orcadian to be accepted into the Guild of Master Craftsmen. Fiona Mitchell, who runs Castaway Crafts in Dounby on the Mainland, is almost evangelical about the quality of Orcadian craftsmanship: 'It is extremely good. We do not accept anything less than excellence. Some people have made poor things here but they don't last long in the business. They get known and they get told. There is a long history on the islands of people spinning their own wool, making their own things. If you make it for yourself then you make it to last, so you make it good.'

The self-preservation element of working as a self-employed creative is important, says Andrew Appleby (better known as 'the Harray Potter': page 103). 'Things are made to last. The islands attract the best people but the ingenuity of Orkney craftsmanship has always been here; it's of a high standard. Orkney has a tremendous energy, you can just feel it all the time'.

The Orkney landscape is conducive to creativity, agrees Alison Moore, a jeweller, also from Dounby. 'It's nice on a good day to just walk down to the beach and soak things up. That's bound to help with inspiration.'

An Orkney Craft Trail is produced each year; an online list of artists and other creatives can be found at w creative-orkney.com. The trail is also signposted around the Mainland. More often than not you will find the artists present in their gallery or studio. They are, pretty much without exception, always happy to chew the cud and mull over their work and indeed Orkney's place in the wider scheme of things. A new development is the emergence of a 'buddy scheme', an innovative mutual back-scratching project, whereby a craft shop or studio on one side of the Mainland promotes another elsewhere. The aim is to encourage visitors to move away from the main tourist sites and explore further around the Mainland and other islands.

George Mackay Brown, the son of a Stromness postman, who became one of Scotland's leading 20th-century authors and poets (see box, page 37). Both writers have been accused of sentimentalism, yet the more you explore their haunts and gain insights into the history of the islands, the more such critiques can sound like those of cosmopolitan academics. Having moved to Westray as a child, Glasgow-born Robert Rendall established a strong reputation as a poet, antiquarian and amateur naturalist. Author of *Country Sonnets*, a collection of songs (some in Orcadian), he was a contemporary and friend of Mackay Brown. Eric Linklater, though born in Wales, spent many years in the islands, and is also firmly lodged in this pantheon: a wide-ranging literary man, he composed novels, short stories and travel books. Linklater also wrote children's tales and won the Carnegie Medal for *The Wind on the Moon*.

More recently, local writers have chosen to place universal themes of love and separation, as well as darker deeds, on the islands. As yet, however, an Orcadian TV noir, in the vein of *Shetland*, has yet to see the light of day.

SEND US YOUR SNAPS!

We'd love to follow your adventures using our *Orkney* guide – why not tag us in your photos and stories via Twitter (🐦 @BradtGuides) and Instagram (📷 @bradtguides)? Alternatively, you can upload your photos directly to the gallery on the Orkney destination page via our website (w bradtguides.com/orkney).

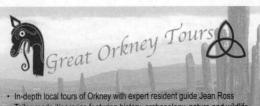

2

Practical Information

WHEN TO VISIT

Orkney is a year-round destination with every season offering reasons to come here. Regardless of date, the natural world always has something for everyone – as does the manmade environment, with festivals, dances and events held throughout the calendar. And it's best not to plan around the expected weather – clement and inclement conditions can transpire at any time of year. A week in July can be damp, cold and soggy; conversely, November may bring clear skies and magical sunsets.

For good reason spring and summer are by far the most popular times to visit. By the start of May, the avian race to breed is on and the sky is full of birdlife; wildflowers are emerging in all their glory along clifftops, in fields and even on roadside verges. The weather warms up and, statistically, this is the driest time of year. High summer brings endlessly long days where, although the sun officially drops behind the horizon for 5 hours or so, there is a magical half-light that hangs on into the small hours. Summer months are also good if you are keen on archaeology, as this is the time when many researchers and students are liberated from university lecture rooms and get a chance to dig up Orkney's landscape. Regular excavations continue every summer at the Ness of Brodgar, on Rousay and Westray – but you may see similar signs of activity anywhere.

By September, autumn is already firmly in place. The modest woodlands sprinkled across Orkney are turning orange and brown, while long skeins of geese cut through the skies as they retreat from the oncoming Arctic winter.

The secret is slowly getting out that late autumn to early spring is as good a time as any to visit Orkney. Yes, the days are shorter and deepest February can sometimes be grim, but wandering around windswept islands and burial mounds at dusk on such days offers an unrivalled opportunity to embrace your inner Neolithic ancestry. Autumn sees an increase in storms: an Orkney *hoolie* (a Scottish term for a gale or storm), with 36 hours of winds that never dip below 70mph, is something to behold – but there again a period of high pressure may allow you to enjoy several successive stunningly clear, still days. Off peak, it is likely you will have the guide to Maeshowe to yourself; in July you will share the minibus that takes you to the site with 30 others. And on the wild side, October is prime pupping time for the colonies of grey seals.

Winter brings a sporting chance of catching the Merrie Dancers, or northern lights – you are more than far enough north to spot them. Stand outside on a clear December night and it can feel like you are in the middle of a planetarium. On the Mainland in particular shops, most B&Bs and hotels and major attractions stay open all year, allowing you to enjoy them without the crowds of high season. As David Loutit, owner of The Creel guesthouse in South Ronaldsay, puts it: 'Orkney is completely different in winter. Yes, it's a little colder, it's a little windier, but the storms are fantastic.'

Most visitors are initially drawn to Orkney by its headline attractions: the **Neolithic sites** of Skara Brae, Maeshowe, the Standing Stones of Stenness, the Ring of Brodgar and Ness of Brodgar – all on the West Mainland – along with the **Italian Chapel**, built by prisoners of war. At this point, most guidebooks conclude their highlights of Orkney. Yet there is just so much more to see, particularly the magnificent North Isles, which are rich in archaeology, birdlife and dramatic coastal scenery, and additionally offer the chance to encounter a very different kind of island life.

It's true enough that the Neolithic sights of the West Mainland really do exceed what may already be high expectations. Without fail, they offer haunting insights into the Stone Age and the peoples who built them and lived and died there. But the glory of the Orkney Islands is that these 'blockbuster' sites are just the headline acts. Several sites located either side of Skara Brae, on the west coast of the West Mainland, should be on your list. These include the **Brough of Birsay**, a defensive headland reached by a causeway only passable at low tide, and the fractured cliffs and seastacks around **Yesnaby**. The **Broch of Gurness** is an extraordinarily complete Iron Age site, far less visited than Skara Brae but where you can actually walk among the remains; it is adjacent to Evie beach, one of Orkney's loveliest stretches of sand. Orkney's 'capital' **Kirkwall** exudes a far greater appeal than most such towns, while exploring the quaysides, higgledy-piggledy streets and art galleries of Stromness should definitely be on your list. The **East Mainland** is much emptier and repays exploration around the rugged headland of Deerness and the sandy isthmus of Dingieshowe.

South of the East Mainland you'll find the **Churchill Barriers**, a feat of urgent wartime engineering that links several islands. Down this way is also **St Margaret's Hope**, a gorgeous pint-sized port with fetching architecture and a strong arts culture. Meanwhile, be sure to walk, drive or take a bus somewhere along the lengthy shoreline of the vast natural harbour of Scapa Flow.

On the western side of Scapa Flow lies the hilly island of **Hoy**, whose key appeal is the beautiful walk through Rackwick Valley and along cliffs to the great sea stack known as the **Old Man of Hoy**. The island's 20th-century wartime history is important: the small port of **Lyness** is the place to learn more.

Do consider a visit to one or two of Orkney's truly wonderful and almost entirely overlooked **North Isles**, a collective term for the ten inhabited islands set in the waters north of Kirkwall. On Stronsay take a walk to the spectacular sea arch known as the **Vat of Kirbuster**. Across the water the island of Sanday offers more than 25 graceful beaches and the alpine-like dunes of **Cata Sand**. There's a strong case for arguing that the **Midhowe Cairn and Broch** on Rousay are the equals of Skara Brae, as well as being free of crowds. Perhaps the most dramatic landscape feature of all is **Noup Head lighthouse** on Westray, perched above shudderingly vertical cliffs jam-packed with seabirds. On the adjacent island of Papa Westray lies the **Knap of Howar**, Europe's oldest house, which was built before Skara Brae and remains as fully intact. Tiny **North Ronaldsay** is the most remote of the islands: it offers the striking spectacle of seaweed-eating sheep that live outside a drystone wall that encircles the island.

At least one **ferry journey** should be on your list, such as the delightful triangular route across Eynhallow Sound between Rousay, Eyre and Egilsay, on the last of which stands lonely St Magnus Kirk. You should also definitely consider taking an **inter-island flight**, the most obvious choice being the short hop from Westray to Papa Westray, which, with a fastest flight time of less than one minute, is officially the world's shortest scheduled flight.

SUGGESTED ITINERARIES

A WEEK Watch the coaches unload their punters who have booked 'Orkney-in-a-day' trips and you are left scratching your head. 'Doing' Orkney in three months would not be enough time to experience everything the islands have to offer. Certainly, you require at least a week here to get a flavour of Orkney. In seven days you should focus your attention on the Mainland, visiting the Neolithic sites at Skara Brae, Ring of Brodgar, Maeshowe and Stenness. Try and spread these out over the week, to avoid getting 'tombed out' (see box, page 25) and so that you can time visits for when crowds are thinner and the weather better. In between, Stromness is worth a day of exploration and you can visit St Magnus Cathedral and the Orkney Museum in Kirkwall. Explore the clifftops at Yesnaby, Marwick Head and the Brough of Birsay, along with the Brough of Gurness. South of Kirkwall, visit the Italian Chapel and St Margaret's Hope. Take a day trip to an island: Hoy, where ferry schedules give you time to walk to the Old Man of Hoy and back, or Rousay.

A FORTNIGHT In two weeks, you can explore the Mainland further, perhaps walking around Mull Head in Deerness and the southwest and eastern coastlines of the adjacent (and connected) island of South Ronaldsay. If the weather looks promising, enquire about short-notice availability for a 'sightseer' flight to an outer island, such as North Ronaldsay, where you stay on the aircraft while it turns around. You'll be out there and back within the hour. You also have time to spend three or four days exploring a couple of the North Isles by ferry – perhaps Westray and Papa Westray, or Sanday and Stronsay.

THREE WEEKS The luxury of three weeks would allow you to stay longer on a North Isle, which is really recommended as way of seeing how island life hangs together. Westray would be a good first choice, with its superb scenery, range of shops and accommodation. If you are really looking to get away from things, head to the emptiness of Eday, which offers rugged moorland walking, or to North Ronaldsay.

TOUR OPERATORS AND GUIDES

Travelling around Orkney by yourself is easy enough. However, a knowledgeable tour guide or operator can certainly enhance your trip. This is particularly the case if you have a special interest in archaeology or wildlife. The majority of local guides are based on the Mainland. Rates are usually in the range of £50–60 per person per day. On the Outer Isles, guides tend to be island rangers whose details we list in the relevant island chapter. Those marked with an asterisk are based locally. The best local guides are really excellent – although others do seem to come and go quite quickly.

Great Orkney Tours* ✆01856 861443; m 07768 165607; e info@greatorkneytours. co.uk; w greatorkneytours.co.uk; see ad, page 40. Orcadian Jean Ross offers excellent & informal tours focussing on everything from birdlife to culture.
Macs Adventure ✆0141 530 4002; (US) +1 844 335 4871; w macsadventure.com. Offers walking & wildlife tours.
McKinlay Kidd ✆0141 260 9260; e hello@ mckinlaykidd.com; w mckinlaykidd.com; see ad, 3rd

colour section. Organises fly-drive; offers self-guided excursions & walks.
My Orkney Tours* ✆01856 831701; m 07710 494187; e marlene@myorkneytours.co.uk; w myorkneytours.co.uk. Lifelong Orcadian Marlene Thomson offers bespoke tours.
Odin Tours of Orkney* ✆01856 751757; m 07541 039321; e meg.lythes@btinternet.com; w odintoursoforkney.com. Offers a wide range of tours with themes such as Neolithic Orkney, wartime

2

Hoy, whisky & Vikings as well as tailor-made trips.
Orcadian Wildlife* ✆ 01856 831240; **m** 07730
004911; **w** orcadianwildlife.co.uk. Excellent &
informed trips led by professional ornithologist
Steve Sankey.
See Orkney* ✆ 01856 870635; **e** info@see-
orkney.com; **w** see-orkney.co.uk. Tours with a
cultural emphasis, taking in World Heritage Sites

along with local food & drink, textiles & crafts. Also
offers bespoke itineraries.
Wildabout Orkney* ✆ 01856 877737; **e** info@
wildaboutorkney.com; **w** wildaboutorkney.com.
Offers tours of the main archaeological sites
as well as wildlife reserves, coastal scenery &
bespoke trips.

TOURIST INFORMATION

The key website is **w** orkney.com, which provides a comprehensive listing of attractions and accommodation. Visit Scotland (**w** visitscotland.com) has a visitor centre in Kirkwall (page 74) but no longer in Stromness. Most hotels and attractions stock leaflets about other sights and events. None of the Outer Isles has a tourist information office; the function is usually served by a battered annotated map, partly sheltered by Perspex and pinned to the toilets or waiting room at the ferry port. Island shops tend to be the de facto centre of information.

MAPS Buy any UK road atlas and you might think that Orkney lies a few miles east of Aberdeen, so rarely do the islands get so much as a page of their own. More specialised and regional maps can be obtained from travel bookshops such as Stanfords (**w** stanfords.co.uk) and local maps of Orkney are also available at the Visit Scotland information centre in Kirkwall. The Ordnance Survey series are also handy – for walkers and cyclists as well as motorists. The Explorer Range maps that cover Orkney are: 461 (East Mainland); 462 (Hoy, South Walls & Flotta); 463 (West Mainland, Stromness & Graemsay); 464 (Westray, Papa Westray, Rousay, Egilsay & Wyre); and 465 (Sanday, Eday, North Ronaldsay & Stronsay). The OS Landranger sheets are 5 (The Northern Isles); 6 (The Mainland); and 7 (The Southern Isles).

RED TAPE

Orkney is part of the UK, so entry requirements only apply to the port at which you arrive in the UK: you can freely travel between the UK mainland and Orkney. After the UK leaves the European Union, documentation requirements for EU citizens may change. Check before travelling. Whatever happens, one principle will apply: once in the UK, you are freely able to travel to Orkney.

CONSULATES AND EMBASSIES The majority of nations, including the US, Canada, Australia and countries from Europe and Asia are fully represented by embassies or high commissions (for Commonwealth members) in the national capital of London. No country has an official presence in Orkney though many have consulates in Edinburgh or Glasgow (**w** visitscotland.com/about/practical-information/embassies-consulates). A full list of contact details can be found at **w** www.gov.uk/government/publications/foreign-embassies-in-the-uk.

GETTING THERE AND AWAY

For somewhere so far north, Orkney is remarkably accessible from the British mainland. Most people travel by car and ferry; train and ferry is a viable option, as is flying (albeit more expensive).

BY SEA Orkney is served by three car-ferry routes and a seasonal foot-passenger ferry. The most popular crossing is the **Scrabster–Stromness** service on the MV *Hamnavoe*, operated by NorthLink Ferries (✆ 0845 600 0449; e info@ northlinkferries.co.uk; w northlinkferries.co.uk). This runs up to three times a day between Scrabster pier, 1.5 miles west of Thurso on the north coast of the Scottish mainland, and Stromness on the Mainland (90 mins; return fares £33.30/16.80/106 adult/child/standard car, excluding driver). Scrabster is 3 hours beyond Inverness by car or bus (Citylink: w citylink.co.uk). A beautiful train line (w scotrail.co.uk) from Inverness serves Thurso but not Scrabster. If you don't want to walk from Thurso, book a taxi (Ormlie Taxi; ✆ 01847 893434; w ormlietaxis.com).

The other major car-ferry route to Orkney runs from **Gill's Bay**, 5 miles west of John O'Groats, to **St Margaret's Hope** on South Ronaldsay. The service is managed by Pentland Ferries (✆ 0800 688 8988; e sales@pentlandferries.co.uk; w pentlandferries.co.uk) and runs up to four services per day on a catamaran. At just 1 hour this is the quickest car crossing to the islands (return fares £32/16/76 adult/child/standard car, excluding driver).

Between May and September, a seasonal foot-passenger ferry (✆ 01955 611353; e contact@jogferry.co.uk; w jogferry.co.uk) operates two to three times a day from **John O'Groats to Burwick** on South Ronaldsay. Prices always seem rather expensive at £40 return (£42 with coach transfer to Kirkwall; children half-price) but the boat, which is aimed at day trippers seeking a taster of Orkney, gets packed out. The journey time is 40 minutes.

You can also travel the **Aberdeen–Kirkwall** route with the NorthLink Ferries service (w northlinkferries.co.uk) that sails between Aberdeen, Orkney and Shetland. This departs Aberdeen 17.00 on Tuesday, Thursday, Saturday and Sunday and arrives in Kirkwall's Hatston Pier (half a mile northwest of the town centre) at 23.00 (on other days, the ferry sails direct to Lerwick in Shetland). Low-season return fares are from £63/31.30/222 adult/child/standard car, excluding driver; higher in peak season. Travelling this route in reverse back to Aberdeen, the ferry operates as a night boat on Monday, Wednesday and Friday, departing Kirkwall at 23.45 and arriving in Aberdeen at 07.00 the next morning. This service provides cabins, evening meals, breakfast and, in summer months, entertainment. Cabin beds are available from £24.30. You can also use this ferry to travel between Shetland and Orkney: the service departs Lerwick at 17.30 and arrives in Kirkwall at 23.00 (single fare £19.75/9.90/82.40 adult/child/standard car).

BY AIR Flights from the UK mainland go only to Kirkwall and are provided solely by Loganair (✆ 0344 800 2855; w loganair.co.uk). The airline handles flights from Glasgow, Edinburgh, Aberdeen, Inverness and Manchester as well as Stornoway (Hebrides) and Lerwick (Shetland). Flights from these locations cost £120–280 return.

If flying from outside Scotland, either from the UK or internationally, you will need to transit through a Scottish airport (the sole exception is Loganair's Manchester–Kirkwall flight) to reach Orkney. In 2019, Loganair took over the Bristol–Aberdeen service, which offers connections to Kirkwall. Through (return) fares are usually in the range of £220–500. They also have a code-share service with British Airways (w ba.com), offering connecting flights from London Heathrow, London City and London Gatwick (via Edinburgh or Glasgow) to Kirkwall. Note that if you buy a flight to the Scottish mainland from elsewhere in the UK (or abroad) and a separate flight to Kirkwall, you may have difficulty in getting check-in staff to check your luggage all the way through and you will have to collect your bags at a Scottish airport and check in all over again; this rarely happens when flying from Orkney but will always be the case with budget airlines that fly between

England and Scotland such as easyJet (**w** easyjet.com) and Ryanair (**w** ryanair.com). Note that when you fly with two airlines who do not have a code share, they have little responsibility for you if the first flight is late and you miss your connection.

BY RAIL Should you be travelling from southern England, say, the most comfortable way to break the back of the journey to Orkney is to take the Caledonian Sleeper (**w** sleeper.scot) from London Euston to Aberdeen (then take the ferry) or to Inverness (then travel by train or hire car to Thurso/Scrabster). Beds in a compartment cost from £70 single.

HEALTH

Tap water is drinkable across the islands. Your chances of getting food poisoning are the same as anywhere in the UK, ie: pretty low. Orkney is fairly low-lying, so generally it is not advisable to drink water from streams as they may only be rarely above human habitation. That said, you can always gather the water and drop a chlorine tablet into your bottle, as you might elsewhere in the world.

Midges certainly flex their muscles in Orkney, though there is nothing remotely approaching the formidable squadrons found in the Highlands and on Skye, or even on the Outer Hebrides. The most vulnerable to the beasties are those who fish in lochs on a calm day. Of more concern should be horseflies, known locally as *cleggs*, whose bites can cause horrendous swellings. Be mindful also of sheep ticks, or *kebs*, should you rummage around in sheep wool at factories or farms. Your chances of contracting orf are low but your GP may be slightly excited and intrigued should you return with the disease, which manifests itself with a mild fever and scabby, puss-filled lesions.

One nasty disease that ticks are increasingly transmitting is Lyme, a bacterial infection often manifested by a circular rash and/or flu-like symptoms and muscle and joint pain. The NHS provides good information at **w** nhs.uk/conditions/lyme-disease. See the box below for information on how to remove ticks safely.

Medical standards in Orkney are as good as anywhere in the UK. Balfour Hospital in Kirkwall is the only major medical centre; a new replacement hospital is being built a mile south of town on the Scapa Road. Depending on their condition, life-threatening cases may be flown to Edinburgh or Aberdeen. All of the outer islands have a GP (doctor) surgery that will offer on-the-day appointments; some island GPs are itinerant and only visit certain days a week, in which case you may

---

TICK REMOVAL

Ticks should ideally be removed complete, and as soon as possible, to reduce the chance of infection. You can use special tick tweezers, which can be bought in good travel shops, or failing this with your fingernails, grasping the tick as close to your body as possible, and pulling it away steadily and firmly at right angles to your skin without jerking or twisting. Irritants (eg: Olbas oil) or lit cigarettes are to be discouraged since they can cause the ticks to regurgitate and therefore increase the risk of disease. Once the tick is removed, if possible douse the wound with alcohol (any spirit will do), soap and water, or iodine. If you are travelling with small children, remember to check their heads, and particularly behind the ears, for ticks. Spreading redness around the bite and/or fever and/or aching joints after a tick bite imply that you have an infection that requires antibiotic treatment. In this case seek medical advice

be better off contacting the Visit Scotland travel centre for current surgery details. For further medical advice, you can contact w NHS24.scot (\111).

SAFETY

Orkney is an extremely safe place to visit and you are unlikely to have any kind of negative experience on the islands. Crime is extremely low (though the theft of Stations of the Cross from the Italian Chapel in 2014 stunned everyone (see box, page 162).

The circumstances in which you should be mindful of risk emerge when you explore the great outdoors. When walking, you should certainly be wary of cattle, which will not be as well versed in the rights of open access as you might be. Avoid getting between a calf and its mother and be particularly cautious in May when most cattle are finally let out of their barns after being cooped up for the best part of eight months. Every year there is a handful of incidents involving cattle trampling people (usually farmers). Use your judgement and certainly keep dogs on a lead when in any field with livestock. Rusty and sharp-edged farm gates are ubiquitous and an easy way to scratch yourself and introduce infection.

Only on Hoy, with its high hills and deep valleys, is the combination of remoteness and bad weather a safety consideration when walking. Always be mindful of cliffs, which can be remarkably adjacent to coastal footpaths in a way you rarely see anywhere in, say, Devon and Cornwall. Another landscape feature that Orkney possesses is the ominous-sounding *gloup*, a large hole near cliffs that drops to the sea. These are very rarely fenced off. Needless to say, avoid walking in fog in their proximity.

Always ask locally which beaches are safe for swimming. The same goes for quicksand, which is rare but can come and go depending on how much water is carried by a burn to the beach.

Be prepared for sudden changes of weather. Orcadian weather can be extreme and winter sees storms with winds exceeding 80mph, even topping 100mph (national news reports of 50mph in the south of England always raise a wry chuckle among Orcadians). That said, when an Orcadian says to you that 'it's a poor day' it means even they consider the weather to be shockingly bad: in such circumstances you are strongly advised to simply curl up with a book and observe the elements from inside; certainly never consider going for a walk or driving to an exposed headland. Such winds can simply tear car doors off.

WOMEN TRAVELLERS Orkney is as safe as any part of the UK for women to travel around. Unwarranted attention is rare and you can walk with confidence late at night in Kirkwall and Stromness and on the more far-flung islands. Indeed, spend a while walking and exploring off the beaten track and you notice locals discreetly looking out for you, purely as a courtesy.

TRAVELLING WITH A DISABILITY Orkney is slowly getting its act together in regard to travellers with mobility issues. Older hotels (which is nearly all of them) have extremely limited facilities and access. All new-build B&Bs and restaurants will provide access to a standard recognisable elsewhere in the UK. Elsewhere, the phrase 'ground-floor rooms available' is deemed sufficient more often than should be the case. That said, you should not let any concerns you have restrict you from travelling to the Outer Isles. You will find much accommodation, and many hostels have ramps and even fully equipped wet rooms (Papa Westray, Stronsay and Hoy stand out in this regard). Infrastructure does its best: even remote airfields will have an access ramp. Where this is not the case, people will be extremely helpful and usually find a way to accommodate travellers with disabilities. While this is not quite the same thing as getting it right in the first place, you will rarely be left to feel overlooked.

LGBTQ+ TRAVELLERS Younger Orcadians are generally open minded and pretty relaxed about sexuality but there is certainly a conservative strain among some older, more traditional folk, particularly in religious circles. Over the past few years the islands have caught unwanted publicity over the occasional refusal to allow a gay couple or those in a civil partnership to share a room. It's hard to tell if these signify a deep-seated cultural prejudice because showing affection to one another in the vast majority of places in Orkney is unlikely to make anyone turn their head.

TRAVELLING WITH CHILDREN My own son, Thomas, once said that Orkney is a good place to show children that sand is not always hot. That sand, however, is to be found on some of the UK's most beautiful beaches; some are so little visited that you may feel as if you own them for a day. Gorgeous strands on the Mainland include those at Evie on the north coast, Waulkmill Bay in Orphir on the south coast and, little more than a mile south of Kirkwall, at Scapa Bay. On the outer islands, Sanday has more than 20 delectable bays while Stronsay and Shapinsay also have fine sands. Perhaps the most beautiful of all is at Grobust on Westray.

Wildlife is so accessible and exhilarating that there's a high chance your brood will return bent on a career in conservation. They – and parents – can also relax knowing that Orcadians will not scowl or snap when children simply go about the business of being children. Families can feel less financially penalised than in other parts of Scotland: B&Bs and self-catering options are usually flexible when it comes to throwing in a camp bed, and child fares on ferries are always half adult prices. The novelty of exploring *airfields* – rather than airports – is one that enchants young people. Take a flight or a ferry as a family and somehow everything gels together into a mild adventure that can leave an imprint on young minds. Taking the sleeper train as part of the journey to reach the islands will only add to this impression.

Low tide exposes rock pools right across the islands, providing magical places to explore with fishing nets (use with care, as inadvertent scraping can damage creatures and their habitats) or a bucket. The pick is the causeway at Brough of Birsay. Fossil hunting is rewarding across Orkney, and children can learn more at the excellent Fossil and Heritage Centre at Burray (page 165). A number of working farms are open to the public and geared towards children, including at Kirbuster and Corrigall on the Mainland. Interpretation is generally done extremely well – Barony Mill on the Mainland comes to mind – and will keep children engaged. Many townships and most outer islands also have good playparks. On bad weather days you can turn to swimming pools in Stromness and Kirkwall, or those on Hoy, Stronsay, Sanday and Westray. The Pickaquoy Centre (page 119) in Kirkwall has an adventure playground and a cinema.

The main cautionary note is that Orkney has a good number of unfenced cliffs. Care has been taken in the text, particularly for coastal walks, to make clear where you may want to be mindful. Don't let this put you off: Orkney's adult population is proof that generations of Orcadian children have managed to surmount such hazards.

WHAT TO TAKE

Implausible as it sounds, it is entirely possible on Orkney to get sunburnt on a clear day in March yet reach for the thermals at the end of May. Whatever time of year you visit, you should therefore pack for all seasons. Wet-weather gear is essential, as are gloves, warm hats and good walking boots. Mosquito repellent is useful though you can buy everything else you need on Orkney – from sunscreen and outdoor clothing to medicines and memory cards. A torch is useful for exploring Orkney's many burial cairns; invariably the ones left on site are flat. Plugs and voltages are the same as in the rest of the UK.

MONEY AND BUDGETING

The currency, like in the rest of the UK, is sterling (£). Generally, you only see Scottish banknotes, though UK ones are also in circulation. You should note that increasingly you may have difficulty using Scottish banknotes in England. Contrary to popular perception shopkeepers are entirely within their rights to refuse to accept them. This is not an issue in major supermarkets.

ATMs can be found in Kirkwall and Stromness, as can banks. On the outer islands, you can generally withdraw money using a debit card at the local post office, while most island grocers will give cashback. Just about all accommodation takes credit cards (though you should check in advance) as do Orkney Island Ferries.

BUDGETING Orkney can be as expensive or as cheap as you choose. If your budget is £25 a day or lower, you can stay at a decent hostel, camp, cook your own food and travel by bus, and just about have change for a dram or pint of beer.

Elect to stay in a mid-range B&B and the costs bump up considerably: eat out as well and you are looking at £70 per person per day. Orkney has few truly luxurious, blow-the-budget options: stay at the best hotels and dine at the best restaurants for lunch and dinner and you will spend about £140 per person per day.

A main course in a pub or hotel restaurant will cost £8–20 (the higher end usually being the catch of the day, or a slice of Orkney beef); a bottle of wine £8–20; a pint of beer is around £3.50. A lunchtime sandwich and coffee will cost £5–7.

Prices for staple products are slightly higher than on the mainland: petrol is 10% higher at around £1.35 a litre (20% higher or more on the North Isles); a pack of local traybakes are around £2.20; a sandwich £1.80–3.50; postcards 80p; a souvenir T-shirt in Stromness £20–25, a print of an eye-catching painting £25; a bottle of water £1; and a local loaf of bread £1.60.

GETTING AROUND

Even how you explore the outer islands is likely to prove a memorable part of your visit. In practice, most people will bring a car simply to cover more ground more quickly; a private vehicle is comfortably the most convenient means of getting from A to B. But even if you do drive, consider complementing your travel with buses or cycling; ferries and air travel also offer unforgettable experiences. Many visitors make the mistake of travelling to the Outer Isles as foot passengers. With the exceptions of Papa Westray and North Ronaldsay, this will severely limit what you can see and do on the islands as bus services are all but non-existent, most sites are located away from the ports and very few have anything that resembles a tourist office. The reality is that most of the outer islands feel too big to take a car to but are just too small to explore on foot. Cycling is a good compromise.

BY CAR Orkney's roads are almost universally good. A comprehensive network of A roads with one lane in each direction reaches most parts of the Mainland and continues all the way down South Ronaldsay via the Churchill Barriers. Be aware that thanks to the many bends, and locals zooming up behind you, motoring on the Mainland requires a good deal of concentration, so whoever sits behind the wheel may miss out on the scenery. Some roads on the Mainland and the majority on the islands are single-track roads with passing places. The latter concept can throw you if you're not familiar with it. The easiest thing is just to have a default attitude of yielding to let others come past. Smiling and waving at fellow motorists makes things all the smoother.

Also be mindful if cars come up behind you as you happily drive along, taking in the views: let people pass at the first and safest opportunity as they may be a key worker such as a firefighter, nurse or doctor on a call. Frustratingly, the empathy that many visitors show in this regard is not always reciprocated. A small minority of Orcadians really floor it and drive aggressively, sometimes haring past you at 80mph and moving out to overtake several hundred yards behind you in what can feel an intimidating statement of intent.

The Mainland has plenty of petrol stations, so you don't need to keep a close eye on the fuel gauge. It's usually best to top up before visiting other islands. Electric-vehicle charging points can be found in Kirkwall (near Tesco), in the car parks at Stromness and at most ferry ports. Several North Isles are pushing hard to provide these too.

Scottish drink-driving laws are strict, with a legal limit of just 50mg in every 100ml of blood compared to 80mg in the rest of the UK. A pint of beer or a large glass of wine is enough to put a typical man over the limit; half-a-pint and a small glass of wine will do the same for a woman.

Car hire Orkney has several hire companies on the Mainland while one-man bands tend to offer options on the Outer Isles. Prices generally seem quite reasonable. See the relevant island chapters for details.

Camper vans There's no denying that driving your own camper van makes for a great experience on Orkney, enabling you to enjoy the freedom of the coast and isolated moors. You should, however, study the road network carefully as even on the Mainland many roads are narrow and twisting and simply unsuitable for camper vans, and will cause you and other motorists a great deal of stress. Surprisingly few camper vans make it to the Outer Isles, which do seem made for exploration in this way.

BY BUS Bus services on the Mainland (and across the Churchill Barriers to South Ronaldsay) are good but rare to non-existent on the Outer Isles. On the Mainland, all major sites can be reached by bus and a good service links Kirkwall and Stromness. Try and get hold of *Travel Times*, an excellent free booklet listing summer timetables for all bus and ferry services. You should find it at the Visit Scotland information centre in Kirkwall (page 74) and the adjacent Kirkwall Travel Centre. The same information is online at w orkney.gov.uk/transport, though picking your way through the clicks and scrolls is a little laborious.

BY FERRY All inter-island ferries are operated by the council-owned Orkney Ferries (\ 01856 872044; e info@orkneyferries.co.uk; w orkneyferries.co.uk; tickets also available from office at Kirkwall harbour ⊕ 07.00–17.00 Mon–Fri, 07.00–noon & 13.00–15.00 Sat). Fares are usually paid on board. Orkney Ferries also offers an Island Explorer pass, which offers ten consecutive days of unlimited travel for foot passengers (£42/21 adult/child) – note that bicycles are carried for free.

The South Isles of Hoy, Graemsay and Flotta can all be reached by ferry. Lyness (halfway down the east coast of Hoy) and Flotta are served by a vehicle ferry from Houton, 8 miles southwest of Kirkwall. A separate foot-passenger service runs between Stromness, Graemsay and Moaness in North Hoy.

The majority of the North Isles (Shapinsay, Stronsay, Eday, Sanday, Westray, Papa Westray and North Ronaldsay) are served from Kirkwall. The exception is Rousay, which is reached from Tingwall, 12 miles west of Kirkwall; this route also takes in Egilsay and Wyre. All these services take vehicles. A separate foot-passenger ferry connects Westray and Papa Westray. You'll sometimes hear people on the Mainland describe – tongue in cheek – the islet of Galt Skerry, just to the north of Shapinsay (the island closest to Kirkwall), as the edge of the civilised world: beyond lies the unknown, Orkney's *Ultima Thule*. Journey times vary from 25 minutes to Shapinsay to 90 minutes for direct sailings to most other islands. Return fares range from £8.50–16 (adult), £4.30–8 (child) and £27–39 (standard car).

In truth, the ferry timetable does itself no favours and can be horribly confusing for the uninitiated. It helps to remember that most islands enjoy at least two services per day, apart from North Ronaldsay, which gets just a Tuesday and Friday sailing. Another useful rule of thumb is that most services operate on a 'there and back' basis from Kirkwall: if you are on Westray and want to go to Stronsay, you must go back to Kirkwall. The main exception to this is the service from Kirkwall to Stronsay, Eday and Sanday. Each of these islands enjoys a combination of direct services from Kirkwall and indirect services that sail via one, or both, of its neighbours. This can resemble a game of musical chairs as the service differs from one day of the week to the next: the logic of this can still bewilder you no matter how often you travel. It can help to bear in mind that the weekly service to the three islands is fixed: the same sailings take place on Monday every week but the Tuesday timetable, also the same every week, will be quite different.

From late June to late August, Orkney Ferries runs 'Sunday Special' excursions from Kirkwall to Eday, Sanday, Stronsay, Westray, Papa Westray and North Ronaldsay. These enable visitors to spend a few hours on an island where normal schedules would either render a visit meaningless or require an overnight stay (though it should be noted that staying on the Outer Isles is one of the most wonderful experiences Orkney has to offer).

From May onwards ferries get booked up well in advance, particularly on Fridays when visitors and commuting islanders returning home swell demand. Hoy is always hugely popular: from April to August you should book the Houton–Hoy route well in advance. If a ferry is full you will be waitlisted. Details and prices of services that run from each island to Kirkwall are listed in the relevant island chapter. One phrase you don't want to hear from the ferry crew when you turn up as a waitlisted passenger with a vehicle is that your chances of getting on board are 'likely improbable', an extremely diplomatic Orcadian way of saying 'forget it.'

Departure times listed in the timetables are known as 'belled times': this is the scheduled time of departure when the tides are not too low. Plenty of routes cross narrow waters so when the tides are too shallow the ferries cannot dock and timetables are temporarily altered. In such cases, timetable changes are advertised well in advance on the Orkney Ferries website. This is particularly the case for North Ronaldsay and Stronsay. Also note that ferries may leave ahead of time if bad weather is forecast in order to complete a journey. The cautionary phrase posted on the Orkney Ferries website when poor weather is expected to disrupt sailings is that services are 'under review', which is as dry an understatement as you can

Sitting on the deck of a ferry, watching islands pass and change shape with every minute that goes by is a quintessential Orkney experience that provides an insight into the vessels' role in island life. Even the most confirmed landlubber should try it at least once.

Nine vessels ply 13 routes to the north and south of the Mainland, from short 25-minute hops from Kirkwall to Shapinsay and 2½-hour voyages to North Ronaldsay. The further out the islands you travel to, the more rural and local the freight, which can range from tractors through ovens to sheep and cattle transporters.

A faint whiff of yesteryear prevails on the services – although this may not be immediately apparent if you arrived in Orkney on the huge MV *Hamnavoe* from Scrabster. Vessels are more than 30 years old; they can look battered and weather-worn, which they are, but the rationale seems to be that if the engines are maintained then there is little need to replace the whole ferry. They sail in most winds up to 50mph (sometimes lesser winds will halt services if they blow directly from the east).

Originally the service was mainly a cargo-based operation, but has evolved over the past 40 years to provide a lifeline for islanders and, in some respects, a means of keeping depopulation at bay. 'If Mrs X knows she can live on an island but have reliable transport to Kirkwall to visit the hospital or other services, then she may choose to live on that island,' says Andrew Blake, Ferry Services Manager. 'If the ferry services did not run then events such as sports days on the northern isles would likely not happen. Ferries provide an element of social cohesion.'

The playful waters north of Kirkwall demand a constant wary eye from shipmasters. 'It can get choppy in the Westray Firth and the Stronsay Sound while the North Ronaldsay route with its low tides is one where the masters really have to think,' says Blake. 'But it makes things more interesting. My view is that a bad day at sea is better than a good day in the office. It comes down to good seamanship – the masters have to think on their feet and may change the route to give passengers an easier journey.'

One person you may wish to thank for your safe passage through the treacherous sounds and currents is a local schoolmaster, Murdoch Mackenzie. In 1705, financed by traders and merchants, he created the Foley of Charts, with a view to making navigation safer. His methods, using symbols to indicate the bottom of the sea and direction of the tides, revolutionised map-making around the world: his symbols are still used on present-day charts.

Orkney's ferry service is undergoing a review that may see the modernisation of the fleet and the introduction of a trial vessel powered by hydrogen produced on Eday and Shapinsay. 'Every captain would like to renew their fleet after 30 years but the fact Orkney is at the forefront of this technology is very exciting,' says Blake.

expect to hear. It's worth signing up for alerts regarding disruption by emailing e textmessages@orkneyferries.co.uk.

BY AIR You can fly from Kirkwall to six of the North Isles, with regular services to Stronsay, Westray, Papa Westray, Sanday and North Ronaldsay, and less frequent flights to Eday. All flights to the outer islands are operated by Loganair (☎ 01856 872494; e orkneyres@loganair.co.uk; w loganair.co.uk). Some flights are direct, others call in at one or more other islands. Note that it is not possible to check through to these islands from flights originating outside Orkney: you need to leave adequate time to reclaim your bags at Kirkwall and check in again. The Westray–Papa Westray route, famously the world's shortest scheduled flight at 1 minute, is not the only flight that you can blink and miss: journey times are usually 8–15 minutes in duration. Detailed information can be found in the relevant island chapters.

LITTLE AIRCRAFT, BIG WINDS

Your journey to Orkney may have taken you through one or two of the UK's more soul-sapping airports; the contrast with Orkney airfields could not be greater. Here the usual formalities are taken seriously but conducted in a relaxed manner. On the North Isles, airfield buildings are barely larger than a garden shed. A fixed routine follows: someone drives along the airfield runway to ensure it is clear of obstructions. The pilot calls the (single!) airport radio controller to confirm he's (at time of writing they are all male) happy with flying conditions. A third airport employee places your bags in the hold. You are rarely even asked for your name – you can only assume that someone, somewhere, knows that you have a ticket. Then the pilot simply pops his head around the door and says, usually with a smile, 'anyone for North Ronaldsay?' Everyone follows him and clambers aboard. You may be asked to mind your head as you duck under the wing.

Flights take place in an eight-seater Britten-Norman Islander. George Mackay Brown described the spectacle of these aircraft taking off 'slowly, like a soft moth in the haze'. Passengers are squeezed tightly together; those in the rear seats may be given headphones to mitigate engine noise.

It never ceases to amaze how often flights take place in what might be considered bad weather. On one take-off experienced by this author in high crosswinds, the *instant* that the wheels left the ground the aircraft made a fierce turn to starboard into the wind; it felt like skateboarding. This, explains Captain Colin McAllister, a veteran of more than 6,000 hours in the Orkney air, is because the Islander's rudder is not fixed: 'you can't lock the rudder the way you can on larger aircraft'. A similarly impressive spectacle takes place when the Islander lands in strong winds, rather like a demented dragonfly.

This may look worrying but McAllister is keen to stress the safety aspect: 'the aircraft can take the weather we fly in'. Islanders can take off in ground-winds of up to 50mph and pilots have special dispensation from the Civil Aviation Authority to fly by day as low as 350ft to be clear of cloud.

Pilots must always have 2 miles of visibility. Although the aircraft have radar, there are no locator beacons on the North Isles airfields, so the pilot must be able to see the runway before he lands. 'We can fly to Kirkwall and Shetland on instruments but the little islands have nothing other than visual references,' says McAllister. 'So we have to be able to see them,' he adds, almost as an afterthought. This leads to not infrequent cancellations, or flights that turn back mid-journey. The concern is less hitting terrain and more of hitting telephone wires. 'We can't just descend in cloud in the hope we might pop out of it in time,' McAllister says.

Flights can seem remarkable value, typically around £32 return (children half-price), dropping to £21 return if you stay a night. Flights do get disrupted (see box, page 53) but, if necessary, the airline always puts on extra flights as soon as conditions allow to avoid leaving you marooned for days on end.

Loganair offers 'sightseer fares' (usually 1½ times a standard single fare) where you fly to the island and back on the same flight, with no stopover allowed. Such trips offer a spectacular aerial view of the archipelago. In most cases, you'll be out and back to Kirkwall in less than an hour. These are bookable only on the day of departure.

BY BICYCLE Cycling on Orkney is a joy – as soon as you get away from the main A roads of the Mainland. Quiet lanes can be found right across the Mainland, the gently undulating landscape is easy to navigate and you can access just about every site of interest on the Mainland by bicycle. The same goes for all the other islands, where traffic is even lighter and you can safely leave your bike by a road edge, spend a day walking the coast and return knowing it will still be there. The only islands that present a physical challenge of any significance are Rousay and Hoy, which have some steep(ish) climbs. Taking your bicycle on the ferries is free and never a problem. The smattering of cycle-hire outlets across the isles (see individual chapters) are good value and always helpful: there's a welcoming two-wheeled community on Orkney.

HITCHING Thumbing a lift is a viable option, especially on the outer islands, where it would be quite unusual to wait for more than a handful of cars to pass before you get picked up.

ACCOMMODATION

The default level of accommodation on Orkney is good and ranges from characterful older properties converted from their original function to new builds that can occasionally be stylish. There are very few places that could be described as truly high-end, and places that charge top-range prices are usually mid-range (but decent) in standards. The Mainland has a huge amount of accommodation, from hotels to B&Bs and self-catering but, even so, it is best to book ahead if you're staying between June and August. On the Outer Isles accommodation is much more limited – something that almost all are trying to address – and you should always ensure you have a bed waiting when you get off the ferry. If you are out on the North Isles and there is a sudden bottleneck – when weather halts the flight and ferries – you will not be left stranded. Someone will always ring around and find you a room.

Prices will generally seem pretty reasonable and not dissimilar to what you would pay on the UK mainland. While most places take credit cards and some can manage online bank transfers, definitely check in advance. Most places stay open all year, though many close around Christmas and New Year.

Most places offer discounts for stays of more than a couple of days and all hotels and B&Bs drop their prices over winter and in the shoulder months of March/April and late September/October. You can usually negotiate quite successfully at these times of year.

Many providers on the Mainland and especially on the offshore islands offer evening meals. These can sometimes be dining experiences that verge on the epicurean and better than many restaurants will offer; more often they will be standard but filling fare. Even those providers that don't formally offer dinner will usually rustle something up if you arrive on a ferry delayed by bad weather.

Codes are used to accompany accommodation listings in this guide. They are meant to give a basic indication of price based on a double room per night including breakfast in high season. Most providers offer discounts for solo travellers and many will also discount for stays of a few days. Please check websites or call ahead of booking to check exact rates. Where proprietors offer dinner to residents, a dining-out code (see box, page 57) is added separately.

£££	£100+
££	£50–100
£	>£50

HOSTELS Orkney has a handful of extremely good, modern and well-run hostels. Even if you don't usually stay in a hostel these are excellent options, which is important since on a couple of islands they are the only accommodation option. Some have small dormitories with shared facilities but most now offer private, recently modernised en-suite rooms. The pick of these are on Hoy, Stronsay, Sanday and Papa Westray.

FAMILIES Generally, families will look to stay in self-catering accommodation that can offer the space both internally and in the form of a croft to run around in. Note that some hotels and pubs are very strict about not allowing under-18s in their bars. Always enquire in advance; usually places that have such rules will offer room service for no extra charge. If you're planning to eat in a pub you may be surprised to see the bar displaying a children's licence. This isn't actually a permission to serve them alcohol but a licence for them to be present in the bar. This is usually a good signal that a place will not get too boisterous.

One irritant is the higher cost of hotel accommodation for any family with more than one child. It's not unusual to find the costs charged per person, which can mean that a four-bed room costs more than a suite elsewhere in the same building. However, many B&Bs positively welcome children and will go the extra mile when it comes to shifting beds around or providing a camp bed; some will switch their B&B into self-catering to give you the run of a house. Staying in one of the island hostels is great fun as they too have family rooms and board games.

CAMPING Unzipping a tent and peering out at an early-morning view of the Orkney landscape is right up there with any UK camping experience. That said, Orkney has curiously few formal camp sites, with just a handful on the Mainland and barely any on the outer islands. Generally, facilities range from sufficient to excellent. Most are well run; some have electric hook-ups. Most often, particularly on the North Isles, campsites are attached to hostels or B&Bs. More informal is the wild camping that you can engage in thanks to Scottish open-access rights (see box, page 61). Remember that, by law, wild camping may be conducted only in small numbers and for no more than two or three nights at any one place. Do not camp in enclosed fields with crops; and try and check with a farmer whether they intend to move cattle into any particular field – unless you want to share your tent with an inquisitive and assertive cow (as does occasionally happen on Orkney). There seems to be just the one traditional stone bothy in Orkney (Rackwick Bay on Hoy).

SELF-CATERING Visitor surveys suggest that self-catering accounts for less than 20% of all accommodation in Orkney but it remains a popular option. Properties are usually detached and roomy, command fine views and come with grounds that are particularly good for children. The best place to look for self-catering accommodation on Orkney is w orkney.com, which has a comprehensive list of properties. The various island websites also list local options.

It is worth considering that the attitude towards self-catering on Orkney is ambivalent. Particularly on the North Isles, locals are worried about the ever-present pressures of depopulation, so may question the rationale of a three-bed property, owned remotely, being occupied for just a few weeks each year. It also says something about changing demographics that old schoolhouses and churches are often among buildings converted to holiday lets. Where self-catering can work best is in instances where an islander, often a farmer, has been able to obtain a grant to renovate an outbuilding, usually to a very high standard.

EATING AND DRINKING

FOOD From local beef to salmon, shellfish, oatcakes, cheese and lamb, food in Orkney has undergone a revolution over the past 20 years. Drawing heavily on the sea and fertile soils, Orkney was promoting local and 'slow' food long before the concepts became fashionable in metropolitan areas of the UK. All local food has a kitemark, 'A taste of Orkney', and it is unusual to come across any restaurant or local shop that does not steadfastly emphasise its Orcadian credentials. Foodies will enjoy indulging in the excellent website w orkneyfoodanddrink.com, which features a comprehensive listing of producers and retailers. An astonishing number of local food outlets and family producers, from bakers to butchers, go back more than 50 years – and some more than 100 years.

Fish and shellfish are ubiquitous and delicious. Look out for fresh shellfish from the Stromness-based Orkney Fishermen's Society: scallops, brown crab (all edible crabs are known locally as *partans*) and lobster, along with langoustines from Scapa Flow plus line-caught mackerel and other fish from Westray. Cullen skink, a traditional Scottish dish of smoked fish, cream and potatoes, becomes a high art in Orkney. Another classic Orcadian dish is clapshot – potatoes and turnips cooked and mashed together, generally served with sausages or salmon.

You will find Orkney **beef** on just about every menu and can also buy it from venerable producers such as E Flett (w eflettbutcher.co.uk) in Stromness and Donaldsons of Orkney (w donaldsonsoforkney.co.uk) in Kirkwall. Almost as common is North Ronaldsay **lamb**, possibly Orkney's best-known food export. The lamb is prized for its salty taste, a flavour that results from the fact the sheep enjoy a diet of seaweed.

Dairy produce is also of high quality. The only Orkney cheese you usually see in supermarkets on the UK mainland is an orange cheddar. This is a shame given that several excellent local cheesemakers are based on the islands. Varieties include crumbly cheeses originally produced by Hilda Seator at Grimbister Farm Cheese (a business now run by Hilda's daughter-in-law, Ann); her flavours include chive, garlic, whisky and walnut. The Orcadian penchant for combining refinement with lip-smacking, calorie-laden dishes probably reaches its apogee in the form of Grimbister cheese served in deep-fried wedges, which you will often encounter in restaurants. Of similarly high quality are the smoked cheddars produced by the Island Smokery in Stromness (w islandsmokery.co.uk), which are flavoured with whisky or apricot or black pepper as well as green tomato chutney. You should look out for Westray Wife, a tangy cheese produced by Wilsons of Westray (w wilsonsofwestray.co.uk).

RESTAURANT PRICE CODES

The following codes are used in the guide to indicate the average price for a main course in a restaurant or local eatery.

£££   £20+
££   £10–20
£   >£10

And check out food produced by students at the University of the Highlands and Islands, marketed under the Orkney Infusions brand, which includes various chutneys.

For somewhere so far north, Orkney certainly has a predilection for **ice cream**. Orkney Ice Cream, produced at the Orkney Creamery outside Kirkwall, comes in 17 flavours and is sold with a ubiquity that rivals Cornish seaside towns.

You can buy free-range **eggs** at the roadside from farms and houses on just about every outer isle plus many places on the Mainland. Along with bread and cakes, these are usually sold alongside honesty boxes.

Those with a **sweet tooth** are well catered for. You will find Stromness-based Argo's Bakery (w argosbakery.co.uk) products all over the mainland, ranging from bere-barley biscuits to fudge, chocolate biscuits and brownies. Argo's also produces the Stockan's oatcakes sold in shops across the Mainland. A little less ubiquitous but no less delicious are the breads and shortbreads from Westray Bakehouse. Such products are fantastic for keeping up energy levels when walking in relentless winds (just to be clear, if you're on holiday you don't need to turn to the winds to justify eating them; they taste just as good in calm weather).

Thanks to long hours of daylight and a relatively mild climate, a surprising range of **fruit and vegetables** can be grown on Orkney, including strawberries, raspberries, potatoes, cauliflower, cabbages and carrots as well as herbs and purple rocket. Rhubarb grows abundantly here.

You can put aside any **dietary concerns** you may have. Most cafés serve gluten-free food and clearly advertise whether they serve vegan food. Most restaurants can cater – some with a little notice – for those with allergies or other concerns. Lest you consider, however, that Orcadian food is too healthy for its own good, you can still buy cheesy chips (or cheesy broccoli), along with sausages cooked with Iron Bru.

Service is generally very good and, refreshingly, is never too slick or polished. However, poor service does occur, and perhaps more so than Orcadians would like to think. Proprietors wave this away, saying that visitors are simply misinterpreting relaxed and informal 'Orcadian' body language: when it happens, it's actually just bad service.

DRINK Island **whisky** is considered a strength, particularly the liquid distilled at Highland Park (w highlandparkwhisky.com), the world's most northerly distillery. Its rival, Scapa (w scapawhisky.com), lies barely a mile south. Good and varied, Orkney beer was riding the craft wave some time before it became fashionable in the rest of the UK. Two local **breweries** will keep real-ale fans content. The players here are Swannay Brewery (w swannaybrewery.com) whose Scapa Special and IPA are perennially popular; and Orkney Brewery (w orkneybrewery.co.uk), whose range includes the signature Dark Island brew and the lighter, citrus-flavoured Corncrake ale. Both breweries are located on the west of the Mainland; you will see their beers sold everywhere and most pubs will have them on draft. In recent years three

gin distilleries have popped up: Kirkjuvagr Orkney Gin (w orkneydistilling.com) on the Kirkwall waterfront; the Orkney Gin Company (w orkneygincompany. co.uk) on Burray; and the Deerness Distillery (w deernessdistillery.com) in the southeast of the Mainland. All three have tapped into the craft gin movement, offering everything from Seville orange- to cinnamon-flavoured liver ticklers.

The national mania for good **coffee** has not passed Orkney by, and you will be able to enjoy beans or ground coffee from Orkney Roastery (w theorkneyroastery. com). Meanwhile, a small, pioneering tea-growing industry has recently begun on Shapinsay (page 199).

PUBLIC HOLIDAYS AND FESTIVALS

Every month – it can seem like every week – brings a festival to the islands. Those most likely to appeal to the visitor are listed below; others come and go, depending on how successful they prove to be. An up-to-date list can be found at w orkney.com/events. In addition to these, you may well come across a small community event to which you will invariably be welcomed. All islands, including the Mainland, have agricultural shows in summer that offer excellent insights into just how important farming is to Orkney. These are often accompanied by entertainment and stalls selling good food.

New Year's Day sees **The Ba'** – roughly, street rugby in Kirkwall (see box, opposite). In February, the **Papay Gyro Nights Arts Festival** (w papaygyronights. papawestray.org) focuses on folktales, landscape and heritage and old Papa Westray traditions. The first festival of the year, it is held during February's first full moon. On 16 April, St Magnus Kirk in Birsay hosts a **St Magnus Day Service** to commemorate the eponymous Orkney earl, martyred in the 12th century. May sees two major festivals: the **Orkney Folk Festival** in Stromness (w orkneyfolkfestival.com) and **Orkney Nature Festival** (w orkneycommunities.co.uk/orkneynaturefestival) held at various locations across the islands. The former is regarded as one of the UK's greatest attractions of its kind, showcasing local talent, attracting musicians from around the world, and offering ceilidhs, workshops and impromptu street performances. The Nature Festival is open to all – not just birders and their ilk. Highlights include a cruise around Hoy on the MV *Hamnavoe*.

June sees **St Magnus Festival** (w stmagnusfestival.com), which features high-quality performances by international orchestras, recitalists and dancers. Atmospheric locations include St Magnus Cathedral and the Italian Chapel. In July, there are three days of jollity – including pipe bands, bouncy castles and face-painting – to mark **Papay Fun Weekend** (w papawestray.co.uk/events.html). **Agricultural shows** dominate in August, with events in Sanday, the East Mainland in Tankerness, Shapinsay, South Ronaldsay and Burray at St Margaret's Hope. The West Mainland show is held at Dounby. The biggest is the County Show at Bignold Park, Kirkwall. Other events include the Riding of the Marches, a tradition revived in the 1980s that celebrates the Kirkwall's charter as a royal burgh and involves horses and riders heading out to Scapa beach.

In September, the **Orkney International Science Festival** (w oisf.org) celebrates stargazing, polar exploration and astronomy along with food events and ceilidhs. October's highlight is the **Orkney Storytelling Festival** (w orkneystorytellingfestival. co.uk); local, national and international storytellers ensure great appeal for both children and adults. On 25 December another game of **Ba'** bookends the year in Kirkwall. **New Year's Eve** in Kirkwall and Stromness is a good deal of fun. Large crowds gather by St Magnus Cathedral and Stromness pier. The New Year is seen in with ships' whistles and church bells.

Talk all you like about Orcadians' hospitality, courtesy and easy-going approach to life. Nothing offers more of an insight into the island soul than The Ba'. Visitors are welcome to watch the game but are actively discouraged from taking part: the event is emphatically neither a tourist event nor a gimmick.

As well as the name of the game, the Ba' is a leather ball that weighs 5.5lb and is filled with cork. Competition takes place on the central streets of Kirkwall between two teams, the 'uppies' and the 'doonies', and can involve 200 players. A doonie is someone born between the line of Old Post Office Lane and the harbour; uppies hail from the other, more inland, side of the line. The aim is to get the Ba' into the other team's goal. Easier said than done, however, as these goals are about half a mile apart; the uppies' goal is near the junction of Makin Street and New Scapa Road by the Catholic church and the doonies' is the harbour. Shopfronts are wisely boarded up. The ball is hurled in the air at 1pm, falls into the scrum and occasionally pops up to see the light of day before disappearing again. Games can take several hours before a winner emerges.

To the outsider the game appears to rest somewhere between a street brawl and rugby. Those who take part, particularly veterans of dozens of Ba' games, swear that nifty footwork, strategic planning, an ability to think three-dimensionally, and even dark arts such as false runs, can help to win the day. Another conclusion would be that luck, size and raw strength each play a role.

Every year one of the participants is awarded the ball at the match end. Norman Kelday, who runs Ardconnel Bed and Breakfast outside Kirkwall, is the proud owner of a Ba', having won a game for the doonies and ended up in the salt water of Kirkwall harbour for his troubles. Norman has played the Ba' since 1981, when he was eight years old. Does he ever get hurt? 'Oh, you get roughed up a bit, but nothing major,' he smiles. 'I've just had the three cracked ribs.'

As well as a men's game, a boys' game is held. Women's games were staged in 1945 and 1946 but never since. Some people disapproved of a spectacle they deemed 'unlady like' but another story (which is possibly not apocryphal) goes that the female participants were so violent that even the most hard-bitten male players were shocked.

SHOPPING

Shops generally open Monday to Saturday 09.00–17.00, although some close at lunchtime on Saturday. Other than some cafés, most places tend to close on Sundays. If a cruise ship is due in Kirkwall on a Sunday, or in March, April or September when some shops keep shorter hours, then they will open their doors to accommodate the surge in visitors.

A handful of the major supermarket chains have made it to the Mainland but more striking is the number of local grocers, butchers, delis and community-run stores. These work hard to provide an excellent service to locals and visitors. They are very unlike the mediocre, overpriced and tired chain-owned shops you often see in rural parts of the UK. Instead, they are well stocked, well priced and overcome sizeable logistical challenges to provide fresh fruit and vegetables. The community shops on Papa Westray, Westray and Eday particularly stand out in this regard.

Winter hours for cafés and restaurants are often shorter and some restaurants will close down between October and April. Generally, opening hours extend in line with the Orkney Islands Ferries summer schedule, which runs from early May until end September. Museums are usually open all year, with shorter winter hours. Opening times for pubs are often variable. They will keep open as long as someone is sitting on a bar stool – but on a quiet night you may find they have locked up early. On the Outer Isles most eateries stay open until the last boat has sailed. If you're arriving late at night it's worth calling ahead to a pub or your accommodation and they may well put together a meal for you.

ARTS AND ENTERTAINMENT

Orkney is something of a magnet both for resident artists and for visiting exhibitions. The major display space is the Pier Arts Centre in Stromness but the town's other galleries (page 81) often host visiting shows. The Gable End Theatre on Hoy attracts troupes and performers from around the world to perform in its 75-seat community auditorium. Across the islands, artists and other crafts folk are only too happy to chat; there is never any pressure to buy.

The Mainland has two cinemas, complemented every few weeks here and on the North Isles by Britain's only mobile equivalent, the Screen Machine (w screenmachine.co.uk). If your visit coincides, buy a ticket: the 'cinema' is housed in an articulated lorry with soft-backed seats and provides a slightly surreal take on the real thing. Some islands also have impressively high-spec projectors and screens they deploy in community halls.

Outside Kirkwall, hotels tend to be the social hub of a community. The difference between a lounge and a public bar – the latter generally more boisterous and often accommodating snooker/billiard tables and a dartboard – is more pronounced than in many other parts of the UK.

OUTDOOR ACTIVITIES

Few places in the UK are so geared up for exploring the great outdoors as Orkney. Outside of Kirkwall and Stromness you are pretty much in the countryside all the time. In addition to walking along rugged headlands and diving the wrecks of Scapa Flow, the islands offer everything from sedate beach strolls and relaxing fishing to more stirring hikes and bike rides. At the time of writing, the only thing missing was an operator offering the more adrenalin-pulsing activities such as coasteering or kitesurfing.

WALKING Walking on Orkney is a joy and among the most rewarding and exhilarating in the UK. Much of the time you will almost certainly have the landscape to yourself, and there are few better places to enjoy wildlife, coastal views and extremely aesthetic hilltops as you ramble along. The range of walking is vast, from decent mountain hikes on Hoy to glorious, endless shoreline walks on all the other islands. Many of the Outer Isles are small enough that walking them is the best way to explore. Scotland's open-access laws also mean you can walk more or less where you wish, so long as you adhere to the countryside access code and respect the privacy of owners.

In other ways, walking on Orkney is a rather different experience to what you may be used to if you hail from England. While there are footpaths, particularly along coastal routes, much of the walking to be had is over open ground, which usually means fields and rough moorland. You need to have good footwear, and be able to read a map and to use a compass. Whatever the time of year, pack warm clothing and waterproofs as the speed with which the weather can change never ceases to amaze. GPS is always useful but remember that batteries go flat and that GPS won't warn you of an impending deep bog or sheer cliff edge. Several coastal paths run hard up against dizzyingly exposed cliffs; such risks are highlighted in the relevant walks featured in this book. Just to add to the fun, overhanging precipices, known as hags, can be found in parts of Westray, Rousay and Deerness on the Mainland.

A good way to ease yourself into walking on Orkney is to join a walk organised by Orkney Ramblers (e orkneyramblers@gmail.com; w orkneypics.com/ramblers). They welcome visitors and will happily suggest walking routes, particularly on the Mainland.

One feature worth noting is that, despite Scotland's open-access laws, simply striking out into the moors and rolling farmland can at times prove fiddly. Blame it on the islands' sizeable livestock industry but all those cows and sheep need to be fenced in. Orkney farmers love barbed wire and they can often seem less keen on stiles. What may appear a reasonably direct route from A to B on foot can become exasperating as you search in vain for a gate or a gap in a fence. In theory you can walk anywhere you wish; in practice you will often end up on a more circuitous route following lanes and roads.

Another thing to bear in mind is Udal Law (see box, page 19), which applies in Orkney (and Shetland). Essentially, open-access provisions do not apply to land subject to Udal Law (namely, privately owned foreshore or beach). In practice, almost no-one objects to you walking along the foreshore. That said, it does no harm to show courtesy and ask permission if opportunity presents itself.

Also bear in mind that there are fewer waymarked or recognised walks than elsewhere in the UK. This means some farmers may not be familiar with your rights, or, if they are, refuse to recognise them. Very rarely, they may choose to deploy intimidating behaviour to drive home the point that you are not welcome. You will also come across 'no entry' signs and bolted gates with mesh affixed to prevent you clambering over. Other tactics include laying fences right up against cliff edges or down to the high-tide mark. You are nevertheless entitled to climb over such gates and obstacles: whether you choose to make a point is up to you but the most constructive approach is to report any issues to Orkney Ramblers. All walks described in this book are on land where walkers are welcome.

FISHING Orkney offers fine trout-fishing; even better, it is free. Good lochs on the Mainland include Swannay and Boardhouse in the far west, Harray near the Ring of Brodgar and Kirbister near Orphir. Remote Heldale Water on Hoy is often revered for the quality of its fish. Stocking policies begun 25 years ago have also had great

Practical Information   OUTDOOR ACTIVITIES   **2**

The UK's northerly waters are not automatically associated with diving, but Scapa Flow is most definitely on the wish list for divers around the world. The main appeal is the wrecks from the German fleet that was scuttled in 1919. Today, you are able to explore seven primary and four secondary wrecks in the waters east of Stromness and south of Scapa Bay. 'The wrecks lie 65–130ft deep so are easily accessible,' says Katie MacLeod, dive manager at Scapa Scuba. 'You don't need to be a technical diver. What you see is amazing – the wrecks are ginormous and they have great historical significance. It can feel like swimming in the bowels of a cathedral. They attract marine life so you might spot seals, conger eels and lobsters.' If diving by yourself, bear in mind that some sites are war graves and off limits.

success on Sanday, Stronsay and Westray. For more information and advice visit w orkneytroutfishing.co.uk.

GOLF Orkney has some wonderful golf courses, typically situated hard by the sea. Visitors are always welcome to play a round. Westray Golf Club, overlooked by the brooding outline of Noltland Castle and adjacent to the unfolding drama of the Links of Noltland archaeological site (page 251), is probably the pick of the bunch.

SCUBA DIVING Orkney is firmly on the bucket list for scuba-divers. The waters around Scapa Flow are excellent for underwater exploration, with the wartime wrecks of three battleships and four light cruisers. The wrecks of the UB116 and a German destroyer just off the Buchanan Battery on the east shores of Flotta are particularly attractive to divers. Training is available for beginners while local experts will take the more experienced around the wrecks of the scuttled German fleet in Scapa Flow. Generally, diving operates out of Stromness (page 74). Operators will provide all gear. Drysuits are advisable: temperatures are a chilly 4/5°C in March, rising, if you're lucky, to the giddy heights of 13°C in August and September.

WATERSPORTS The islands' countless bays make for wonderful kayaking, canoeing or stand-up paddleboarding. Highlights include the geos and caves off the east coast of Shapinsay. The larger lochs on mainland can also be idyllic.

MEDIA AND COMMUNICATIONS

The local **newspaper** is a venerable weekly (published every Thursday), *The Orcadian* (w orcadian.co.uk). Unusually for newspapers in the age of free internet news, the publication retains considerable stature within the community. BBC Radio Orkney operates at 93.7Mhz on FM as well as online. Local news and music are interspersed with feeds from BBC Scotland. Out on the isles, look out for grassroots bulletins such as the *Sanday Sound*, the *Stronsay Limpet* and *Auk Talk* (Westray), which provide up-to-date developments on events, openings and closures.

Mobile and **broadband** connections are improving all the time. Roughly 75% of all households in Orkney now have fibre. Kirkwall has 4G mobile and you can get a signal across most of the Mainland. Good mobile reception, usually 2G and 3G, can be found across all the outer islands and is especially decent if you are in sight of the huge Cloudnet mast on Sanday. The erection of a mast, scheduled for 2019, on

North Ronaldsay, should improve matters further. Internet is more variable on the Outer Isles but increasingly most B&Bs and self-catering places offer Wi-Fi, though speeds can range from 0.5–10Mb/s.

Mail to the UK mainland is delivered remarkably quickly, often arriving the next day, or the day after at the latest.

CULTURAL ETIQUETTE

The most striking feature of Orcadians that visitors take away with them is just how straight-talking they seem. There is a prevailing absence of cynicism, or 'side', that makes most encounters with Orcadians an uplifting experience. 'I love the fact there isn't really a class system,' says Teresa Probert of Isle of Auskerry (see box, page 204). 'People value you for your skills and your actions rather than your possessions.'

CRUISE SHIPS – THE DOUBLE-EDGED (NEOLITHIC) SWORD

Twenty years ago just a handful of cruise ships visited Orkney every year. That number swelled over the first decade of this century to 60. In 2018, 170 cruise ships docked at Hatston Pier outside Kirkwall, some carrying 5,000 passengers. Well before then, non-cruise visitors were already complaining that their experience of major sites such as Skara Brae and the Italian Chapel was being ruined by multiple coaches disgorging human cargo.

Cruise ships divide islander opinion as well. Some Kirkwall shops are geared very largely to the cruise trade; others dread passengers accessing Wi-Fi while dawdling over coffee.

'It's an ongoing issue. Cruise ships are a 21st-century travel phenomenon. As the world gets wealthier, more people will want to travel and see wonderful places such as Orkney,' says Stephen Watt, district architect for Heritage Environment Scotland (HES).

Yet cruise ships are merely symptomatic of Orkney's increasing popularity. Visitor numbers to Skara Brae have rocketed from 68,000 (2010) to 110,000 (2017), a rise of 61%. The Ring of Brodgar is proving even more popular, with numbers rising from 110,000 in 2015 to 141,000 in 2017. That said, the problem only applies to a handful of major sites. Along the road from Maeshowe and Brodgar, you may be alone enjoying the magnificent, 5,000-year-old Unstan chambered tomb (page 109).

The past couple of years has seen co-ordinated action between the cruise-ship industry, HES (which owns 33 sites across Orkney) and the Orkney Tourism Group. They aim to strike a balance and think strategically. Measures include timed ticketing for Maeshowe, and separate entrances for cruise and individual visitors at Skara Brae. Sympathetically designed portable toilets here have further helped to relieve the queues.

The same approach is being applied to other key sites. At the Ring of Brodgar, a new car park is helping and a footpath connects Brodgar to Stenness, helping to diffuse numbers at any one site.

'It is a balancing act. We want people to enjoy, learn from and appreciate these sites – but we still have a responsibility to conserve and care for them,' says Watt. 'Increasing numbers of visitors inevitably has an impact on the condition not only of the monuments, but also the surrounding area. The sites themselves are not under threat – it's the overloading that can confound the visitor experience.'

Individual travellers – who still make up the vast majority of visitors to Orkney – are often advised by their accommodation provider not to visit a site when a cruise is booked in. Visit Scotland's office in Kirkwall is also extremely helpful in this regard and will offer useful alternative suggestions.

The debate continues as to whether transport infrastructure across the islands should be upgraded to make it easier for coaches to move around. Many oppose this. 'We don't want to build two-lane roads,' says Alan Tulloch, owner of the Standing Stones Hotel, which lies at the heart of the UNESCO World Heritage Site. 'Our quaint roads are what they are.'

Apart from reciprocating in kind, there are a few easy measures you can take to leave a good impression – much of what Orcadians ask of you amounts to basic courtesy and common sense.

While many of Orkney's thousands of ancient monuments are freely accessible – a decent number are even signposted – many are located on private land. Despite Scotland's open-access laws (see box, page 61), it remains the done thing to ask permission from the landowner before seeking out a particular site. Pleasingly, it's unusual for such a request to be turned down. Never park in front of farm gates or what appear to be unused farm lanes: you will soon appreciate just how frequently they are used. Don't forget to close gates after you. Always be mindful of taking photographs in appropriate circumstances: Orkney's churches are incredibly romantic but local upset has been caused by people sufficiently gauche or self-obsessed to take pictures with selfie sticks during funerals.

TRAVELLING POSITIVELY

Cause and effect are certainly at work in Orkney, and visitors have a significant role to play in the islands' future. This applies to how and where you choose to spend your money: supporting local shops, particularly grocery stores and island hubs, can make a meaningful difference to the prospects of them staying open. In turn, that has an impact on the quality of islanders' lives.

Despite their increasingly popularity, these islands are not a destination for mass tourism; islanders are not geared up for that and most of them do not wish to be. This can mean things don't always go to plan. Service is generally very good but – like anywhere – can come under pressure when overwhelmed by more visitors than they are used to. The wild swings of Orcadian weather are a fact of life and, indeed, a large part of the appeal for many visitors. Yet some people will find it unnerving to experience a big storm in a remote landscape.

When you draw up a wish list of things to do on Orkney, you may find that Plan A doesn't always work out. Above all, that weather usually has the final say in how your holiday will unfold. But do you *need* everything to go like clockwork and expect – or want – to be able to access the internet at a drop of a hat? Reciprocating the courtesy and phlegmatic approach extended to you when things go awry matters a good deal; islanders will take note of how you respond to such situations. Just accept that Plan A may have to be ditched and Plan E, or even Plan Z, may rise to the top of the list. Come with an open mind, ready to respect and embrace local attitudes and you will be welcomed into a distinctive culture like no other in Britain.

Part Two

THE GUIDE

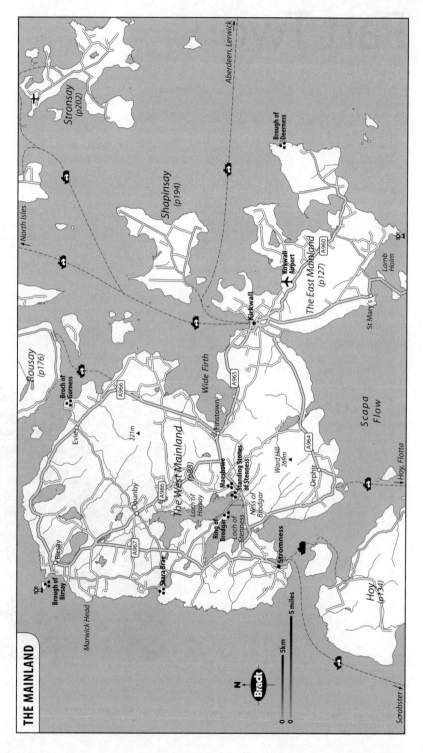

3

The Mainland

By far Orkney's largest island, the Mainland is where the vast majority of visitors spend most of their time in Orkney. This is for good reason as the range and diversity of interest is astonishing, running along an archaeological timeline from the Neolithic, Bronze and Iron Ages to Pictish and Norse sites as well as incorporating wild landscapes, beautiful beaches and remote moorlands. This is the island where you will find Orkney's 'blockbuster' sites: Skara Brae, Maeshowe, the Ring and Ness of Brodgar and the Italian Chapel are all justifiably world famous. It's impossible, however, to visit them and ignore the simply breathtaking landscape of valleys, ridgelines, steeling cliffs and sweeping bays among which they lie. Quite simply, there is an almost ineffable magic to the Mainland that stirs the imagination of just about everyone who visits. Narrow your eyes and it's not a huge – or necessarily pretentious – jump to envisage this landscape peopled with Neolithic tribes and smoke rising from cooking fires across the intermittent flatlands, or a wooden boat making landfall laden with fish speared from the abundant waters.

The island stretches for 25 miles from east to west and, at its maximum extent, 18 miles north to south. The Mainland is divided into two; everything west and southwest of Kirkwall is referred to as 'the West Mainland'; the land east of the town is, logically enough, 'the East Mainland'. The name originates from the Norse moniker, Meginland ('main island'), though those peoples also tended to refer to it as Hrossey ('island of horses').

Most major tourist sites are located in the West Mainland, which also accounts for around 60% of the island's landmass. The East Mainland is much smaller, predominantly given over to farming and, even though it has a handful of impressive sites, less visited.

The island is subdivided historically into several parishes, some of which also have a township, or village, of the same name. Examples include Birsay, Evie, Dounby and Orphir.

HISTORY

The Mainland's appeal to modern-day visitors is directly related to its historical importance at the heart of Orkney. From the earliest settlers, who managed to make it up the coasts of Britain and across the Pentland Firth, to 20th-century wartime sites, the island history is bound up with what you see today. Exactly when people first arrived on the Mainland is uncertain but, if, as is thought, they hailed from the northern plains of Doggerland, the area that connected Britain to continental Europe, then their first landfall may well have been on what today is the East Mainland and natural harbours such as those that have eventually grown into Stromness and Kirkwall. The sandstone bedrock that underlies much of the

Mainland provided fertile growing conditions and gave rise to peoples who had sophisticated belief systems and rituals and who left behind an extraordinary number of sites, such as Skara Brae, Maeshowe and the Ring of Brodgar.

Over time, even though such sites fell into disrepair, or were overwhelmed by the elements, the Mainland remained a good place to live with the lochs of Stenness and Harray providing fish. As the climate worsened – some time after 2200BC – blanket peat began to dominate, pushing out the birch and alder trees, making it harder for communities to hold on. From this time until the Iron Age, there is remarkably little evidence of permanent villages. After 2200BC evidence is scant for villages or indeed any settlements. The one exception is the remarkable Knowes of Trotty (page 103), a collection of 12 Bronze Age burial mounds located south of Dounby.

THE SCUTTLING OF THE GERMAN FLEET

The scuttling of the German fleet in midsummer 1919 was a dramatic event that sent reverberations across Europe. At the time of the Armistice, the captured German fleet of 74 ships was escorted to Scapa Flow. On 21 November 1918 the Germans were ordered to lower the national flag on their ships. The crew numbered 25,000, many mutinous. The majority were sent home, leaving a skeleton crew of 1,700 to maintain the ships during negotiations over the peace settlement.

Time passed interminably slowly for the captive crew. In Stromness Museum you will find a poem by Torpedo-Obermatrosen Heintze, on torpedo boat S60: 'Four months I have lingered in Scapa/How long can this misery last?/Barren rocks are my only lookout/What horrors their shadows cast!/Wild ducks fly on high/And for freedom I sigh.'

As talks dragged on with little apparent prospect of resolution, the German commander Ludwig van der Reuter grew increasingly restless. On 17 June he sent a secret letter to his commanding officers to make preparations to scuttle: they were to open all hatches and watertight doors.

He wrote that his officers were 'to make immediate preparations for scuttling all ships, to ensure their sinking as soon as possible after the receipt of command'. He added: 'if our government accepts the peace terms and agrees to surrender the ships, I will deliver them to the enemy – to the eternal disgrace of those who have placed them in this position.'

When the German government collapsed van der Reuter concluded that there was no prospect for a peace agreement and decided to authorise the scuttling. He was unaware that a new German government had been formed and had agreed to resume talks. On 21 June he sent the signal. The SMS *Friedrich der Grosse* was the first to sink at noon; by 5pm, 52 ships had been sunk and the rest were beached. Over the years different theories have emerged as to just how van der Reuter was able to execute his plan: the case has been made that it actually suited both sides for the ships to be scuttled, so that they did not fall into, or remain in, enemy hands. Wreaths washed up – most likely having been laid on the ships before they were sunk – were made from flowers unobtainable in Orkney, which has fuelled some of the conspiracy theories (the wreaths were intended to mark the loss of the ships, rather than humans – while no German drowned during the scuttling, nine were shot and killed by British soldiers as they rowed on lifeboats to shore as the drama unfolded).

When the Picts moved into Orkney around the 6th century, the Mainland, the largest of the islands, was their logical stronghold and this is the time when a centre of power first began to be established on the Brough of Birsay (page 95). From the 9th century onwards, the Orkney Earls established their grip. Birsay and Orphir were both important to them but, after the conflicts that led to the murder of Earl Magnus Erlendsson in 1117 (page 188), the seat of power was moved to Kirkwall. Various characters, such as Earl Patrick (page 123) in the 17th century, proved extremely adept at exploiting their rule of the islands for dubious purposes. In the 18th century, the Mainland became an increasingly important international trading base, particularly for the Hudson's Bay Company, which used it to recruit sailors and stock up on food and water before heading for Canada and the Arctic.

During the 20th century, the Mainland's strategic position, commanding northern shipping routes, meant that it found itself catapulted into national importance during the world wars. Fortifications were built on many headlands and they and much other military infrastructure remains in place today. While more recently oil and renewables have provided employment, farming remains the dominant industry and is an ever-present backdrop to any journey around the Mainland.

GETTING THERE AND AWAY

The Mainland (along with South Ronaldsay, page 167) is the gateway for all arrivals from the rest of the UK. Even if your final destination is one of the Outer Isles, you must travel there via the Mainland, by ferry or air.

BY FERRY Three vehicle and one passenger ferry route grant direct or swift access from the UK mainland to the Mainland of Orkney: Scrabster–Stromness, Gill's Bay–St Margaret's Hope, John O'Groats–Burwick and Aberdeen–Kirkwall. For details of fares and crossing times, see page 45.

Ferries to other Orkney islands Ferry services to other Orkney islands operate from and to (Orkney) Mainland; you cannot reach them directly from the UK mainland. Services are run by Orkney Ferries (✆ 01856 872044; e info@ orkneyferries.co.uk; w orkneyferries.co.uk) whose office (⊕ 07.00–17.00 Mon–Fri, 07.00–noon & 13.00–15.00 Sat) and main terminal are located at Kirkwall harbour, in front of the Kirkwall Hotel [117 D2].

Ferry routes to the North Isles of Sanday, Eday, Stronsay, Westray, Papa Westray and North Ronaldsay depart from the pier on the east side of Kirkwall harbour [117 B1]. The ferry to Shapinsay departs from the adjacent pier (west side) [117 C2] and has its own access road for vehicle drivers and foot passengers. Ferries for Rousay and the islands of Egilsay and Wyre depart from Tingwall [88 E2], 12 miles northwest of Kirkwall, just off the A966. For the South Isles of Hoy, Flotta and Graemsay, you have two options. The vehicle and passenger ferry for Flotta and Lyness (Hoy) departs from Houton, 10 miles southwest of Kirkwall and just west of the township of Orphir along the A964. Meanwhile, a foot-passenger service sails from Stromness [89 B6] to the Moaness Pier in the north of Hoy, calling at Graemsay. A slightly reduced service runs on all routes during the winter months (late Sep to early May).

Details and prices of services between each island and Kirkwall are listed in the relevant island chapters.

BY ROAD The islands of Burray and South Ronaldsay, as well as the Italian Chapel, are connected by road to the East Mainland by the series of causeways known as the Churchill Barriers.

BY AIR Kirkwall Airport is 3 miles southeast of the town, off the A960 [89 G6]. For details of services, see page 45. The airport has separate procedures for inter-island flights and for services to the UK mainland. The café (⊕ 06.30–19.30 Mon–Fri, 06.30–15.30 Sat, 10.30–19.30 Sun, shorter hours in winter) provides hot meals as well as proper coffee, cakes and smoothies. The adjacent bar, with its local whiskies, beers and gins is – unusually for an airport bar – on the landside of the security checks and therefore also open to the non-flying public (a notice to this effect stands outside the entrance to the airport off the A960). If you've left your souvenir purchases to the last minute then the airport shop may come to your rescue, selling a good selection of jewellery, art and knitwear.

GETTING AROUND

BY CAR The Mainland's roads are generally good, with one lane in each direction on all the arterial routes that criss-cross the island. Almost all the major roads eventually go through or skirt around Kirkwall. From Kirkwall to Birsay on the west coast is a distance of 22 miles; it is 15 miles from Kirkwall to the northern tip of South Ronaldsay. The two major towns, Kirkwall and Stromness, are 17 miles apart (roughly a 30-minute drive).

The West Mainland's major roads traverse the south, the middle and the north. The A roads sometimes change their number for no obvious reason, which can occasionally be a little confusing, but the destinations are all extremely logical and as direct as can be given the lochs, hills and farmland around which the roads must weave. The main road through the southwest of the island is the A965, which runs from Kirkwall via Finstown to Stromness; this passes to the southeast of the lochs of Harray and Stenness and provides access to the Ring of Brodgar, Maeshowe and the Standing Stones of Stenness. The A964 runs from Kirkwall along the south coast through Orphir and is a scenic, if slightly slower, route to Stromness. The A967 then picks up the baton and heads north from Stromness, furnishing access to the west coast, Skara Brae and Birsay.

The north of the West Mainland is served by the A966 that runs from Finstown, via the parishes of Rendall and Evie, to Birsay. The journey from Kirkwall to Birsay along this route is 27 miles (45mins). Another useful road is the A986, which cuts through the middle of the West Mainland and is the best way to reach Dounby. Maeshowe and its adjacent Neolithic sites are around 25 minutes from Kirkwall and 15 minutes from Stromness; Skara Brae is 35 minutes from Kirkwall, 25 minutes from Stromness.

Distances are much shorter on the East Mainland. The main road is the A960, which runs past the airport and connects the parishes of Tankerness and Deerness. This road gets downgraded to the B9050 a mile east of Dingieshowe. From Kirkwall to the extremity of Mull Head in Deerness is 14 miles (30mins).

Electric charging points can be found in Kirkwall and Stromness and at the Houton ferry pier.

Car hire By and large, rates are reasonable: expect to pay around £250 per week in high season for a small car and £300 for an estate car. You should book in advance in the summer months when demand is high.

Reliable companies include:

🚗 **Colin Gregg Cars** Hatston Industrial Estate, Grainshore Dr, Kirkwall; 📞 01856 870900; e colin@ colingreggcars.co.uk; w colingreggcars.co.uk

🚗 **Drive Orkney Car & Van Hire** Grainshore Rd, Kirkwall; 📞 01856 877551; e info@ driveorkney.com; w driveorkney.com

🚗 **Orkney Car Rental** Offices at airport & Junction Rd, Kirkwall; 📞 01856 875500; e airportcarental@wrtullock.com; w orkneycarrental.co.uk

BY BUS
A good bus service radiates out of Kirkwall and, with a little planning, it is possible to see most major island attractions by bus. This is less plausible in winter when many services are reduced and also geared towards schoolchildren and commuters. A slimmed-down service runs on Sundays. For up-to-date timetables visit w orkney.gov.uk/transport or w stagecoach.com.

The most popular bus routes are X1, which runs between Stromness and Kirkwall then south to St Margaret's Hope on South Ronaldsay; and number 4, the Kirkwall–airport service, which runs every half hour and takes 15 minutes. Number 3 also runs to the airport en route to Tankerness and Deerness. The other main service is the 8S, which runs from Kirkwall to Skara Brae via Maeshowe, Stenness and the Ring of Brodgar. The easiest day to explore the major Neolithic wonders is Saturday when the bus runs four times. Other routes include number 6, which serves both the Tingwall ferry (for Rousay) and the northwest of the Mainland, including Evie and Birsay; and number 2, which takes 20 minutes to reach Houton (for the Hoy ferry) from Kirkwall. Number 5 serves Houton from Stromness and takes 15 minutes. If you're based in Stromness, service 7 is handy for getting to Birsay and Dounby. Sample one-way fares from Kirkwall include: Stromness (£3.35); St Margaret's Hope (£3.15); and Birsay (£3.65). Return tickets are 1½ times the price of a single and children travel half price. Seniors must be in possession of a Scottish senior bus pass to travel for free.

BY TAXI
Several taxis run to the airport, around Kirkwall and Stromness, and between the two. Approximate fares include: Kirkwall–airport (£8); Kirkwall–Stromness (£25–30); and Skara Brae or Birsay to Kirkwall (£35–38).

Ab's taxis m 07437 332012
Bob's taxis 📞 01856 876543

Craigies taxis 📞 01856 878787
Harbour taxis 📞 01856 490185

BY BIKE
The terrain of the Mainland makes cycling easy enough; only the central moors involve any need for uphill puffing. The smaller roads are generally quiet and allow you to explore not just major sites such as Maeshowe and Skara Brae but rarely visited lochs to the west, such as Hundland and Swannay. Often your only companions will be avian, most likely a curlew. The only downside is the speed of drivers on many of the A roads, which will quickly shatter any vision of riding along in a rural idyll. By and large, and with a little planning, you can knit routes together that broadly avoid these arterial routes.

If you need to hire a bike, it's worth checking out the following:

🚲 **Cycle Orkney** [117 B5] Tankerness Ln, Kirkwall; 📞 01856 875777; e cycleorkney@ btconnect.com; w cycleorkney.com. A range including electric bikes (£20/10 adult/child).

🚲 **Orkney Cycle Hire** [78 B5] 54 Dundas St, Stromness; 📞 01856 850255; e info@ orkneycyclehire.co.uk; w orkneycyclehire.co.uk. From £10/day (inc children's bikes).

♿ Trek & Travel [117 D3] 15–17 Bridge St, Kirkwall; ☎01856 874505; ⏱ 09.00–17.15 Mon–Sat, 12.30–16.00 Sun. Hires out a range of bikes for £15/day & is also useful for outdoor gear (including shoelaces for hiking boots).

TOURIST INFORMATION AND TOUR OPERATORS

There is no tourist office in Stromness but you will find many flyers and brochures at the main Stromness ferry terminal [78 D2] (⏱ 05.30–16.45 & 20.15–23.45 Mon–Fri, 07.30–16.45 & 20.15–23.45 Sat & Sun), which facilitates the NorthLink services (☎ 0845 600 0449; w northlinkferries.co.uk) to Scrabster.

For a full list of guides and tour operators see page 43.

Dawn Star Boat Trips ☎01856 876743; e dawnstar@orkneyboattrips.co.uk; w orkneyboattrips.co.uk. Boat tours of the East Mainland are available on the *Dawn Star* run by Laurence Tait. They take in the gloup (blowhole) off Deerness, the Brough of Deerness & Mull Head.

Kirkwall Visit Scotland Centre [117 B4] ☎01856 872856; e kirkwall@visitscotland.com; ⏱ Easter–Sep 09.00–18.00 daily; Oct–Mar 09.00–17.00 Mon–Sat. Friendly & helpful staff who will book you rooms, give advice on eating out & provide bus timetables. It's also well stocked with souvenirs from fudge to woollen scarves.

Northerly Marine Services [117 C2] ☎01856 252998; m 07825 459242; e paul@northerlymarineservices.co.uk; w northerlymarineservices.co.uk. Based out of the Corn Slip in Kirkwall, this outfit offers bespoke boat trips to islands not served by Orkney Islands Ferries, such as Fara, Eynhallow & Auskerry, as well as more general tours of Scapa Flow & waters north of Kirkwall plus evening cruises with light meals of local salmon & cheese. It also operates a tender so can drop you off on an island & pick you up later. Prices work out at about £30/head per trip for evening & general tours; a trip to Eynhallow is around £250 divided between 4 or more people.

Orkney Trike Tours m 07861310139; e john@orkneytriketours.co.uk; w orkneytriketours.co.uk; see ad, page 66. Offers chauffeur-driven tours of the Mainland – but with a difference, in a classic trike. Tours are bespoke but include a romantic evening summer option, visiting Yesnaby & finishing at the Ring of Brodgar at midnight.

Scapa Scuba [78 B5] Lifeboat House, Stromness; ☎01856 851218; e diving@scapascuba.co.uk; w scapascuba.co.uk; ⏱ usually May–Sep. For scuba-diving, Scapa Scuba offers guided tours around the wrecks & light cruisers of Scapa Flow as well as shore-diving. Also provides a 'try-a-dive' course for beginners aged 10 & above. For hard-hat diving, Andrew Hamill of Leviathan International (page 81) offers courses for beginners & excursions for the experienced.

STROMNESS

> The street uncoiled like a sailor's rope from north to south,
> And closes swarmed up the side of the hills.
>
> *Per Mare: The Stromness Pagent, George Mackay Brown*

Orkney's second-largest and most attractive settlement, Stromness is a stone-built port hunkered down in a sheltered harbour. At its heart is a tight-knit huddle of houses, quaysides and slipways all but embedded in the granite ridge of Brinkies Brae, which towers above them. An 18th-century imprint underpins the town – apparent in the three-storey terraced houses that are topped with triangular gable ends of crow-step design. At ground level, these houses open hard on to the street or abut narrow alleys that face stone waterside piers, jetties and nousts. Overall, the town, which has just over 2,000 residents, has a pleasingly weathered yet warm appearance.

Stromness translates from Old Norse as 'headland in the tidal stream' and you can almost see the ghosts of young men preparing to sail on whaling adventures to the Arctic or ready for service with the Hudson's Bay Company. That sense of yesteryear is augmented by the smell of peat- and wood-burning stoves and the ever-present sloshing of the sea.

Rather like Kirkwall, a single narrow street threads its way through the heart of Stromness, changing its name (John Street becomes Victoria Street then Dundas Street and finally Alfred Street) as it meanders towards the Ness headland. From the west, a series of lanes tumbles down the hillside, feeding the main street like streams, many of them with elegiac names such as Puffer's Close (named after James Leask, a 19th-century town crier nicknamed 'Puffer'), Boys Lane, Khyber Pass, Millar's Steps, Hellihole Road and Free Kirk Lane. The narrowest of such lanes qualify as a 'clos', an Orcadian word for a narrow passageway between two buildings.

Stromness is curtailed to the east by the harbour of Hamnavoe, or Haven Bay, which, together with the adjacent islands of Outer and Inner Holm, has provided shelter and refuge from weather and attack since Viking times. The town has a different vibe to Kirkwall – and it is a vibe, for this is an artistic settlement of some stature. In the town's early days, you clearly had to have something about you to both survive and thrive here, and that spirit is still apparent. Consequently, Stromness manages to maintain the feel of a pioneer town.

STROMNESS CASTAWAYS

Given how many people have sailed across the world from Stromness, it is unsurprising that a good number found themselves in the soup. Several ended up marooned on tropical islands, embracing local mores. Their number included John Renton, born in Stromness in 1848. Aged 20 he was 'shanghaied' (kidnapped) and forced on to a boat collecting guano in the Pacific. He managed to escape and drifted for 1,100 miles over 34 days before reaching the coast of Malaita in the Solomon Islands. Adopted by a local leader and accepted into his family, Renton was later picked up by a passing European ship and returned to Stromness. Undeterred, he sailed to work in Australia but was killed in a skirmish in Vanuatu in 1878.

Another Stromness inhabitant, Eliza Fraser, had an even more dramatic life. Pregnant with her fourth child (she left her other three with a Presbyterian minister in Stromness), she accompanied her husband, an Orkney sea captain, to Australia in 1836. North of the continent the ship fell victim to the shallows of the Torres Strait and was swept on to an unchartered reef. A few days later she gave birth to her child who soon died. Eliza and her husband were, she later reported, 'enslaved by aboriginals'. A spear wound hastened her husband's death; for her part Fraser maintained she was manhandled, abused and tortured. The reality may be a little more ambiguous, as other reports suggest the indigenous peoples were merely protecting her, smearing her body with lizard grease to keep her warm and treating her suppurating sores with fire sticks. She was finally rescued by an Irish convict who persuaded the islanders that he was her 'spirit wife'; she returned home and dined out with some financial success on her experience. Posterity, however, has suggested that her accounts were misleading and helped cement the canard that aboriginal peoples were inferior and primitive. Nevertheless, her name was subsequently honoured in Australia's Fraser Island and Eliza Reef.

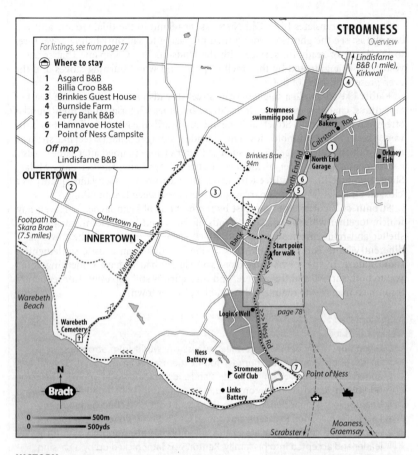

page 78

Where to stay
For listings, see from page 77

1 Asgard B&B
2 Billia Croo B&B
3 Brinkies Guest House
4 Burnside Farm
5 Ferry Bank B&B
6 Hamnavoe Hostel
7 Point of Ness Campsite

Off map
Lindisfarne B&B

STROMNESS
Overview

OUTERTOWN

Lindisfarne
B&B (1 mile),
Kirkwall

Stromness
swimming pool

Argo's
Bakery

Cairston Road

North End
Garage

Orkney
Fish

Brinkies Brae
94m

North End Rd

Footpath to
Skara Brae
(7.5 miles)

Outertown Rd

INNERTOWN

Warebeth Rd

Back Road

**Start point
for walk**

Warebeth
Beach

Warebeth
Cemetery †

Login's Well

Ness
Battery

Stromness
Golf Club

Links
Battery

Ness Rd

Point of Ness

N

Bradt

0   500m
0   500yds

Scrabster

Moaness,
Graemsay

HISTORY Neolithic imprints in Stromness are rare but the general assumption is that any prehistoric communities would have settled on the more sheltered Cairston shore, immediately east of the present-day town. We then have to wait for the *Orkneyinga Saga* to narrate tales of Viking skirmishes in the 1150s; apart from mention of a few settlements and inns, little is known of who and what came and went here in subsequent centuries.

Whaling and trading are responsible for the development of the town. Stromness began to evolve as a harbour town in the 16th century at a time when international trade was increasingly taking the northerly route around Britain. By the 18th century it had become an important source of water, food and recruitment for the Hudson's Bay Company, which acted as a de facto government for parts of North America and monopolised the lucrative Arctic fur trade. From the 1770s, the whaling industry also provided employment, with ships bound for the Davis Strait between Greenland and Nunavit in Canada. By 1786 the town had 34 whaling ships registered. According to historian Bryce Wilson in *Stromness, A History*, even though the town can look as though it has been planned out as a model village, this was not the intention; instead the only plan was to fit as many buildings as possible into the narrow uneven strips between the hill and the sea.

The herring industry injected further impetus into the economy in the late 1800s, bringing an extra 5,000 people into the town every year. Some of the great pioneering explorations began or finished here, including the ill-fated Franklin expedition (see box, page 84) in search of the Northwest Passage, which set sail from Stromness in 1845; meanwhile, Captain Cook's ships, *Resolution* and *Discovery* made their first British landfall here after his death.

GETTING AROUND Stromness could not be more suited for exploration on foot: everything is within a 20-minute walk of the ferry port and a walk from the top of town to the headland at Point of Ness at the southern end will take little more than 30 minutes. Rather like Kirkwall, it's a little surprising that much of the narrow main street through Stromness permits access to vehicles. Access, though, is really intended for residents, deliveries and for dropping off suitcases at accommodation. During the working day, parking is only permissible for 30 minutes in any one hour and traffic wardens are highly motivated; it's best you leave your car at the main car park by the ferry terminal, on the left as you enter the town from the north.

WHERE TO STAY Stromness's accommodation is for the most part closeted along the length of the main street so a stay here leaves you well placed to enjoy the town's sizeable entertainment options. Many townhouses have now been converted to self-catering; a full list can be found at w orkney.com.

When leaving Stromness for the UK mainland, a little-used but novel and helpful option is to sleep on board the MV *Hamnavoe* while it is docked (w northlinkferries.co.uk/offers/hamnavoe-bed-and-breakfast); you then take the early-morning departure for Scrabster. A cabin sleeping up to four people costs £49.50 per person. As well as removing the need for a crack-of-dawn departure from your accommodation, this offers a slightly surreal experience as you can rattle around the ship more or less on your own.

Top range

The Ferry Inn [78 C2] (12 rooms) 10 John St; ✆ 01856 850280; e info@ferryinn.com; w ferryinn.com; ⏱ closed winter. All rooms en suite, 2 with baths. Owners Karen & Gareth Crichton, who also run The Shore in Kirkwall & The Royal Hotel & Harbourside Guest House in Stromness, worked here as students. Go for the attic-style rooms located on the 3rd floor, which are more spacious with great views of the harbour or down Victoria St towards Hoy. **£££**

The Royal Hotel [78 B3] (11 rooms) 53–55 Victoria St; ✆ 01856 850342; e info@royalhotelstromness.com; w royalhotelstromness.com. Recently refurbished hotel with friendly staff. All rooms en suite, the most appealing of which are on the attic level, as they have views high across the harbour. Also includes 2 self-contained annexes. Has 3 bars & a sheltered beer garden. **£££**

The Stromness Hotel [78 C2] (42 rooms) 15 Victoria St; ✆ 01856 850298; e info@stromnesshotel.com; w stromnesshotel.com; ⏱ Apr–Sep. Stoutly facing Stromness harbour,

with a turreted sandstone façade & Doric columns, this landmark hotel exudes yesteryear charm across 4 floors. Built in 1941, it is full of faded character, from the revolving brass door to high ceilings & the *fin de siècle* ambience of its public areas. The rooms are adequate & functional but lack the style of the rest of the hotel. Rooms 2 & 3 are the pick, their bay windows overlooking the harbour. Room 2 is equipped for travellers of limited mobility. **£££**

Mid range

Asgard B&B [map, opposite] (2 rooms) Cairston Rd; ✆ 01856 851699; e dawn@stromness-orkney.co.uk; w stromness-orkney.co.uk. Really welcoming owners make your stay special. Well-appointed en-suite rooms (1 sgl, 1 dbl) with superb views downhill over town, the harbour & the Hoy hills. **££**

Billia Croo B&B [map, opposite] (3 rooms) Innertown; ✆ 01856 851195; e seona@billiacroo.com; w tinyurl.com/billia-croo. Clean & tidy mix of dbls & trpls; hearty b/fasts. **££**

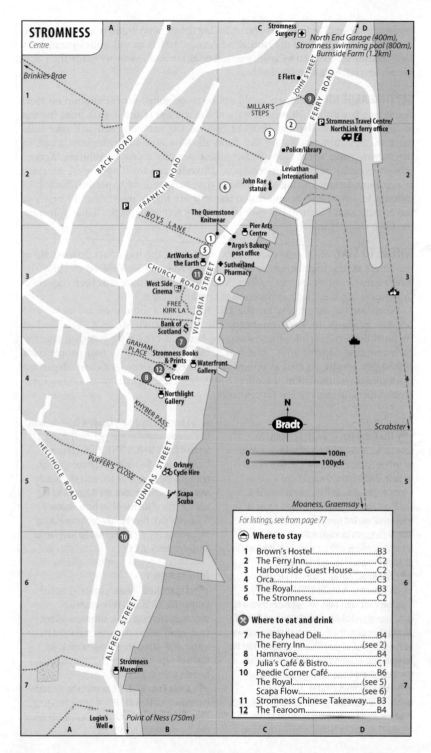

STROMNESS
Centre

Brinkies Brae

Stromness
Surgery

North End Garage (400m),
Stromness swimming pool (800m),
Burnside Farm (1.2km)

E Flett

MILLAR'S
STEPS

9

Stromness Travel Centre/
NorthLink ferry office

BACK ROAD

FRANKLIN ROAD

BOYS LANE

Police/library

Leviathan
International

John Rae
statue

The Quernstone
Knitwear

Pier Arts
Centre

Argo's Bakery/
post office

ArtWorks of
the Earth

Sutherland
Pharmacy

CHURCH ROAD

West Side
Cinema

FREE
KIRK LA

VICTORIA STREET

Bank of
Scotland

GRAHAM
PLACE

Stromness Books
& Prints

Waterfront
Gallery

Cream

Northlight
Gallery

KHYBER PASS

HELLIHOLE ROAD

PUFFER'S CLOSE

DUNDAS STREET

Orkney
Cycle Hire

Scapa
Scuba

N

Bradt

Scrabster

0 ──────── 100m
0 ──────── 100yds

Moaness, Graemsay

ALFRED STREET

Stromness
Museum

Login's
Well

Point of Ness (750m)

For listings, see from page 77

🛏 **Where to stay**

1	Brown's Hostel	B3
2	The Ferry Inn	C2
3	Harbourside Guest House	C2
4	Orca	C3
5	The Royal	B3
6	The Stromness	C2

✖ **Where to eat and drink**

7	The Bayhead Deli	B4
	The Ferry Inn	(see 2)
8	Hamnavoe	B4
9	Julia's Café & Bistro	C1
10	Peedie Corner Café	B6
	The Royal	(see 5)
	Scapa Flow	(see 6)
11	Stromness Chinese Takeaway	B3
12	The Tearoom	B4

✳ 🏠 **Brinkies Guest House** [map, page 76] (4 rooms) Brinkies Brae; ☎01856 851881; m 07729 394828; e brinkiesguesthse@btinternet. com. All rooms en suite or with private facilities. Charming ambience from Yvonne Harrold who justifiably takes pride in her service. B/fast is a combination of bere bannocks, fish & cold meats. Located a short, steep hike up the southern edge of Brinkies Brae. **££**

🏠 **Burnside Farm** [map, page 76] (3 rooms) A965, immediately north of Stromness; ☎01856 850723; w burnside-farm.com; ⊕ Easter–Oct, informally open in winter, call ahead. Working farm located at the town's northern entrance. Run by Robbie & Joy Ritch; Robbie was born & bred on the farm. The 3 dbls are comfortable & smart; 2 overlook Stromness & Scapa Flow. **££**

✳ 🏠 **Ferry Bank B&B** [map, page 76] (1 room) 2 North End Rd; ☎01856 851250. A classic Orcadian experience of friendly host & attention to detail. Traditional & friendly ambience, cosy room, beautifully decorated with fresh flowers. Located at north end of town; harbour views. **££**

🏠 **Harbourside Guest House** [78 C2] (6 rooms) 7 John St; ☎01856 8519699; e info@ ferryinn.com; w ferryinn.com. Smart & tidy rooms including trpls; popular with cyclists. **££**

🏠 **Lindisfarne B&B** [89 B6] (4 rooms) Lindisfarne; ☎01856 850082; m 07825

751538; e info@stayinstromness.co.uk; w stayinstromness.co.uk/lindisfarne. All rooms en suite with modern décor; some have dormer-window views. Guest lounge has aspect over Stromness harbour & Stenness Loch. Located north of town centre. **££**

Budget
🏠 **Brown's Hostel** [78 B3] (6 rooms) 45–47 Victoria St; ☎01856 850661; w brownsorkney. co.uk. Mix of private dbls, trpls & family rooms. Kitchen. Bang in centre of town & open all year. **£**

🏠 **Hamnavoe Hostel** [map, page 76] (6 rooms) 10a North End Rd; ☎01856 851202; m 07717 745360; e info@hamnavoehostel.co.uk; w hamnavoehostel.co.uk. Mix of bunk beds & private rooms, good lounge & kitchen. **£**

🏠 **Orca Hotel** [78 C3] (6 rooms) 76 Victoria St; ☎01856 850447; e dfischler@ymail.com; w orcahotel.moonfruit.com. All rooms en suite. Exclusive hire option for 11–16 guests. Closed winter. **££**

Camping
⋀ **Point of Ness Campsite** [map, page 76] Point of Ness; ☎01856 850907; e stromnesscs@ orkney.gov.uk; w tinyurl.com/point-ness; ⊕ Apr–Sep. Sited on the shore, overlooking Stromness, 1 mile from the harbour. Offers both pitches & electric hook-ups; toilets, showers & washing amenities.

✗ **WHERE TO EAT AND DRINK** You can eat heartily and often really rather well in Stromness. A good seasonal restaurant and several cafés supplement the fare offered by the town pubs, which tend to serve quality that is often a cut above the standard you might expect. The pub bars are busy for much of the year, with seasonal visitors supplementing the perennial local clientele.

Mid range
✗ **The Ferry Inn** [78 C2] Same contacts as hotel; ⊕ noon–14.00 & 17.00–21.00 daily, closed in winter. Excellent hostelry that serves food several notches higher than typical pub grub. Shortlisted for regional pub & bar of year in Scottish travel awards 2017. Bar & dining area recently refurbished with a nautical theme to resemble a ship deck, even with a sail draped from the ceiling. Gets busy in summer but hardworking staff keep it running smoothly **££**

✗ **Hamnavoe** [78 B4] Leslie's Close; ☎01856 850606; ⊕ May–Sep 19.00–22.00 Tue–Sun.

Excellent family-run restaurant managed by Sarah & Neil Taylor. Tucked up a small lane off Victoria St. Small, so booking essential. Dishes include haddock in lobster sauce & a generous local cheeseboard. **££**

✗ **The Royal Hotel** [78 B3] Same contacts as hotel; ⊕ all day. Has an à la carte restaurant with a short but fine menu. Lounge bar offers more standard but decent pub fare. **££**

✗ **Scapa Flow** [78 C2] Same contacts as The Stomness Hotel; ⊕ noon–14.00 & 17.00–20.30 daily, closed winter. Food can be really rather good in this restaurant on the 1st floor of The

Stromness Hotel. Mains include sea bass & lobster (£20) or scallops & black pudding gratin (£18). Top it off with the hotel's signature Baileys & fudge cheesecake. Book ahead to get a table overlooking the harbour. If it's chilly, they light the log fire, even in May. The place mats, portraying the hotel in its early 20th-century heyday, are something of a design classic & conveniently for sale. ££

⬛ **The Tearoom** [78 B4] 19 Porteus Close; ⏲ 10.00–16.00 Mon–Sat. Newish family-run café serving good food. Brunch until 11.30; best is high tea (£12pp, featuring a cake stand & finger sandwiches). Kerry Sinclair maintains good service despite high demand from day trippers. ££

Cheap and cheerful

✕ **Stromness Chinese Takeaway** [78 B3] 63 Victoria St; m 07584 678038; ⏲ Oct–Mar 16.00–22.00 daily; Apr–Sep noon–14.00 & 16.00–23.00 daily. Decent & filling portions covering usual range of Chinese fare. £

⬛ **Julia's Café & Bistro** [78 C1] 20 Ferry Rd; ✆ 01856 850904; e Julia@juliascafe.co.uk; w juliascafe.co.uk. ⏲ 09.00–15.00 Mon–Sat, 10.00–17.00 Sun. Conservatory-style café/bistro; a venerable Stromness institution. Good location with views of harbour's coming & goings. B/fasts until 11.30, also good sandwiches, roast beef & salads. Look out for specials such as coconut & coriander soup. Outside tables in summer. Good place to mark your Orkney arrival or departure. £–££

⬛ **The Bayhead Deli** [78 B4] 103 Victoria St; ✆ 01856 851605; ⏲ May–Sep 10.00–17.00 Mon–Sat, 11.00–16.00 Sun; Oct–Apr closed Sun. Friendly shop serving gamut of foodie delights from pheasant & pancetta pies to antipasti & fine coffee. Small seating area; best place in town for take-away coffee. £

⬛ **Peedie Corner Café** [78 B6] 3 Alfred St; ⏲ 16.30–19.00 Fri & Sat. Handy chip shop take-outs. £

ENTERTAINMENT AND NIGHTLIFE All the hotels have public bars that provide social hubs of an evening. The pint-sized Flattie Bar at The Stromness Hotel is a cosy choice; unlike the hotel itself, it stays open all year. The Stromness's Hamnavoe bar on the first floor is a good option for drinks with a view (it operates under the same ceiling as the Scapa Flow restaurant). The Ferry Inn always seems to be buzzing and the Royal Hotel has three bars and a sheltered beer garden.

FILM REVIEW BY PING-PONG

As you leave the West Side Cinema in Stromness you are invited to take a ping-pong ball and place it in baskets numbered from one to five to indicate how much you liked the film (one: it should never have been made; five: you'd take it to movie heaven). 'It guarantees us really good rates of feedback so we know if the films are popular,' explains Mark Jenkins, chair of the cinema's trust. The idea came from one of the first films the cinema screened, *Ping Pong*, the story of an over-80s table-tennis championship; it is typical of the quirky thinking required to run an independent cinema on a northern Scottish island.

Other measures involve the encouragement to bring a bottle and – preferably cold – food, and to watch the film at tables rather than in rows. 'At most cinemas people go in, watch the film and walk away; it's not usually a space to talk about the film,' says Jenkins. 'In winter it becomes very much "our cinema". People may sometimes say they didn't think much of the film but it's always a great night.'

In 2018, when Mark heard Bill Murray was in Orkney, he invited him to a screening of *Isle of Dogs* where the actor, to the initial incredulity of those watching, stood up and introduced the film. 'A cinema screen has four corners and I like to think we are always pushing at those corners for new ways to make the cinema work,' says Mark. 'We do take risks.'

The innovative **West Side Cinema** (w wscinema.wordpress.com) operates from the Town Hall on Church Road [78 B3]. Established in 2012, it has quickly become a Stromness institution, screening a mixture of major releases, films and documentaries. Film nights are a highly social event and you are encouraged to bring a bottle. Don't expect the latest releases; you will enjoy a good film and convivial company. Tickets on the door only.

SHOPPING

Art and souvenirs Art studios, galleries and knitwear shops stand cheek by jowl the length of Stromness. Unlike elsewhere, you never endure any sales pressure, which can sometimes make you wonder how anyone in Stromness makes a profit. Many outlets have become attractions in their own right, with artists usually in situ and happy to talk about their work. This convivial approach reaches something of a crescendo during Stromness shopping week (w stromnessshoppingweek.co.uk) in mid-July, effectively a festival of arts, crafts and music that culminates in a firework display.

A random exploration of various studios might include:

ArtWorks of the Earth [78 B3] 59 Victoria St; ✆01856 851308; m 07900 982612; e Jeanne@ artworksoftheearth.com; w artworksoftheearth. com; see ad, page 66. This gallery showcases the work of the charismatic US-born painter Jeanne Bouza Rose (see box, page 82), who produces captivating & oddly moving woodblock prints of Stromness town & Orkney landscapes. She also sells jewellery by Francis Garrioch, a silversmith who bases her work on local archaeology.

Cream [78 B4] 23 Graham Pl; ✆01856 851628; ⏱ Apr–Sep 09.30–17.30 Thu–Sat; Oct–Mar 10.00–16.00 Mon, Tue, Fri & Sat. This is the home of artist Sally Lynch who use watercolours to striking effect. Among her *oeuvres*, Sally depicts Orkney's birdlife through linear images of oystercatchers & curlews that blend slightly abstract depictions with naturalistic, elemental landscape colours. 'I simplify the birds to capture their character,' says Sally. 'I'm feeling quite birdy at the moment,' she adds, laughing.

✳ **Leviathan International** [78 C2] 14a Victoria St; ✆01856 850395; m 07876 71847; e andy@leviathaninternational.com; w leviathaninternational.com; ⏱ May–Sep 09.00–18.00 Mon & Fri–Sun, 07.00–18.00 Thu; Oct–Apr 09.30–17.00 Mon–Wed, Fri & Sat, 07.00–17.00 Thu; see ad, page 66. Located by the quayside, this is no ordinary souvenir shop. Owners

Lesley Clark & Andrew Hamill embroider T-shirts for local sports clubs and schools as well as visitors. Wide & imaginative range of reasonably priced arts & crafts as well as diving equipment. Ice cream all year. Opening times are a guide only; often open much longer. In summer the Hamills put up a marquee & sell crab & lobster rolls.

Northlight Gallery [78 B4] Graham Pl; ✆01865 851194; e cary@carywelling.co.uk; w northlight. artweb.com; ⏱ 11.00–17.00 Mon–Sat. Not-for-profit exhibition space for creative projects from a rota of artists-in-residence.

The Quernstone Knitwear [78 C3] 41 Victoria St; ✆01856 852900; e info@quernstone.co.uk; w quernstone.co.uk; ⏱ May–Sep 09.30–17.30 Mon–Sat; Oct–Apr 10.00–17.00 Mon–Sat. Stylish, often Nordic & original knitwear. Intriguing approach to manufacture sees garments passed from knitter to knitter & across various Orkney islands for different stages of production. Sister shop across the road at 38 Victoria St (similar opening hours) has more of a gift-shop theme.

Waterfront Gallery [78 B4] 128 Victoria St; ✆01856 850644; w waterfrontgallery.co.uk; ⏱ Oct–Apr 11.00–16.00 Mon, Wed, Fri & Sat; May–Sep 09.30–17.00 Mon–Sat; also occasionally 11.00–16.00 Sun. Displays a fine range of work by local artists & collectives.

Books The town also has an excellent bookshop, **Stromness Books and Prints** [78 B4] (1 Graham Pl; ✆ 0856 850565; e grahamplace1@hotmail.com; ⏱ Apr–Sep 11.00–18.00 Mon–Sat, occasionally Sun; Oct–Mar noon–18.00 Tue–Sat). This shoebox-sized gem brims with stock and has been running for the best part of

Stromness spent much of the 18th and 19th centuries sending people to the Americas. Some, however, have come the other way, including painter Jeanne Bouza Rose, who displays her woodblock creations at the ArtWorks of the Earth Gallery on Victoria Street (page 81). Her striking work features finely outlined scenes of Stromness's huddled streets and houses as well as sea and landscapes amid monumental skies. A trained art teacher, Jeanne first came to Orkney in 1984. 'I gravitated to the Standing Stones. I knew that Stonehenge was fenced off; I very much appreciated that here they were free,' she recalls.

You can't help but notice that some of Jeanne's work is rather large, involving unstretched canvasses sometimes bolted to the wall. 'The usual stretched canvas curtailed my expression,' she says. This has perhaps reached its logical conclusion in a 44ft × 5ft painting of Hoy, which arose from the view from her window when she first arrived on Orkney. During the summer of 2018, she was artist-in-residence at the Ness of Brodgar archaeological dig.

'Every colour is possible in Orkney, even if it is fleeting. See the pink, then blink and it's gone. Look at my pictures and you may say that not all colours of the sky there are necessarily possible at the same time; but they do exist and you will see them. Some of the shades of yellow and orange here can look impossible but there was one day over Hoy when everyone was texting each other and saying they had just seen that combination of colours.'

By and large Jeanne eschews painting outside – 'it will either start raining hail or your paper will be blown across the harbour' – and instead works in her studio from photographs she takes. Jeanne paints in oil and watercolours – the latter for her huge skies – but she has also developed a unique local style, which she calls the Orkney woodcut print. For this, she uses an ingenious implement to press the ink into the paper: a pebble from the beach wrapped in North Ronaldsay wool. If you wish to learn more, Jeanne is always happy to chat and also offers workshops explaining her woodcut technique.

50 years (the name of an earlier owner, J Broom, is inscribed on the lintel above the entrance). 'I sell a bit of absolutely everything,' says manager Sheena Winter, including a good range of Orkney history, guides and fiction. Also on display but not for sale ('They're part of the history of the shop,' says Sheena) is a collection of age-old Orkney guides and leaflets, including a 1950 guide to Skara Brae produced by the Ministry of Works.

Food shopping

Argo's Bakery [78 C3] 50–52 Victoria St; 01856 850245; w argosbakery.co.uk; May–Sep 07.30–18.30 Mon–Sat; Oct–Apr 07.30–17.30 Mon–Sat. Housed within a more general grocers. Argo's has another shop at its factory site (Cairston Rd; 07.30–16.00 Mon–Fri, 08.30–14.00 Sat) that serves good b/fast rolls. Small seating area. Handy if you're arriving or leaving town early.
E Flett [78 C1] John St; 01856 850309; e enquiries@eflettbutcher; w eflettbutcher.

co.uk; 07.00–17.00 Mon–Fri, 07.00–16.30 Sat. Butcher for more than 150 years, sourcing locally reared meat. Takes preorders for self-catering & has frozen homemade ready meals.
Orkney Fish [map, page 76] Garson Food Park; 01856 850870; e contact@orkneyfishshop. co.uk; 09.00–13.00 Mon & Sat, 09.00–16.00 Tue–Fri. Excellent fishmongers, selling everything from monkfish to salmon & lemon sole. Ideal for self-catering.

OTHER PRACTICALITIES

$ **Bank of Scotland** [78 B4] 99 Victoria St;
⊕ 10.00–15.00 Wed & Fri

✚ **Stromness Surgery** [78 C1] John St;
✆ 01856 850205. Stromness has no hospital of its
own; you will need to head for Balfour Hospital in
Kirkwall (page 120).

✚ **Sutherland Pharmacy** [78 C3] 74 Victoria
St; ⊕ 09.00–17.30 Mon–Wed, 09.00–14.00 Fri
& Sat

✉ **Post office** [78 C3] In Argo's Bakery;
⊕ same hours

Police [78 C1] John St, just up from the Pier
Arts Centre

Petrol [map, page 76] North End Garage, North
End Rd (by roundabout at top of town) ⊕ 08.00–
21.00 Mon–Sat, 10.00–20.00 Sun

Other amenities Perfect for families on rainy
days, Stromness swimming pool (North End Rd;
✆ 01856 850552; ⊕ times vary) has a pool, fitness
suite, sauna & steam room.

WHAT TO SEE AND DO Given that Stromness essentially comprises a single street
that runs parallel to the shore and harbour for a mile or so, the town is remarkably
packed with interest. Browse a few artists' studios and galleries, visit the museum
and the Pier Arts Centre, have a coffee here, a sandwich there, and you can happily
occupy yourself for a day or more. This is the kind of town you can find yourself
coming back to time and time again during a stay on Orkney.

Exploring the town is easy: simply walk down the main street (in its various
incarnations) until you meet the headland of Ness. The road snakes its way
between the jumble of houses, shops, cafés and galleries. Beneath your feet local
flagstones add to the town's character – even more so because below them lies a
network of smugglers' tunnels said to be blocked up nowadays. House windows
are tiny and set back in thick walls – precautions necessary when building in an
area prone to wild weather. As you walk along, stepped or steep and narrow lanes
cut uphill away from the water; these are worth skipping a little way up, although
they all eventually run into the residential backdrop of Stromness rather than
leading to anywhere in particular – the one exception to this being the route up
to the hill of Brinkies Brae (page 86). If you're interested in guided tours, consider
Story Telling & Heritage Tours ✳ (✆ 01856 841207; peatfire@orkneyattractions.
com; w orkneystorytelling.com); John Brook and Lynn Babour offer a good range
of folklore and historic tales, walking along Stromness streets and further afield.

In a town of such venerable history and architecture, one of Stromness's most
impressive attractions turns out to be the modern **Pier Arts Centre** [78 C3]
(✆ 01856 850209; e info@pierartscentre.com; w pierartscentre.com; ⊕ May–Sep
10.00–17.00 Mon–Sat; Oct–Apr 10.30–17.00 Tue–Sat; free). This truly excellent
museum has a permanent collection of international importance, bequeathed
by its founder Margaret Gardiner, a close friend of sculptor Barbara Hepworth.
Hepworth of course established herself in Cornwall and, accordingly, the St Ives
School has a strong presence here, including Hepworth's carved slate sculpture,
Two Forms (Orkney) and works by Patrick Heron, Alfred Wallis and Hepworth's
husband Ben Nicholson.

As you meander around the town, you'll notice how Stromness is adorned with
blue plaques of varying degrees of interest; perhaps the most eye-catching is at
2 Alfred Street, on the façade of what was once both known as Mrs Humphry's
House and a makeshift 19th-century whaling hospital, the site of treatment for
'scurvy-ridden whale men' who had endured the horrors of a vitamin-deprived
Arctic winter. Where Dundas Street becomes Albert Street look out for the plaque
commemorating the former office of Hudson's Bay agents who registered Orcadians
for what often proved to be one-way trips.

3

The **Stromness Museum** [78 A7] (01856 850025; e custodian@
stromnessmuseum.co.uk; w stromnessmuseum.co.uk; ☉ Apr–Oct 10.00–17.00
daily; Nov–Mar 11.00–15.30 Mon–Sat; £5/1/10 adult/child/family) is located
at the southern end of town. Victorian in layout, the museum is housed in the
former town hall. On the ground floor you can see the original design with raised
platforms for speakers and entertainers. The museum is a gem, packed with high-
quality displays and intriguing accounts of people and events that have shaped
the town. Pride of place goes to the Skara Brae Buddo, a Neolithic stone figure
carved from whale bone. Just under 4 inches high, the buddo has eyes, a mouth,
a navel and two holes that extend through the figure, perhaps for suspension.
After being mislaid for many years, in 2016 the buddo was chanced upon amid
a box of artefacts in the museum's archaeological stores. As the museum puts it,
the buddo is in elite company, for it is just one of a handful of known figures from
the British Neolithic.

World War I features prominently. The scuttling of the German fleet in Scapa
Flow in 1919 (see box, page 70) is detailed, attended by memorabilia such as clocks
from the sunken ships. There are also mournful accounts of great British losses
such as HMS *Hampshire* (see box, page 99), HMS *Vanguard* and HMS *Royal Oak*
(see box, page 161). Memorabilia includes a cross from the *Vanguard*, which sank
in 1917 after an internal explosion, with the loss of 843 crew, part of the torpedo
fired at the *Royal Oak*, and a portrait of 17-year-old Frank Potter, lost at sea on
HMS *Hampshire* in 1917. There are also cabinets displaying a necklace of human
teeth brought back from the Solomon Islands by Stromness sailor Jack Renton, as
well as accounts of other local adventurers (see box, page 75). The most famous
Stromness resident to leave the port was Dr John Rae (see box, below) who gets the
lion's share of the ground floor of the museum, including a display of his original
cloth boats, plus moccasins and husky whips brought back from the Arctic by the
Hudson's Bay Company.

ORKNEY'S GREAT ARCTIC EXPLORER

Hugely charismatic and fearsomely tough, the explorer Dr John Rae staged
some of the 19th century's great pioneering expeditions across the Arctic.
Born in 1813 in Orphir, east of Stromness, he studied medicine before joining
the Hudson's Bay Company in 1833. From 1846 to 1854, he undertook
several expeditions to the Arctic. On one, he identified a strait (later named
after him) between Boothia and King William Island that established the
'Northwest Passage' to the Far East. On the same trip, by consulting Inuit
at Pelly Bay and studying objects, he discovered the gruesome fate of the
Franklin expedition of 1845, a venture infamous for the desperate explorers
resorting to cannibalism. Before finally returning to Orkney, Rae found time
to survey Greenland in 1860. In all, he travelled more than 13,000 miles in
the Canadian Arctic and mapped 1,800 miles of coastline. He scoffed at
Royal Navy expeditions for being lavishly but ill-equipped for their journeys.
Instead, Rae travelled on foot, sleeping in the open or in snow houses and
surviving on his hunting skills. A statue of Rae lies in St Magnus Cathedral.

Plans are afoot to convert Rae's birthplace, the magnificent but crumbling
Hall of Clestrain in Orphir into a centre celebrating his life and times
(w johnraesociety.com) as well as commemorating other less heralded
Orcadian and Arctic explorers and the peoples of the Arctic rim.

Distance: 11 miles; time: 5–6hrs
Start: Victoria St, Stromness town centre
Finish: Skara Brae visitor centre ✪ HY235188
OS Map: Explorer 463 Orkney West Mainland
Bus (for return from Skara Brae): the 8S connects Skara Brae to Dounby and Kirkwall (a service earlier in the day does go to Stromness but is usually too early for most walkers); from either Dounby or Kirkwall take the 7 to Stromness. For timetables visit w orkney.gov.uk/transport.

Probably Orkney's signature walk, this is a lengthy but rarely strenuous hike up the western coast of the Mainland. Beginning in the port of Stromness, it covers scenery that gets increasingly dramatic the farther north you head and takes in the fractured cliffs of Yesnaby before dropping down into Skara Brae. Note there are no facilities until you reach Skara Brae. The route is partly along the coastal path and partly over open ground. In Stromness, simply follow signs south along Victoria Street for the West Coast Trail, which takes you out of town past the Ness Battery and Warebeth. After 7 miles you reach the sea stacks at Yesnaby, then the Broch of Borwick, which is more dramatic from afar than close up. (Be careful if you enter via the capstone, as the broch has no back to it.) A mile or so north, you reach the conspicuous cairn on Ward Hill. The view of Skara Brae from here is an oddly timeless one. The enduring backdrop of whaleback hills makes the dimensions of this world-famous site seem rather modest. Just as striking is how the landscape, although indeed timeless, has been altered in the intervening millennia by nature rather than humans, for when Skara Brae was occupied the coast was much farther out and you would have been able to walk more or less straight across to Marwick Head on dry land.

Just beyond the museum you reach the site of **Login's Well** [78 A7], which served as the last watering place on this side of the Atlantic for Hudson's Bay Company ships between 1670 and the 1890s. In 1780 Cook's ships *Endeavour* and *Discovery* loaded their fresh water from here, as did the ill-fated Franklin expedition in 1845. The well was sealed up in 1931.

Another important site not to be missed is the **Ness Battery**, located above the coast a mile south of Stromness Museum. Visits are by guided tour only (m 07759 857298; e info@nessbattery.co.uk; w nessbattery.co.uk; ⊕ Apr–Sep, 3–4 times a week; £6). The battery operated in both world wars – though it was dismantled in the interwar years. After the outbreak of World War II, six batteries defended the western entrances to Scapa Flow, all controlled from a Fire Command at Ness Battery. Concrete remains of searchlight emplacements can be seen among the rocks along the shore. Ness is the only British battery to have kept its original huts. In one, the Mess Hall, you will find the famous painted mural with colourful scenes of rural English life, and a depiction of the hills of Hoy over which the gunners' challenge to the enemy is painted in bold letters: 'Come the three corners of the world in ships and we will sink them!' It's easy to draw parallels with the Italian Chapel at Lamb Holm (page 162). There the POWs turned to Christian iconography; at the battery, British soldiers depicted a home counties' landscape of orchards, women and children. To reach the battery on foot, walk south from Stromness Museum,

Distance: 4½ miles; time: 2–2½hrs
Start/finish: corner of Church Rd/Victoria St
OS Map: Explorer 463 Orkney West Mainland

This superb walk takes in the coast and a hundred years of military history while providing a strong geographical context for the importance of Stromness. Walk south along Stromness's main street until you finally leave the houses behind and the cobbles become a paved road. Where the main road bends right, keep straight, passing through the campsite right by the sea towards the headland known as Point of Ness. Unusual circular rings on the shoreline are part of a wave-energy generation scheme. At night, the glow of the 'golden doughnuts' – as they are known locally – is visible from town.

After enjoying fine views over Stromness, across to Graemsay and to Hoy, go through a gate on to the headland. Wartime remains are everywhere here: by the headland you can see Volunteers' Battery and the remains of gun emplacements. The beacon across the water is Hoy Low lighthouse on the island of Graemsay. About half a mile along the coast from the Point of Ness you come to the Links Battery, one of six that guarded the west entrances to Scapa Flow during World War II. The golf course on the right was laid out in 1923. The 10th hole is known as 'Battery' as it is played over World War I gun emplacements. Slightly west along the shore is the sole remaining searchlight emplacement, while a Nissen hut now houses the lawnmower for Stromness Golf Club. Just across the track, a grassy mound is all that remains of the accommodation camp.

Wildlife here is outstanding. In spring and summer gannets plunge into the waves, great skuas skirt the shores for eggs and the verges are bursting with

past the campsite and on to the coastal path. Pass the Links Battery and after half a mile you'll see the battery's paved parking area.

The granite mound of **Brinkies Brae** (308ft/94m) acts as a bulwark, protecting Stromness against westerly winds. A short, sharp climb to its summit will take 30–40 minutes: the easiest route is to begin at Victoria Street, head up Church Road, cross Franklin Road, and keep uphill along Christie's Brae. Turn right along Back Road then turn left up Downie's Lane. Bear left immediately and climb steps on to the moorland then keep ahead on the clear path uphill. When you reach a gap in a drystone wall, turn right with the wall on your right to make for the cairn and trig point. The summit offers superb views over the Mainland, Hamnavoe, the adjacent islands of Outer Holm and Inner Holm, Graemsay and Hoy.

THE WEST MAINLAND

Everything west and southwest of Kirkwall is referred to as the West Mainland. Here you will find many of Orkney's most iconic attractions. The Neolithic sites of Skara Brae, Maeshowe, the Standing Stones of Stenness and the Ring of Brodgar are all here, as is the unfolding drama that is the Ness of Brodgar. The natural beauty is staggering, from the bird colonies and fracturing coastal landscapes of Marwick Head and the Castle of Yesnaby to waves crashing on to the rocks at the Bay o' Skaill. An important broch is located at Gurness while the tidal island of Birsay provides a suitably elemental crescendo to the Mainland's western limits. In between

meadowsweet, sea pink and bird's-foot trefoil. Harbour and grey seals loiter on the foreshore at low tide. In winter, turnstones pad around the shingle, flocks of curlews dangle above the fields and the snow line on the Hoy hills is diamond sharp.

As you pass a car park below Ness Battery, the coastline fragments, exposing serrated skerries at low tide. Just beyond a second car park you reach Warebeth cemetery, the final resting place of author George Mackay Brown (see box, page 37). Heavily eroded, the cemetery all but overhangs the sea. The most eye-catching tomb is the cairn-like structure that houses the remains of the father of explorer John Rae (see box, page 84). Take the grassy footpath immediately to the east of the cemetery (✪ HY237084). Follow this to join the road that heads steeply uphill along Warebeth Road. When you reach a junction by a sign for Outertown, dogleg across and take the lane uphill. Follow this as it winds through farms for 300yds; at a quiet T-junction the lane squeezes between two houses and descends as a paved lane. Brinkies Brae and its summit are now visible up to the right. Bear right at a minor junction then immediately left to walk along the road, keeping Brinkies Brae up to your right. About 100yds after a 'passing place' sign look for a narrow gap on the right between fields where a stony footpath cuts uphill by a dyke. After 200yds this emerges on to open moorland with the cairn directly ahead along a clear path. You can keep ahead to the cairn or squelch a few yards to the right to follow the obvious ridgeline (which offers superb views). From the cairn, face the sea and turn right, keeping the drystone wall on your left for 200yds. At a gap in the wall turn left up the brow before dropping down steps to reach Downie's Lane. Turn right along Back Road and then left down Christie's Brae, which quickly becomes Church Street. You are back in Stromness.

are serene lochs overlooked by a moorland spine that runs through the heart of the West Mainland.

Travelling around the West Mainland it's easy to assume that the region is densely populated; in fact, just 2,500 people live here. This emptiness becomes more apparent to the southwest, where the parish of Orphir runs along the shores of Scapa Flow: this area is delightful, little visited and capped by the serene saltmarsh beauty of Waulkmill Bay.

While many of the above sites are near each other, avoid trying to see them all in a day or two as you will find yourself rushed and may well become ensnared within the pinch points of cruise-ship coaches. You can easily justify a full week to explore the West Mainland.

 WHERE TO STAY Most places on the West Mainland are no more than 20–30 minutes from anywhere else on the island, so you don't need to pay too much attention to staying adjacent to any particular sights on your list.

Top range

☀ 🏠 **Merkister Hotel** [88 C3] (16 rooms) Loch of Harray; 📞 01856 771366; e merkisterhotel@gmail.com; w merkister. com. Welcoming hotel enjoying a wonderfully secluded position overlooking the Loch of Harray.

Former home of poet Eric Linklater & run by the same family since 1974. All rooms (15 en suite) are well appointed & comfortable; the best have views of the loch & include 3 ground-floor suites suitable for people with limited mobility. Homemade biscuits in bedrooms. Guest lounge

The Mainland THE WEST MAINLAND

3

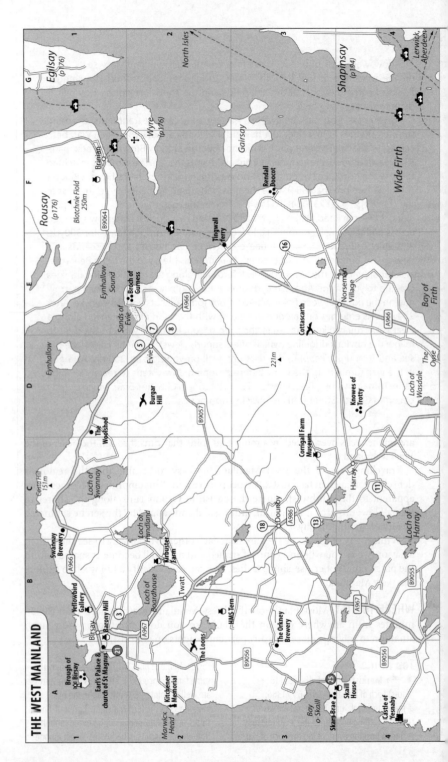

THE WEST MAINLAND

Egilsay
(p176)

Rousay
(p176)

Blotchnie Field
250m

B9064

Eynhallow
Sound

Eynhallow

Sands of
Evie

Brough of
Birsay

Earl's Palace &
church of St Magnus

Yellowbird
Gallery

Birsay

Barony Mill

Swannay
Brewery

A966

Gerta Hill
151m

Loch of
Swannay

The
Woolshed

Burgar
Hill

Evie

Broch of
Gurness

A966

Tingwall
ferry

Wyre
(p176)

Brinian

North Isles

Gairsay

Wide Firth

Shapinsay
(p194)

Lerwick,
Aberdeen

Rendall
Doocot

Norseman
Village

Bay of
Firth

A966

The
Ouse

Loch of
Wasdale

Cottascarth

221m

Knowes of
Trotty

Corrigall Farm
Museum

Harray

Loch of
Harray

B9055

Dounby

A986

Loch of
Hundland

Kirbuster
Farm

Twatt

Loch of
Boardhouse

A967

HMS Tern

The Loons

B9056

The Orkney
Brewery

A967

B9056

Kitchener
Memorial

Marwick
Head

Bay
o' Skaill

Skara-Brae

Skaill
House

Castle of
Yesnaby

B9057

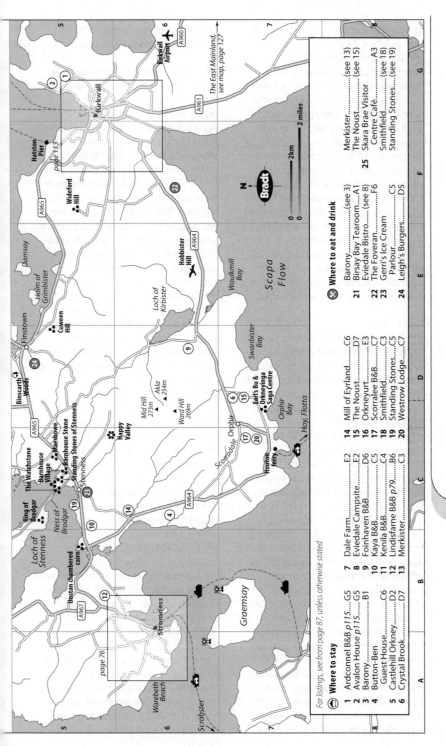

For listings, see from page 87, unless otherwise stated

🏠 Where to stay

1 Ardconnel B&B *p115*.......G5
2 Avalon House *p115*.......G5
3 Barony.................................B1
4 Button-Ben
   Guest House....................C6
5 Castlehill Orkney............D2
6 Crystal Brook..................D7
7 Dale Farm.........................E2
8 Eviedale Campsite..........E2
9 Foinhaven B&B................D6
10 Kaya B&B..........................C5
11 Kenila B&B.......................C4
12 Lindisfarne B&B *p79*.....B6
13 Merkister..........................C3
14 Mill of Eyrland...............C6
15 The Noust.........................D7
16 Orkneyurt........................E3
17 Scorralee B&B.................C7
18 Smithfield.........................C3
19 Standing Stones..............C5
20 Westrow Lodge...............C7

✕ Where to eat and drink

      Barony.................................(see 3)
21 Birsay Bay Tearoom.....A1
      Eviedale Bistro............(see 8)
22 The Foveran....................F6
23 Gerri's Ice Cream
      Parlour.............................C5
24 Leigh's Burgers...............D5
      Merkister.......................(see 13)
      The Noust......................(see 15)
25 Skara Brae Visitor
      Centre Café.....................A3
      Smithfield.......................(see 18)
      Standing Stones............(see 19)

has bar with honesty box & guests can use the boats for fishing. £££

🏠 **Standing Stones Hotel** [89 C5] (17 rooms) Stenness; 📞01856 850449; e info@ standingstoneshotel.co.uk; w standingstoneshotel. co.uk. Hotels close to great sites can so often be complacent. Fortunately, the opposite applies at this excellent & friendly hotel. Orkney's only purpose-built hotel, it opened in 1991 on the site of the UK's first 'kit hotel' (shipped from Norway but razed by a fire in 1989). Rooms are recently refurbished & decorated with tasteful standing-stone themes. The pick is probably room 18 with balcony, jacuzzi & panoramic view of the Neolithic sites. Hotel does not cater for tour groups, a policy that embellishes the relaxed atmosphere. 'We are trying to be a hotel first, not on a coach tour, and we need to look after locals as much as visitors,' says owner Alan Tulloch, a former distributor for Orkney ice cream. Dinner available. ££–£££

Mid range

🏠 **Barony Hotel** [88 B1] (8 rooms) Birsay; 📞01856 721327; e info@baronyhotel.com; w baronyhotel.com; 🕑 May–mid-Sep. Great location above the shores of Boardhouse Loch. Mix of en-suite rooms & those with shared facilities. Ground-floor room is partly suitable for people with limited mobility. ££

🏠 **Button-Ben Guest House** [89 C6] (4 rooms) Button Rd, Stenness; 📞01856 850794; e button-ben@outlook.com; w buttonbenguesthouseorkney.com. Luxurious & richly decorated rooms, all en suite. Wonderful location, eyeballing Hoy across Scapa Flow. Owners May Harper & Tony Henry are welcoming; with their b/fast & traybakes, you won't go hungry. A handrail & ramp for travellers with limited mobility should be in place by the time you read this. ££

🏠 **Castlehill Orkney** [88 D2] (4 rooms) Evie; m 07802 473927; e info@castlehillorkney. co.uk; w castlehillorkney.co.uk; see ad, 3rd colour section. Smartly furnished, en-suite rooms in modern building. Superb location high on Burger Hill overlooking Eynhallow Sound; 3 rooms have views of sea, rear room of the Birsay Moor RSPB reserve. Host Denise goes beyond the call of duty in offering a warm welcome & advice on local activities. She will happily talk to you about the challenges of 'extreme gardening' in Orkney's rugged climate & show you her walled garden. Hot

tub in conservatory is an unexpected bonus. Dinner available: 2 courses, £20; 3 courses, £25. ££

🏠 **Crystal Brook** [89 C7] (2 rooms) Orphir; 📞01856 811469; e sarah@crystalbrookorkney. com; w crystalbrookorkney.com. Designed vaguely like a Viking longhouse, with both rooms well-appointed dbls. Friendly hosts provide all-day nibbles for you to graze as you come & go. ££

🏠 **Dale Farm** [88 E2] (2 rooms) Evie; 📞01856 751454; e sally@dale-farmhouse.co.uk; w dale-farmhouse.co.uk. Building has served as a church manse, post office & farmhouse during its 160 years of existence. Retains ample character with thick walls, panelled flooring & bay windows. Views across to Rousay from upstairs. Welcoming hosts Sally & Tim Wootton offer tours around the islands while Tim, a wildlife artist (w tim-wootton.blogspot.com) also holds courses on sketching birds. ££

🏠 **Foinhaven B&B** [89 C6] (3 rooms) Orphir; 📞01856 811249; e info@foinhaven.co.uk; w foinhaven.co.uk. Fantastic position overlooking Waulkmill Bay. Spacious rooms, all en suite, sleeping 3–4 & suitable for families; 2 have views of Scapa Flow. Also 3 adjacent self-catering properties sleeping 3–6 people (from £50/night; £) ££

🏠 **Kaya B&B** [89 C5] (2 rooms) Kaya, Stenness; 📞01856 850120; w tinyurl.com/kaya-b-b . The well-appointed en-suite rooms offer views of the Ring of Brodgar; 1 dbl & 1 twin, the latter suitable for travellers with limited mobility. Good location, just back from the Stromness–Kirkwall road. Friendly welcome from South African owner Rachel Boonzaier (Kaya means 'welcome' in Zulu), who will be happy to convert 1 room with fold-out bed & cot to accommodate family of 4. ££

🏠 **Kenila B&B** [88 C4] (3 rooms) Harray; 📞01856 771431; e sheila@kenila.com; w kenila. com. Superb location near the north shore of Loch of Harray, a pebble's throw from the larger stones at Stenness & Brodgar. Snug rooms: dbl, sgl & family. Play area outside. ££

✳ 🏠 **Mill of Eyrland** [89 C6] (5 rooms) Stenness; 📞01856 850136; e info@millofeyrland. com; w millofeyrland.com. Converted mid-19th-century watermill – restored with great attention & sympathy – oozing atmosphere. The 4-poster & *chaise longue* make Mill Burn the pick of the rooms, though all are tasteful. Restored fittings turn up all over property & include watermill outside,

3 original quernstones in guest lounge & grain chutes in b/fast room. Gorgeous garden & fine setting. **££**

🏠 **The Noust** [89 C7] (3 rooms) Gyre Rd, Orphir; ✆ 01856 811348; e thenoust@gmail.com; ⏱ May–Sep. Comfortable rooms, all on 1st floor: 2 dbls, 1 twin, all en suite. **££**

🏠 **Scorralee B&B** [89 C7] (3 rooms) Scorradale Rd, Orphir; ✆ 01856 811268; e margaretclouston@btinternet.com. Bungalow on working croft high above Scapa Flow in Scorradale. Well-appointed cosy rooms: 2 dbls, 1 twin, all en suite. **££**

🏠 **Smithfield Hotel** [88 C3] (6 rooms) Dounby; ✆ 01856 771215; e info@smithfieldhotel. co.uk; w smithfieldhotel.co.uk. Simply furnished rooms in snug hotel with mix of dbls & twins, 5 en suite. Located on crossroads in middle of village. **££**

🏠 **Westrow Lodge** [89 C7] (2 rooms) A964, just south of Scorradale Rd, Orphir; ✆ 01856 811360; e westrowlodge@rovingeye. co.uk; w rovingeye.co.uk/westrowlodge.html.

Distinctive, Norwegian-style timber property (you can't miss the solar panels on the roof). Both rooms stylish & spacious with internal wood cladding; 1 has jacuzzi bath. Good location a mile west of Orphir village. Superb views across Scapa Flow. **££**

Camping

⛺ **Eviedale Campsite** [88 E2] Evie; ✆ 01856 751714; e info@eviedale-cottages.co.uk; w eviedale-cottages.co.uk. Tents & small camper vans only. Amenities include toilets, showers, washing-up block & freezer. **£**

⛺ **Orkneyurt** [88 E3] The Old School, Rendall; ✆ 01856 751261; e bookings@orkneyurt.com; w orkneyurt.com. Based on a Mongolian *ger*, the 'glamping' option comprises a single yurt made from sustainable wood & heavy-duty canvas. Interior features a wood-burning stove, is decorated with carpets & includes a dbl bed & an African bedroll for any children. Daily & weekly rates available. **££**

✗ WHERE TO EAT AND DRINK
Top range

✗ **The Foveran** [89 F6] St Ola; ✆ 01856 872389; e info@thefoveran.com; w thefoveran.com; ⏱ mid-May–mid-Sep 18.00–20.30 Mon–Sat, 18.00–20.00 Sun. Considered among Orkney's best eateries. Seafood platter of smoked salmon with beremeal oatcakes is a signature dish, as is catch of the day (always local). Other imaginative dishes include cauliflower & chickpea cakes. Perhaps finish off with a raspberry cranachan. All this amid superb views across Scapa Flow to South Ronaldsay. Arrive in good time so as to linger over pre-dinner drinks in the lounge. Wheelchair access. Also has 8 rooms, though none has views of Scapa Flow & they can come across as very much an afterthought with less attention paid to them than should be the case. A great pity as b/fasts here are lovely too. **££–£££**

Mid range

✗ **Barony Hotel** [88 B1] Same contacts as hotel; ⏱ 18.30–20.30 daily. Dinner (must be booked in advance, as must crab & lobster) served in the lounge bar of this hotel. Mains range from seafood pie to Thai curry & sirloin steaks. **££**

✳ ✗ **Merkister Hotel** [88 C3] Same contacts as hotel; restaurant ⏱ May–Sep 18.00–20.00 daily; bar meals ⏱ all year noon–14.00 & 17.30–20.30 daily. Meat sourced from local Dounby butcher, fish from Westray by head chef & co-owner Jacqui Smith, who runs hotel with sister Lorna Munson. DBB available. A nice touch is that Jacqui takes just 1 booking per table for dinner, meaning you can sit down at 19.00 if you wish & watch the sunset over the water without being kicked off by later bookings. Reservations essential. **£–££**

✗ **The Noust** [89 C7] Same contacts as hotel; ⏱ 17.00–23.00 Tue–Thu, 17.00–01.00 Fri & Sat, 12.30–22.00 Sun. Menu resists temptation to be too clever, featuring basics served with some panache, ranging from hot smoked salmon salads to chilli con carne & plum crumble. Bar area with good range of beer, wine & whisky. **£–££**

✗ **Smithfield Hotel** [88 C3] Same contacts as hotel; ⏱ 17.00–20.00 daily. Offers pub mains with a more ambitious range including Orkney beef cooked in local beer. Spacious bar with full range of beers, spirts & wines. Look out for unique wallpaper – formed from a petition several hundred names long to prevent pub from closing in 1899. Also café (🕐 11.00–15.00 daily) at the front offers chowder, wraps & pub favourites. **£**

✖ **Standing Stones Hotel** [89 C5] Same contacts as hotel; 🕐 all day. Excellent restaurant offers à la carte & pub meals in more informal lounge. Unusual high tea (Sun) combines roast chicken/mixed grill & cakes – and it works. **££–£££**

Cheap and cheerful

✳ 🍽 **Birsay Bay Tearoom** [88 A1] Birsay; ☎ 01856 721399; e georgina@birsaybaytearoom. co.uk; w birsaybaytearoom.co.uk; 🕐 Apr–May & Sep 10.30–17.00 Thu–Mon; Jun–Aug 10.30–17.00 daily; Oct–Mar 10.30–15.30 Fri–Sun. Offering the proverbial brew with a view, this fine tearoom is perched on the unpromisingly named Mount Misery & looks out across the eponymous bay with a magnificent panorama that takes in Marwick Head to the south & the Brough of Birsay to the east. Offers salmon salads at afternoon tea (£10) & excellent berry biscuits made from the local bere barley as well as rose cakes. You are likely to see seals hauled out on the foreshore. One of those places where everything just feels right. Strongly recommended. **£**

SHOPPING
Supplies
Most island stores have post offices, which formally or informally keep the same hours as the shop. For basic supplies, try:

Baikie's Stores Finstown; 🕐 07.00–19.00 Mon–Sat, 11.00–17.00 Sun
Mistra Evie; 🕐 08.00–18.00 Mon–Sat, 10.00–19.00 Sun
Palace Stores Birsay; 🕐 10.00–17.00 Mon–Sat, noon–17.00 Sun; shorter hours in winter. This is a useful general store, also selling Westray crab sandwiches.
Sutherland's Garage Stenness; 🕐 07.30–19.00 Mon–Fri, 08.00–19.00 Sat, 10.00–18.00 Sun. As well as a petrol station, this is also a handy general store.

Breweries
The Orkney Brewery [88 A3] Quoyloo; ☎ 01856 841777; e info@orkneybrewery. co.uk; w orkneybrewery.co.uk; 🕐 10.00–16.30 Mon–Sat, 11.00–16.30 Sun. Sells flagship beers including Orkney Gold & Dark Island.

🍽 **Eviedale Bistro** [88 E2] Evie; ☎ 01856 751714; e info@eviedale-cottages.co.uk; w eviedale-cottages.co.uk; 🕐 Easter–Aug 11.00–15.30 Wed–Sun. Soups, sandwiches & good coffee from small & rather engaging café. Has plans to open in evenings in 2019, offering meals including sourdough pizzas. **£**

🍽 **Gerri's Ice Cream Parlour** [89 C5] Stenness; 🕐 Apr–Sep 10.30–19.00 Mon–Fri, 10.30–17.00 Sat, 11.00–18.00 Sun. Located in the orange house on A965 road in Stenness, close to the turning for Maeshowe visitor centre. **£**

🍽 **Leigh's Burgers** [89 D5] Finstown; 🕐 08.30–14.30 Tue–Sat, 10.30–14.00 Sun. Located in lay-by opposite cemetery. Certainly not your run-of-the-mill burger van. Leigh Dowie serves mouthwatering burgers & bacon rolls of impressive ingenuity from her mobile van. All produce locally sourced; eggs come from chickens that sometimes scuttle across the road. If you're peckish, the Rossini burger – a double burger with bacon, duck pâté, cheese & blueberry sauce – should fill you up. **£**

🍽 **Skara Brae Visitor Centre Café** [88 A3] 🕐 Apr–Oct same hours as centre, usually closes just before centre; usually closed winter, check ahead. Good food include scones & some hot meals. **£**

Swannay Brewery [88 C1] Near Birsay; ☎ 01856 721700; e cheers@swannaybrewery.com; w swannaybrewery.com; 🕐 10.00–16.00 Mon–Fri. Sells good range of IPAs & pale ales.

Art and crafts
The Woolshed [88 D1] Benlaw, Costa; ☎ 01856 751305; e thewoolshed@btinternet.com; w creative-orkney.com. Sells a creative array of knitwear & felt goods, ranging from felt cafetière covers to hand-knitted waistcoats, with many products utilising the natural colours of North Ronaldsay fleeces.
Yellowbird Gallery [88 B1] Birsay; ☎ 01856 721360; w yellowbirdgallery.org; 🕐 all year, 'most days, most of the time,' says artist Lesley Murdoch. Based in an appealing traditional stone Orkney longhouse a mile east of Birsay on the A966, this gallery sells eye-catching originals & prints, drawing on local birdlife & the Brough of Birsay, which fills the view from the studio of Lesley & her partner Jon Thompson.

WHAT TO SEE AND DO There is a lot to see on the West Mainland, both along the coast and inland. The places and sights described below broadly follow a route that starts at the junction of the West and East Mainland – Kirkwall – and heads northwest, proceeding anticlockwise around the West Mainland. It starts on the coast, working its way from Kirkwall via Finstown and Birsay to Marwick Head and Skara Brae (although doesn't quite reach Stromness, which we have already covered). It then ducks inland to cover first Dounby and the moors, then the Neolithic World Heritage Site. Finally, it heads back to Kirkwall via a couple of areas in the south of the West Mainland. It's worth noting that this is not a fixed itinerary but instead a series of geographically grouped places of interest. You certainly should not attempt to see everything described here in a single day.

The coast from Finstown to Birsay

Finstown [89 D5] Heading west from Kirkwall for 3 miles along the A965 around the Bay of Firth you come to Finstown. Apart from a handy post office and grocers, the only reason to stop here is to explore **The Ouse** [89 D5], an attractive inlet of brackish water that lies to the west of the A966 bridge. Tidal currents surge underneath the bridge to create an important sliver of saltmarsh. You can walk for 600yds or so around the northern and western edges of the inlet, looking out for herons and redshank, while high tide sees wigeon feeding on the banks. This is also a good place for sea aster.

A more substantial there-and-back **walk** of 5 miles (2hrs) runs through Binscarth Woods just above Finstown towards the moors around Dounby. If you have a car, park in one of the spaces on the right of the A965 just uphill from the Pamona Inn. Walk uphill for a further 100yds, passing through a kissing gate, and follow the clear grassy path gently downhill towards the gate that leads into Binscarth Wood. A delightful woodland of mature sycamore, ash and beech overhangs the path while a gurgling stream keeps you company. Later on, you skirt the edge of lonely Loch of Wasdale where there are fine views along the burn to the sea. The walk takes the route of the St Magnus Way (see box, page 100); you can follow the waymarkers until you turn around at Refuge Corner (at a bend on the A986). If you fancy walking only one way, take the X1 bus to Refuge Corner then walk down to Finstown – easier on the legs and with the side-benefit of glorious views across the Firth and the North Isles.

Above Finstown – and unmissable from the road – is the chambered cairn of **Cuween Hill** [89 D5]. Accessed by the back road from the village to Kirkwall, Cuween commands a cinematic view of the Bay of Firth (the two small uninhabited islands in the middle distance are the Holm of Grimbister and Damsay). Its open aspect conveys a genuine sense of place; it seems logical that in the distant past people would have wanted to bury their dead here. Cuween also offers an intriguing insight into the religious practices of the Neolithic: during excavations, along with the remains of eight people, the skulls of 24 dogs were found. These were possibly of totemic importance and hint at a similar veneration to that of the sea (or white-tailed) eagles on South Ronaldsay (page 173).

Rendall and Evie In Finstown the A966 turns sharp north off the main Stromness road to run parallel to the Bay of Firth. For company, you have the sizeable lumps of Gairsay and Wyre occupying Eynhallow Sound. After 6 miles – and just after passing through Norseman Village – you come to a signpost for the Tingwall ferry (for Rousay). This is also the access point for the parish of **Rendall**, which bulges into the sound. If you've ever wanted to take a 3-mile diversion down a minor road to see a medieval dovecote, now is your chance: the 17th-century, beehive-shaped and five-tier **Rendall Doocot** [88 F3] was built to house the pigeons that provided meat for the wealthy family residing in the nearby Hall of Rendall. The doocot is adjacent to a small car park (✪ HY423206). The area should lend itself to walking – particularly given the fine views of Gairsay and Rousay – but you are constantly frustrated by farm gates and fences. It's a far easier and perfectly pleasant walk to follow the unclassified road that loops around Rendall. You can ask the driver of the No 6 Tingwall bus to drop you at the turn for the doocot on the A966, follow Gorseness Road above the coast to the doocot for 3 miles, then continue for another 2 miles along the same lane to the Tingwall ferry and take the bus back to Kirkwall.

As you head northwest along the coast, following the A966, the next parish (and small township) is **Evie** [88 D2]. A signposted road winds down to the shores of Eynhallow Sound, the narrow strait with powerful tidal currents that separates the Mainland from Rousay. Right on the promontory you will find the delightful Sands of Evie, also called Evie beach. This is one of the prettiest beaches on the Mainland – a stretch of golden sand either side of a burn with a shimmering aquamarine tinge to the waters when the sun shines.

Just around the headland from the beach, the **Broch of Gurness** ✳ [88 E2] (w tinyurl.com/broch-gurness; ⊕ Apr–Sep 09.30–12.30 & 13.30–17.30; £6/4.80) stands proud over the sound. This substantial broch, 65ft in diameter and 25ft in height, is rare in Scotland in that it is surrounded both by defences and a village of 14 houses; a good deal of all three elements remain. The site was only uncovered in 1929 and then by accident: Robert Rendall, the poet and antiquarian, was sketching while sitting atop a stool on a grassy mound; a stool leg sank into the ground, and a quick rummage revealed a staircase leading down into the broch. The site is 2,000 years old and, unlike Skara Brae, you can make your way into the heart of the broch and walk among the stone slabs that made up the sleeping quarters. On the east side of the site a line of rocks protruding from the greensward marks the site of a Viking cemetery that subsequently occupied the site. A shamrock-shaped dwelling on the west edge of the site suggests that the Picts also had a farmstead here. Rangers on site are helpful, informative and interesting to chat to.

Continuing west, the landscape is dominated by **Costa Hill** [88 C1], visible for miles around. There is a short, sharp access track off the A966 up its flanks (✪ HY309295) to the summit at 495ft (151m), which yields outstanding views across Eynhallow Sound to Rousay and south right across the mainland with a backdrop of the hills of Hoy. There is just the one catch: there is nowhere to park for a mile either side along this fast road; in practice you will need a co-operative partner with a car or an understanding bus driver in order to visit.

Located on the east shore of the Loch of Boardhouse, a couple of miles east of Birsay village, **Kirbuster Farm** ✳ [88 B2] (✆ 01856 771268; ⊕ Mar–Oct 10.30–13.00 & 14.00–17.00 Mon–Sat, noon–17.00 Sun; free) is a thoughtfully preserved (rather than restored) farmhouse and one of Orkney's unsung gems. Kirbuster, meaning 'church farm', offers a truly absorbing insight into life as lived continuously in the same house for more than 400 years. When the last occupants died in the 1960s, the house was rescued from becoming yet another Orkney ruin by George Argo (who also founded the islands' bakery empire). The farm is centred upon the *firehoose*, the last of its kind in northwest Europe, where the family would share space with cattle. Peat smoke hangs in the air as you inspect the stone-floored room that was the centre of family life: among eye-catching features is the *neuk* bed, placed in a recess and remarkably similar to the Neolithic beds seen at Skara

Brae and the Broch of Gurness. The house is unusually large for its time, as was the farm surrounding it. Adjacent buildings include a parlour room; outside, rather randomly, is a putting green.

Birsay [88 B1] Located on the northwest coast of the Mainland, the parish of Birsay can feel a long way from Kirkwall. Perhaps it is the soothing influence of the succession of unheralded but picturesque lochs, including Hundland and Swannay, that you pass to get here, but the impression derived is of the quiet and laid-back atmosphere you find on the Outer Isles. Even on a busy summer's day, Birsay never seems overrun. And this despite the area harbouring several impressive places of interest.

The main reason to visit is the elemental, immensely beautiful and very special **Brough of Birsay** ✳ [88 A1], a tidal island and defensive headland. The brough is a place apart in all senses, not only separated from the Mainland by a causeway but also bursting with wildlife and home to a distinct history. Drivers will find plenty of parking either by the causeway or back in Birsay village, half a mile south along the shore.

Accessible only by causeway 2 hours either side of low tide, the brough is of vital historical importance. A concrete path leads two-thirds of the way across the causeway (at one time there may have been a natural land bridge to the mainland). After this you pick your way across the stones, gravel and super-slippery seaweed. Otherworldly rock formations form wave-pummelled patterns and pull away in symmetry towards a turbulent sea. If a child were asked to draw a rock pool, they

THE BERE NECESSITIES

Bere is an early form of barley, also known locally as *bear, bygge* or *big*. Bere has four to six rows of ears and very long awns; in contrast barley has just two rows and shorter awns. For many years it was assumed that bere was introduced to Orkney by the Vikings (*bygg* is Old Norse for barley) but recent finds at Skara Brae and Unstan suggest that bere has been present for at least 5,000 years and is in fact an early strain from which barley evolved or was cultivated. Bere is certainly ideally suited to Orkney; its 90-day growth period and tolerance to wet weather makes the most of Orkney's all-too-brief but daylight-laden summers. These properties have counted against bere as the grain has thwarted attempts to be grown at more southerly latitudes. Often bere was stored in a gimmet (or kist), a wooden chest. The child of the family with the cleanest feet would sometimes be required to pad the bere down so that no insects or rats could work a way in. It was subsequently ground into beremeal. In the 16th century, the Orcadian diet was characterised by bannocks and ale derived from beremeal; even the children drank a weak brew called *pleenk*. In its heyday, there were 50 bere mills across Orkney, and most parishes had at least one mill. Bere fell out of favour when barley, offering 50% higher yields and being more suited to mechanised agriculture, gained the upper hand. In the 1850s, as Orkney farming moved from grain production to the grass-fed beef industry, bere almost disappeared altogether. Now Barony is the only bere mill remaining, and yet the future of bere looks surprisingly rosy. Bere has been identified as a 'superfood'. Its high levels of folate (Vitamin B12, which prevents anaemia) has attracted the interest of foodie and health-food outlets so demand is again steadily increasing.

3

would draw those you find along the causeway: endless, overlapping and brimming with sealife.

The brough is looked after by Historic Environment Scotland (w tinyurl.com/brough-birsay; ⊕ all year; £5/3, although not always applied). You'll find the brough's archaeological interest located immediately across the causeway where the neatly tended grass hosts substantial Pictish remains overlaid with a Norse settlement. That the Picts had a presence here is evidenced by the discovery of a pin bone and a stone carved with fighters underneath Pictish symbols (now in the National Museum of Scotland).

The Vikings considered the Brough of Birsay the seat from which to rule Orkney. Viking remains include Norse houses from the 10th to 11th centuries, along with the remnants of a nave, chancel and cloister from a 13th-century church that was home of Earl Thorfinn the Mighty, the most powerful of the Orkney earls. The brough may also be the site of Christchurch, the burial place of Thorfinn's grandson Magnus, who was murdered in 1116 (more recent theories suggest Christchurch may have been located near the current location of St Magnus Kirk in Birsay village).

The wider brough is worth exploring, something best done by following the clear coastal paths around its perimeter. Be mindful with children of sheer and sudden cliff edges. There is much thrilling coastal drama, with ledges and headlands – both easy on the eye – swooping seawards against the backdrop of Marwick Head and Yesnaby to the south.

Birdlife here is simply amazing: the *peep-peep* of oystercatchers echoing across the cliffs and causeway will linger long after you have left. Most visitors search for the puffins that nest here, though they do so in lesser numbers than historically. Fulmars and guillemots are abundant. Don't overlook the magnificent spectacle of gannets parading past and slicing into the sea surface for fish; be aware also of the sporting chance you have of spotting orcas running the tides between Birsay, Gurness and Rousay. In spring, the brough is smothered by flowers such as sea pink.

The village of **Birsay** lies a mile southeast of the brough and is built around the ruins of the 16th-century **Earl's Palace** [88 A1] (⊕ daylight hours; free). Constructed in Renaissance style, this comes complete with projecting towers, archery butts and a turnpike staircase around an open courtyard. The palace was built by Earl Robert Stewart, the illegitimate son of James V. The glory soon faded and by 1700 opulence had turned to decay, thanks mainly to the activity of Robert's notorious son, Earl Patrick (who built the Earl's Palace in Kirkwall; page 122); Patrick and his own son were executed for treason for their part in an armed rebellion against James VI. Across the road is the rather austere **church of St Magnus** [88 A1]. You can get the key to enter from the Palace Stores grocers just around the corner.

Just inland from Birsay, on the A967 by the western shore of the Loch of Boardhouse lies **Barony Mill** ✳ [88 B1] (✆ 01856 771276; e miller@birsay.org.uk; w birsay.org.uk; ⊕ May–Sep 11.00–17.00 daily; free), a thoroughly engaging restored mill operated by the Birsay Heritage Trust. Established in 1873, the photogenic mill, complete with giant waterwheel, produces traditional Orcadian beremeal (see box, page 95), a type of flour made using bere, an ancient and local variety of barley. Informative guided tours last 15 minutes and are delivered with panache by enthusiastic staff who talk you through the process of drying the grain and milling. Try not to stumble over the huge quernstones used for the latter: some 5ft in diameter, these cost three times a miller's annual salary and their cost gave rise to the phrase 'a millstone around the neck'. Around 50 acres of bere is grown during the summer months on nearby fields; it is mainly sold to local bakers (beremeal biscuits are commonplace on the island) and breweries.

Along the A967 just south of Birsay village you will come to **HMS Tern** [88 B2] (m 07342 202530; e info@hmstern.co.uk; w hmstern.co.uk; guided tours May–Aug, see website for times; £6/4), also known, perhaps a little unfortunately, as Royal Naval Air Station Twatt, after the local village of the same name (from an Old Norse word meaning 'parcel of land'). Accessed via Bryameadow Road, HMS Tern was a key airfield during World War II and provided training facilities for the Royal Navy. Tours take in the control tower, cinema and fire station and reflect the prodigious efforts to restore the site by the Birsay Heritage Trust (w birsay.org.uk).

The west coast from Marwick Head to Skara Brae and Yesnaby
Some of Orkney's most scintillating coastal scenery is located along the west coast. The drama begins south of Birsay with the ascending contours of Marwick Head that dip down to the sea at Skara Brae and swoop upwards once more at Yesnaby. This represents an 8-mile promenade of cliffs of giddying proportions, some lush and smooth, others so brutal it can feel as if you are poking around in the Earth's rib cage. At any time of year this is a wild, end-of-the-world landscape: in winter, storms smash into the jagged cliffs; in spring, the race to breed brings ruthless avian conflicts, with Arctic and great skuas mercilessly targeting other breeding seabirds.

Marwick Head [88 B2] Three miles south of Birsay, a signposted lane off the B9056 heads west toward the coast and Marwick Head. For decades, this promontory has been spoken of in hallowed tones on account of its magnificent seabird colonies; it is the RSPB's flagship reserve on Orkney. In recent years, the number of birds has dropped disturbingly; nevertheless, in spring the air can still seem filled with the confetti-like assemblage of kittiwakes and fulmars.

The bay of Mar Wick, which extends in front of the car park, is exceptionally scenic. At low tide, water is trapped by the reef-like shape of the exposed rocks, known as the The Choin (from the Old Norse word *tjörn*, meaning large pool). To the north, the cliffs of Marwick Head lurch up abruptly from sea level. Wildlife is

THE DISAPPEARING BIRDS

Despite appearances in some lucky parts of Orkney, many species of bird are under pressure – locally, nationally and internationally. This is particularly true of seabirds. Kittiwake numbers at Marwick Head have declined markedly and visibly over the past decade or so from 17,000 to 2,000. Elsewhere, they are under the cosh too – and are now considered threatened with global extinction. This is due in large part to warming seas, which are prompting their key prey, the sand eel, to move further north. Moreover, the fish's own breeding season is increasingly out of kilter with that of the kittiwake. The same issue affects puffins while great skuas have been recorded hunting seabirds (rather than forcing them to relinquish their catch), suggesting they too are responding to a decline in the availability of sand eels. For more information, including ways in which you can help, visit w tinyurl.com/puffin-project. Inland from the coast, it can feel as though you see curlews everywhere, but they too have declined by as much as 40% in recent years. The causes are varied but are due mainly to farming practices, weather changes and predation.

A WALK UP TO MARWICK HEAD

Distance: 2½ miles; time: 1½–2hrs
Start/finish: Marwick Head car park, ⊕ HY229241
OS Map: Explorer 463, Orkney West Mainland

At 285ft (87m), the cliffs of Marwick Head require some puff to reach. The effort is worthwhile, though, both for superb views along the way and – in spring and summer – the spectacle of thousands of seabirds (kittiwakes, guillemots, razorbills, fulmars, cormorants and others) beavering to and from their nests. You are also likely to see seals hauled out far below. On a clear day you can just about make out the Old Man of Hoy to the south and Westray (north). The scenery is stunning: fragmented sandstone cliffs crumble and tumble into the sea, leaving exposed ridges and sheer drops on which seabirds somehow find space to nest.

A clear path arcs north around the shore before the climb begins. Most of the climb is well away from the cliff edge. Only as you approach the Kitchener Memorial does the path narrow a little and take you by the cliff edge. Although it's far from the tightrope stuff experienced in other parts of Orkney, those without a head for heights may decide to take in the view from here then return to the car park.

Offshore is the site of one of Britain's worst naval disasters, the 1916 sinking of HMS *Hampshire* with the loss of 737 crew and passengers (see box, opposite). The castle-like Kitchener Memorial [88 A2] is a landmark visible from much of the West Mainland; erected in 1926, it stands 48ft high. In 2016, to mark the centenary of the ship's loss, the Orkney Heritage Society restored the memorial and commissioned a commemorative wall inscribing names of all those who died. The intention is, says an inscription, 'to better remember' *all* who lost their lives. (The Kitchener Memorial is just that, a monument to one man; the original epitaph mentions that 736 others perished only in its final sentence.)

About 100yds beyond the memorial, follow the signposted path right through a gate and downhill along a grassy track – keep an eye out for hares scampering around the adjacent fields – to a small car park where there stands a deck gun salvaged from the wreck of the *Hampshire*. Turn right along the lane towards the shore, then bear left to retrace your steps behind the beach to the car park.

---

abundant: in winter, swans and ducks such as wigeon and red-breasted merganser can be seen in the lagoon-like water; meanwhile, greylag geese and curlew feed in shoreline fields alongside the ever-present oystercatchers. In summer the sky is filled with fulmars, while Arctic skuas and great black-backed gulls patrol the skies. Also look out for the rare great yellow bumblebee (see box, page 12).

Skara Brae [88 A3] (w tinyurl.com/skara-brae18; ⊕ Apr–Sep 09.30–17.30 daily; Oct–Mar 10.00–16.00 daily; £6.50/3.90; Apr–Oct ticket includes admission to Skaill House) Many much-heralded sites can be a let down when you finally visit them: not so Skara Brae, which is managed by Historic Environment Scotland. Britain's earliest known Neolithic village, dating back more than 5,000 years, Skara Brae is simply haunting. A visit comprises a walk through an excellent interpretation

On the evening of 5 June 1916, HMS *Hampshire* was sailing from Scapa Flow to Russia on what is thought to have been a secret mission for Lord Kitchener, the minister for war (best known for his finger-pointing recruitment posters declaring 'Your country needs you'). In Force 9 seas, the ship hit a mine less than 2 miles from the memorial. The *Hampshire* sank so quickly that of the 749 passengers and crew, just 12 survived. Kitchener's body was never found.

That anyone at all was spared is extraordinary: they were swept violently into sharp-edged gullies at the cliff base. The Stromness lifeboat and local people were desperate to attempt a rescue but were forbidden amid fears that secret documents on board the *Hampshire* might fall into the wrong hands; less than a week before, the ship had taken part in the Battle of Jutland. Today, the ship is honoured as a war grave and diving is forbidden. You can learn more at w hmshampshire.org.

The *Hampshire* was not the only vessel sunk by German mines as many fishing drifters were deployed for duties such as minesweeping. On 22 June 1916 the *Laurel Crow* hit a mine and sank with the loss of all nine men. One of those on board was George Petrie from Burray, the only Orcadian to die in either sinking.

centre, a reconstruction of one of the Neolithic houses, and a short stroll to the village itself, perched hard above the magnificent setting of the Bay o' Skaill, with headlands pulling away to the north and south.

Occupied from 3100–2500BC, Skara Brae predates the Pyramids of Giza by 600 years and Stonehenge by 1,000 years. The site re-emerged during a storm in 1850, some 4,400 years after it had been abandoned. What you see today represents two distinct phases of occupation. Houses 6, 9 and 10 probably date to the earliest community, around 3500BC, which survived for a few hundred years. The site was then abandoned for several hundred years before being occupied again from 2900–2500BC.

This open-air location is fragile, so you are not permitted to walk among the houses; instead you must follow walkways around the top of the site, which provide excellent and close-up views. There is good wheelchair access. It's worth remembering that this perspective can give a misleading impression of how Skara Brae would have appeared while in use: the village was most certainly not subterranean.

In all, there are eight houses of similar design, with a single room entered from a roofed passageway that, like a street, linked each dwelling. Each house had the same internal layout, with stone beds to the side, a central hearth and a dresser opposite the entrance. While this uniformity brings to mind a modern building development of identikit houses, it also provides a possible insight into the psychology of those who built them and lived there: harmony may well have been essential to the functioning of the village. This sense is reinforced by the fact that no single house is obviously larger or more ostentatious than any other: this was a community where, most likely, people treated each other more or less as equals.

Skara Brae probably supported 50–100 people; each house was most likely home to a single family. The exception is house 8, which is thought to have been a workshop for making stone tools and pottery. The best-preserved and most substantial dwelling is house 1, where you can peer down and examine the central hearth, beds and dressers of stone slabs as well as stone tanks embedded in the sand that were used for preparing fish bait. Occupants used bracken and deer skins to make their 'furniture' comfortable. For food, they hunted deer, gathered berries and reared pigs, sheep and cattle. Stone food boxes were lined with clay to act as refrigeration. Whalebone arches were used to secure doors.

At the height of its occupation, Skara Brae was almost certainly much larger and would have reached out across the bay to the headland, with a freshwater loch in between. Geophysical surveys have established that the settlement also extended further inland. It's thought that coastal erosion led to the loss of fresh water, which, in combination with encroaching wind-blown sand, contributed to the abandonment of the site. Other possible factors were disease, warfare and climate change. It was warmer when Skara Brae was established, leading to the hypothesis that strengthening winds and woodland clearance – creating scrub and grasslands – may have further sealed the site's fate by making it ever harder to grow crops and secure shelter.

You can learn more about Skara Brae and study an impressive collection of artefacts in the visitor centre. These include a whalestone slab with an oval hole in its centre, pendants made from whales and walruses, geometric designs and shards of pottery. Other more enigmatic objects, amorphous in shape, were small enough to be held in the hand and may have been of religious significance. The centre impressively resists the temptation to leap to sensational conclusions. Since the inhabitants bequeathed no written evidence, archaeologists are careful to distinguish between what is known or can be safely deduced from the finds they make, and what might be called 'informed conjecture'.

Between the visitor centre and the Neolithic site stands a replica house worth visiting. Complete with roof and a shadowy half-light it feels, apart from the concrete flooring, remarkably realistic.

THE ST MAGNUS WAY

A new long-distance route across the Mainland, the St Magnus Way, (w stmagnusway.com) was established in 2018 and is closely linked to the life and times of the eponymous saint (see box, page 188) who is so central to Orkney's history. Running for 55 miles, it is intended as a pilgrimage route – think the Camino de Santiago in Spain. In practice, it is likely to prove a magnet for walkers in general as it fills a long-awaited gap for a well-waymarked route across the island. St Magnus Way takes the most scenic route wherever possible and includes the fetching coast around Evie and Birsay, the shores of Scapa Flow and empty moorlands in between.

Divided into five sections, the route starts in Evie in the north of the island, following the journey of Magnus's body as it was carried from Gurness to Christ Kirk in Birsay. On the second section, the Way turns inland to Dounby, following Magnus's bones as they were later moved from St Magnus Kirk in Birsay to St Olaf's Kirk in Kirkwall, awaiting the completion of the cathedral that now bears his name. The third section traverses the heart of the island via Binscarth Wood to Finstown; subsequently it follows rough heather ground across Lyradale and a scenic off-road coastal stretch from the Breck to Houton in the parish of Orphir on the southern coast. Finally, the trail tracks east along the shores of Scapa Flow to Kirkwall and St Magnus Cathedral. The walk is not always easy going – indeed, is quite tough in places – as, it could be argued, a pilgrimage should be. The wry observation of the route authors that 'you should expect to get wet and discouraged at least once each day during your pilgrimage' is something of a leitmotif for walking on Orkney in general.

The inland backdrop to Skara Brae is punctuated by the grim, grey outline of **Skaill House** [88 C3] (**w** skaillhouse.co.uk; ⊕ Apr–Sep 09.30–17.30 daily; Oct 10.00–16.00 daily; ticket included in Skara Brae entry). Most visitors decline the option of visiting the house but it is certainly worth a brief visit. While from the outside it looks every inch a stage set from a Hammer House of Horror movie, inside it is more homely, presented as it was in the 1950s. Dating to the 1620s, Skaill House has been tinkered with by lairds over the centuries and includes an eclectic mix of items for inspection, from a dinner service presented by Captain Cook to a colonial-era tiger skin to end all tiger skins. The house is also magnificently spooky, creaking and groaning as if the building is sighing to itself. Staff, including the sceptical, and some visitors swear to have seen benign ghosts, including a mysterious woman in black. To further stoke the imagination of the credulous, the southern wing of the house stands on a pre-Norse burial ground.

Yesnaby South of Skara Brae, a collage of collapsing cliffs and monumental slabs of rock work their way up and down the coast around Yesnaby. There are two ways to inspect this superb landscape: on foot along the coast from Stromness in the south (see box, page 86), or via the 2-mile-long track signposted from the B9056. This approach 'road' is also a good place to look out for short-eared owls either sitting on or quartering over the fields. Some maps, including the Ordnance Survey, don't mention Yesnaby (⊕ HY220161): the road end is by the Hill of Borwick, 2 miles south of Skara Brae.

From the car park by the wartime battery, the most spectacular scenery lies to the south. The Brough of Bigging, a huge brow of a headland, juts out into the sea, its exposed sandstone cliffs gently yielding to the pounding ocean. A 15-minute walk south along the coastal trail leads to the impressive sea stack known as the **Castle of Yesnaby** (115ft/35m) [88 A4], which is used by climbers to get their eye in before tackling the Old Man of Hoy. It is distinguished by its two 'legs' – the sandstone columns on which it stands. A mile further south (⊕ HY216134) is another mighty stack, **North Gaulton castle**, which is of similar height but far wider.

Yesnaby is also renowned for its coastal vegetation. Its maritime heath and grassland are considered among the best in Europe; the flora includes ling, bell heather, crowberry and spring squill (whose blue star-shaped flowers emerge en masse in April and May).

The interior: Dounby and the moors
Inland, the landscape of the West Mainland is characterised by peat, interspersed by distinctive mounds and small hills of boulder clay; these are particularly visible around Harray Loch.

Dounby [88 C3] The main village on the West Mainland, Dounby is scattered around a crossroads where the central A986 meets the moorland roads from Stromness and Evie.

Dounby is small but vibrant, with a Co-Op, butcher's, petrol station and handy post office (⊕ 09.00–13.00 & 14.00–17.30 Mon–Wed & Fri, 09.00–13.00 Thu, 10.00–13.00 Sat). The village is also something of a craft hub. On the main A986 at Rose Cottage is **Castaway Crafts** (✆ 01856 771376; **e** castaway_crafts@hotmail. com; **w** castawaycrafts.co.uk; ⊕ all year 10.00–18.00 Mon–Fri, 10.00–16.00 Sat; also May–Sep noon–16.00 Sun) selling soaps, candles, pottery, glasswork and knitwear. It is run by Fiona Mitchell, who asserts her outlet to be the most Orkney shop on the islands, with '99%' of her goods made on the islands. 'I asked people to provide me with a few things and it has just grown,' she says. In her workshop Fiona makes cushions and other items from Harris tweed, drawing on her experience of working with tweed on the eponymous Hebridean island. 'This used to be the last tailor shop in Orkney so it's nice in a way to put it back to its original use by bringing in the sewing machines,' she laughs.

Just a few yards north of Castaway Crafts and signposted off the main road is the studio of jeweller **Alison Moore** (✆ 01856 771511; e hello@alisonmoore.co.uk; w alisonmoore.co.uk; ⏱ 09.00–17.00 Mon–Sat; see ad, 3rd colour section) who makes distinctive jewellery from gemstones. Alison's jewellery is noticeable for the fact that she resists the temptation to punctuate her work with Viking galley ships or seabirds. Instead, she produces intriguing work that uses gemstones to reflect the light and mood of the Orcadian landscape. Some of her jewellery is entwined, to reflect the island's scarce woodlands; other works use sky-blue topaz to capture the light of sunny days at low tide on Evie beach. Her labradorite range is iridescent and harks back to the whaling days of Orkney (one boat returned from the Arctic and dumped a heap of labradorite on the Holm of Stromness). Alison trained as a geologist and had a science-based career, 'so gemstones and minerals were my thing,' she says. She moved to Orkney, having 'run away to Skye to get married' and is mainly self-taught. 'I just started to make jewellery in my spare time. The designs are quite simple, I try not to over-complicate things.' Now she has enough demand to have trained up local people. 'It works really well for all of us. We're quite flexible, the staff can fit in work around the school run, or they can pop off and buy a sheep at the auction mart – that's what happens on Orkney.'

Harray [88 C4] The parish of Harray – and the tiny hamlet of the same name – is located on and around the A986 that runs from Birsay across the heart of the Mainland. Set back from the archaeological intensity of Brodgar, Stenness and Maeshowe, this can be a pleasant place to explore. One place not to miss is **Fursbreck Pottery** (✆ 01856 771419; e info@orkneypottery.co.uk; w orkneypottery.

BIRDWATCHING ON THE WEST MAINLAND

No great skill is required for watching wildlife on the West Mainland. You'll see it wherever you walk, cycle or drive. That said, the RSPB (w rspb.org.uk/orkney) manages several reserves and hides that not only offer fine birdwatching opportunities but are set in places of great natural beauty. The reserve at **Burgar Hill** [88 D2] (⊕ HY343262) provides one of the very few UK hides where you can watch breeding red-throated divers. The hide at **The Loons** [88 A2] (⊕ HY245244) is a special place for rare UK species such as pintail and black-tailed godwit. Some 50 pairs of hen harrier nest on the West Mainland, and the RSPB hide at **Cottascarth** [88 E3] (⊕ HY367198), on the moors east of Dounby, has huge windows that are superb for watching these birds, which are almost extinct in England but thrive on Orkney. The easiest way to reach Cottascarth is to follow the A966 north from Finstown towards Rendall and Evie, then, just after passing through Norseman Village, take the signposted turning inland for Dounby. After half a mile, follow signs to the right to a car park beyond Lower Cottascarth farm. The hide is a further 600yds on along a good path. The hide is named after Eddie Balfour, an Orcadian naturalist who grew up on a local farm at Rendall and instigated the world's longest-running raptor study – right here. Spring sees the birds 'sky-dancing' and the ghostly male dropping food to its mate; in winter there is the haunting sight of the birds coming to roost in the heather at dusk.

co.uk), which provides the studio of Andrew Appleby. Perhaps understandably, Appleby has been unable to resist the temptation to call himself 'the Harray Potter', although he maintains that he came up with the moniker before J K Rowling's books were published. Enter his studio, however, and you might assume that the wizards of Hogwarts have indeed been let loose on the place. Dominated by a giant kiln, the shelves are heaving with replica Neolithic grooved ware, vases and goblets. Andrew's work is eye-catching and impressive, and he provides engaging company. 'I was a potter from the age of three, when I was taken to a pottery in Kent. When I grew up I ended up running it. The smell of clay does it for me: it's a musty, muddy scent. I always loved the hessian sacks the clay came in.' Inspired by his father, who spent World War II on the islands, Andrew hitchhiked to Orkney with his brother, funding the trip by selling pottery for £100. 'I was completely spellbound by the colour of the Orkney landscape and by the folk who lived here,' he recalls. He eventually relocated for good, living in an old chicken barn. 'I was starving in Kent so I decided I may as well starve on Orkney.'

Andrew's wide-ranging and eclectic designs are intended to be all things to all people (and indeed, to all tourists). 'I decided I was going to make pottery that people wanted to buy: little animals for a child, a vase for flowers for a grandmother and jugs for people who wanted to use them.'

The **Loch of Harray** [88 C4] (known locally as simply Harray Loch) runs for 5 miles and its shores are a pleasant place to park your car or bicycle, have a picnic and simply watch what turns up. An intricate ecosystem prevails on the shoreline, with aquatic plants, such as mare's-tail, shoreweed and water-milfoil, that are essential for food or breeding material for ducks. More than 30 pairs of mute swan nest around Harray and adjacent Stenness. Thousands of greylag geese use the loch as a roosting site on winter nights. Generally, you will see the geese at the southern end of the loch; the geese used to then head on to mainland Scotland but with a warming climate Orkney's grass now grows all year. As a result many greylags are 'short-stopping' (staying put) on Orkney, rather than expending energy on a further flight south. Harray is also home to diving ducks such as tufted duck and pochard, which primarily feed on invertebrates such as small molluscs and larvae of insects. They are joined in autumn by goldeneye and scaup that fly in from the Baltic and other northerly places; the largest of the diving ducks on Harray is the red-breasted merganser. In spring, Harray is a fine pace to enjoy abundant shoreside flowers such as lady's smock and ragged robin.

The A986 skirts the east shores of the Loch of Harray, and 2 miles south along it from Dounby – signposted to the right – stands the restored **Corrigall Farm Museum** [88 C3] (✆ 01856 771411; ⊕ Mar–Oct 10.30–13.00 & 14.00–17.00 Mon–Sat, noon–17.00 Sun; free). Comprising a byre, stable and a house adapted and furnished as they would have been in the early 19th century, this is an excellent place to tangibly experience how Orkney life felt until relatively recently. The house is more than 200 years old and features an 'oot-by' (scullery) and 'seller' (from the Old Norse 'sair', meaning sleeping quarters) complete with box bed. Outside you can inspect a range of agricultural implements from turnip choppers to ploughs.

A mile or so south along the A986 from the farm, at a crossroads (✛ HY327161), it's well worth taking the quiet road north signposted for Howe. A short walk from the end of this road leads to extraordinary but little-visited **Knowes of Trotty** [88 D4], Scotland's largest Bronze Age burial site. The quirky-sounding name derives from the Old Norse 'Trow Marsh' ('marsh of the goblins'), a nod to the chilling tales and superstitions that are so often associated with such sites. If you are travelling here by No 7 bus, ask to be dropped at the A986 crossroads at Howe; this only

Orkney clay is not widely regarded as being of high quality; this means that Andrew Appleby (aka 'the Harray Potter', page 102), for example, buys his raw materials from Stoke-on-Trent. 'The local clay is not good for turning. It's difficult to use so it had to be supported all the time,' he says. Andrew found that mixing Orkney clay with duck fat made it more malleable. 'It set fast and was watertight, it could be used without being fired.' Appleby believes that this may well be the technique that Neolithic Orcadians deployed. 'They knew their stuff. I think sometimes archaeologists forget that,' he says. 'They were making pots that were perfectly adequate for them – what they needed for survival. They weren't making it for display in John Lewis or in a museum. Such vessels have emerged from excavations at the Ring of Brodgar, he points out. 'There is a risk of judging our predecessors but they were at the forefront of the technology of the time. It's plausible they even used some of the pits like a tandoori oven, putting charcoal in them and laying a spit roast above.'

adds another half a mile to the walk (check timetables, however, as the bus only runs at the beginning and end of the working day). Otherwise, park in the space opposite the second road on the left. From here, continue down the lane to Howe. You'll reach a house where the road turns left; keep following the road until it turns right after 100yds, at which point keep straight ahead, walking on to a peat track, with a fence on your left. The track plods towards what look from a distance to be indistinguishable hillocks. After half a mile, just after the third stretch of boardwalk, you reach the first grassy burial mound. Climb this stumpy knoll for a fine view of the entire site: a further 11 mounds fork out ahead of you in a 'v' shape for 800yds. Gold discs found here once adorned residents' buttons. You can go further if you wish, but the trail comes and goes and you will soon be breasting heather. From May to June you also risk disturbing nesting birds, so you may judge that seeing the knowes from the first hill is sufficient.

The heart of Neolithic Orkney World Heritage Site With their faintly delineated drystone-wall boundaries, the sheep-nibbled hills that flank the Finstown–Stromness road can bring to mind the Yorkshire Dales. Yet here, along a thin neck of land between the lochs of Harray and Stenness, in a natural amphitheatre formed by the hills of Hoy to the south and the backbone of Orkney's moorland, lies one of Europe's richest Neolithic landscapes.

The epicentre of this extraordinary density of ritual prehistoric sites lies along and near the B9055, 5 miles northeast of Stromness, where you will find the Ring of Brodgar, the Ness of Brodgar, the Standing Stones of Stenness and Maeshowe chambered cairn. Each site is visually striking: these are not just bumps and lumps where you must take a guide's word that they look impressive or are important. Evidence garnered by your own eyes will tell you that you are looking at a landscape unchanged for more than 5,000 years. Their collective significance was recognised by latter-day civilisation in 1999 when UNESCO accorded them – together with Skara Brae, 6 miles west – World Heritage Site status.

With the exception of Maeshowe, you are free to explore the sites at any time of day or night. Midsummer is particularly popular, not just on account of the inevitable magnetism of the solstice but because the drawn-out evenings provide a half-light that raises the atmosphere of this landscape a further notch or two.

The sites are managed by Historic Environment Scotland (☎ 01856 841732; e orkneyrangers@hes.scot; w historicenvironment.scot). Free guided tours of both Brodgars and Stenness take place each week from June to September; Maeshowe can only be visited on a guided tour. Check the HES website for times.

The Ring of Brodgar [89 C5] Set on slightly raised ground, the Ring of Brodgar Stone Circle and Henge features 36 monoliths (originally perhaps 60), 27 of which still stand today (the remainder lie prone or in fragments). The monoliths vary considerably in size: some are oblong, others thin and slender, still more resemble stumpy incisors. Scottish geologist Hugh Miller described them as 'an assemblage of ancient druids'. All are made of old red sandstone and range from 7ft to 15ft in height. Although they can look damaged or deliberately cut at an angle, this is actually a natural feature resulting from fracturing or erosion (you can see this for yourself at spots such as the cliffs at Yesnaby). The stones form a near-perfect circle 340ft in diameter. The stones are surrounded by a rock-cut ditch, which was once 7ft deep and 21ft wide. While the site is often described as a henge, this is contested by some archaeologists on the basis that henges usually have an external bank, which is absent in the case of Brodgar.

Brodgar's exact age is uncertain as it has never been fully excavated, but it was probably erected 4,000–4,500 years ago. It is thought to have been a convening place for ceremonies, feats and for commemorations of the dead. There is no clear

SAVING THE RING OF BRODGAR

With more than 140,000 visitors a year, the Ring of Brodgar is comfortably Orkney's most-visited archaeological site. And justifiably so: not only is it mesmerising and stirring, but it is also free. Unlike at Stonehenge (or indeed Maeshowe), you need neither pay nor book an entry slot: Heritage Environment Scotland (HES), which owns the site, is keen to keep it that way.

The challenge HES faces is the literally heavy footfall that has led to compaction, saturation and ultimately destruction of the turf, occasionally turning parts of the site into a slippery, unwalkable bog. In response, HES has come up with an innovative solution which it hopes will allow more-or-less unfettered access. After consulting with English Heritage, which owns Stonehenge and has faced similar pressures, HES has cultivated a wear-resistant rye grass. Initially this was grown on the UK mainland but proved unable to cope with the shock of Orcadian weather when planted there; now the turf is grown at the end of the runway at Kirkwall airport. Perforated pipes laid under the grass drain the water away. The intention is that in high season half of the area inside the Ring will be 'rested' for five days while visitors walk around the other half. The outer path around the Ring should be accessible at all times. In low season, visitors will be able to walk pretty much as they wish.

Other measures include encouraging people to visit the other tumuli on the site and to visit with local rangers. 'You actually get a better view and sense of the ring from outside than inside,' says Stephen Watt, HES district architect, who hopes these measures will suffice. In the longer term, should numbers keep rising, a visitor management centre on the scale of the one at Skara Brae cannot be ruled out, though this may be based in Kirkwall rather than adjacent to the site. 'There's always conflict between conservation and inviting the public; it's something we wrestle with,' says Watt.

3

Distance: 2 miles; time: 2hrs
Start/finish: Ring of Brodgar car park ✪ HY295135
OS Map: Explorer 463 Orkney West Mainland

The spectacle and stature of the Ring of Brodgar and Stenness ensure that they are at the centre of exploration of the UNESCO World Heritage Site. It is tempting to dash between the two. Their setting is important, however, rather than coincidental. A walk between the two and their adjacent areas not only enables you to put them in a geographical context but also to admire the breathtaking wildlife.

Begin from the car park just north of the Ring of Brodgar and follow the boardwalk to the site. After walking around the circle, head south to Salt Knowe and take the clear grassy path just to its left, heading for Loch of Stenness. By the loch bear left with the shore on your right. Harbour seals can sometimes be seen in the waters, reminding you that the loch is – just about – a saltwater intrusion from the open sea. On the inland fields you are almost certain to see curlews, or to pick them out in the air by tracing their mournful gurgling call, along with lapwings, skylarks and oystercatchers.

The wildlife benefits from intentionally supportive farming, which involves grazing with cattle or sheep and rotational cultivation. Flowers thrive; their number includes bird's-foot trefoil, yellow rattle, self-heal, lousewort, eyebright and, from May to late July, the purple spikes of northern marsh orchid. In summer you may spot a rarity, the great yellow bumblebee. Just in front of a farmhouse, the path turns sharp left and leads down to the road. Cross with care and turn right to pick up the footpath by Loch of Harray parallel to the road. You soon pass the Ness of Brodgar up to your right. Follow the road for 300yds before returning to the grassy path and passing the huge Watchstone to your right. After visiting Stenness, follow a signposted path leading north to Barnhouse. Just behind the settlement is a small council-run birdwatching hide, which offers good viewing of the Loch of Harray. The RSPB (w rspb.org.uk/orkney) often offers guided watching here. This is a good spot in spring to hear the rasping song of sedge warblers and also reed bunting, a bird that has, despite a recent partial recovery, declined in huge numbers nationally but is doing well on Orkney as local farming encourages its winter food supply of weed seeds. From here, retrace your steps, a distance of a mile or so, to the car park.

evidence that Brodgar is particularly aligned with the solstices, but it may well have charted the cycles of the moon or sun. While the adjacent lochs enhance the atmosphere of a visit – and are occasionally accorded some kind of ceremonial significance – the Loch of Stenness was only formed 500–1,000 years after Brodgar was erected. Before this, the site was set in a marshy landscape, harder to reach (there are two clear causeway entrances to the Ring) and accordingly enjoying a high status.

The site of Brodgar is kept company by several burial mounds set back from the main stones. Just across the road from the circle is **Plumcake Mound**, which was excavated in 1854 to reveal two stone cists (burial coffins), inside each grave was an urn with cremated human remains. The largest mound is **Salt Knowe**, just

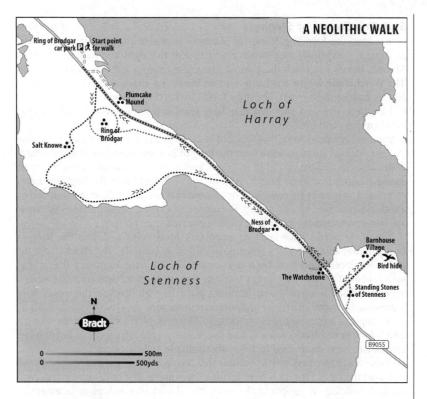

Ring of Brodgar car park 🅿️🚶 Start point for walk

Plumcake Mound

Loch of Harray

Ring of Brodgar

Salt Knowe

Ness of Brodgar

Barnhouse Village

Bird hide

The Watchstone

Standing Stones of Stenness

Loch of Stenness

N

Bradt

0 — 500m
0 — 500yds

B9055

southwest of the Ring; unexcavated, it is a similar size to Maeshowe and may in time yield yet another Neolithic tomb.

The Ness of Brodgar [89 C5] (w nessofbrodgar.co.uk; ⊕ Jul & Aug, check website for times; free) The strip of land that runs between lochs Harray and Stenness is known as the Ness of Brodgar. Archaeologists are uncovering new and significant archaeological finds all the time here. About half a mile east of Brodgar, the Ness of Brodgar is an unfolding site whose importance increases with every annual dig. The Ness was completely unknown until 2002 when a geophysical survey revealed evidence of a huge complex at least 5,000 years old and comprising huge stone buildings up to 75ft in length with walls 14ft thick. Excavations began the following year, and finds so far include Neolithic art scratched or etched into stone, painted stonework, polished mace heads and axes, and huge amounts of animal bone. The Ness was in use for at least 1,000 years and is thought to have been a meeting place for worship, the exchange of ideas and trade. The site has so far been defined by thick walls through which were only permitted people of great standing and suggest a place of significant spirituality. Geophysical scans have identified a series of houses, or even temples, within the Ness that were covered with domed roofs. Either way, this was the site of an organised and sophisticated society. The slightly raised nature of the site is believed to be the result of thousands of years of layers of buildings and middens of food, farm and household waste, including that left by those earlier peoples who used the site where the Ness was constructed. You can't normally access the Ness site but during the summer months archaeologists working on the site provide free tours and a scaffolded viewing gallery is erected.

Standing Stones of Stenness [89 C5] Located half a mile east of the Ness of Brodgar, the Standing Stones of Stenness is one of the earliest stone circles in Britain, comprising four stones rising to 13ft in height and dating to at least 3100BC. Before you reach these you'll pass the enormous 19ft monolith known as **The Watchstone**, by the road and right on the Brig o' Brodgar (where the lochs of Harray and Stenness meet). The stone forms part of the Stenness site and is thought to have been one of a pair that may have formed part of a ceremonial walkway between there and Brodgar.

Stenness is fenced from livestock but visually you could make a case for saying that the site is more impressive than the Ring of Brodgar. Stenness comprises three dominating monoliths up to 14ft in height, kept company by a fourth smaller stone. At their centre is a stone hearth. Although it is thought that the ring was never completed, originally there were 11 or 12 stones set out in an ellipse, surrounded by a wide ditch crossed by a causeway. The name comes from 'Stein-nes', the Old Norse for 'stone promontory'. Finds here include grooved ware pottery.

The circle would have been an important focal point and, like the Ring of Brodgar, may have enjoyed a ceremonial and ritual purpose. The effort to put the stones in place would have been monumental: it has been estimated that it may have taken 50 people six months working flat out to move and erect the stones, using driftwood ramps to lever them into place. As with Brodgar, this would have represented a major enterprise and social commitment.

A couple of important sites are close to Stenness. North of the stones, along a 200yd-long grassy track, you will find the reconstructed settlement of **Barnhouse**. The houses here, discovered in 1984, are similar in style to Skara Brae but date to the same era as Stenness, so it's plausible that the people who lived here also erected and used the circle. The 13 houses include the remains of a once-substantial, two-roomed building. A geophysical survey has shown that village once extended towards Maeshowe. Note that the site is a reconstruction, rather than the real thing. It appears that, when the houses were abandoned, they were deliberately demolished for reasons that remain unclear.

Visible to the southeast of Stenness, half a mile away and close to Maeshowe chambered cairn, is the **Barnhouse Stone** (⊕ HY312121). Standing alone in a field, 10ft high, the stone is in perfect alignment with Maeshowe: on the winter solstice, the sun is directly above the stone when its rays shine into the entrance of Maeshowe. The stone takes time to access – it's a lengthy walk via the church lane immediately to its north – and, as it has few remarkable features in its own right, is generally best viewed from afar.

Maeshowe [88 C5] The final major element of the UNESCO site is the chambered cairn of Maeshowe, a tomb or passage grave built 5,000 years ago and today covered by a grassy mound. The site is fenced off in a field half a mile north of the Standing Stones of Stenness and can only be visited on an escorted 1-hour tour (w tinyurl. com/maeshowe-cairn; ⏲ May–Sep 09.30–17.30; Oct–Apr 10.00–16.00 daily; evening tours on some dates Jun–Aug; £6/3.60; tickets can be bought in advance). The visitor centre (on the A965, just south of the B9055; be wary if crossing as this is among the fastest roads in Orkney) has a mixture of print and virtual-reality interpretation, which enables you to do a little homework before visiting the site. Note that Maeshowe is popular and gets booked up well in advance during summer. The sunset tours are atmospheric and can be that little bit quieter.

Maeshowe derives from 'howe' (Old Norse for 'hill') though the meaning of 'maes' is less certain (the Norse called it Orkahaugr, the Ork Mound). The site lies within a circular ditch which may originally have been much deeper and contained water, thereby perhaps physically and symbolically separating the world of the dead from that of the living. The mound contains a large stone passage leading to an elaborate stone-skinned chamber with side cells. A singular feature is that the passageway and main chamber were constructed to align with the setting sun for the winter solstice as well as for the three weeks either side. At these times, the light of the sun shines down the passageway, steadily moving towards the back of the main chamber and illuminating the side cell at the rear (cameras are set up that stream the setting sun from different angles; you can see this in real time at **w** maeshowe.co.uk).

The entrance passage is 30ft long, but not high so most people will need to stoop slightly to progress through into the chamber. A single giant sandstone slab forms the walls either side of the passage. The chamber walls are formed of flagstone and corbelling. The tomb was excavated in 1861 by archaeologists who found scant remains. Over the years, however, an extraordinary outline has emerged of the people who built and used the tomb. Even though much remains uncertain, archaeologists are now clear that this was an advanced, intelligent civilisation. This was not a structure simply thrown together: engineers and mathematicians must have been needed to work out weights and angles; astronomers to align the opening with the solstice sunset.

The actual purpose of Maeshowe is unclear. It may have been a way to celebrate the shift from darkness to the lighter months of the year. More complex theories suggest that the bodies of important dead were left outside the chamber to decompose to skeletons during the year, whereupon the bleached bones were laid in the chamber to be transported to the afterlife when the solstice sun fell upon them. After several hundred years of use, it seems that beliefs may have changed and Maeshowe was closed up.

At least 3,000 years passed before there was any further significant occupation. In the mid-12th century, the Vikings arrived, breaking through the roof and leaving a legacy of wall-to-wall runic writing. They used two alphabets: stick-like characters and more fan-shaped writing. The meanings of the runes, including parts written in coded language, thwarted academia for decades until they were unpicked by Professor Michael Barnes, one of the world's foremost runologists. The writing includes references to a woman called Ingeborg who is 'a great show-off'. The Vikings left other imprints, including an intricate and perfect etching of a dragon or a griffin, complete with a foliated tail and pointed ears. A crusader's cross is equally enigmatic.

South of Stenness Across the busy A965 from the Standing Stones of Stenness, a minor lane (signposted to a craft shop) reaches a dead end by a small parking space and the entrance to **Happy Valley** ✳ [89 C5] (**w** orkneycommunities.co.uk/HappyValley), a beautiful miniature woodland (just 7 acres). Framed by drystone walls, the wood includes stone seats and bridges over a gurgling burn. The air is full of birdsong from the gathering of oak, ash and sycamore. The garden is the work of Edwin Harrold, who lived here from 1948 and devoted his life to turning an impoverished sliver of scrubland into one of Orkney's rare woodlands. He actively encouraged Orcadians to visit and enjoy it. Since his death in 2006, the garden has been maintained by volunteers (the Friends of Happy Valley) and is open to all.

About half a mile south of the major sights along the A965 is the less heralded but arguably just as fascinating **Unstan chambered cairn** [89 B5] (**w** tinyurl.com/unstan-cairn). This small mound, similar in shape to Maeshowe, is located on the edge of the Loch of Stenness with dramatic views across to Orphir and Hoy. It's a stunning position but, located next to a working farm, the cairn simultaneously comes across as ordinary, as though it were still in use. Excavated in 1884 and again in 1934, the cairn has had a modern roof installed to keep it from collapsing. Entering is an awkward fit – the passage is so narrow and low that you must waddle or pad through on all fours rather than simply crouch. Inside is a main chamber, subdivided into stalls by upright stone slabs and a smaller chamber that is too tiny to squeeze into. Two crouched skeletons were discovered in this smaller chamber while a jumble of human bones was found in the compartments of the larger chamber. The decorated pottery featuring fine grooved lines found here has given its name to a style known as Unstan ware, though the rationale for them remains unclear – they may have contained food to accompany the dead into the afterworld or served as offerings to the gods.

Orphir and the south The A964 heads southwest out of Kirkwall and offers superb views of Scapa Flow and the Mainland's surprisingly hilly hinterland. The shoreline between Scapa and Stromness is well worth exploring. About 6 miles out of Kirkwall, look for the signposted turn for **Waulkmill Bay** [89 D7], an attractive rump of sand squeezed between the moors of Hobbister and Veness Hill. If you're coming by car, you can park in several places along this lane. Just across from the toilets a stepped path descends to the bay. The sands all but disappear at high tide but the water is considered safe for swimming. The sands are also a wonderful spot for collecting the abundant seashells that get washed up. The head of the bay lies half a mile away by Forkers Gill: to reach it you need to take the narrow track through the gorse by the first small parking space on the lane off the A964 (⊕ HY384075). At the head of the bay lies Orkney's largest area of saltmarsh, which is home to beautiful fronds of sea arrowgrass and sea milkwort. The bay is part of the RSPB's **Hobbister Hill reserve** [89 E6], which you can explore further on a 2-mile circular walk. To start this, walk down the lane past the toilets towards Crook and follow the waymarkers on the left across Hobbister Hill. Where the path begins to loop back along the coast, you may well hear cuckoos in spring by the Burn of Vam. The peat cuttings you pass are the handiwork of the landowner, Highland Park Distillery, which burns the peat to give its whisky a light smoky aroma.

The parish of Orphir – pronounced 'Orfa' – is dominated at ground level by the vastness of Scapa Flow and the Loch of Kirbister and from on high by Ward Hill (883ft/269m) and Mid Hill (897ft/273m). The coast and adjacent hinterland are exceptionally scenic. Even the major road (A964) ploughing through it does not detract from the sense that this is a hidden corner of Orkney. Orphir village is scattered over quite a distance. Just before you reach it from the east, you'll see the **Toumal Gallery** (m 07810 720981; e ingridgrieve@toumalart.co.uk; w toumalart. co.uk; ⊕ Apr–Oct 10.30–17.00 Thu & Fri, other times call ahead) on the right, home to artist Ingrid Grieve. Her studio is ludicrously idyllic: a blue wooden shed with picnic bench and commanding one of Orkney's best views, taking in just about the whole of Scapa Flow right across to Barth Head in South Ronaldsay, with the foreground infilled by Flotta, the background by Hoy. Grieve's trademark paintings of stirring landscapes are deservedly popular and capture scenes of wild weather and dramatically changing light. She took a roundabout route to painting. 'It was something I always wanted to do,' she says. After running the Scorrabrae Inn, she worked as a home care co-ordinator for the Islands Council. 'Someone said to me that I now had a job for life, at which point my heart sank,' she says. She applied for college, dusting off a couple of old paintings from under the bed to impress the admissions officer. 'I was 43 and had no idea where to start,' she admits. Today Grieve works mainly with water-based oils on canvas. Generally, she will go for a walk and take pictures with a camera to work from. Although she explores all of the Mainland, she mainly focuses on Birsay and the Bay of Skaill but has also featured Westray and Hoy. 'I just go for a walk. I see light, colours, a cloud and feel I have to paint it. It's just a feeling that you get.' People are referenced in her paintings though they never feature. 'I will paint a farm that has been there for thousands of years,' she says. 'There's not a lot of detail, it's all about the atmosphere. I like the low landscape you get on Orkney. There are no trees, so you see a lot more. We have sea and lochs around us so the light is somehow reflected more.' But then the day can change. 'I love a good storm,' Grieve admits. 'It makes me quite happy. It can be beautiful, then half an hour later it's just one big black sky, the wind's got up and the waves are crashing on the bay.'

The back road that runs through Scorradale, from Orphir towards Stromness, is a fine touring destination yet little visited. Operating like a chicane for the A964, which it leaves just west of Orphir village and rejoins at Clestrain, west of Houton Pier, the road offers views of the Mainland's moorland scenery that can take you by surprise if you've been focusing on the Neolithic blockbusters by the shores of the lochs of Harray and Stenness. The moors here, a little frustratingly, are not particularly geared up to walking, but a peat track from the side of the road near the pass (✛ HY322965) winds its way for 600yds to the Hill of Midland where you can enjoy commanding views of Scapa Flow, Hoy and Stromness.

COASTAL WALK FROM THE BÚ

Distance: 2 miles; time: 1–1½hrs
Start/finish: Orkneyinga Saga Centre ✛ HY335044
OS Map: Explorer 463 Orkney West Mainland

While in the area you can take in a fine walk along the shores of Scapa Flow. This is a circular route from Orkneyinga Saga Centre to Breck, returning along quiet roads though farmland and woodland. Walk past the Bú, through the cemetery and follow the sign for Breck alongside a stream. Cross the footbridge and keep to the path as it winds around the coast hard above the low cliffs that line Scapa Flow. In spring and summer these cliffs are popular with nesting seabirds. Rocky shores are wonderful for low-tide exploration – look out for crabs, sea anemones, starfish and the slippery butterfish. In winter you will often see rafts of ducks on the inshore waters, in particular gangs of juvenile male eiders, their distinctive lichen-green, black and white plumage just beginning to emerge. The views are tremendous, taking in the hills of Hoy and the eastern boundary of Scapa Flow in the form of the Churchill Barriers and South Ronaldsay. By a field edge, turn right up an open grassy track, waymarked by a post with a cross above a wave. After 200yds turn left along a paved track. The panorama here is glorious with the sweep of Swanbister Bay to your right and the twin peaks of Ward Hill and Akla framing the view ahead. The track passes through a modest yet delightful woodland of sycamore, rowan and contorted beech. Here you can leave the road and follow a winding path for a short while before it returns you to the road. Keep ahead past Gyre Farm on your left, turn left at the junction and follow the road downhill back to the car park.

3

Just south of the A964 lies the unmarked site of the **Battle of Summerdale**. This was the last battle fought on Orkney, on 19 May 1529. James Sinclair led an uprising in protest against feudal land-ownership and took control of Kirkwall Castle. King James V sent an army left by the Sinclairs of Caithness to quell the rebellion but they were wiped out with the Orkney battalion suffering, so the story goes, just the single loss: a young man who dressed in the clothes of a defeated opponent and was killed by his own side in a case of mistaken identity.

In the centre of Orphir village turn left by the war memorial and continue past The Noust (page 91), which serves as pub, post office and accommodation. Where this minor road forks, bear right and you soon come to the **Orkneyinga Saga Centre** [89 D7] (⊕ Apr–Oct 09.00–18.00 daily; free), which has a small but fine exhibition on the great Icelandic tale of Norse life in Orkney (see box, page 35). Rather charmingly, the centre is unstaffed, leaving a 17-minute film to recount juicier bits of the saga, including entertaining tales of the dark deeds committed by the various Jarls (Norse earls). A short stroll behind the centre brings you to the modest remnants of the 12th-century Earl's Bu, which, according to the Norse sagas, was where Earl Haakon Paulsson built his great hall. The lumps and bumps that poke out from under the turf are thought to be part of the earl's drinking hall. Just beyond, within a cemetery that also contains war graves, you reach the modest but historically significant remains of a 12th-century **church**, Orkney's only surviving medieval round church. The unusual shape is thought to be based upon the Church of the Holy Sepulchre in Jerusalem, to where Haakon hurried to atone for his sin of having Magnus murdered on Egilsay (see box, page 188). One theory is that the shape of the church inspired him to have the round church built on his return. The church survived until the 1750s. When it was demolished, a rune-inscribed stone was discovered and later translated as 'the church is not good'.

KIRKWALL

If you arrive on the Mainland at Stromness it is easy to explore the island without even visiting Kirkwall. This would be a pity: while you probably have not selected Orkney to spend your holiday in a town, Kirkwall has a good deal going for it, including an excellent museum that will help join the archaeological dots of many of the sites you visit, along with the unique St Magnus Cathedral and a vibrant nightlife driven by strong musical traditions. With a population of 9,000, Kirkwall can feel decidedly metropolitan after the rest of the Mainland.

The town's Old Norse name of Kirkjuvagr means 'church bay', which is sometimes mistaken to be a reference to St Magnus Cathedral. In fact, the name dates back even further to a kirk built by Norse inhabitants more than 1,000 years ago.

A natural harbour provides a fetching waterfront and an embracing arm round the Bay of Kirkwall. At the centre is the port, where ferries are squeezed in between the town's modest fishing fleet, flanked on either side by a backdrop of hotels, sometimes boisterous bars, B&Bs and industrial estates.

Much of the town is huddled – for weather-related reasons – behind the bulwark of the harbourside hotels. Essentially, two main roads form the frame of Kirkwall's attractions and retain the outline of its medieval street plan. The waterfront comprises the conjoined Shore Street and Harbour Street; meanwhile, running through the heart of the town is a single street that changes its name from Albert Street to Broad Street and Victoria Street. (It's worth noting that while the narrow dimensions and flagstones of parts of this road give the impression of it being pedestrianised, it is in fact open to traffic.)

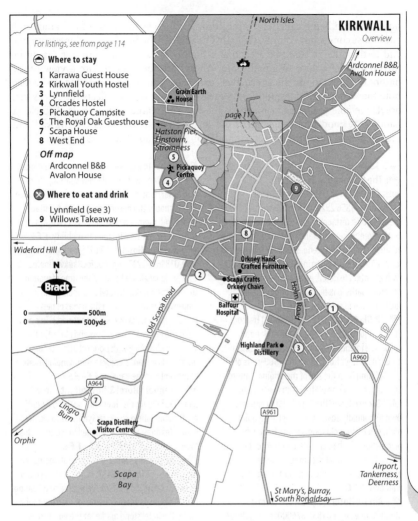

page 117

KIRKWALL
Overview

For listings, see from page 114

⊜ **Where to stay**

1 Karrawa Guest House
2 Kirkwall Youth Hostel
3 Lynnfield
4 Orcades Hostel
5 Pickaquoy Campsite
6 The Royal Oak Guesthouse
7 Scapa House
8 West End

Off map
 Ardconnel B&B
 Avalon House

✖ **Where to eat and drink**

 Lynnfield (see 3)
9 Willows Takeaway

Wideford Hill

N

Bradt

0 ————— 500m
0 ————— 500yds

North Isles

Ardconnel B&B,
Avalon House

Grain Earth
House

Hatston Pier,
Finstown,
Stromness

Pickaquoy
Centre

Orkney Hand
Crafted Furniture

Scapa Crafts
Orkney Chairs

Balfour
Hospital

Highland Park
Distillery

Old Scapa Road

Holm Road

A960

A964

Lingro
Burn

Orphir

Scapa Distillery
Visitor Centre

A961

Scapa
Bay

St Mary's, Burray,
South Ronaldsay

Airport,
Tankerness,
Deerness

The Mainland KIRKWALL

3

In contrast to its tight-knit centre, Kirkwall has a surprisingly sprawling hinterland punctuated by a suburban layout of functional and austere pebble-dash architecture. Although a few B&Bs can be found away from the harbour, the waterside and vicinity are where you will spend the majority of your time in the town.

GETTING AROUND Kirkwall's centre is compact and everything you might wish to see and do is within easy walking distance. St Magnus Cathedral, for example, is a 10-minute walk from the North Isle ferry terminal. The only location not so easily reached on foot is the Hatston Pier terminal (for ferries to Shetland and Aberdeen); an integrated bus service takes passengers to and collects them from the ferries as they arrive and depart. The bus starts and finishes at the Kirkwall Travel Centre.

WHERE TO STAY The striking feature about accommodation in Kirkwall – as across Orkney more widely – is that few of its hotels are purpose-built: most began life as anything from hospitals to schools and residential homes. Accordingly, the town's hotels end up being called anything from 'distinctive' to 'quirky' to 'characterful' and, most commonly, 'quintessentially Orcadian'. A bedroom may slope from one end to the other, a staircase ascend at a slightly rakish tilt, a promising wardrobe turn out to be a door to a bathroom. Always ask for a room with a view of the harbour or the moors; the alternatives may leave you staring at pebble-dash. Also note that 'top range' does not always mean 'best' but rather reflects the prices that hotels are able to charge as business guests form a large part of their clientele. A handful of good mid-range B&Bs are located on the outskirts of Kirkwall, but included here. Self-catering accommodation can be found at w orkney.com.

Top range

🏠 **The Storehouse Restaurant with Rooms** [117 D4] (8 rooms) Bridge St Wynd; 📞01856 252250; e info@ thestorehouserestaurantwithrooms.co.uk; w thestorehouserestaurantwithrooms.co.uk. New addition to Kirkwall's scene, set inside a converted former 19th-century herring store. Furnished with attention to detail, eg: walk-in showers or generous baths, oak flooring & original features such as wooden supports. **£££**

🏠 **St Ola Hotel** [117 C2] (6 rooms) Harbour St; 📞01856 875090; e enquiries@stolahotel. co.uk; w stolahotel.co.uk. Pint-sized but smart hotel on harbour front. More than 500 years old, this building is on the site of the original 'Inns of Sinclair', built by one of the Scottish earls who ruled Orkney during the 14th & 15th centuries. Owners candidly advise those seeking a quiet night's sleep to avoid rooms at the back, which, being above the bar, are often noisy into the small hours. The 2 rooms at the front are quieter & have gorgeous views over the harbour through bay windows. **£££**

🏠 **Albert Hotel** [117 C3] (18 rooms) Mounthoolie Ln; 📞01856 876000; e enquiries@ alberthotel.co.uk; w alberthotel.co.uk. This well-run hotel benefited from a fire 10 years ago that required a rebuild across 3 floors (confusingly, lift buttons still go up to 9th floor) & means all rooms on the second floor have a stylish, dormer & loft feel. Striking 3-cornered exterior belies a large building (comparison with a Tardis is readily made). Mixture of twins & dbls. 1 room on 2nd floor suitable for travellers with limited mobility issues & includes a wet room. Pick is the superior deluxe with balcony. All rooms en suite. **££–£££**

🏠 **The Ayre Hotel** [117 B3] (51 rooms) Ayre Rd; 📞01865 873001; e info@ayrehotel.co.uk; w ayrehotel.co.uk. Probably the closest thing Kirkwall has to a conventional purpose-built hotel. The hotel wing was added a few years ago to the pub & bar; it makes for a good, comfortable choice. Tidy & thoughtful décor including art & vintage photos. All rooms en suite. 1 dbl & 1 twin apt suitable for guests with limited mobility. **£££**

🏠 **Kirkwall Hotel** [117 C2] (36 rooms) Harbour St; 📞01856 872232; e enquiries@kirkwallhotel. com; w kirkwallhotel.com. At the time of writing the landmark Kirkwall Hotel was undergoing long-overdue renovation in the hands of new owners (but it remains open for business). This may finally do justice to Kirkwall's 'grand old lady': the sandstone building, with Doric columns standing guard at its entrance, enjoys a commanding location at the centre of the harbour. **££–£££**

🏠 **Lynnfield Hotel & Restaurant** [map, page 113] (10 rooms) Holm Rd; 📞01856 872505; e office@lynnfield.co.uk; w lynnfield.co.uk. Rated 4-star; features antiques & panelled lounges. Close to Highland Park distillery. **££–£££**

🏠 **The Orkney Hotel** [117 B6] (30 rooms) 40 Victoria St; 📞01856 873477; e info@orkneyhotel. co.uk; w orkneyhotel.co.uk. Venerable hotel dating to 1670, built as a family home for merchant John Richa; the lintel stone marker at the entrance is carved with his initials. Do not be put off by the functional entrance. Inside, the hotel blooms into a wide lobby & grand staircase. Running over 3 floors, narrow corridors eventually wind their way to rooms. The pick is the 4-poster (room 213); some rooms are more spacious, with prices to reflect this. **££–£££**

🏠 **The Shore** [117 D2] (17 rooms) Shore St; 📞01856 872200; e eatandstay@theshore.co.uk; w theshore.co.uk. Comfortable, modern & fully equipped rooms, all en suite. Bright larger rooms at the front are a good choice for families & have harbour views. Snug lounge with fire a good choice for a quiet drink before dinner. Recommended. **££–£££**

Mid range

⌂ **Avalon House** [89 G5] (5 rooms) Carness Rd; ☎01856 876665; e enquiries@avalon-house. co.uk; w avalon-house.co.uk. 4-star with 2 dbls, 2 twins, 1 family room. Another lovely choice, set back from the shore (but no sea views) a mile from Kirkwall. Run by Marina Anderson & Mike Findlay. Cosy, spacious rooms with plush bedding. B/fast room adorned with Mike's impressive canvas landscape prints of Orkney. Small snug corner contains books & information. **££–£££**

⌂ **West End Hotel** [map, page 113] (10 rooms) 14 Main St; ☎01856 872368; e info@ westendkirkwall.co.uk; w westendkirkwall.co.uk. Rather charming hotel in a Georgian building with filigree balcony over the entrance. Just 10mins walk from town centre. Run by same team as the St Ola Hotel & recently renovated. Full of quirky recesses & ample character. Medical bits & bobs in the lounge pay homage to the hotel's 1840s incarnation as Kirkwall's 1st hospital. Pick of the rooms is spacious Richan suite with its superking-sized bed. 1 room suitable for guests with limited mobility. **££–£££**

⌂ **Ardconnel B&B** [89 G5] (4 rooms) Craigiefield Rd; ☎01856 876786; m 07725 565943; e ardconnel@hotmail.co.uk; w bed-and-breakfast-kirkwall.co.uk. Excellent B&B run by Theresa Guthrie & Norman Kelday. All rooms warm, homely & well appointed. Guest lounge with TV for guests' use; hearty b/fasts. Beautiful location a mile east of town, with views over harbour & Whiteford Hill. Surrounding fields often full of curlews & geese. Owners very good company & helpful: will alert you if cruise ship is in town & suggest sights off the beaten track to ensure a quiet day's sightseeing. Norman is also the proud owner of the 2011 Ba' (see box, page 59). 1 room suitable for guests with limited mobility. **££**

⌂ **Karrawa Guest House** [map, page 113] (6 rooms) Inganess Rd; ☎01865 871100; e stay@karrawaguesthouseorkney.co.uk; w karrawaguesthouseorkney.co.uk. Cosily & immaculately furnished guesthouse, located on A960 airport road, a mile south of town centre. Run

by ever-helpful Albert & Aileen Bruce. All rooms en suite, with TV & Wi-Fi. 1 room downstairs suitable for less mobile guests & has ramp access. Family room sleeps 4 but can squeeze in camp bed for a 3rd child. **££**

⌂ **The Royal Oak Guesthouse** [map, page 113] (8 rooms) Holm Rd; ☎01856 877177; e info@ stayinkirkwall.co.uk; w stayinkirkwall.co.uk. All rooms en suite. B/fasts can be enjoyed from a dining room overlooking Scapa Flow. Mix of sgls, dbls, twins & family room. **££**

⌂ **Scapa House** [map, page 113] (3 rooms) St Ola; ☎01856 874639; e bs.wylie39@btinternet. com. Modern & smartly furnished. Although 2 miles from town centre, location is good, being just a short walk from Scapa Beach & adjacent to Scapa distillery. **££**

Budget

⌂ **Kirkwall Youth Hostel** [map, page 113] Old Scapa Rd; ☎01856 872243; e kirkwall@ hostellingscotland.org.uk; w tinyurl.com/kirkwall-youth-hostel. Mix of shared & private rooms. **£**

⌂ **Orcades Hostel** [map, page 113] Muddisdale Rd; ☎01856 873745; e orcadeshostel@hotmail.co.uk; w orcadeshostel. co.uk. Secluded with own small, neatly tended grounds. Mix of twins & dbls. Located by Pickaquoy Centre. **£**

⌂ **The Peedie Hostel** [117 A3] (8 rooms) Ayre Houses; ☎01856 875477; e kirkwallpeediehostel@ talk21.com; w stayinkirkwall.co.uk. Former fishermen's cottages recently renovated to high standard. Mixture of sgls, twins & 4-bed rooms, with 3 kitchens & 3 bathrooms. Small but comfortable lounge on 1st floor with one of the best sea views in town. **£**

Camping

⋏ **Pickaquoy Campsite** [map, page 113] Pickaquoy Centre; ☎01856 879900; e campsite@ pickaquoy.com; w pickaquoy.campmanager.com. Large site with 80 pitches including 30 hook-ups. Just a pity it's not more rural. **£**

✗ **WHERE TO EAT AND DRINK** Dining in Kirkwall is pretty egalitarian. Even places that come close to or achieve fine dining don't seek to match the quality of food with ludicrous prices or over-polished service. You will eat well at some of the hotels but almost as splendidly in one or two of the cafés. If it's pub grub you're after, you will not be short of options.

Expensive

✖ Garden View and Royal Cask [117 B6]
Same contacts as hotel; ◷ noon–14.00 &
17.30–19.30 daily. The Orkney Hotel boasts 2
eateries: the more casual Royal Cask downstairs
& the formal 1st-floor Garden View restaurant.
Same menu in both, including starters such as
Grimbister cheese fritters & mains such as chicken
in whisky & pepper marmalade as well as Orkney
lamb. The hotel also offers an extraordinary
5-course whisky-tasting menu, taking in 5 malts
between steaks & other dishes. Advance booking
only (£130). **££–£££**

✖ Harbour View [117 C2] Same contacts as
hotel; ◷ noon–16.00 & 18.00–21.00 daily. The
restaurant at the Kirkwall Hotel serves top-class
cuisine including Kirkwall crab-cake starters, mains
of local monkfish with Thai spices & puds such as
'Shorkney', combining raspberry mousse, mint &
shortbread. If you still have room, sign off with an
ensemble of Orkney cheeses, including Grimbister
& Westray Wife. In high season, book up to 2 weeks
ahead. **££–£££**

✖ Lynnfield Hotel [map, page 113] Same
contacts as hotel; ◷ noon–14.00 & 18.00–20.30
daily. Highly regarded restaurant. Menu light on its
feet, ranging from spiced sweet-potato samosas to
house special Holmy Lamb, which comes roasted or
in a stew. Offers 70-bin wine list. **££–£££**

✖ The Shore Hotel [117 D2] Same contacts as
hotel; ◷ 17.30–20.30 daily. The Shore's restaurant
is truly excellent; chefs get to show their flair.
Starters include haddock risotto or Orkney crab
tartlets while mains range from monkfish with
asparagus wrapped in Parma ham to scallops with
crab linguini. The Belgian chocolate tart with local
ice cream will send you waddling on your way.
Not cheap but a good choice for a special occasion.
££–£££

**✖ The Storehouse Restaurant with
Rooms** [117 D4] Same contacts as hotel;
◷ 10.00–22.00 Mon–Sat, 11.00–22.00 Sun. Top-
notch fine dining including starters of Orkney beef
carpaccio followed by chorizo & bean cassoulet
with Westray salmon. Desserts range from lemon
tart to classic Orkney ice-cream sundae. Vegan &
gluten-free options. **££–£££**

Mid range

✖ The Ayre Hotel [117 B3] Same contacts
as hotel; ◷ noon–14.00 & 18.00–21.00 daily.

Serves standard fare, eg: scampi, lasagne & steaks
(£11–24). If there are no cars parked in front, the
conservatory annexe at front offers views over the
harbour & sea walls. **££–£££**

✖ Neuk [117 C3] Same contacts as Albert Hotel;
◷ noon–14.00 & 17.00–21.00 daily. Menu ranges
from pizzas to seafood pie & pizzas. **££–£££**

✖ St Ola [117 C2] Same contacts as hotel;
◷ noon–21.00 Sun–Fri, noon–02.00 Sat. The
ground floor of the St Ola has recently had a facelift
to good effect. Among the few hotels to serve food
all day. Good food in bright & breezy surroundings
including chive fishcakes (£6.50); chorizo & black
pudding salad (£9), burgers, fish & chips etc. Serve
b/fast rolls (£2.45) ◷ 10.00–15.00 Sat & Sun.
Adjacent snug bar serves real ales, 9 whiskies & 13
gins. Photos of local ships in high seas will make
your environs seem that little bit cosier. **££**

✖ The Real Food Café & Restaurant [117 B5]
25 Broad St; ☏ 01856 874225; e info@judithglue.
com; ◷ 09.00–18.00 Mon–Sat, 10.00–18.00 Sun;
Jun–Aug until 21.00. At the back of the Judith Glue
shop (page 119) & open the same hours. Good
sandwiches, taster board of Hickory ham, smoked

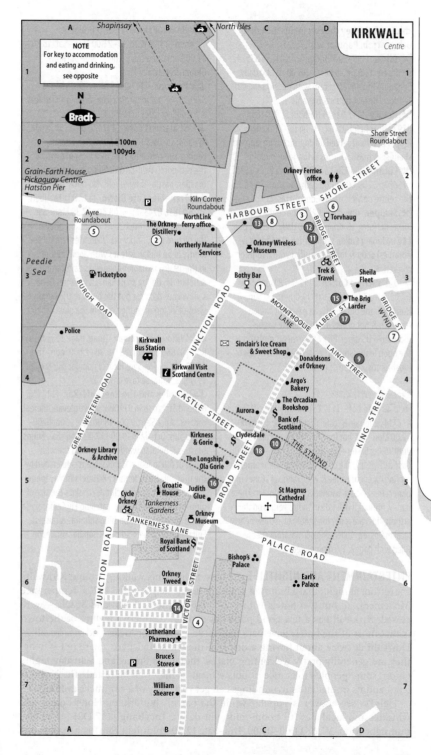

KIRKWALL
Centre

NOTE
For key to accommodation
and eating and drinking,
see opposite

Bradt

N

0 _____ 100m
0 _____ 100yds

Shapinsay

North Isles

Shore Street
Roundabout

*Grain-Earth House,
Pickaquoy Centre,
Hatston Pier*

Orkney Ferries
office

SHORE STREET

HARBOUR STREET

Kiln Corner
Roundabout

Ayre
Roundabout
⑤

The Orkney
Distillery
②

NorthLink
ferry office

Northerly Marine
Services

⑬ ⑧   ③
        ⑫
        ⑪

⑥ Torvhaug

BRIDGE STREET

*Peedie
Sea*

🏠 Ticketyboo

Orkney Wireless
Museum

Bothy Bar
①

Trek &
Travel

Sheila
Fleet

⑮ • The Brig
      Larder
⑰

BRIDGE ST

⑦

BURGH ROAD

JUNCTION ROAD

MOUNTHOOLIE
LANE

ALBERT ST

LAING STREET

• Police

Kirkwall
Bus Station

Kirkwall Visit
Scotland Centre

✉ Sinclair's Ice Cream
   & Sweet Shop

Donaldsons
of Orkney

Argo's
Bakery

⑨

KING STREET

GREAT WESTERN ROAD

CASTLE STREET

Aurora •

• The Orcadian
  Bookshop

Bank of
Scotland $

Orkney Library
& Archive

Kirkness
& Gorie

Clydesdale $

⑱ ⑩

THE STRYND

The Longship/
Ola Gorie
⑯

Cycle
Orkney
🚲

Groatie
House

*Tankerness
Gardens*

Judith
Glue

BROAD STREET

St Magnus
Cathedral
✝

TANKERNESS LANE

Orkney
Museum

Royal Bank
of Scotland $

PALACE ROAD

JUNCTION ROAD

Orkney
Tweed

VICTORIA STREET

Bishop's
Palace

Earl's
Palace

⑭

④

Sutherland
Pharmacy ✚

P

Bruce's
Stores •

William
Shearer •

chicken & Orkney cheese; mains including Orkney crab. Popular with locals. £–££

✗ **Dil Se** [117 C3] 7 Bridge St; ☎01856 875242; w dilserestaurant.co.uk; ⏲ 16.00–23.00 daily. Engaging Indian restaurant with decent range of Tandoori dishes, baltis & biryanis. £

✗ **Helgi's** [117 C2] 14 Harbour St; ☎01856 879293; w helgis.co.uk; ⏲ noon–21.00 daily. Proper pub food served all day, including smoked shellfish & mash; churros & fudge for pudding. £

✗ **Lucano** [117 B6] 31–33 Victoria St; ☎01865 875687; ⏲ 09.00–21.00 daily. Tucked away from the centre on Victoria St. Good pizzas. £

✗ **Skippers Bar** [117 C2] Same contacts as Kirkwall Hotel; ⏲ noon–21.00 daily. Decent pub fare including Cullen skink (smoked haddock & potatoes) soup & tortillas stuffed with haggis or chicken. £

✳ 🍴 **Archive Coffee** [117 D4] 8 Laing St; ⏲ 08.30–17.00 Mon–Sat, 11.00–16.00 Sun. Housed in the old library, an excellent choice for lunch & hot drinks in atmosphere vaguely recalling a US diner. Pick of the meals probably the open leafy sandwiches layered with heaps of mushrooms, cheese or meats. £–££

Cheap and cheerful

✳ 🍴 **Café Lolz** [117 C5] The Strynd; ☎01856 877714; e lorraine@cafelolzat21.co.uk; ⏲ 10.00–17.00 Mon–Sat, hot food noon–14.00, cold food until 15.00; Easter–Sep also open 11.00–15.00 Sun. Cosy café (Lolz is the owner Lorraine's nickname) serving excellent coffee & wide range of scones (inc gluten-free) & bere bannocks made from local bere barley. Although deli side of things verges on artisan, this café is not too snooty to eschew hearty local mains, eg: Cullen skink & macaroni cheese filled with haggis. Recommended. £

🍴 **Harbour Fry** [117 C3] 5 Bridge St; ⏲ noon–14.00 & 16.30–21.00 Mon–Sat, 16.30–21.00 Sun. Good fish & chips, large portions. Gluten-free available. £

🍴 **Pomona** [117 D3] 9 Albert St; ☎01856 872325; w pomonacafe.co.uk. Among the oldest & friendliest cafés in town. £

🍴 **St Magnus Café** [117 B5] Broad St; ☎01856 873354; ⏲ 09.30–15.30 Mon–Sat. Friendly council-run café offers the best view in town of the cathedral. Well-priced, filling fare including toasties, pasties & filled rolls. No cards. £

🍴 **Trenabies Café Bistro** [117 D3] 16 Albert St; ☎01856 874336; ⏲ 08.30–17.30 Mon–Sat. Charming café. If the bas-relief designs above the picture rails, brickwork & cubicles remind you faintly of an Italian café it's with good reason. In the 1930s, Trenabies opened as Café Central & Gelateria, run by an Italian, Livio Zanre. Good sandwiches & coffee but the best are the huge slabs of Victorian sponge cake in the glass cabinet. £

🍴 **Willows Takeaway** [map, page 113] Willow Rd; ☎01856 875371; ⏲ 16.30–22.00 Mon–Thu, 16.30–22.45 Fri–Sun. Hugely popular fish & chips as well as Chinese take-away. £

🍴 **Wrigley and The Reel Café/Bar** [117 C5] 6 Broad St; ☎01856 971000; w wrigleyandthereel.com; ⏲ Apr–Sep 09.00–18.00 Mon–Sat, 10.00–17.00 Sun; Oct–Mar 10.00–17.00 Mon–Sat. Soups, toasties & Belgian waffles are among the wide range of filling foods at this vibrant café owned by the musical sisters Jennifer & Hazel Wrigley (page 35). Snacks & nibbles including cookies the size of ping-pong bats & the eye-catching Fly Cemetery (a baked shortbread entombing sultanas & raisins). Full range of coffees & teas. A popular venue for live music. £

ENTERTAINMENT AND NIGHTLIFE It's hard to imagine, walking around Kirkwall's shorefront at night, that a hundred years ago, at the height of the 1920s' Temperance Movement, all but two hotels with public bars – the Kirkwall and St Ola – were closed. Kirkwall has a few good pubs but another distinctive feature of the town is that most of the hotels have bars that serve as pubs for locals and visitors alike. Don't think twice about having a drink in the bar somewhere you're not staying: they are generally pretty welcoming places, though as Friday and Saturday nights go on, some people's tolerance of boisterousness may well be tested. The harbour front and its immediate surroundings can get very busy of a summer's evening.

Helgi's (see above) is popular while the bar of the Orkney Hotel boasts 900 whiskies and local ales (⏲ noon–midnight daily). **Torvhaug** [117 D2] (⏲ 11.00–midnight Mon–Wed, 11.00–01.00 Thu–Sat, 12.30–midnight Sun) is a traditional bar, just across the narrow neck of Bridge Street from **Skippers Bar** (see opposite); both offer the full range of liver-ticklers and get lively as the night goes on. The front bar at the **Ayre Hotel** has a licence for children, so it generally has a relaxed ambience with local beers and pool tables.

A little further from the harbour, and part of the Albert Hotel building, is the **Bothy Bar** [117 C3] (⏱ 11.00–midnight Mon–Wed, 11.00–01.00 Thu–Sat, noon–midnight Sun; over-18s only). Don't be deterred by the formidable solid door, as it leads into a half-timbered snug offering real ales and music most Sunday evenings. You can eat here (same menu and hours as Neuk; page 116).

For **Orcadian music**, you should definitely gravitate to Wrigley and The Reel Café/Bar (see opposite), which hosts the Orkney Accordion and Fiddle Club on Wednesdays and the Orkney Strathspey and Reel Society on Thursdays, the latter offering faster tunes and jigs. The Reel opens up the stage to anyone who wants to play on Saturday (⏱ 20.00–late) while on the second Friday of the month it hosts a song night. In May and June the **Orkney Traditional Music Project** (w otmp. co.uk) holds lunchtime concerts every Saturday in St Magnus Cathedral. Regular concerts and entertainment are held at the Pickaquoy Centre (w pickaquoy.co.uk) while **The Sound Archive** (8 Laing St; same details as Archive Coffee; see opposite) occasionally puts on live music and events.

SHOPPING There's a good deal more to Kirkwall than shops oriented to the cruise market – although those most certainly do exist.

Aurora [117 C4] 69 Albert St; ☎01856 871521; w aurora-jewellery.com; ⏱ Apr–Sep 09.00–17.30 Mon–Sat, noon–16.00 Sun; Oct–Mar 09.30–17.00 Mon–Sat. Showroom for the work of local silversmith Steven Cooper whose designs include eye-catching Viking galleys & seabird earrings.

Judith Glue [117 B5] 25 Broad St; same contacts as The Real Food Café & Restaurant (page 116); ⏱ 09.00–18.00 Mon–Sat, 10.00–18.00 Sun. Wide range of souvenirs from Orkney & beyond.

The Longship/Ola Gorie [117 C5] 7–15 Broad St; ☎01856 888790; w olagoriejewellery.com; ⏱ 09.30–17.15 Mon–Sat. 2 conjoined & joint-owned shops straddling a narrow alleyway. The Longship sells wide mixture of fabrics, throws, pottery & other crafts, while Ola Gorie sells high-quality jewellery by local silversmiths.

✴ **The Orcadian Bookshop** [117 C4] 50 Albert St; ☎01856 878000; e bookshop@orcadian.co.uk; w orcadian.co.uk; ⏱ 09.00–17.00 Mon–Fri, 10.00–17.00 Sat. A truly outstanding bookshop & the go-to place for books produced by the ever-excellent Kirkwall publishers. Also stocks wide range of fiction & there's a small art gallery on the 2nd floor. An immensely reassuring place for bookshop fans who fear for their fate in an era of online shopping.

The Orkney Distillery [117 B3] Ayre Rd; ☎01865 875338; e info@orkneydistilling.com; w orkneydistilling.com; ⏱ tours noon & 14.00 Mon–Sat, £8–£15. Purveyors of Kirkjuvagr Orkney Gin; the latest distillery to open its doors in Orkney.

Orkney Tweed [117 B6] 23 Victoria St; ☎01856 872063; e nancy@orkneytweed.co.uk; w orkneytweed.co.uk; ⏱ 10.30–16.00 Mon–Sat. Stylish & modern: think baseball caps as well as flat caps.

Scapa Crafts Orkney Chairs [map, page 113] 12 Scapa Court; ☎01856 872517; e Jackie@ scapacrafts.co.uk; w scapacrafts.co.uk; ⏱ 09.00–17.00 Mon–Fri, 09.00–noon Sat. Walking half a mile south from the town centre leads you to Kirkwall's hive of furniture making, home to Jackie & Marlene Miller, who have been making bespoke Orkney chairs for the best part of 30 years (see box, page 38). Pretty much across the road you will find **Orkney Hand Crafted Furniture** (Dellovo, New Scapa Rd; ☎01856 872492; m 07742 428727; e fraser@orkneyhandcraftedfurniture.co.uk; w orkneyhandcraftedfurniture.co.uk; ⏱ 09.00–17.00 Mon–Sat), the workshop of Fraser Anderson. Both craft shops welcome visitors.

Sheila Fleet [117 D3] 30 Bridge St; ⏱ 09.00–17.00 Mon–Sat. Kirkwall showroom for one of Orkney's major jewellers (page 128).

Food shopping While national supermarket chains have a presence in Kirkwall you will find local stores proudly selling island and UK-wide produce. All those mentioned below broadly open standard hours in the week and on Saturdays.

Argo's Bakery [117 C4] 44 Albert St. Serves hot soup to take away as well as a formidable range of brownie-type delights & biscuits.

The Brig Larder [117 D3] w jollysoforkney. co.uk. On the corner of Bridge St and Albert St is Orkney's largest deli, stocking local produce as well as foodie treats from across the UK and Europe. 3 shops operate under its roof: **Craigies** serves meats including chicken & steak pies, & bacon & cheddar sausages; **Scott & Miller** sells high-quality wines; & **Jollys of Orkney** is a seafood specialist where you can pick up smoked salmon, fresh oysters (£1.10 each) & frozen meals (handy if self-catering), which include lasagne or quiches for 2 (£5.25) & desserts such as Orkney fudge cheesecake (£4.75; contains 4 servings). Jollys also sells local oatcakes, chutneys, jams & locally roasted coffee.

Bruce's Stores [117 B7] 55 Victoria St. Another local independent store selling fresh sandwiches, local bread & beer.

Donaldsons of Orkney [117 C4] 38 Albert St; w donaldsonsoforkney.co.uk. This butchers is a firm favourite with locals & sells its own cured bacon & sausages & also makes black pudding & even Parma-style ham.

Kirkness & Gorie [117 B5] 7–15 Broad St; w kirknessandgorie.com. A smaller alternative to The Brig Larder, but just as well stocked with local produce (from fudge to local beer), this is squeezed down an alleyway between the Longship/Ola Gore outlets. It is run by Duncan McLean, who also runs the Orkney Wine Festival (w kirknessandgorie.com/orkney-wine-festival) every May, so it is no surprise that his shelves are also replete with extremely good and vintage wines.

Sinclair's Ice Cream & Sweet Shop [117 C4] 37 Albert St; ⊕ May–Sep 09.00–17.00 Mon–Wed, 09.00–20.00 Thu–Sat, noon–16.00 Sun; Oct–Apr 09.00–17.00 Mon–Sat. Good old-fashioned sweet shop, worth knowing about if you're a family. Upstairs is a small parlour café serving soups, milkshakes & smoothies.

William Shearer [117 B7] 71 Victoria St; w williamshearer.co.uk. This is worth a visit for the insight it offers into the needs of islanders when it comes to agricultural & fishing equipment.

OTHER PRACTICALITIES Several **banks** with cash machines can be found along Albert Street and Victoria Street. These include Bank of Scotland, Royal Bank of Scotland and Clydesdale Bank.

✚ **Balfour Hospital** [map, page 113] New Scapa Rd; ☎ 01856 888000; w ohb.scot.nhs.uk. 10mins' walk from town centre. New hospital being built 400yds further down the road.

✚ **Sutherland Pharmacy** [117 B7] 43 Victoria St; ⊕ 09.30–17.30 Mon–Sat

✉ **Post office** [117 B4] 15 Junction Rd; ⊕ 09.00–17.00 Mon & Wed–Fri, 09.30–17.00 Tue, 09.30–12.30 Sat

Police [117 A4] Burgh Rd; ☎ 01786 289070

Petrol [117 A3] Ticketyboo, Ayre service station ⊕ 08.00–20.00 Mon–Sat, 13.00–17.00 Sun; automatic pump 24hrs. Also specialises in selling

prams. In answer to the obvious question, the owner replies: 'we had a big space to fill, so we looked around to see what wasn't being sold in town'. A good example of how Orcadian quick thinking has long seen the islands through thick & thin.

Other amenities Public toilets are on the waterfront between Shore St Roundabout & the ferry office [117 D2]. Kirkwall Swimming Pool is on Willow Rd, & there's another one in the sports centre (& cinema!) complex at the Pickaquoy Centre (Muddisdale Rd; w pickaquoy.co.uk).

WHAT TO SEE AND DO Kirkwall's oldest and most venerable sites are clustered around the junction of Albert Street and Palace Road.

St Magnus Cathedral [117 C5] (**w** stmagnus.org; ⊕ Apr–Sep 09.00–18.00 Mon–Sat, 13.00–18.00 Sun; Oct–Mar 09.00–13.00 & 14.00–17.00 Mon–Sat, Sun service 11.15; donation requested) With a spire that can be seen from out in the Bay of Kirkwall, this cathedral represents the historical and cultural heart of the town. The cathedral was founded in 1137 by Earl Rognvald, nephew of St Magnus, and is dedicated to the eponymous 11th-century earl, who was canonised upon his murder. Originally part of the Archdiocese of Nidaros (modern-day Trondheim in Norway), the cathedral was given to the people of Kirkwall by King James III of Scotland after Orkney became part of Scotland in 1468. At the time, it was located close to the foreshore, to make getting stone to the site straightforward; over the

---

CHAIRS OF STRAW   *With thanks to Jeanette Park for historical information.*

Chair-making is a distinctively Orcadian craft, rooted – to some extent literally – in the earth of the island. A visit to the Kirkwall workshop of Jackie and Marlene Miller, who have been making bespoke chairs from driftwood, straw and oak for nearly 30 years, shows why this is the case. They welcome visitors and will invariably be working on a chair when you arrive.

Each Orkney chair is bespoke and easy on the eye, thanks to wooden legs and arms and knitted-straw backing. There are three basic designs: a low rounded stool; the low-backed chair, which rises to the shoulder; and the hooded chair, or Heided-Steul (from 'heid', the local word for 'head', and 'steul', from the Old Norse for stool).

The reality is that Orkney chairs were nothing special to 19th-century Orcadians; they were simply the logical thing to make from materials to hand. All were easy chairs, pulled in front of the croft hearth on a cold night. Chairs that rose to the shoulders or higher gave protection against draughts as straw is an ideal insulator that retains body heat; this way a man could rest his weary body after a day on the fields. The arms of the chairs can seem low but were the perfect height for women's chores, for example allowing easy movement of the elbows for knitting. They also gave an unhindered view of the room, of children playing and the pot bubbling on the fire. Due to the lack of trees on Orkney, driftwood was often used and still occasionally pops up. One log, a Douglas fir, was washed up on the Mainland and identified as having come from a tree on the west coast of the United States. 'That tree certainly had a story,' says Jackie. 'Orkney houses were quite poorly insulated and draughty; these chairs kept the wind out,' says Jackie, patting the back of one. 'You are nice and cosy sitting in these.'

The chairs got a boost from the Arts and Crafts movement, whose idiom was 'truth to materials' and quality craftsmanship. Interest in them grew after May Morris, daughter of William Morris, a founder of the Arts and Crafts Movement, visited Orkney.

Today they are made from imported oak or walnut and finished with linseed oil. Nothing is wasted. The discarded chaff from the straw is given to a farmer for bedding, the oats for the hens; in return the Millers get eggs.

A chair takes up to three weeks to make and orders come from all over the world. With prices starting at £1,100, they are not cheap but when you factor in the labour and skill involved, it's clear why costs are higher than at your local furniture centre. 'It just takes time,' says Jackie. 'It's very hands on, it's delicate work, you can't rush it. It matters, there is a history to it.'

centuries, land reclamation means it now stands 500yds away from the sea. Today, St Magnus is a parish church of the Presbyterian Church of Scotland, and therefore technically no longer a cathedral.

The cathedral is a striking building made from red and yellow sandstone. The outstanding handiwork is thought partly attributable to the involvement of the stonemasons who built the exquisite cathedral at Durham. The masons left their insignias around the cathedral and volunteers will help you pick out ravens, green men (sculpted faces of deities and sprites), dragons, a squatting female figure known as a Sheela-na-gig and a crow's foot.

The cathedral also gives you a glimpse into the intense pride you find across Orkney. Wandering around, you will find the accumulated equivalent of Poets' Corner in Westminster Abbey – memorials to George Mackay Brown (see box, page 37), Eric Linklater, Edwin Muir and Robert Rendall. Elsewhere there are striking carvings including the tomb of Dr John Rae (see box, page 84), who discovered the Northwest Passage (his grave, to the rear of the cemetery, is more nondescript).

The cathedral is an intensely atmospheric building: details include the unsettling Mort Bord (depicting death in a shroud) that dangles from a pillar; the brass bell recovered from HMS *Royal Oak*, which sank in Scapa Flow in 1939; a 13th-century gravestone; and arched tombs and headstones that line the walls on either side of the nave, transept and chapel.

Historically this was a popular place of pilgrimage and a square pillar just to the right of the organ is said to house St Magnus's bones, which were transported from Birsay to Kirkwall in the 1150s (some say the apparent injuries to the skull do not match those described in the *Orkneyinga Saga*, which recounts Magnus's death; see box, page 35). There's a fine stained-glass window halfway up the north transept which depicts St Magnus holding a green palm frond (a symbol of martyrdom). The beautiful west window, though dating to only 1987, is equally impressive and depicts an axe (the weapon used to kill Magnus) at the top of its arch. On the south side of the choir, look above head height for the unsettling Marwick's Hole, a dungeon where women accused of witchcraft were held.

It's definitely worth taking the guided tours to the top ($\oplus$ 11.00 & 14.00 Tue & Thu; £8; 1hr) for the view of the town, surrounding landscape and islands.

Bishop's and Earl's palaces [117 C6] (w historicenvironment.scot; $\oplus$ Apr–Sep 09.30–17.30 daily; £5/3) Across Palace Road from the cathedral stand these two ruins, which are equally impressive in different ways, though you need to put your imagination to harder work to envisage the **Bishop's Palace** as it originally looked. Founded in the 12th century, around the same time as the cathedral, Bishop's Palace is by some 500 years the older of the two. This was the grand residence of the medieval bishops of Orkney and built to the same design as the Haakon Hall in Bergen (Norway). The most outstanding features remaining are the circular tower and, internally, a spiral staircase that leads to a striking viewpoint over the town (be warned that the staircase terminates abruptly, with just a low barrier separating you from thin air). A small road, Watergate, separates the two palaces; the arch that once stood over the road was removed, turned sideways and inserted into the walls of the Bishop's Palace in 1877 when the lane was widened.

The neighbouring **Earl's Palace** is more visually impressive. With its fractured gables abruptly fronting thin air and remains of projecting oriel windows, it is very much in the style of the French Renaissance. It's worth exploring inside to take in the atmospheric dungeons and impressive central hall. For all its opulence, the Earl's Palace was built from the traditional materials of vanity and falsehoods

– anything, in fact other than money. The palace was the prized domain of Earl Patrick, the illegitimate cousin of Scotland's James VI (James I of England). Patrick was nicknamed 'Black Patie' for good reason. A man whose income was unable to support his opulent tastes, he instead commanded the building of the palace on the back of menace and aggression (some historians play down his infamy, pointing out that, like the Vikings, his history was recorded by his worst enemies). The palace was completed in 1605 but Patrick had little time to enjoy it as he was ordered to hand it over to the authorities in 1607 and later imprisoned. He was indicted for treason, along with murder, oppression and thefts of land in 1610 and accordingly lost his head in 1615. His demise marked the end of the last ruler of Orkney who played an independent political role.

Orkney Museum ✳ [117 B5] (✆ 01856 873191; w tinyurl.com/orkney-museum;
⊕ May–Sep 10.30–17.30 Mon–Sat; Oct–Apr 10.30–12.30 & 13.30–17.00 Mon–Sat; free) A short walk downhill from the medieval quarter is Tankerness House, once the site of a pre-Reformation manse for the Roman Catholic clergy of St Magnus Cathedral, and now home to this excellent museum. Accompanying you all the way from prehistory through to the 20th century, this charming museum is a treasure trove. You may well be surprised by the quality of artefacts on display; the sort of items that might easily have been snaffled by a UK mainland museum include Pictish symbol stones adorned with eagles and hippocamps (a hybrid horse with a fish tail), a carved whale bone plaque and burial cists with human skeletons buried in a crouched position. There is a small but well-stocked bookshop and collection of souvenirs by the entrance.

The formal **Tankerness Gardens** just behind the Orkney Museum are of modest dimensions but a pleasant place to sit in good weather. Amid the rock garden you will find **Groatie House**, the spire of a summer house constructed from the ballast of the wrecked pirate ship *The Revenge* (run aground by the pirate John Gow; see box, page 221). The spire is quite a sight, adorned with European cowrie shells, and known locally as Groatie Buckles. If you are researching your family history and ties to Orkney then the **Orkney Library and Archive** [117 A5] (44 Junction Rd; ✆ 01856 873166; e archives@orkneylibrary.org.uk; w orkneylibrary.org.uk) behind the museum is useful, with a strong genealogy archive.

Around the harbour Near the harbour at Kiln Corner at the top of Junction Road, you'll find the small but gently engaging **Orkney Wireless Museum** [117 C3] (✆ 01856 871400; w owm.org.uk; ⊕ Apr–Sep 10.00–16.30 Mon–Sat, 14.30–16.30 Sun; £3/1). Many items, such as an early radar screen, relate to the involvement of Scapa Flow in the two world wars. Displays include inlaid vanity boxes made by Italian prisoners of war from material they salvaged while building the Churchill Barriers.

Immediately west of the harbour is the **Peedie Sea** [117 A3], a lake created by a natural shingle spit (now reinforced by concrete) with a curious inner paved ring that functions as a large duck pond. This is actually a pleasant place for an early-morning leg-stretcher to work up an appetite for breakfast and, in winter, you are likely to see long-tailed duck, pochard, redshank and other shoreline birds.

Grain Earth-House [map, page 113] (Off Scotts Rd, at the junction of Swordfish & Skua rds; collect the key from Judith Glue shop, 25 Broad St; free) One of Orkney's more unusually located archaeological sites is this Iron Age structure, sited in the improbable location of Hatston Industrial Estate half a mile northwest of the town

centre. Although small, this subterranean structure, discovered by accident by a ploughman in 1827, is very much worth visiting. After a short flight of steps (bring a torch) you squeeze through a narrow passageway to reach a chamber propped up by four pillars. Used by farmers 1,500–2,800 years ago, it was probably a food store although a case has been put for a ritualistic provenance (the underworld was important to Iron Age peoples in ways that are still not yet entirely understood).

Other sights A pleasant square of green space can be found on Willow Road, just beyond Archive Coffee on Laing Street, where a modest woodland bestrides a stream. This **park** brims with snowdrops in winter and is full of birdsong in spring. Evening at any time of year brings the haunting cawing of rooks going to roost.

Don't forget to look above the shopfronts in the centre of town, where the lintels and façades rise above the mundane. A stroll here, particularly along Victoria Street, repays interest for the mixture of faded façades that have seen better days and older buildings, such as 17th-century grain stores. Other buildings, such as those around Mounthoolie Lane, off Albert Street, seem ripe for the gentrification they would likely get further south. Here, they look and feel like an authentic part of the town. You will often see the founding date of the house – usually 16th–18th centuries – imprinted on the sandstone lintel. Opposite the Brig Larder at the junction of Bridge Street and Albert Street is **Parliament Close**, the site of Orkney's Norse Ting (parliament). The Scottish parliament met here in 1540 during a visit by James V.

Around Kirkwall A couple of sights worth exploring lie just south of Kirkwall. Located 1½ miles south of the cathedral on Holm Road (the A961 to Burray and South Ronaldsay), an industrial assemblage of warehouses, pagoda-like turrets and road-bridging pipes signals the **Highland Park Distillery** (✆ 01856 874619; e tours@highlandparkwhisky.com; w highlandparkwhisky.com; ⊕ 10.00–17.00 daily; shorter hours in winter). The world's northernmost distillery (by a mile or so), Highland Park is also the sixth-oldest in Scotland, dating to 1788. In the best traditions of such enterprises, it began as an illegal still-on-a-hill (High Park) outside Kirkwall run by Magnus Eunson, part-time bootlegger, part-time clergyman. Tours are good value and much more entertaining than many such experiences, mainly on account of the traditional methods, equipment deployed and your proximity to the machinery. The barley is laid on the floor and aerated by staff who use shovel-like implements known as shiels. These maltings are then gently roasted over peat cut from Hobbister moors in Orphir, then mixed with yeast in huge wooden washback tanks. After working its way through 18ft-high (5.4m) copper sills that are a cross between ear trumpets and swans, the whisky is left to macturate (mature with flavour) in handmade casks seasoned with Andalusian sherry. This process takes from three years and a day (for a single malt) to more than 30 years. Depending on the tour you've selected, after visiting the warehouses (which host 40,000 casks), you are invited to swig between up to three drams. Highland Park is something of a pilgrimage site for whisky lovers; 30,000 visitors from as far away as Yukon and Japan take the tour each year.

Just southwest and below the distillery is Kirkwall's own beach, the south-facing **Scapa Bay**. The northeast corner of the bay is given over to a memorial garden for a famous ship, the *Royal Oak* (see box, page 161), along with a cenotaph. (A large green buoy marks the war grave of the ship and is visible from the clifftops 2 miles south of the bay in Holm.) There's a waterfall here and fine views down Scapa Flow. On a calm day this spot can feel like the headwaters of a great lake rather than open sea. Nearby, visible above the western cliffs and located just off the A964 by Lingro

Distance: 6 miles; 3hrs
Start/finish: Peedie Sea, Kirkwall ✦ HY445112
OS Map: Explorer 43, Orkney West Mainland

A walk to the summit of Wideford Hill, looming large over Kirkwall, is an excellent choice for a first Orkney wander as it offers elements of everything the islands have to offer: a smattering of archaeology, superb views and a bit of bog.

Walk clockwise around Peedie Sea, crossing into Muddisdale Road by the Pickaquoy Centre. Follow this road as it branches left past Orcades Hostel; the breeze-block backdrop is unprepossessing. After 400yds keep ahead as the road forks, and 150yds further on, bear left on to the Muddisdale footpath, which winds through woodland home to downy birch, a native Orkney tree. The summit of Wideford Hill is visible directly ahead. The path weaves up to a road where you turn left. Walk on the grass verge for 200yds, then turn right up a farm track signposted for Wideford Hill. Keep ahead for about a mile as you gently ascend to a minor road. Keep ahead uphill. After 150yds, where the road flicks to the left, keep straight along a thin grassy track, heading straight uphill with the telecoms structures on your left. Shortly afterwards, keep left where the path forks. This bit is almost always boggy but walkable. Here you may catch a hare unawares and will almost certainly see skylarks and ravens.

With its telecoms paraphernalia, the summit (738ft/225m) is no work of beauty – but offers excellent views. Scapa Flow sweeps away southwards, meeting the severe, rolling flanks of Keelylang Hill. A topograph puts the hill and Orkney in perspective: the North Isles, from Shapinsay (5 miles away) to North Ronaldsay (34 miles) may be visible – but you'll need good atmospheric conditions to see Fair Isle (62 miles), or Cape Wrath, 75 miles southwest on the British mainland.

Wideford chambered cairn is located on the hill's northwestern flank. It is possible to reach the cairn via tracks over the hill but these are often indistinct and it's hard going over the peat-squelch. Instead, head downhill (with Kirkwall to your left) for 400yds, passing an abandoned house, to reach a small car park and information point. Follow the path as it winds gently downhill for three quarters of a mile, the flagstones soon yielding to peat. The ring-fenced cairn is signposted. It dates to around 3000BC and has been likened to Maeshowe. The chamber is 9ft high and partly cut into the hillside. You can access the chamber down a stepladder through the trap door. The effort is worthwhile as dropping into the cairn is an extraordinary sensation; cold and dark with only torchlight enabling fleeting glimpses of the rectangular surroundings.

From the cairn, return to the car park and follow the road downhill past the telecoms building then retrace your steps to Kirkwall. The view of the town is impressive; the spire of St Magnus rises above a mass of buildings that looks to have its metaphorical collar turned up against the elements.

Burn, is the **Scapa Distillery Visitor Centre** (✆ 01856 873269; e scapa.admin@ pernod-ricard.com; w scapawhisky.com; ⊕ Apr–Sep 09.30–17.00 Mon–Sat, 12.30– 17.00 Sun; shorter hours in winter; tours available). Founded in 1885 and restored in 2004, it produces a less peaty single malt than most.

The East Mainland is oddly overlooked by the majority of tourists, even though you must skirt it en route to the Italian Chapel (page 162) and the port of St Margaret's Hope. While the region lacks the density of archaeological sites found elsewhere, there is ample coastal beauty and drama amid an area defined by the headlands of Tankerness and Deerness. The former is low-lying and indented by bays where the sloshing of tides is rarely out of earshot; Deerness is more imposing with startling clifftop paths that will shake you out of any reverie induced by the dozy farming landscape below. With a population of just 1,360, the region is uncluttered, and you are likely to have its fracturing coastline of semi-detached headlands more or less to yourself. From Kirkwall to the tip of Deerness is around 12 miles and 20 minutes by car. Bus 3 runs from Kirkwall to Deerness.

 WHERE TO STAY, EAT AND DRINK *Map, opposite*
The emptiness of the East Mainland is reflected in its dearth of accommodation and eating options.

Mid range
St Mary's Inn Guesthouse (6 rooms) St Mary's; ☎01856 781786; e shonamike@ btinternet.com; w orkneytheinnguesthouse.co.uk. Recently refurbished; welcoming hosts. Ask for a room with a view of Scapa Flow. **££**

✱ **Straigona B&B** (3 rooms) Tankerness; ☎01856 861328; e enquiries@straigona.co.uk; w straigona.co.uk. Among the finest B&Bs on the Mainland. Comfortable rooms, all en suite with local soaps. Nothing is too much trouble for owners Julie & Mike Rickards. Excellent b/fasts including option of goose or buffalo sausages. Nice touches include unlimited traybakes made by Julie, perfect after a

day hiking & sightseeing. Strongly recommended. Also serves good evening meals. **££**

Cheap and cheerful
Å Deerness Community Campsite ☎01856 741317; m 07493 812345. Pitches for caravans & tents; washing facilities.

Kirk Café ☎01856 861203; e info@ sheilafleet.com; w sheilafleet.com; ⊕ 09.00– 17.00 Mon–Sat, 11.00–16.00 Sun. Eye-catchingly designed café in a converted church – pews as tables, chairs infilled with stained glass from windows. Salads, bere bannocks with salmon. Hot drinks & cakes. **£**

SHOPPING
Deerness Stores Junction of B9050 & Newark Rd; ⊕ 09.00–18.00 Mon–Wed, Fri & Sat, 07.00– 18.00 Thu, 11.00–17.00 Sun. Well stocked & good for picnic items. Petrol pumps outside keep the

same hours. Located a mile east of Dingieshowe. **Holm Shop** St Mary's; ⊕ 09.00–13.00 Mon–Fri. Local grocery store, handy to top up for lunch & dinner.

WHAT TO SEE AND DO The attractions to be found in the East Mainland are overwhelmingly elemental. The two peninsulas of Tankerness and Deerness are conjoined by the stirring isthmus of Dingieshowe, while the lonely B9050 leads eventually to the coastal beauty of Mull Head, the nearby Brough of Deerness, a thrillingly unstable rock stack and the rather spooky gloup, a vertical inland hole that plunges all the way to the sea. Elsewhere, calmer scenery can be had along the delightful beaches of Newark Bay.

Tankerness The westernmost parish of the East Mainland, and the location of the busy Kirkwall airport, Tankerness pushes deep into Shapinsay Sound and forms the eastern edge of the huge Inganess Bay. **Inganess beach** (officially known as the Sands of Wideford) is a lovely sheltered spot off the airport road (take the Inganess

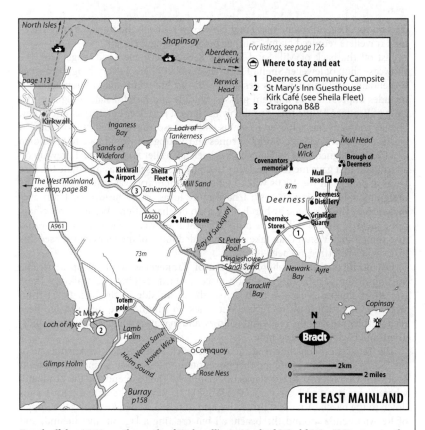

For listings, see page 126

Where to stay and eat

1 Deerness Community Campsite
2 St Mary's Inn Guesthouse
  Kirk Café (see Sheila Fleet)
3 Straigona B&B

THE EAST MAINLAND

Road off the A960 a mile south of Kirkwall). A wrecked World War II Destroyer, the *Juanita*, sits just offshore; it was sunk as a blockship for Scapa Flow, then recovered with a view for salvage. When the price for scrap metal declined, the *Juanita* lost her value and has wallowed here ever since. Inganess Bay is the start for a serene walk amid woodland and marshland. Go through the stile behind the car park right by the beach (✥ 477086) and pass a small loch. On a sunny day you may be treated to a hyperactive show from Orkney dragonflies (page 12) or you may see one of the short-eared owls that live in the rough vegetation around the airport. Cross the main road with care and pick up the path opposite, passing thickets of willow, rowan and dog rose before arriving after half a mile at Wideford Burn. Return the same way. The whole walk is a little over 2 miles and should take about an hour to complete. For those who fancy a longer stroll, a map at the car park outlines an extension, an easy 3-mile circular route mainly using quiet lanes.

Ask locally about developments at the Iron Age site of **Mine Howe**, 2 miles south of the airport off the A960 on Churchyard Road. The site, once open to visitors, is currently firmly closed until further notice. The interior was reached by descending 29 narrow and slippery steps which turn back on themselves halfway down. Three human burials were found here prompting theories suggesting that the site had a ritual purpose, possibly to commune with sprits from the underworld. In 2000, Channel 4 TV's Time Team had a root around the site, which is surrounded by a deep ditch. Adjacent to Mine Howe is **Long Howe** (also closed at the time of writing), an elongated glacial mound with two Bronze Age cists on top. Legends relate that Long Howe was home to the *trows*, Orkney's fairy folk: travellers required Dutch courage before passing their lair.

Just off the back of Mill Sand lies the Kirk Gallery and Café (page 126), the showcase shop of jeweller **Sheila Fleet**. The jewellery here – everything from rings to pendants and earrings – is designed with no little flair and is often subtle: it includes impressions of marram grasses, wildlife and tasteful slate designs of the Ring of Brodgar. While this is probably the largest jewellery enterprise on Orkney, Sheila's company has achieved its status without resorting to what might be called 'vertical jewellery', clichéd works of runes and Vikings. 'I would hate to be known as a Celtic designer,' says Sheila, who has been a jeweller for 50 years. 'I grew up on a farm and that gave me responsibility to do things myself. I was fortunate because I was at college in the 1960s when being 'contemporary' was just unfolding. The designing side of things is easy; I have more ideas in my head than I can ever make.' Everything is done by hand; there is no mechanisation. 'We are a workshop, not a factory,' she says. 'We'd be more efficient if we were a factory but we would lose something.' Visitors can take part in guided tours of the workshop to see this process at work (free; no need to book).

Just north of the workshop, the **Loch of Tankerness** swallows up a sizeable portion of the parish. This is a good place for birdwatching and walking. There is a short signposted access path across the south side of the loch (start from ⊕ HY514085) that leads to Yestay. With luck, in summer you may see and hear reed warblers among the reeds and willows, and may pass northern marsh orchids. There and back is a barely a mile.

The Tankerness coastline is attractive. **Rerwick Head**, which represents one of the 'horns' of the East Mainland that pokes out into Shapinsay Sound, is a pleasant spot with views across to sea stacks off Shapinsay. The road ends by the headland, where there is a small car park (⊕ HY538117). Beyond the gate a path wends down to the beach. A natural protective arm of raised stones, known as the Rough of Rerwick, curls around the beach, all but creating a lagoon. Just behind, and unmissable, are gun emplacements and observation posts from World War II. Wide ledges jut out into the sea here; a little further a colony of cormorants occupies a tussock-covered promontory.

Dingieshowe

A narrow isthmus, fortified by the dunes of Dingieshowe, links Deerness to Tankerness and hence the rest of the East Mainland. (OS maps don't use the name Dingieshowe: the east of the isthmus is formally Taracliff Bay and the west is Sandi Sand.) The south-facing beach is wonderful: in sunshine it is the quintessential sandy idyll; when the winter storms blow in, nowhere in Orkney is more dramatic. The gorgeous natural portrait of the isthmus is completed by St Peter's Pool, an enclosed embayment, and, a little further northwest, the Bay of Suckquoy, an intertidal saltmarsh. The name Dingieshowe is a corruption of the Norse 'Ting' and 'Howe', meaning 'Parliament Mount'; this refers to the defensive structures and broken mounds under the dunes, which is where Norsemen would meet to pass laws and settle feuds. The bay here was the scene of gruesome conflict in 1135 between Earl Rognvald, nephew to Magnus, and Earl Paul the Silent, when their rival ships were bound together and hand-to-hand fighting ensued. While the Silent One won the day, Rognvald was to become Earl the following year.

The dunes are under threat from erosion; in what may prove the last roll of the dice, fences have been installed and marram grass planted while visitors are asked to stick to paths. The hope is that this will prevent the dunes from collapse and the sea from making a decisive incursion across the isthmus.

Deerness The easternmost of the East Mainland's two great headlands, Deerness bursts into the sea at Dingieshowe. This is an empty part of the Mainland, given over to farming and wildlife; the latter benefits from a combination of heath,

A WALK AROUND MULL HEAD

Distance: 5½ miles (circular); 3hrs (including visit to the Brough of Deerness)
Start/finish: Mull Head car park ✪ HY590080
OS Map: Orkney East Mainland Explorer 461

The landscape of Deerness is as diverse and exhilarating as anywhere in Orkney, so a walk around the headland takes in the striking contrasts of farmland, moors, coast and a smattering of fens. This is not a walk for young children as unprotected cliff edges indent much of the route, some of them well hidden, even on the west coast of this headland, where the cliffs are less visually dramatic.

From the car park head east along the track to the gloup and then along the grassy path to the brough, passing spectacular slab-like ledges of rock that slice into the sea. As you head beyond the brough you enter a coastline that is being thoroughly dismantled by sea and wind. High cliffs fall dizzyingly into the sea, geos cut deep inland and everywhere the strata of the sedimentary rocks of eastern Orkney are thrillingly exposed. To the south lies the island of Copinsay; as you look north the horizon is framed by Stronsay and, behind that, the long spindly outline of Sanday.

The route is clear, if sometimes boggy, and leads on to **Mull Head nature reserve**. In spring and summer, the wildlife here makes for an outstanding spectacle: oystercatchers, lapwings and curlews nest in the fields; bonxies, Arctic skuas and Arctic terns nest on the moors; puffins, fulmars and kittiwakes nest among the cliffs; and gannets sweep past offshore. The strong tidal currents of Mull Head make for rich feeding grounds so attract many cetaceans, including orcas, Risso's dolphins, white-beaked dolphins, long-finned pilot whales and minke whales. You will almost certainly see both UK seal species here. Mull Head has never been ploughed; its abundance of wildflowers contrasts hugely with the snooker-table farmlands you travelled through to get here.

The path turns southwest along the coast, dipping down to burns lined by creeping willow as the cliffs finally begin to shrink. The pepper-pot column on the brow south of Den Wick bay is the **Covenantors memorial**, dedicated to the victims of a shocking 17th-century event. The Covenantors were a Presbyterian Christian movement named for the National Covenant they signed to set out their opposition to religious changes imposed by Charles I. The covenantors took part in the Civil War against the Crown but were defeated in 1679 at the Battle of Bothwell Brig. The 257 prisoners who survived their subsequent internment were dispatched to work as slaves in the Americas. As their ship rounded Orkney it was wrecked. The captain ordered the prisoners to remain locked below decks where most of them drowned; 48 were released by a crewmate who unlocked their cell.

Follow the path as it turns inland behind the monument. After half a mile, turn left at the car park and take the grassy track to the side of the minor road. Where this ends, turn right and follow the lane back to Mull Head car park.

fens and coast that rewards exploration on foot. The inhabitants were historically referred to as 'skate-rumples' (the provenance is unclear: 'rumple' is an old word for the inedible part of a fish).

The most arresting spectacle in Deerness is the **gloup**, or blowhole, located on the northeast coast (⊕ HY595079). To reach it, drive to **Mull Head** car park at the end of the B9050. A useful information centre is located across the road from the car park in a single-storey brick building (which also houses toilets). Follow the short, wheelchair-accessible path towards the coast for 200yds. The gloup – 80ft deep, 90yds long and 80ft wide – has collapsed on its landward side, allowing a thrilling glimpse through a cleft in the rock to the sea beyond. The water seems to rush and bulge into the gloup, even on a calm day. In spring and summer, fulmars and kittiwakes somehow find ledges on which to nest. A couple of wooden fences create viewing platforms from which you can take in the spectacle in safety.

You can walk further north along the coast for a mile to reach the **Brough of Deerness**, one of the most scintillating combinations of nature and archaeology you will find across Orkney. The path is generally clear and good, though rocky and boggy in parts. The brough comprises a sea stack of sedimentary rock that has all but crumbled free from the rest of Durness. On its top, clearly visible from the coastal path, is a tiny 11th-century Norse stone chapel, measuring just 10ft high and 15ft wide.

The brough can be admired from afar but if you have a head for heights you can follow the narrow path that sidles up the side of the stack for some 50yds. (You first descend down the coastal path along a narrow trail that drops almost to the shore before rising again on to the brough; as you ascend, there's a rope chained to the rock to steady you against the precipitous drop seawards.) Around the site of the chapel are the remnants of more than 30 dwellings and outbuildings, including defensive stone walls dating to 600BC–AD400. The stack is known to have been home to a Pictish community; a coin from Anglo-Saxon times has also been recovered. Recent finds include a stone gaming-board and antler playing-pieces. During the Middle Ages, religious activity continued and people were seen walking around the stack, scattering pebbles and water. Indentations visible in the grass are thought to be of more recent origin – having resulted from the use of the brough as target practice during World War II.

A special place for birdwatching is the exquisite **Grindigar Quarry** ✳, which gives the chance to see goldcrest and firecrest, the UK's joint-smallest birds, and, in spring, hardy African migrants that make it this far north, such as chiffchaff. Now reclaimed by nature, with help of some thoughtful planting, this tiny enclosure (⊕ HY580063) is located 200yds west of the New Lighthouse crossing towards the end of the B9050. Just 600yds further down this same branch road is **Deerness Distillery** (☎ 01856 741264; e sales@deernessdistillery.com; w deernessdistillery. com; ⊕ 14.00–18.00 Tue–Sun), which has a small shop and runs tours.

The southern shores of Deerness are much calmer than Mull Head and make for some easy walking and beachcombing. A mile or so east of Dingieshowe, take the right-hand turning signposted for the geo and jetty; these lead down to the crescent of white sand that is **Newark Bay**, where a large natural slipway is exposed at low tide. Newark Beach is a gorgeous sweep of sand. It is the locus for one of Orkney's more enduring and endearing tales of encounters with 'selkies' (page 36). One night a young man saw a group of 'people' dancing on the beach. On closer inspection he saw they were selkies who had lain their seal skins on the sand. The man stole one of the skins; it turned out to belong to a beautiful selkie girl who had to follow him as long as he possessed her skin. They were married and had children. One day, he left the skin unguarded in a chest; when he returned from a fair with the children, both the skin and his wife were gone. Whenever the children played on the beach, a seal would swim up to the shoreline and could be heard sobbing.

Another car park on the east side of Newark Bay bookends the beach. From here, there is an easy walk along low coastal banks for a mile or so to the sands at **Ayre**. Sand martins nest above the shore and, on calm days, the bay is often full with resting seabirds. The island of Copinsay (see box, above) lies just a couple of miles offshore. At Ayre a rough path continues, under the gaze of wind turbines, for a further half mile to the headland at Point of Ayre.

St Mary's The southern end of the East Mainland is infilled by the parish of Holm (pronounced 'ham'), punctuated by the village of St Mary's. A totem pole on the eastern edge of the village is a striking and unexpected landmark overlooking the first Churchill Barrier. The pole was erected in 2007 and emerged from a First Nation and Orcadian community project which saw a group of Squamish helping local adults and children to carve characteristic bird and human faces into the wood. The Loch of Ayre, immediately west of the village is another good place to see birds; kingfishers and short-eared owls often scout around for a meal.

The oldest building in St Mary's is a storehouse dating to 1649, located just east of the village. It was originally built as a corn store and used by crofters to temporarily hold the produce that they gave to the local laird as payment against their rent (known as *skat*, the tax payable under Udal Law; see box, page 19).

Rose Ness The southernmost tip of the East Mainland, and indeed of the Mainland, is marked by the lighthouse on the headland of Rose Ness above Mirth Hilly. You can walk part or all of the way to the headland. Follow the minor road past Wester Sand and Howes Wick (which are both pleasant places to pause). From the road end at Cornquoy (✪ ND522999), follow the peat track south into the moors for fine views over Holm Sound and back north over Deerness, Shapinsay and, on a clear day, Stronsay.

4

Hoy, South Walls and Flotta

Hoy is unlike anywhere else in Orkney. The first island many visitors see as they sail from the UK mainland, Hoy is the wildest and most rugged of all Orkney's islands, its contours defined by glowering sea cliffs of breathtakingly sheer dimensions. You will find Orkney's highest peaks here – and the name of the island, appropriately enough, comes from the Old Norse 'Haey', meaning the 'high island'. Separated from the UK mainland by the notoriously fearsome tidal currents of the Pentland Firth, Hoy lies barely 2 miles south of the Mainland of Orkney, across a combination of sounds and deeps that coalesce into the harbour of Scapa Flow.

At some 22 miles north–south and 6 miles east–west, Hoy is the second-largest Orkney island. Yet with a population of just 470 it can feel almost unpopulated. More than 90% of the island's land mass – just about everything apart from the settlements scattered in the far north and along the east coast – has been left to its own devices, the heather ungrazed for the best part of 50 years. This interior is as close to wilderness as you can find in the UK.

Across this visually arresting landscape birds of prey and farmland birds flourish in an elemental, sometimes sub-Arctic glacial environment. The coasts and shallow waters of some of Orkney's islands can, on a sunny day, stir vague comparisons to a Caribbean idyll. With its glaciated valleys and bone-hard whaleback hills, however, no-one will ever make the same claim for Hoy.

At the southern end of Hoy lies **South Walls**. Although sometimes assumed to be conjoined with its larger neighbour, it is actually a discrete narrow island tethered to its larger sibling by a manmade causeway. The island has an atmosphere all of its own and is characterised by softer and low-lying scenery. Here, at the port of Longhope, you will find these islands' most substantial – a relative term – community.

Flotta, meanwhile, is arguably Orkney's most accessible and underrated small island. Dominated by a flare stack that can be seen from most vantage points around Scapa Flow, it has an important military history, a fine coastal trail and seascapes with a unique perspective of Orkney and the British mainland. The island is easily reached by the regular Houton–Hoy ferry and is most definitely worthy of a day trip.

HISTORY

Unlike a great deal of Orkney, surprisingly little is documented about Hoy's prehistory. Neolithic peoples will surely have lived here and used the lee of the hills for shelter and fished on its shoreline. But the only substantial evidence found so far is the chambered cairn known as the Dwarfie Stane (page 141), which has been dated to as far back as 3500BC. A smattering of Bronze Age burial mounds on South Walls are in the process of being excavated and are likely to offer more

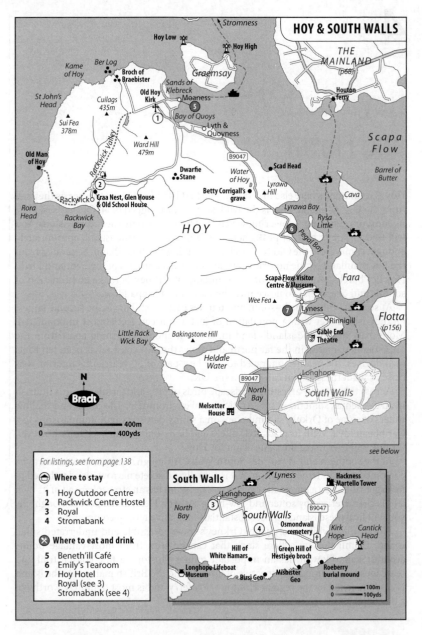

THE
MAINLAND
(p68)

Houton
ferry

Scapa
Flow

Barrel of
Butter

Cava

Rysa
Little

Fara

Flotta
(p156)

Stromness

Hoy Low

Hoy High

Graemsay

Kame
of Hoy

Ber Log

Broch of
Braebister

Sands of
Klebreck

Old Hoy
Kirk

Moaness

St John's
Head

Cuilags
435m

Bay of Quoys

Sui Fea
378m

Ward Hill
479m

Lyth &
Quoyness

B9047

Scad Head

Dwarfie
Stane

Water
of Hoy

Lyrawa
Hill

Betty Corrigall's
grave

Old Man
of Hoy

Rackwick

Craa Nest, Glen House
& Old School House

Lyrawa Bay

Rora
Head

Rackwick
Bay

HOY

Pegal Bay

Scapa Flow Visitor
Centre & Museum

Wee Fea

Lyness

Rinnigill

Little Rack
Wick Bay

Bakingstone Hill

Gable End
Theatre

Heldale
Water

B9047

Longhope

North
Bay

South Walls

see below

Melsetter
House

N

Bradt

| 0 | 400m |
| 0 | 400yds |

For listings, see from page 138

Where to stay

1 Hoy Outdoor Centre
2 Rackwick Centre Hostel
3 Royal
4 Stromabank

Where to eat and drink

5 Beneth'ill Café
6 Emily's Tearoom
7 Hoy Hotel
   Royal (see 3)
   Stromabank (see 4)

South Walls

Lyness

Hackness
Martello Tower

Longhope

North
Bay

South Walls

B9047

Osmondwall
cemetery

Kirk
Hope

Cantick
Head

Hill of
White Hamars

Green Hill of
Hestigeo broch

Longhope Lifeboat
Museum

Birsi Geo

Misbister
Geo

Roeberry
burial mound

| 0 | 100m |
| 0 | 100yds |

insights into how people lived on these islands during that time. Remains of Pictish square-barrow cemeteries have been found on both Hoy and South Walls but, as is the case with much of the Pictish presence on Orkney, little more is known of them than this.

The Vikings certainly made good use of the sheltered bays around Hoy's coastline; the island was an important seat during the era of the Orkney Earls. Key battles from these times may well have been staged on Hoy. The Norse scribe Snorri

With its rugged scenery, hills and an impressive coastline that embraces both the Pentland Firth and Scapa Flow, Hoy is something of a walker's paradise, not least thanks to Scotland's open-access laws. Most of the island's easily walkable hikes are described in detail later in this chapter. Elsewhere, you are free to walk where you wish, though this generally involves what is locally termed 'heather walking': yomps over open ground, bouncing on the springy heather and avoiding the bogs that can lurk in between.

That said, you can't help feeling that with a little effort, much more of the island's wilderness could be opened up to the hiker. Perhaps it's a combination of geology, weather, lack of heavy footfall and economics: without large numbers of visitors, paths will quickly be reclaimed by the elements; without walkable paths rather than ubiquitous open ground, those visitor numbers are unlikely to be sufficient to justify the investment in the creation of sturdy paths. The two obvious exceptions to this are the trails to Rackwick (page 141) and the Old Man of Hoy (see box, page 145) where the number of walkers has resulted in investment in the paths. Yet from the Old Man of Hoy an enticing path leads up to St John's Head but no further; meanwhile further south, a trail along Hoy's whaleback peaks would surely become one of the UK's finest skyline walks. The experienced hiker, comfortable with true isolation and arduous conditions, will take the current landscape in their stride but the majority of walkers will baulk at such undertakings. Outdoor tourism has been identified as key to Hoy's sustainable future; as visitor numbers increase, perhaps the picture will change for the better.

Sturluson wrote of an eternal battle on Hoy in which those who were killed were reborn each night; as with many such tales, the mythical and magical details are likely to contain within them the seed of a genuine, enduring conflict. In 995 Kirk Hope in South Walls was the scene of one of the most significant events in Orkney's history when the pagan earl, Sigurd the Stout, was converted to Christianity, a decisive act that established Orkney as a Christian kingdom.

Hoy is also punctuated with impossibly romantic-sounding names that point to these Norse influences: the Sands of Klebreck (from 'klette', meaning 'rocky', and 'breck', meaning 'slope'); Glifters of Lyrawa ('glifter' means 'hill-face'); and the Red Hill of Sneuk (from the Old Norse 'snokr', or 'snout').

The islands' geographical location as a western bulwark for Scapa Flow has long lent Hoy strategic military importance. During the Napoleonic Wars, Longhope was a rendezvous for the convoys of British merchantmen sailing to the Baltic. Distinctive Martello towers – still standing today – were built to safeguard the ships at anchor against attacks from American privateers and French vessels. During the 20th century's great wars, Hoy came into its own, serving as the base for the Royal Navy's Grand Fleet during both World War I and World War II.

GETTING THERE AND AWAY

Despite Hoy's military history, there is no airfield; nor is there a land bridge. Accordingly, the only way to get here is by sea. This involves one of two Orkney Ferries services, both starting from the Mainland of Orkney. The main service, the MV *Hoy Head* ro-ro ferry, runs up to six times a day from Houton, southwest of

Hoy's sandstones are harder than those anywhere else on Orkney, enabling formation of the island's signature towering cliffs. These are Upper rather than Middle Old Red Sandstone and are better able to withstand relentless pummelling from the Atlantic. As the sandstone erodes at different rates, narrow ledges emerge that enable seabirds to nest. Elsewhere, Hoy has weathered into a rugged landscape of whaleback hills sufficiently high in both altitude and latitude to have generated their own glaciers during the last Ice Age – you can see reminders of this in northwest Hoy's corries and wide glaciated valleys. Unlike much of Orkney, where peat moorlands and rough pastures have been reclaimed for farming, Hoy's hills are carpeted with upland heath. This has enabled rarer Arctic-Alpine plants, such as stone bramble and purple saxifrage, to flourish.

Hoy forms a major part of the Hoy and West Mainland National Scenic Area, a Scottish designation accredited to important natural landscapes of high conservation value. Meanwhile, Hoy RSPB reserve covers almost 10,000 acres of moorland. Birdlife is magnificent: the island boasts seven or eight pairs of peregrine, which prey on seabirds. This diet may explain the falcons' sadly low breeding success rate as biologists believe they are ingesting pollutants from seabirds that have consumed plastics (see box, page 155). Seabirds you are very likely to see from April to July are kittiwake, fulmar, puffin and razorbill, while guillemot and shag can be seen year round.

Kirkwall, to Lyness (single fares: passengers £4.25/2.15 adult/child, return fares double; £13.60 standard car). Journey time is around 35 minutes for non-stop services; those that stop at Flotta (off the east coast of Hoy) take up to 1½ hours. The number 2 bus runs from Kirkwall travel centre to Houton to connect with the ferry (20mins). Note that the first sailing of the day to Houton actually departs from Longhope, the small community in South Walls, and the last arrival terminates there. Between May and late August you should book any car well in advance.

A second service – for foot passengers only – sails five times daily. It navigates a route from Stromness across Hoy Sound, via Graemsay to Moaness Pier in northeast Hoy (£4.25/2.15 single; 25mins). This is the ferry to take should you intend to walk to the Old Man of Hoy in a day: it lands you much closer – and even then, the walk is pretty long and time-consuming (see box, page 145). Although sailings dwindle to just two daily at weekends, they bookend the day so you still have enough time on the island to complete this hike.

GETTING AROUND

Hoy is much larger than you might think. It's 12 miles from the settlement of Hoy to Lyness and a further 7 miles from there to Longhope on the western edge of South Walls. As the island bus only runs from Lyness to Longhope – and there has never been a service running the length of the island – you will need a car to cover most of what the island has to offer. The very largely single-track B9047 follows the east coast from Hoy to Longhope. The only access into Hoy's interior is the single-track road that peels off west just above Moaness Pier to reach Rackwick, 4½ miles away. The only petrol station on the island is located at Longhope and is closed on Sundays.

Amid Hoy's high-cliff drama, you might easily overlook the island's shores and lowland farmland. Lapwing, with its distinctive 'quiff', is among the most common birds, thriving in fields of barley, oats and potatoes. Here too are skylark, twite (a northern version of linnet) and snow bunting, which depend on winter stubble for sustenance. Curlew flit between moors and lower-lying farmland. Ungrazed moorlands are perfect for hen harrier and merlin, a pint-sized raptor that scouts for small birds, dragonflies and even moths. Hoy boasts more than 1,400 pairs of great skua (bonxie; Orkney holds an astonishing 17% of the global population). On inland lochans you may spot a majestic red-throated diver. Mountain hares were introduced to Hoy in the 6th century and thrive to the extent there are thought to be around 30 individuals per square mile. You have a good chance of spotting otters along the Scapa Flow coastline and in the Rackwick Burn. They also come inland across low-lying farmland in search of fresh water for bathing.

Orkney may not be widely known for its woodland but substantial tracts of rowan, aspen, willow and birch survive in places such as the gullies in Berriedale, along which a footpath runs from Moaness to Rackwick. Curiosities abound, with botanists often exercised by plant communities more commonly associated with mountain areas, such as least willow and yellow mountain saxifrage. The island's seven species of dragonfly include the distinctive gold-ringed which thrives on boggy pools. To help you enjoy Hoy's wildlife, consider joining a RSPB guided walk (℡ 01856 850176; w rspb.org.uk/orkney; spring to early autumn).

A community bus (℡ 01856 701356; w tinyurl.com/hoy-bus; times vary) travels up the B9047 from Lyness to Longhope. From May to early September Albert Clark runs a minibus that meets the Moaness ferry and takes visitors to Rackwick (℡ 01856 791315; £3 single). This considerably shortens the walk to the Old May of Hoy.

Cycling is a good option if you're reasonably fit but Hoy can be hard going. As well as its size, the island has more climbs than you might expect: an uphill slog in high winds from Pegal Bay to Lyrawa Hill will leave its mark on the casual cyclist.

TOURIST INFORMATION

Given Hoy's sizeable appeal to visitors you may be surprised at just how sleepy it is, particularly in terms of information provision. Don't expect to arrive on the last ferry and hop on a bus to your accommodation. You will also spend a long time searching for any signs 'to the beach'. Extremely rudimentary, out-of-date information boards are at Moaness, Longhope and Lyness piers. The best sources of local information on current transport options are the websites w hoyorkney.com and w orkneycommunities.co.uk/IOHDT. Otherwise, in North Hoy, Old Hoy Kirk (⊕ all year) offers decent information, displays photographs and stages regular exhibitions (page 140). Emily's Tearoom and Wild Heather Crafts (page 139) is comfortably your best bet for news about local events. Emily herself is extremely helpful.

TOUR OPERATORS A good tour operator on the island is Steven Rhodes, who runs **Island Tours of Hoy** (℡ 01856 701632; m 07887 995730; w islandtourshoy.com; Thu only). Steve runs a standard tour (£49/24.50 adult/child) that takes in sights from Lyness north, and a Maxi-tour (£59/29.50 adult/child) that includes South Walls. Bring a picnic to enjoy as you chat to Steve on Rackwick Beach.

THE UNINHABITED ISLANDS OFF HOY

The ferry journey from Houton to Lyness is extremely picturesque: the panorama of Hoy shifts from a ridgeline of high hills to an indented coastline that occasionally heaves upwards to form sheer cliff faces. The ferry also passes three uninhabited islands: Cava, Rysa Little and Fara. Rysa Little is blanketed in heather and may only ever have been sporadically inhabited, possibly in summer. Cava and Fara, meanwhile both supported substantial communities into the early 20th century. When the German fleet was scuttled in Scapa Flow in 1919 the islanders enjoyed rich pickings from the flotsam that emerged, including binoculars, typewriters and, inevitably, whisky. More than 200 military personnel were stationed on Cava and Fara in World War II so military structures abound too.

Fara means Sheep Island. According to the 1881 census, it was home to a dressmaker, a knitter, farmer/schoolteacher and a boat carpenter. Exploring the island, you can pick out the remnants of peat-cutting, occasional roofless stone crofts, boat nousts and stone piers. The name Cava comes from the Old Norse 'Kalf-ey' (Calf Island). Rather than relating to livestock, the word refers to small islands next to larger. (Several other Calf Islands are scattered across Orkney.) The last residents left Cava in 1945. Fara was sold in 1965; two resettled on Cava until 1993.

To the east as you pass Cava lies a tiny islet, Barrel of Butter – appropriately named, as at one time the annual rent for its ownership was a barrel of butter. These waters are also a wonderland for birdwatchers. Winter brings Slavonian grebe, great northern diver and little auk. In summer, the air is full of fulmars, bonxies and the occasional puffin. Keep an eye out in the water for porpoises and grey seals; the latter often haul out by the Scad Head Battery. A boat operator such as Northerly Marine Services (page 74) may offer a bespoke tour to and around the islands; otherwise the best option is simply to take a round trip as a ferry passenger on the Lyness ferry.

WHERE TO STAY   Map, page 134

For an island of international renown, Hoy has remarkably little accommodation: two hostels in the north (both excellent and run by Orkney Islands Council) and two hotels on South Walls. There is also a stone bothy at Rackwick, which, overlooking a bay backed by high cliffs, enjoys as good a view as anywhere in Orkney. There's a toilet here and fresh water.

For self-catering suggestions visit w hoyorkney.com/visiting/accommodation.

Hoy Outdoor Centre (8 rooms) Hoy; 01856 850907; e stromnesscs@orkney.gov.uk; w tinyurl.com/hoy-centre; ⊙ all year. Spacious en-suite rooms with 4 beds, good shared kitchen & social area. Rooms & hostel can be booked for exclusive use. Great location overlooking Scapa Flow & Stromness & surveyed by the brooding mass of Ward Hill. Recommended. **£**

Rackwick Centre Hostel (2 rooms) Rackwick; 01856 850907; e stromnesscs@ orkney.gov.uk; w tinyurl.com/rackwick-outdoor-centre; ⊙ Apr–Sep. 4 beds/room. Shared kitchen & common room. Housed in former school building. Stunning location above Rackwick Bay. More basic than Hoy counterpart but well maintained. **£**

Royal Hotel (3 rooms) Longhope; 01856 701276; ⊙ for accommodation, Apr–Dec. Dating to 1900 & the closest thing in South Walls that comes to a landmark building, it has seen better days but ticks over convivially enough. En-suite rooms have faded grandeur of thick carpets, wood-framed beds & heavy curtains (possibly unchanged from the time George V & Edward, Prince of Wales, slept here while inspecting the Grand Fleet in 1915). **££**

🏠 **Stromabank Hotel** (4 rooms) Longhope; ☏ 01856 710494; e stromabankhotelhoy@gmail. com; w stromabank.co.uk. En-suite rooms, neat & tidy with TV. Two upstairs rooms have coastal views, 1 overlooks moorland; 1 downstairs suitable for travellers with limited mobility (but no view). Run by sisters Roz Ware & Rachel Wilkins, both former nurses who fancied a change of career. Roz moved from Norfolk 5 years ago after marrying an Orcadian. 'Orkney gets under your skin,' she says. Plans for a campsite in the grounds should have come to fruition by the time you read this guide. **££**

✖ WHERE TO EAT AND DRINK

✖ **Royal Hotel** Longhope; ☺ Jan–Easter 17.00–late Thu–Sat; Apr–Dec noon–14.00 & 17.00–20.00 daily. Restaurant serves standard chip-based fare (fish, curry & chicken). The bar is a good social hub if you are down this end of the island (☺ 17.00–01.00 daily). **£–££**

✖ **Stromabank Hotel** Longhope; ☺ Apr–Sep noon–14.00 & 18.00–20.30 daily; Oct–Mar 18.00–20.00 Fri & Sat, noon–14.00 Sun (other days by arrangement). Restaurant has superb views across Scapa Flow to Switha. Good food ranges from sweet potato & pepper soup (£4.50) to North Ronaldsay lamb (£14). Traditional Sun roast; fish & chip take-away (☺ 16.00–18.30 Sat). The bar has a proper pub feel with a hearth & dartboard (☺ Apr–Sep 18.00–midnight daily; Oct–Mar 18.00–late Mon & Thu–Sat). **£–££**

🍽 **Beneth'ill Café** Moaness; ☏ 01856 791119; e admin@benethillcafe.co.uk; w benethillcafe. co.uk; ☺ Apr–Sep 10.00–18.00 daily. Located 400yds uphill from the pier, in the shadow of Ward Hill (try saying the café name out loud and you'll see why it is so called), this excellent choice serves lentil soup, paninis, scones, traybakes & crumbles. Based in attractive stone building; large garden comes into play when the sun shines. **£**

✱ 🍽 **Emily's Tearoom** 1½ miles north of Lyness; ☏ 01856 791213; ☺ Apr–Sep 10.00–17.00 Mon–Sat; Oct–Mar 11.00–16.00 Fri–Sat. A welcome gem. Idyllic setting overlooking Mill Bay, with outdoor tables & decking for good weather. All-day b/fast, waffles, soup, good wraps, homemade cakes & excellent milkshakes. Call ahead to book the meal of the day. Located in same building as Wild Heather Crafts (page 140). Both are run by Emily Smith, who stopped 'working in accounts' in Kirkwall to move to Hoy. 'The café was something I always wanted to do. I've travelled a lot around the world & you pick up ideas about what you like & what other people like. There was a need for somewhere to get a cup of coffee & good hot food in this part of the island.' **£**

🍷 **Hoy Hotel** Lyness; ☏ 01856 791377; w hoyhotel.co.uk; ☺ 19.00–22.00 Mon–Thu, 19.00–01.00 Fri & Sat, noon–14.00 & 19.00–23.00 Sun. The hotel's fortunes have waxed & waned; at the time of writing, things were looking down rather than up. No longer a hotel, nor serving food, but its bar can be entertaining on a busy night (although deadly grim when not). Worth keeping an eye on, however, as someone will surely exploit its potential & wartime history (page 148). **£**

ENTERTAINMENT

A weekend of music and dance, **The Hoy Hoolie** (w hoyhoolie.com) takes place every other year from the end of July to early August. From June to August the Orkney Traditional Dance Association (w orkneycommunities.co.uk/OTDA) performs monthly reels and jigs in Hoy Kirk. Given Hoy's palpable sense of emptiness, the excellent **Gable End Theatre** (North Walls; w orkneycommunities. co.uk/IOHDT, click on 'calendar') comes as a surprise. This 75-seat theatre screens films fortnightly and attracts performers from around the world. It also has a welcome bar.

As with accommodation, sources of provisions are thin on the ground: don't expect to walk off the ferry and into a shop: the single grocers on the island is the well-stocked **J M F Groat & Sons** merchants and grocers (✆ 01856 701273; ⏱ 09.00–12.30 & 14.00–18.00 Mon–Sat) in Longhope. Just bear in mind that if you're based in North Hoy, it's a 20-mile journey when you run out of milk. Just about your only option for souvenirs is **Wild Heather Crafts** (✆ 01856 791213; w spanglefish. com/wildheathercrafts; ⏱ Apr–Sep 09.30–16.30 Mon–Sat; Oct–Mar 11.00–15.30 Fri & Sat) just north of Lyness. Sharing premises with Emily's Tearoom, this fine little shop sells locally made items such as wreaths made from sea glass and shells, upcycled local furniture and paintings by island artist Joan Roadwell. 'Many artists are hobbyists; they don't make enough to sell in Kirkwall so I'm keen to give them a place to be seen,' says owner Emily Smith.

OTHER PRACTICALITIES

✚ **Hoy and Walls Surgery** Longhope; ✆ 01856 701209
✉ **Post office** Operated from the village shop J M F Groat & Sons, Longhope; ⏱ 09.00–12.30 & 14.00–18.00 Mon–Sat

Petrol Operated from J M F Groats & Sons; details as above

WHAT TO SEE AND DO

NORTH HOY The scattered settlement of **Hoy** radiates from Moaness on the northeast coast, where the tiny pier offers mooring for the regular Stromness foot-passenger service. Two attractive beaches are located either side of the pier. To the north is the better choice, the **Sands of Klebreck**, which covers a broad sweep of the bay. Park with care on the verge above the bay. Just south of the pier is the **Bay of Quoys**; more rugged and with rock pools to explore, it is atmospheric on a windswept day. Getting to it is awkward: walk down the lane immediately north of the beach, then walk past the house at the end of the lane and on to the rocks.

Well worth a visit, **Old Hoy Kirk** stands proud and prominent on the ridge 600yds above the pier; it serves as a historical archive. Built in 1891, it was sold to the Friends of Hoy Kirk in 2003. The surviving pulpit comprises wooden panels thought to come from the Spanish Armada while the cross was made from wood recovered from HMS *Vanguard*. The kirk is a good place to read up on the latest archaeological activity by the Orkney Research Centre for Archaeology (ORCA). In addition, there's a mishmash of sketches of island flora, amateur island weather reports and an account of Hoy botanist James Sinclair, a plant hunter who explored the Far East and established a herbarium, now held at the Royal Botanic Garden in Edinburgh. The RSPB has a small display in the back room.

The fractured coastline at the northern tip of Hoy provides an elemental setting for the remains of the **Broch of Braebister**. Reaching it takes a little time, although it makes for a pleasant, easy walk. There's no parking along the track (technically, this is still the B9047) that leads to the broch; instead start from the car park by the water-treatment works at the start of the Rackwick Valley trail. Walk for 1¼ miles to the lane end in front of a cottage. Unusually for Hoy, there is a waymarker sign here directing you to the left of the cottage, over a gate, through a field and over a stile, all in quick succession. The broch is just below you; a 9ft-high mound is all that remains of an Iron Age fort that once protected this promontory. The walk is probably more rewarding for its views: nearby, in the chasm by Muckle Head, is the vast lozenge-shaped seastack of **Ber Log**, which resembles a listing tanker. High above and to the west is the fractured and breathtaking outline of the **Kame of Hoy**, whose natural arch mesmerises passengers on the MV *Hamnavoe* as they sail between Stromness and Scrabster.

The other points of interest in North Hoy are further west around the township of **Rackwick**, which can be reached from the east coast either on foot along a valley path or a road running parallel beneath the southern flank of Ward Hill.

Just over 2 miles along the road to Rackwick is a small car park (✪ HY243009), from where you can walk to the **Dwarfie Stane**, one of the most remarkable ancient cairns – even by Orcadian standards. Lying on moorland half a mile from the south side of the road (but visible from it), the cairn is signposted and reached by a good track comprising boards, flagstones and intervals of squelchy but walkable bits. Dwarfie Stane is Britain's sole prehistoric rock-cut chambered tomb. Parallels with other tombs on mainland Europe date it to 3500–2500BC. Measuring 25ft by 12ft, the stane was formed from an ice-transported block delivered from adjacent hills, and inspired part of Sir Walter Scott's novel *The Pirate*; Scott put it down as the residence of a Norse dwarf called 'Trolld', from whom the stane gets its name.

A narrow passage has been hewn out which leads – although a bit of a squeeze – to two chambers and a stone ledge that is sometimes identified as a stone pillow. The exact purpose of the stane is unclear but it may have been a burial site: archaeologists who explored the stane in the hope of discovering disarticulated human remains were beaten to it by earlier plunderers. The stane has another curiosity: on its south side a Victorian traveller, Major William Mouncey, has carved an inscription in Arabic that reads: 'I have sat for two nights and have found peace'. For good measure, Mouncey etched his name on the stone in Latin. Returning to the road you are confronted by the shockingly severe contours of Ward Hill. There is a palpably ancient feel to this part of Hoy: much of the landscape looks as it must have done when the Dwarfie Stane was in use.

A pair of white-tailed eagles, thought to have moved in naturally from the north coasts of Scotland, has nested in the cliffs above the stane for several years. After several years with no success, in 2018 one of them was spotted with a new mate. That June the uplifting news emerged that Orkney's first white-tailed eagle for 145 years had hatched. Assuming the birds return, the RSPB will operate a seasonal viewing point here (for updates visit **w** rspb.org.uk/orkney).

Rackwick Valley and township
West of the Dwarfie Stane, the road peters out at **Rackwick**, a township scattered alongside a burbling burn, hemmed in by sheer cliffs and Arctic-looking mountains and overlooking a magnificent beach – in total, an almost impossibly idyllic setting. Among those drawn here were the artist Sylvia Wishart and the composer Peter Maxwell Davies, who both lived in Rackwick crofts; the latter was inspired by the landscape to write the children's score *Songs of Hoy*. Nowadays, the township is an eclectic mix of working farms and three small but fascinating museums. Several renovated self-catering properties are counterbalanced by a number of abandoned, semi-demolished and decaying 19th-century houses.

If driving, you should park in the ramshackle car park just behind the beach (✪ HY203993). You can also **walk to Rackwick** through the valley that runs to the north of Ward Hill. This is a magnificent, easy stroll through a valley of shudder-inducing yet beautiful geology. As you walk it is easy to see how the valley

A HIKE UP WARD HILL

Distance: 4 miles; time: 2½–4hrs return
Start/finish: car park east of Sandy Loch in North Hoy ⊕ HY223034
OS Map: Explorer 462 Hoy, South Walls & Flotta

At 1,570ft (479m), Ward Hill is Orkney's highest point. Although consequently an inviting climb, it is an awkward one. What's more, only its height defines this peak as a 'hill'; in every other sense it looks and feels like a mountain. The upper reaches welcome you with a sub-Arctic glaciated environment so a walk up its sleep slopes should be treated with respect. Fortunately, the pay-off outweighs the effort: arguably the best view to be had in Orkney and a high chance of seeing mountain hare (which sport white winter coats as late as May) bounding ahead of you.

There is no clear path to the summit; instead it's a case of yomping upwards over open ground. One recognised approach leads up the southern ridges from near the Dwarfie Stane but this involves a ferociously steep ascent that verges on scrambling. Instead, the best option for most walkers is on the south side. From Sandy Loch car park, head west along the Rackwick track, passing Sandy Loch, with the austere flanks of Ward Hill up to your left. To find the least steep and least boggy approach, keep on the track to its highest point (⊕ HY215026), 400yds west of the end of the loch. From here strike out across open ground on a compass bearing of south-southeast. Looking up at the hill, keep Water Glen to your left and the austere gloom of Red Glen well to the right (this also makes things easier in May and June when bonxies nest around Sandy Loch; they will quickly let you know should you stray too near their nests).

A stone about two-thirds of the way up to the skyline is a helpful locator – it is quite conspicuous once you pick it out (on closer inspection it is shaped remarkably like a chair and makes a good resting place). The first half mile is easy going over sprigs of heather. Then the heart-thumping ascent begins, with two false skylines to test your spirits. Higher up, the ground becomes stonier and easier, then boggy once more, before, perhaps unexpectedly, a clear stone path nudges you up to the summit plateau. The largest of several cairns at the top has a trig point and an adjacent shelter behind which to huddle from any wind.

The views are outstanding: you can see right across the Orkney archipelago from Stromness to the Brough of Birsay, Westray and, on the skyline, North Ronaldsay. In fact, you can see every island with the exception of Rysa Little, which ironically is the closest. Return the same way, taking care as the steep boggy slopes can be extremely slippery.

inspired composers, artists and poets. From Moaness Pier to Rackwick is just over 4 miles, which takes 2 hours (one-way). The track follows the old post road across streams in a secluded valley sprinkled with clusters of hardy trees. It threads between Ward Hill and Cuilags, both prominences wind-stripped and scarred by frost and gales. Soon after leaving the paved road you pass Sandy Loch. Red-throated divers nest around here while bonxies gather on its waters. Rackwick Burn gurgles heartily as it escorts you through the valley; footbridges help you skip across its waters. The path coils through the valley to reach Berriedale Wood, Britain's most northerly natural woodland. Pollen analysis suggests that native woodland was widespread in Orkney until 5000BC. The track joins the road from the east coast for the last 400yds and heads into Rackwick.

However you reach Rackwick, it is difficult to resist heading straight for the bay, which stretches for the best part of a mile and is impossibly scenic. To the south, the beach crashes abruptly into the base of a solid lump of rocky headland known as Point of Craig-gate, behind which a series of pleasingly geometric headlands poke out, including Santoo Head and Sneuk Head. Towards this southern end, the bay comprises sand made from pure quartz – one of just three places in Scotland it can be found (Skye and Rum are the others). Run along this stretch of the beach and you can feel the sand reverberate under your feet. Looking north, the land sweeps high, taking hikers towards the Old Man of Hoy. In between, the tide seems to brush waves into the shore; 100yds offshore, a sudden drop in the seabed creates waves out of calm waters (accordingly, at low tide, you should swim with caution). The shoreline comprises boulders and seaweed-smothered rock pools tenanted by ducks, cormorants and gulls. However, a tiny insect might interfere with your reverie on a warm summer's day: Rackwick is among the few places on Orkney where midges really run rampant when the wind drops.

Back from the shore and on the north side of Rackwick you will find three small museums (⊕ daily; free, but donations invited). Memorabilia on display at each is less than spectacular but recreates a picture of yesteryear in a remote township on the edge of Britain. Located by the main access path to the Old Man of Hoy is the **Craa Nest (Crow's Nest)**, a collection of three single-storey turfed houses with items such as a straw-backed Rackwick chair and box beds. These were once home to the Thomson family; it's said that the founding Thomson was a survivor of a slave ship wrecked off the Orkney coast in 1679. Oral history passed down by Rackwick families tells how he somehow escaped from his locked cell on the ship and ended up in Rackwick. A slightly meandering family history relates how one descendant went on to invent the suspender belt.

Just east from the Craa Nest, over a burn and by a small coppice of downy birch, stand the **Glen House** and the **Old School House**. The former holds a small archive of early 20th-century photographs, a stove and other Edwardian items. More eye-catching is the schoolhouse, which operated from 1724 to 1841. In the early days, children bought a slice of peat a day in lieu of payment for their education. Later, even this was insufficient and there was no island education from 1841 to 1879. Outside is a collection of mid-20th-century farmyard equipment deployed for hay-raking or ploughing up turnips.

PETER MAXWELL DAVIES

The composer Peter Maxwell Davies – a one-time Master of the Queen's Music – lived more than half his life on Orkney. He resided in a croft called Bunatoon in Rackwick from 1974 to 1988, when he moved to Sanday. Davies embraced the rural life, cutting peat, helping with lambing and volunteering as a coastguard. Attracted to the sense of community and local arts, he would integrate traditional Orkney and Scottish songs and dance into the narrative of his music. He also took inspiration from calling birds and the brightness of mackerel shoals. 'Max', as he was known, also put a good deal of George Mackay Brown's work to music, including *From Stone to Thorn*, and composed an opera, *The Martyrdom of St Magnus*, based on Mackay Brown's *Magnus*.

The Old Man of Hoy Most people who reach Rackwick are bent on a nose-to-nose view of the iconic sandstone column that features in every tourist brochure to both Orkney and Scotland. Standing 450ft (137m) high, this is Europe's tallest sea stack. Buffeted by ever-turbulent waves at its base, it makes for an absorbing and thrilling spectacle. To see it, you have to walk to it (see box, opposite).

Rising from a pedestal of dark basalt lava, the Old Man comprises fragile Old Red Sandstone intermingled with layers of flagstone that create distinctive slab-like ridges upon which nesting fulmars look tiny. Geologists reckon that the Old Man is a relatively recent creation: maps from 1600 and 1750 only portray a headland here. Even more recently, he had two 'legs' that created a natural arch before one 'limb' was swept away by a storm in the early 19th century. This same combination of ocean and geology means that sooner rather than later the Old Man of Hoy will tumble into the sea. The name is – possibly – one of the few Gaelic names in Orkney, perhaps originating from 'allt' ('cliff') and 'maen' ('stone'). The summit was first conquered in 1966 by Sir Chris Bonington, Tom Patey and Rusty Baillie. At the top the trio built a cairn and lit a fire; Patey later reported that 'in our enthusiasm, it got out of hand and only collective action saved us from the inconvenience of a fast abseil down melting nylon'.

THE EAST COAST Hoy's east coast is traversed by the often dramatically scenic B9047, which roller-coasters its way from sea level up to moorland edge before swooping through low-lying farmland. With a car, this delightful journey could easily turn into a day or two's exploration. Wildlife is all around, from hen harriers patrolling the moors to meadow pipits bouncing along the verges. Meanwhile, the view across Scapa Flow and its many islands is ever-changing. The route described here proceeds from north to south.

Leaving North Hoy southwards, the route passes tiny hamlets such as Quoyness and Lyth and gives fine views of Graemsay island (see box, page 146). The first site worth exploring is **Lyrawa Hill**, 4 miles south of Hoy village; follow the signpost along a rough track. Views across Scapa Flow are stunning: overlooking an area

CLIMBING THE OLD MAN OF HOY

The 1966 ascent captured the public imagination to such an extent that it was repeated for the BBC in 1967 as the first live programme of its kind. More than 20 million viewers tuned in over three days to watch the climb. Sir Chris Bonington's achievement was marked by a song composed by South Walls islander Billy Budge, who, in a stream of consciousness, imagined the sea stack being taken to the United States to marry the Statue of Liberty. Other climbs quickly followed. In 1968, inspired by the TV film, seven-year-old Roy Clarkson and his father Arthur climbed it in a day, drinking Ribena at the top. The first woman to summit was Christine Crawshaw. A blind man, Red Szell, has also climbed the Old Man. In 2008, three climbers took 7 hours to climb up and then just 10 seconds to BASE jump down. In 2017, a novel approach was taken by Alexander Schulz, who walked a 591ft-long wire from Hoy across to the summit. In 2018 Edward Mills, an eight-year-old boy from Dunnet, just across the Pentland Firth, climbed it in a fundraising campaign for his mother Bekki who was diagnosed with terminal breast cancer. There's a tin box containing a book on the summit where those who make it can sign their name.

Distance: 5½ miles return; time: 2hrs
Start/finish: Rackwick car park ✪ HY203993
OS Map: Explorer 462, Hoy, South Walls & Flotta

The stunning walk to the Old Man is easy going along one of Orkney's few well-maintained paths. A breathtaking climax leaves you peering over an immense watery void. While the Old Man is the goal, the walk offers ample natural beauty throughout. Seven species of orchid are found in the moors, along with Alpine bearberry. The birdlife is rich too: curlew bubbles, bonxies (and the smaller Arctic skua) patrol the skies and puffins flicker offshore from May to July. Should you stray too close to skua nests, adults will dive-bomb you unpleasantly.

From Rackwick car park, follow signs for the Old Man, heading towards the sea then along a waymarked track that zigzags up to the main path. Flagstones underfoot make the going generally good as you contour around Moor Fea hill. The climb mostly complete, you are confronted with plateau-like moorland, incised by a path stretching to the skyline. Down to the west, a waterfall drains Stourdale Burn off the sheer and angular cliffs at Rora Head. Before long you see the top half of the Old Man.

As you approach the end of the path, the cliffs taper to a point. The pole here is intended to stop you walking into thin air in mist. Take care with children, in particular. The clifftop provides IMAX-like views of the entire stack. The colour scheme is striking: mustard-yellow rock stack inlaid with the pinks of thrift and the greens of sea mayweed and scurvy grass that tenaciously colonise its ledges.

The wider setting is equally sensational. Look north and the land pulls away across vanishingly empty moorland to the summits of Sui Fea (1,240ft/378m) and Cuilags (1,427ft/435m). At St John's Head, at 1,128ft (335m) the UK's highest vertical cliff, Hoy tumbles into the sea. For walkers wanting a less nerve-shredding but equally unimpeded view, follow the narrow path north for 200yds towards St John's Head, where the cliffs are a little less, well, edgy. St John's Head, too, has been climbed, a feat seemingly as implausible as ascending the Old Man.

Return the same way to Rackwick. The RSPB asks you to avoid disturbing nesting bonxies and divers by not following diversions to Rora Head.

Walking from Moaness Pier (where the foot-passenger ferry from Stromness arrives) along the valley to Rackwick (page 141) adds a further 9 miles (4hrs) in total to the Old Man walk. If intending to do this, take the first ferry of the day. Another unhurried day-hike option is to use the seasonal bus (page 137) from Moaness to Rackwick, walk to the Old Man and then stroll back to the pier.

Hoy, South Walls and Flotta **WHAT TO SEE AND DO**

4

known as Bring Deeps, you can really appreciate Scapa Flow's vastness, with a backdrop of Orphir on the Mainland and, 18 miles east, South Ronaldsay. Lyrawa Hill looks down on an important World War II anti-aircraft defence battery, **Scad Head**, which formed part of the Scapa barrage and battery. From the car park the battery is distant but clearly visible above the shore; it comprises four circular concrete emplacements in a semicircular arc around a central command post. At its height, this barrage, which also comprised units on Flotta and Hoxa Head on

South Ronaldsay, took less than 3 minutes to fire a curtain of 1,800 shells to a height of 32,000ft, turning the skies around Scapa Flow black. An information board recounts the observations of those who took part, including Reginald Brimicombe, who noted how 'all the fire and thunder in Dante's *Inferno* was let loose.' After April 1940 the Luftwaffe never made a significant raid on the fleet at Scapa Flow.

Just 200yds south along the road from Lyrawa Hill, a short boardwalk leads to a conspicuous grave, marked by a fibreglass tombstone and ringed by a white picket fence. This is the resting place of **Betty Corrigall**, whose intensely sad story speaks volumes about the times – the 1770s – in which she lived. Aged 27, Betty became pregnant; she was unmarried and the father ran away to sea. In her shame, Betty twice tried to take her own life; the second time she was successful. In the 18th century, convention denied burial on consecrated ground for suicides and the lairds of Melsetter refused her a burial. Instead, she was laid to rest on the boundary of Hoy and North Walls parishes. Her body was disturbed several times, sometimes accidentally by peat-cutters, at other times by ghoulish servicemen during World War II. Military commanders moved her grave 50yds and covered it with a concrete slab to prevent further intrusion. In 1949 an American minister erected a wooden cross and a fence. In 1976 Betty was finally given a headstone and a second service. Her grave lies behind an ineffably serene loch, the **Water of Hoy**, a place of singular beauty whose edges overflow and gently tilt peaty water into a roadside stream. Red-throated divers sometimes nest here.

Continuing south, the road passes Lyrawa Bay, a small area of saltmarsh popular with waders and ducks. The views west and south are austere, with stark moorland pulling to a skyline framed by the peaks of the Red Hill of Sneuk and Genie Fea. The road then twists and turns over a stone bridge above **Pegal Bay**. A couple of picnic tables are positioned here above the burn that feeds the bay; to view the modest falls, pass through the gate. The promising path here soon peters out by a sheer drop to the burn. Once you are back on the road, the scenery opens out into the wide, picturesque Mill Bay before you reach the settlement of Lyness.

Lyness During World War II, the small port and township of Lyness was the main UK shore base for servicing the home fleet and, by 1940, more than 12,000 military and civilian personnel were stationed here. Battleships, aircraft carriers and smaller craft all required re-supply and repair, and their personnel needed recreation. Lyness is among the most historically important military sites in the country. Accordingly, it is a place of near-pilgrimage for surviving veterans, their relatives and the many people wishing to explore a key wartime location and pay homage to those who served and fell in defence of their country.

The remains of the base are scattered around and above the modern-day pier on the east coast of the island, roughly halfway between the township of Hoy in the north and Longhope on South Walls in the south. Interest is centred on the **Scapa Flow Visitor Centre and Museum** (w tinyurl.com/scapa-visitor), the collection of wartime memorabilia in its forecourt, a huge storage tank, the site of the former cinema and NAAFI canteen, and, a short walk away, Lyness naval cemetery. A mile or so west, up the side of the hill of Wee Fea, stand the collapsing ruins of the World War II communications centre.

At the time of writing, all sites are closed for major refurbishment (due to open in mid–late 2020) that includes a new-build museum, café and enhanced self-guided Lyness Wartime Trail. Nevertheless, you are free to wander around the grounds and the perimeter of the closed buildings, and good guided tours still run around

WALK TO SCAD HEAD

Distance: 3 miles (return); time: 2hrs
Start/finish: Lyrawa Hill car park ⊕ HY284997
OS Map: Explorer 452 Hoy, South Walls & Flotta

The substantial remains of Scad Head Battery can be reached on an enjoyable walk from Lyrawa Hill. Even if you are not particularly interested in the minutiae of wartime architecture, this is a gorgeous hike through heather to the coast. The vibrant wildlife contrasts with the rather sobering accounts of the battery's activities: expect to glimpse skylark, perhaps red grouse and even snipe.

The route is nicely signposted. From the car park, walk through the gate and follow the path as it descends – sometimes steeply – through slippery bog and sprigs of heather. After half a mile, the path meets a wide track descending from the left: this is an old tramway (which substituted for a road to the battery). Turn right downhill along this. After 400yds, where the tramway widens and bears left, take the clear but narrow track slightly right as it contours towards the battery buildings. Scottish Access Law requires that you do not enter the buildings, but the combination of observation posts, gun emplacements engine room and searchlight stations make for a striking, if rather mournful, spectacle.

Walking a little further east is worth the effort. Rather than the wide green path to the shore, follow the narrow track through heather just above the last gun emplacement. After 200yds, down on the shore you will see remains of the metal net curtain that formed a defence boom draped right across Scapa Flow. Grey seals frequently haul out on the rocks: stay well back from the edge to avoid disturbance. In late autumn, seals pup here. To return, retrace your steps up the tramway. This time, keep ahead uphill all the way to the main road for more fine views. Go through the gate and turn left to return to the car park.

the sites, beginning from Lyness ferry waiting room (☎ 01856 791300; e museum@orkney.gov.uk; ⏰ Mar–Apr & Oct 10.00–16.30 Mon–Sat; May–Sep 10.00–16.30 daily; booking advised, £5.50). Meanwhile, a small temporary exhibition on the history of Lyness operates from Hoy Hotel (⏰ Jun–Sep, times vary; see contact details for the wartime trail, above).

Given its importance, Lyness can be surprisingly confusing at first: there is a lot to take in, signposting is imperfect, the site is quite large and it's easy to find yourself gazing at what you think is a wartime building of importance only to realise it is a modern-day aquaculture centre or a cargo depot.

The **visitor centre and museum** are located at the top of the access road to the ferry jetty, in the **old pumphouse** where four oil tanks were constructed in 1917. The wide forecourt is draped with anti-torpedo netting, anti-aircraft guns and, most strikingly, the propeller and shaft of HMS *Hampshire*, which was sunk by a mine in 1916 (see box, page 99). Weighing 35 tons, the propeller and shaft were recovered by a German salvage ship in 1985.

Steps behind the museum lead up to the ginormous **oil tank**, which in 2020 will house an audiovisual display of Scapa Flow's key events. From 1936 to 1939, as war loomed, a further 12 storage tanks were added to store the vast quantities of fuel needed to power the home fleet.

To the right of the visitor centre, reached by a 200yd-long path alongside a railway track, are the **Romney huts**. Home to a large steam pinnace (a tender boat attached to a warship), these are thought to have belonged to Admiral van Reuter, who scuttled the German fleet at the end of World War II (see box, page 70). The pond you walk by to reach the huts is a former quarry, from which materials for construction works at Lyness were hewn. On the opposite side of the museum and visitor centre, a twin-stone memorial honours those who died in the Arctic convoys of 1941–45, the inscription written in English and Russian.

The pier that today serves the Houton ferry from the Mainland also has wartime origins. The need for a larger pier was identified before 1939 but only completed in 1944. The time and money involved led to it being labelled the Golden Wharf. Today, as well as serving the ferry, the pier is a base for testing tidal energy; various futuristic-looking tubes and pipes are often seen floating in surrounding waters.

Lyness has more to offer beyond this central hub. As you take the B9048 from the pier up towards the B9047 spinal road, you will see a red corrugated iron building on the left. The site was also home to a cinema and NAAFI canteen. The building is in a state of complete collapse: you could easily dismiss it as an abandoned farm building. Some 400yds further up the road, at the junction with the B9047, is the Hoy Hotel, which stands on part of the site of the old Haybrake Camp, where the Women's Royal Naval Service (the 'Wrens') lived. By 1945 1,500 Wrens were stationed on Hoy.

Two other nearby wartime sites are worth exploring. Follow the B9047 north for 600yds to reach **Lyness Naval Cemetery**, which commemorates more than 600 war dead. Sailors began burying fallen comrades here in 1915; more than 440 from World War I lie here. As with all Commonwealth war graves, it is immaculately kept. There's a monument to those who died on HMS *Malaya* at the Battle of Jutland on 31 May 1936 and to HMS *Vanguard* (page 21), as well as unmarked graves commemorating the dead of HMS *Hampshire*. Other graves record simply the resting place of 'a boy'. A small group of German graves are maintained in the north corner of the cemetery; a further solitary grave, to German combatant Johannes Thill, lies in the south corner.

High above Lyness, just below the summit of **Wee Fea**, is the **old communications block**, where a number of Wren personnel were stationed. To reach it, drive across

A WALK EXPLORING LYNESS AND WEE FEA

Distance: 3 miles; time: 2hrs, plus 2hrs visiting time
Start/finish: Scapa Flow Visitor Centre ✪ HY310945
OS Map: Explorer 462 Hoy, South Walls & Flotta

While you can drive between all the sites at Lyness, exploring them on foot is a viable option and allows you to combine inspection of wartime locations with superb views of Hoy and Scapa Flow, complemented by uplifting wildlife.

Begin at the visitor centre. After exploring the site and the adjacent Romney huts and oil tank, walk past the Arctic convoys memorial and uphill along the B9048 towards the B9047. Pass the Navy, Army and Air Force Institutes (NAAFI) site. At the B9047 crossroads, go straight ahead past the Hoy Hotel. Continue for 1½ miles, cross the cattle grid and turn left above the communications block. From this point all the old naval fleet anchorages are visible. Continue for 200yds to the viewpoint and picnic site.

Return the same way; before you turn right downhill past the plantation, walk straight ahead on the track for 400yds to the underground wartime storage tanks. Then retrace your steps downhill. After crossing the cattle grid, take the path that leads into the rear of Lyness Naval Cemetery. Exit through the main entrance and turn right then first left along the minor lane. Take the first right passing a nondescript brick building that once housed the naval base squash courts. Stay on the lane to arrive back behind the visitor centre, the Romney huts and the pond.

Wildlife here can be exquisite: ironically, the crumbling concrete and railway ballast have produced a lime-rich environment that allows calcium-loving plants such as kidney vetch and fairy flax to thrive. Frogs and toads – Orkney's only native amphibians – reside in the pond, and you may spot great yellow bumblebees or butterflies such as the meadow brown and common blue fluttering against a backdrop of tormentil and crowberry.

the T-junction of the B9047 and the B9048, past the Hoy Hotel. Continue for 1 mile, crossing a cattle grid. At the far corner of a conifer plantation on your left, turn left along an increasingly rough road above the communications block. The site is closed but, just beyond, a picnic spot provides a magnificent view both of Lyness and Scapa Flow.

A mile or so south from Lyness along the B9047, a signpost indicates the tiny, near-deserted settlement of **Rinnigill**. This merits a fleeting visit both for its wartime importance and an astonishing smashed spectacle. During World War II, Rinnigill, located across Ore Bay from mission control, was effectively an extension of Lyness operations. What you see today are the fractured remains of a concentration of research, training, supply and maintenance buildings that were home to hard-nosed war preparation. Among the activities was a hydrogen-production plant that provided gas for barrage balloons that were launched to force enemy aircraft to fly higher. These resulted in fewer direct hits by Nazi forces on intended targets; the only drawback was that strong Orcadian winds blew away so many balloons that they had to be constantly replaced. The firefighting school saw 36,000 personnel trained to deal with blazes on confined replica ships. Similar skills were learnt at the Important Training Centre, which taught naval staff how to

With the exception of Lyness and Scad Head, there is surprisingly scant official interpretation or signage related to the wars on Hoy. Air-raid shelters, gun emplacements, pill boxes and observation posts abound but only occasionally do you come across even a homespun fingerpost sign to alert you to them. Even this is usually put in place either by volunteers or locals, possibly in proactive response to endless questions from visitors. Perhaps it's the enormous cost of restoring and preserving such buildings – or entirely dismantling them – that has created this state of affairs. Rinnigill (page 149) is a good example: given adequate – admittedly, astronomic – funding, it would be a fascinating place to explore with the right interpretation. That said, there is also an awful lot of mundane military remnants scattered around. If every location where a commander played ping-pong with his subordinates were documented, even the most avid military historian might lose the will to live. To put it another way: this author has visited just about all such sites so that you don't have to.

respond to torpedo attacks. You can explore the paths but there is no interpretation and access is pretty much universally forbidden to the shattered buildings as well as the steel pier that serviced the hydrogen plant. The best perspective of Rinnigill is actually from back across the bay at Lyness, where a helpful locator map pinpoints the various buildings.

One anachronism here, located at Crockness beyond the eastern end of Rinnigill, is a Martello tower, constructed during the Napoleonic wars. It is one of a pair, the other located on South Walls (page 154). Don't waste your time seeking it out, however: it is privately owned, near-derelict and lies behind aggressive farm dogs and fences. Its sibling on South Walls is a far better bet.

SOUTH HOY Heading south, just before the causeway to South Walls, you may spot a grand house of sandstone gables and a grey-slate roof behind a walled garden, reached by a narrow drive to the right. This is **Melsetter House**, an exquisite three-storey country mansion – and somewhat unexpected in such a remote location. Built in 1898 by William Richard Lethaby, the Arts and Crafts architect, the house was fashioned on the site of a two-storey, L-shaped laird's abode that dates to 1738. That original property was home to the Moodie family, who owned much of Walls parish from the 16th century to the 1820s. Lethaby was commissioned to give the place a makeover by Thomas Middlemore and Theodesia Mackay, a renowned embroiderer and weaver, who were disciples of William Morris. The latter's daughter, May Morris, subsequently visited the refashioned Melsetter and described it as 'a sort of fairy palace on the edge of the northern sea, a wonderful place, remotely and romantically situated, with its tapestries and its silken hangings and its carpets'. The interior is beautifully preserved, from the vaulted morning room to contemporary stained glass in the chapel. The fine walled garden is among the oldest in Orkney. At the time of research, the house was closed following the death of the most recent owner but relatives were hopeful of reopening in 2019. To check on the status, contact J M F Groat & Sons grocers in Longhope (page 140).

SOUTH WALLS The island of South Walls has long been connected to Hoy by a natural gravel bar known as the Ayre. In 1912 a more substantial half-mile road

A WALK IN REMOTE HOY: HELDALE WATER AND THE WEST COAST

Distance: 7¼ miles; time: 5hrs
Start/finish: by entrance to access road to treatment plant ✪ ND284913, 3 miles south of Lyness
OS Map: Explorer 462 Hoy, South Walls & Flotta

For a taste of Hoy's remoteness and a glimpse of its hard-to-access interior, take a walk up to Heldale Water and beyond to exquisite Little Rack Wick where a tiny beach and utter seclusion await. This, however, is a tough walk, involving a good deal of ploughing through and over heather and only suitable for the very fit and those with experience of such robust conditions.

Located deep in the moors and hills of southwest Hoy, Heldale enjoys a stunning position. The first 1½ miles are easy enough, as you simply walk gently uphill along the access road to a water-treatment plant and communications tower. (The road is in an utterly appalling condition, so do not be tempted to shorten the walk by driving to the water; you will have better things to do than changing a tyre on these moors. There is plenty of space to park where the access road meets the B9047.)

You may well see hen harrier or peregrine hunting across the moors. The best view of the loch is your first – from the brow of the hill. When you reach the loch side, turn right and follow the east and then the north shore (mainly over open ground) and make for the summit of Bakingstone Hill (✪ ND253928). From here, descend towards the sea, heading west-northwest towards the burn where you can pause at a pool (though not for long on a calm day, as the midges will instantly find you). Keep the burn to your right and head to Little Rack Wick Bay. The easiest return route is to retrace your steps: you could head south to the geo and come back along the southern shore of Heldale Water but the heather here can be formidable, testing the endurance of most walkers.

causeway was constructed to permanently link the two. Nevertheless, the island is viewed as a separate community and offers a striking contrast to brooding Hoy. The island name is a corruption of 'Sooth Waas' ('Southern Voes', a 'voe' being a narrow sea inlet, of which South Walls has many). The island was important in Norse times, as it was one of the first safe harbours that the Vikings could reach on the travels from Scandinavia.

Activity centres upon the township of Longhope, where you will find a shop, petrol, a hotel, a doctor's surgery and not a great deal else (see pages 138 and 140). Longhope, however, is an attractive place to pass through as it is scattered along the hillside running above North Bay, a sweeping inlet that pushes into Scapa Flow.

Geographically, the rolling landscape of South Walls is more like other Orkney islands than Hoy. Most of the island is given over to farmland. South Walls crams plenty of appeal into its small size (3½ miles by 2½ miles). It played an important role in Orkney's conversion to Christianity, has a surprising number of prehistoric sites, an imposing lighthouse and an impressively crenulated south coast. More recent history saw Longhope operate as the shore headquarters for the Grand Fleet in World War I; it is from here that the massive 'dreadnought' battleship fleet was dispatched to the Battle of Jutland in 1916. South Walls's easternmost point, Cantick

THE LONGHOPE LIFEBOAT TRAGEDY

On 17 March 1969, coxswain Dan Kirkpatrick and his seven crewmen responded to a distress call from a Liberian steamship, the *Irene*, that was in difficulty in heavy seas east of South Ronaldsay. In the early evening they launched their lifeboat, the *TGB*, aiming to traverse the tempestuous Pentland Firth. Contact with the lifeboat was lost at 22.00; a relief boat deployed to locate her was driven back by heavy seas. The *TGB* was found the following day, upturned, a few miles southwest of Tor Ness. The speculation is that a single 100ft wave had overturned the vessel. The bodies of seven lifeboat men were recovered, the eighth never being found. Meanwhile, the *Irene* had run aground near Grimness with all crew safe.

The impact on the local community was devastating. Almost every local family was left bereaved. One of the museum curators, Michael Johnson, lost his father and uncle; the current coxswain Kevin Kirkpatrick lost his father and grandfather (the Longhope lifeboat has had a serving Kirkpatrick since 1874 – Kevin's son and daughter are now among the 20 current volunteers). The disaster led the RNLI to introduce a role limiting the number of related crew members responding to any single emergency; it also triggered a redesign of future lifeboats so that they were self-righting.

Head, is one of the best places in Orkney for whale-watching and for spotting the orca pods that patrol the waters of the Pentland Firth for unwary seals.

Just before you cross the causeway on to South Walls, take the sharp turn to the right and then immediately left along the minor road by the shore through the township of Brims. A mile along here, where the road ends, you reach **Longhope Lifeboat Museum** (w longhopelifeboat.org.uk/museum/index.htm; ⊕ on request, call Geordie ☏ 01856 701431). The museum is built within the structure of the island's second boathouse, which served for 93 years; the remains of the first, dating to 1874, still stands on the Ayre and is used by local fishermen to store crabs and lobsters collected from inshore creels. Pride of place in the museum goes to the 1930s lifeboat, the *Thomas McCann*, which was bought for the princely sum of £1 by the trust that runs the museum; although no longer in service, every now and then she is launched into Aith Hope. Various memorabilia and harrowing paintings of crew at work adorn the walls. You'll find the current lifeboat, the *Helen Comrie*, afloat at Longhope Pier on South Walls. There is a saddening account of the Longhope lifeboat disaster of 1969 (see box, above) as well as a more uplifting display of successful rescues. A memorial to the eight men who died stands in the Osmondwall cemetery at Kirk Hope.

With the exception of Hackness Martello Tower and Battery (page 154), the main sights of South Walls can be inspected in the course of a delightful walk centred upon the southern half of the island. This will take around 4 hours and covers 8 miles. The first 5 miles are occasionally tough going but provide sensational views of geos, natural arches, sea stacks, waterfalls and the thrilling – or perhaps chilling – spectacle of gloups, where inland holes drop right to the sea. The last section is a glorious stroll along a quiet lane lying on the backbone of the island. Alternatively, if you have a car, access lanes mean that the archaeological sites described here are never more than a few hundred yards' walk from the main road. The best place to start is the car park at the east end of the causeway (⊕ ND293893).

Follow the footpath sign and take the track as it climbs gently uphill with the sea on your right. Almost immediately South Walls lays on a geological feast: the

The Heart of Neolithic Orkney World Heritage Site includes an astonishing cluster of stones and structures.

top left New discoveries are commonplace at the Ness of Brodgar, where one of Europe's largest ongoing archaeological digs is taking place (O) page 107

top right Maeshowe chambered cairn is said to date back 5,000 years (VS/KL) page 108

above The reconstructed settlement at Barnhouse illustrates a once-substantial Neolithic village (SS) page 108

below The Ring of Brodgar boasts 36 monoliths of all shapes and sizes (SS) page 105

above left   The rusting blockships found in Scapa Flow were deliberately sunk to protect the islands against enemy intrusion during the two world wars (TP/S) page 166

above right   Hackness Martello Tower on South Walls illustrates how Orkney's importance as a military base stretches back for centuries (SS) page 154

left   Balfour Castle dominates the waterfront of the island of Shapinsay (SS) page 197

below   Visible from much of the West Mainland, the Kitchener Memorial commemorates all those who lost their lives in the 1916 HMS *Hampshire* disaster (VS/KL) page 98

above left Arctic explorer Dr John Rae was one of the islands' most famous residents (VS/KL) page 84

above right Located on remote Papa Westray, the Knap of Howar is the oldest preserved stone house in northern Europe (SS) page 260

below Discovered by accident in 1929, the enigmatic Broch of Gurness once commanded a village and enjoys a dramatic setting above Evie beach (SS) page 94

above left Oatcakes are just one of the islands' many local foods (O) page 57

top right Jewellery making is a popular craft on Orkney and features many highly skilled silversmiths (O)

above right Chair-making is an age-old Orcadian handicraft (O) page 121

below Ferry journeys, such as the spectacular crossing from Scrabster to Stromness, are a feature of everyday life in Orkney (VS/PT) page 45

above left — Orkney's pioneering spirit is sometimes reflected in shop fronts, such as here in St Margaret's Hope (MR) page 169

above right — The Orkney Museum in Kirkwall offers an insight into Orkney life from prehistory right through to the 20th century (VS) page 123

right — Performances featuring traditional Orcadian music are plentiful in Kirkwall and elsewhere (O) page 119

below — Stromness is Orkney's second-largest but most attractive settlement (CVM/S) page 74

above left   Arctic terns are often spotted diving for fish along Orkney's shorelines (O) page 10

above right   The heather moorlands of the Mainland are home to around 65 pairs of hen harrier (O) page 10

left   Puffins breed on the islands between May and July (O) page 9

below left   Mill Loch on Eday is home to one of the UK's densest populations of red-throated diver (O) page 216

below right   Known by its Norse name of 'bonxie', the great skua is a common sight on coastal heaths (MM/S) page 10

top | North Ronaldsay sheep are famous for living on the island's beaches and off a diet of seaweed (O) page 277

above left and right | You're likely to see Eurasian otters along the shores of Scapa Flow (VS/PT and O) page 13

below left | Harbour seals are identified from their grey counterparts by their dog-like faces (O) page 12

below right | Orkney has far more beef cattle than people (SS) page 13

top   There's plenty of fun to be had messing around in boats on Orkney; sailing is a popular activity in Stromness harbour (O) page 62

left   The rockpools at the tidal causeway of the Brough of Birsay will keep children busy for hours (O) page 95

below   Orkney offers some of the UK's most rewarding walking routes thanks to its exhilarating landscapes, such as here in Hoy's Rackwick Valley (O) page 60

heavily indented coastline is in a constant state of battle with the sea, with ravines and geos eating into the land and offering nesting ledges for fulmars. Although the track seems to disappear now and then, you can always see it in the middle distance. Occasionally it hugs the cliff edge; if this makes you uncomfortable, use open ground to put some distance between yourself and the sea.

Views across the Pentland Firth take in the cliffs of Dunnet Head and the ski-slope dimensions of Duncansby Head, the most northeasterly point on the British mainland. In the middle of the firth lies the low-lying island of **Swona** while closer is the small, shapely island of **Switha**, which rises fetchingly at its southern end to the giddy heights of 91ft (see box, below).

Halfway along the route, the coastal path enters the **Hill of White Hamars**, a Scottish Wildlife Trust reserve. Grasslands by the cliffs here have never been ploughed or sprayed with fertilisers, so they are rich in plant and animal life. More than 180 types of wildflowers have been identified here, including Scottish primrose, tufted vetch and ragged robin. Late summer sees common blue and meadow brown butterflies emerge.

Around **Birsi Geo**, the scenery somehow manages to become even more dramatic. The cliffs may not be as high as those at Marwick Head, North Hoy or on Westray but they are infinitely varied: a striking sea stack, The Candle, rises adjacent to other huge stacks and arches that have been left behind by a retreating coast. Vast polished plates of rock tilt at rakish angles into the sea. Two well-signposted (though unfenced) **gloups** lie in wait along the path; peek into their depths if you have the nerve. At **Misbister Geo**, stepped ledges allow you to easily access the shore at low tide and explore the rock pools. Look back west from here and you will spot a waterfall pouring from a burn.

Just before a drystone dyke, above **Hesti Geo**, you reach a green mound that smothers the remains of a substantial broch, known as the **Green Hill of Hestigeo**, a quarter of which has been lost to the sea. A further 400yds east lie the covered remains of the **Roeberry burial mound**. From 2009 to 2011, excavations by the Orkney Research Centre for Archaeology unpicked a complex history. At its heart lay a round stone barrow with stone-line boxes or burial cists. There was also a square revetment wall; parts of the site form a marked change in barrow architecture.

4

SWONA, SWITHA AND STROMA

From Cantick Head, three mellifluous-sounding and uninhabited islands can be seen in the Pentland Firth. The furthest east is Swona, home to prehistoric and Norse remains. The tidal races around the island are often fearsomely turbulent and can jolt you out of your reverie if you are travelling on the Pentland Ferries service from Gill's Bay to St Margaret Hope. With binoculars you may pick out abandoned houses and cattle: Swona was inhabited up until 1974, at which point eight cows and a bull were left behind. Now feral, the cattle – a crossbreed of Shorthorn and Aberdeen Angus – have been classified as a new, distinct breed. They are the only herd of beef cattle to truly live wild. Switha, a mile east of South Walls, is so important for wildlife that it has been designated a Special Protection Area, particularly for its winter population of barnacle geese. Both islands are administered by Orkney Islands Council. In contrast, Stroma, the largest of the three and positioned to the south, is part of Caithness – and has been for some 500 years. The last family on Stroma – who operated the lighthouse – left in 1997.

In 995, the bay of Kirk Hope witnessed one of the most important acts in Orkney's history. The ruling and pagan earl Sigurd Hlodvisson (known as Sigurd the Stout) converted – or was 'coerced' is another interpretation – to Christianity. Olaf Tryggvasson, a Viking chieftain and claimant to the throne of Norway, was fresh from raiding the Hebrides and the Isle of Man, which were also part of Sigurd's domain. Olaf was bound for Norway to seize the crown there and his missionary zeal probably included a bit of realpolitik in that it would prove useful to have Sigurd as an ally rather than a rival. Conversion would help this aim. Sigurd was threatened with execution if he refused to convert; for good measure Olaf threatened to ravage Orkney with 'fire and steel' should he refuse. Unsurprisingly, Olaf agreed to be baptised. As a precaution, Olaf took Sigurd's son into captivity to vouchsafe the conversion but the boy soon died. This appears to have stretched Sigurd's faith to the limit. According to another Norse saga, *St Olaf's Saga*, it seems that 'after his death Earl Sigurd showed no obedience or fealty to King Olaf'.

While the barrow has Bronze Age features, there are suggestions it has underlying and surviving Neolithic origins.

Less than half a mile further on, you reach South Wall's eastern extremity, **Cantick Head lighthouse**, built by the Stevenson family in 1858. Keep on the outside of the wall and fence then, as the headland turns north, cross the stile further downhill to join the road. Follow this as it sweeps around alongside the beautiful oval-shaped bay of **Kirk Hope**.

On the left look for another substantial mound, originally thought to have been a broch but actually a large Neolithic or Bronze Age burial mound. It could well produce surprises when finally excavated. Keep ahead on the road to reach **Osmondwall cemetery**, just above the head of the bay. This is the resting place of the Longhope lifeboatmen who died in the 1969 tragedy (see box, page 152). The bronze statue of a lifeboatman stands high above the surrounding graves and is accompanied by the inscription 'Greater love hath no man than this; that he lay down his life for his fellow men'. The cemetery also houses several war graves from World War II, including that of Ernest Barber, whose headstone describes 'a boy' on HMS *Dreadnought* who died in 1915. He was barely 16 when he signed up.

Just above the cemetery is an exquisitely carved stone seat depicting the story of the conversion to Christianity of Orkney earl Sigurd Hlodvisson. The four panels depict the arrival of Olaf Tryggvasson, on a mission to convert the earl, and the tragic tale of how Sigurd's young son was taken hostage and died in captivity (see box, above).

The return to the causeway and the end of the walk is much shorter than the outward leg, traversing the spine of South Walls for nearly 3 miles along the unclassified road that passes Stromabank Hotel. This gives glorious views across the landscape you've just walked through.

Located on the northeast coast of South Walls, the **Hackness Martello Tower and Battery** (w tinyurl.com/hackness-martello; ⏲ Apr–Sep 09.30–17.30 daily; £5/3) enjoy a superb vantage point overlooking Scapa Flow. As there is no bus service, you must drive or walk the 2½ miles from Longhope along the B9047 and quiet country lanes (the site is well signposted). The tower is evidence that Hoy and Orkney were strategically important military locations well before the world wars. They were built during the Napoleonic wars in response to attacks by American privateers and French warships on British merchant ships going to and from the Baltic. A convoy system was assembled in Scapa Flow to protect the merchantmen with naval defences (including the Hackness Tower and Battery) established to protect the anchorage, although, ultimately, they never saw action. You can climb to the top of the tower to explore both its slightly sepulchre-like interior and the battery. That said, in both cases it is the views that catch your eye rather than the internal remnants of the sites.

FLOTTA Flotta is the ugly duckling of Orkney's inhabited islands, dismissed by those who have not been there or are put off by its flare stack, designed to release any pressure that builds up in pipelines and which, at 223ft in height, is visible from miles around. Cast your gaze away from the ever-flickering flame, however, and you'll encounter an island rich in wartime sites, boasting a fine coastal trail and a meaningful expanse of moorland, which, like Flotta's cliffs and inlets and surrounding seas, is important for wildlife and rewarding for wildlife-watching. The island has also added to Orkney's archaeological compendium: the Flotta stone, 5ft by 2ft and inscribed with a Celtic cross and dating to the 8th century, was found on the island (it's now housed in the National Museum of Scotland).

Don't dismiss that flare stack too readily either: it, and the oil terminal to which it is tethered, are the source of much of Orkney's modern-day wealth. Well served by ferry (from Houton, part of a triangular route that also takes in Lyness on Hoy; £4.25 passengers; page 135) and reasonably sized (just 3 miles by 2 miles), the island is easily visited on a day trip. This is Orkney's most underestimated and overlooked island.

The ferry journey from Houton to Flotta is one of the best ways to see Scapa Flow wildlife and appreciate this natural harbour's vast dimensions. Expect to spot guillemots, eiders and gannets all year and little auks in winter. The ferry docks at Gibraltar pier right in front of the oil terminal. There is a small hut here that brims

4

PLASTIC IN SCAPA FLOW

The waters of Scapa Flow appear idyllic: seals hauled out or pupping, the abundance of seabirds, and ground-nesting birds on the surrounding shores all suggest a waterscape in good health. Yet even Scapa Flow has not been able to escape the curse of plastic. Nationally, the issue of plastic has deservedly – if belatedly – entered public and political consciousness. But the fact that plastic ends up in such a remote backwater says a good deal about the pervasive nature of the problem.

In 2018, new research found that sediment samples from beaches around Scapa Flow have a level of tiny plastic waste – known as microplastics – similar to that of industrialised waterways such as the Clyde and the Firth of Forth. All 100 samples collected from 13 sites around Scapa Flow contained tiny fragments of thin plastic bags, clothing and microbeads from cosmetics. These are easily mistaken for food by fish and seabirds. Dr Mark Hartl, associate professor of marine biology at Heriot-Watt University, said the results of the Scapa Flow research were 'surprising' given its sheltered location: 'The fact that a relatively remote island has similar microplastic levels to some of the UK's most industrialised waterways was unexpected, and points to the ubiquitous nature of microplastics in our water systems.'

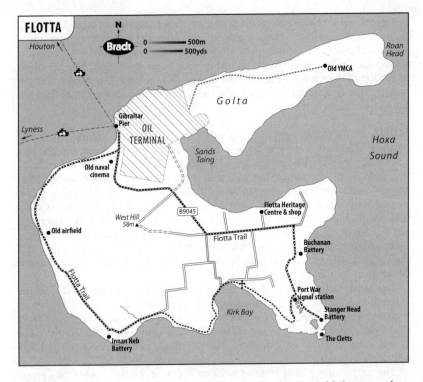

with information on Flotta (just about all the outer islands could do worse than copy Flotta's template). The best way to explore is to follow the Flotta Trail, which runs around the southern two-thirds of the island (8 miles; 4–5hrs). The moorland peninsula of Golta, northeast of the terminal, can also be explored along a track.

Proceeding anticlockwise, the trail leads past the ruins of the **old naval cinema** and woodland originally planted by Naval Ratings during World War II, reportedly 'to relieve the crushing monotony'. Many ratings were to die in combat, and the woodland was restocked with 50,000 trees (including sycamore and elder), only when the oil terminal was built. This is a good place to see goldcrests.

The trail then follows the road past the airfield to reach the various emplacements of the **Innan Neb Battery**, which defended Switha Sound in both world wars. An anti-shipping boom, comprising rugged wooden boxes connected by hawsers and metal spikes, ran all the way across the sound to near Hackness Martello Tower on South Walls.

Shortly afterwards, the trail leaves the road and embarks on a delightful coastal route along the edges of **Kirk Bay**. You can usually see right across the Pentland Firth to Duncansby Head. On a clear day you can pick out the outline of Ben Royal, far to the southwest.

After passing the church, a short climb above steep-sided House Geo leads to Port War signal station. During World War II this co-ordinated shipping movements and submarine detection; today it is an eerie place, littered with skeletons of water towers and a turfed air-raid shelter. Close by – just follow the lane north for 300yds to the T-junction and turn right – lies **Stanger Head Battery**. Although rather desultory – the battery serves as Flotta's dump – it is worth persevering to the grassy track at the headland, which leads to a fine viewpoint of two sea stacks, the Cletts,

For more than 40 years the protected waters of Scapa Flow have proved ideal for bringing ashore oil from North Sea oilfields. The huge 395-acre site on Flotta began operating in 1977. At its peak, 10% of UK oil output reached land here. The oil still comes, though a 30in-wide, 135-mile-long pipeline below the sea. It is treated, pumped into tankers and shipped around the globe. More than 33 crude-oil tankers dock here each year, and arriving vessels are escorted by tugs based in Scapa Bay. As North Sea reserves have dwindled, Flotta now also handles oil from the western waters off Shetland. Scapa Flow has also become one of the primary locations in Europe for ship-to-ship transfers of crude and fuel oils as well as liquid natural gas.

Among the paraphernalia visible at the site are seven large storage tanks, capable of holding up to a million barrels of oil. The most prominent feature, though, is the Flotta flare, and you will see it burning day and night from much of the coastline of Scapa Flow. The flare is part of the safety system for the site and is designed to prevent pipelines and equipment from over-pressurising due to what oil terminal literature euphemistically describes as 'unplanned upsets'. In the event of any emergency, the flare will burn off any reserves.

one of which looks remarkably like a woodpecker. The large quarry you pass here provided the stone for construction of the terminal.

Turning north from Stanger Head the road provides one of very few viewpoints from which both Stromness and Kirkwall are visible. Down to the right lie the well-preserved ruins of **Buchanan Battery**, with a detector tower, crew shelters, engine houses and searchlight platforms. Along with Stanger Head, the Hoxa and Balfour batteries on South Ronaldsay, this defended Hoxa Sound.

The trail turns west along the island road and 300yds further on it is worth turning right to visit **Flotta Heritage Centre** ✱ (⏱ Apr–Oct 09.00–19.00 daily; Nov–Mar 10.00–17.00 daily; donation requested). Housed in an immaculately restored 1940s cottage and barn, this is among the best centres of its kind in all of Orkney. The cottage houses period furniture while the barn is full of memorabilia, expertly presented, that ranges from historic photographs of Flotta folk digging up potatoes ('lifting tatties') to items deeply personal to islanders. You are left with a sense of the unassuming yet immense pride that islanders feel in their own and their island history.

Next door is **Flotta Shop** ✱ (⏱ 09.30–11.30 & 16.45–17.45 Mon–Wed, Fri & Sat, 09.30–13.00 Thu), which offers a real step back in time, with long wooden shelves, lined with wallpaper, bending under the weight of goods. Cheese is cut with a guitar string. Should you need it, the shop also acts as the island post office (same hours).

If you have time before the ferry departs, you can explore the moors of **Golta**, east of the oil terminal. To do so, you need to call security at the terminal (☏01856 884359). There are two entrances, one right by Gibraltar pier and the other just southeast of the terminal by Sands Taing. While there are tracks here and there through the moors, the easiest walking involves following the single-track lane across the north side of Golta. If you've viewed Golta from Buchanan Battery, you may have seen what looks like a circle of standing stones or a deserted medieval church standing lonely on the moors; this is actually the old YMCA, now utterly ruinous. Peregrine, rock pipit and stonechat are among the birds you may see here. From the terminal to the YMCA and back is a distance of almost 3 miles, though the going is easy.

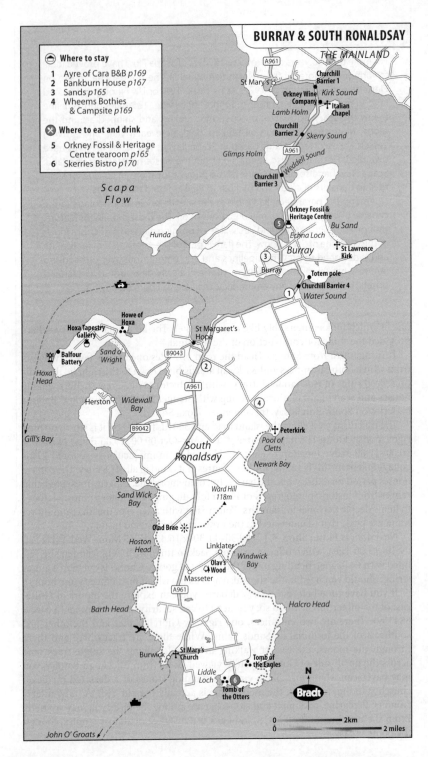

BURRAY & SOUTH RONALDSAY

THE MAINLAND

A961

St Mary's

Churchill Barrier 1

Orkney Wine Company

Kirk Sound

Italian Chapel

Lamb Holm

Churchill Barrier 2

Skerry Sound

A961

Glimps Holm

Weddell Sound

Churchill Barrier 3

Orkney Fossil & Heritage Centre

Bu Sand

Echna Loch

Burray

St Lawrence Kirk

Hunda

Burray

Totem pole

Churchill Barrier 4

Water Sound

Scapa Flow

Howe of Hoxa

Hoxa Tapestry Gallery

St Margaret's Hope

Balfour Battery

Sand o' Wright

B9043

Hoxa Head

Herston

Widewall Bay

A961

Gill's Bay

B9042

Peterkirk

Pool of Cletts

Newark Bay

South Ronaldsay

Stensigar

Sand Wick Bay

Ward Hill 118m

Olad Brae

Hoston Head

Linklater

Olav's Wood

Windwick Bay

Masseter

A961

Barth Head

Halcro Head

Burwick

St Mary's Church

Tomb of the Eagles

Liddle Loch

Tomb of the Otters

N

Bradt

John O' Groats

0   2km
0   2 miles

5

Burray and South Ronaldsay

Known as the Barrier Isles, Burray and South Ronaldsay dangle off the southeast shores of the Mainland, connected by a series of causeways that also link the smaller islands of Lamb Holm, Glimps Holm and Hunda. For many visitors, these islands provide their introduction to Orkney as they contain the arrival points for the foot-passenger service from John O'Groats and the car ferry from Gill's Bay. The islands host a couple of Orkney's most popular attractions in the shape of the delightful Italian Chapel and the breathtakingly located Tomb of the Eagles, but otherwise they see very few visitors. This is partly because the fast spinal road can quickly sweep new arrivals north through the islands to the attractions of the Mainland; and also because to see what these islands have to offer you need to turn off the main road.

HISTORY

Prehistoric peoples settled on the coasts of these islands at least 5,000 years ago and their legacy is seen in several tombs scattered around, mostly on South Ronaldsay. The islands have always been accommodating to those looking to live off the land and raise livestock; early farmers would have settled here with cattle and sheep. The Picts also had a presence, particularly on Burray, where they built so many brochs that these gave the island their modern name (page 4). Christian worship is thought to have been established on the islands before the Vikings arrived; much later, 17th-century records show nine churches on South Ronaldsay alone.

The Vikings certainly made themselves known here. The Howe of Hoxa on South Ronaldsay is said to be the burial spot for a 10th-century earl, Thorfinn Skull-Splitter. In 1889 a huge Viking hoard, dating to the late 10th century, was uncovered on Burray. This included bullion, silver coins and interlocking bracelets of a distinctive Scottish form known as 'ring-money'; most of the hoard is now on display at the National Museum of Scotland.

The islands boomed in the 19th century with the rise of the herring industry; at that time St Margaret's Hope was able to sustain more than 20 shops, compared to the three general stores of today.

Like on Hoy, 20th-century wars have left their stamp on the islands. The most visible impact is the extraordinary engineering feat that is the Churchill Barriers that protected Scapa Flow but also joined islands with the Mainland. Defensive batteries were built on South Ronaldsay and several hundred troops were stationed here, many overseeing the Italian POWs who were requisitioned to the task. Social impacts also followed: journeys to Kirkwall that had taken all day were now possible in less than an hour, while with attention diverted to the Mainland, many

THE CHURCHILL BARRIERS

During World War I, defending Scapa Flow involved the placement of blockships (see box, page 166) to deter enemy vessels from penetrating the eastern edges of the natural harbour. It wasn't long after World War II was declared, however, before their inadequacy was lethally exposed. On 13–14 October 1939, U-47, a German submarine, slipped undetected into Scapa Flow in 1939 and launched a torpedo attack on HMS *Royal Oak* with the loss of 833 crew (see box, opposite).

This was a shattering blow, and not just for the scale of the death toll. The Royal Navy had referred to Scapa Flow as 'The Holy of Holies': if Scapa Flow was not safe, then the whole British fleet was not safe. Without an effective fleet, Britain faced defeat. The importance of securing Scapa Flow could not be overstated. Winston Churchill, at that time the First Lord of the Admiralty, visited Orkney and ordered the construction of four permanent barriers to fill the watery gaps between the Mainland and South Ronaldsay. Just two entrances to Scapa Flow, to the south and to the west, were to be left open.

Work began in May 1940 and was carried out feverishly and at a time of high national anxiety as France was about to surrender to Nazi Germany. But this was to prove no easy task, as the engineers Balfour Beatty had to work amid strong tidal currents in narrow and deep waterways. The project involved quarrying 580,000 tons of rock and placing 66,000 concrete blocks, created from 333,000 tons of concrete.

Aerial cableways called blondins (after the famous French tightrope walker, Chares Blondin) were used to drop rock-filled cages into the channels. The bulk of each barrier, like an iceberg, lies under the surface, up to 59ft deep. More than 2,000 men worked on the barriers: 700 Orcadians, British and Irish labourers were later joined by 1,300 Italian prisoners of war.

The four causeways are numbered from north to south: 1 Kirk Sound (between the East Mainland and Lamb Holm); 2 Skerry Sound (between Lamb Holm and Glimps Holm); 3 Weddell Sound (between Glimps Holm and Burray); and 4 Water Sound (between Burray and South Ronaldsay). All channels were sealed between May 1942 and June 1943.

The barriers have transformed accessibility across the islands. They have also changed the local environment. Sand previously gently washed through Scapa Flow has morphed into beaches by barriers 3 and 4, entombing some ships scuttled here. The dunes east of barrier 4 have been stabilised by marram grass and the rubbery oyster pant (which yields a pink bell-shaped flower in summer); they are now home to Orkney's main colony of little terns. Wave dynamics also appear to be changing and there are concerns that the causeway has become more dangerous to cross during high winds. In 2016, barriers 3 and 4 were listed by Historic Environment Scotland in recognition of their national and international importance.

local shops closed, as, in time, did schools. The fact livestock and grain no longer had to be exported by boat triggered an increase in land prices; these have been further pushed up by the fact the islands have latterly become an attractive base from which to commute to Kirkwall.

GETTING THERE AND AWAY

The islands provide two of the gateways to Orkney from the rest of the UK. Pentland Ferries operates a vehicle service from Gill's Bay near John O'Groats to St Margaret's Hope, while a seasonal foot-passenger ferry runs from the small pier at John O'Groats to Burwick (page 45).

GETTING AROUND

Initially, exploration of these islands can be confusing: the main road is so fast that you can be at the other end of the island chain before you know it. With four barriers to traverse – as well as a coastal stretch in Burray that does a passable imitation of a barrier – it can take a while to work out where one island ends and another begins.

The A961 runs all the way from Kirkwall to the tip of South Ronaldsay. It leaves the East Mainland immediately south of St Mary's village and crosses a causeway on to Lamb Holm; it then traverses Glimps Holm and Burray before entering South Ronaldsay just above the village of St Margaret's Hope and continuing to the island's southernmost tip. It is 17 miles (30mins) from Kirkwall to St Margaret's Hope. Burwick is a further 7 miles south, about 10 minutes by car.

As for buses, service XI runs regularly from Kirkwall to Burray village (22mins) and St Margaret's Hope (30mins). For timetables visit **w** orkney.gov.uk/transport). There is no public transport east or west off the main road, nor any further south, nor is there a local taxi service on the barrier islands. A Kirkwall company (page 73) will charge around £60 to pick you up from Burwick on South Ronaldsay and take you to Kirkwall. Bear this in mind if planning one-way walks; alternatively, your accommodation hosts will often be happy to pick you up.

TOURIST INFORMATION

The back room of Robertson's Coffee Hoose & Bar on Church Road in St Margaret's Hope (page 168) is stocked with leaflets and other information about Burray, South Ronaldsay and further afield. The café staff will also give advice.

5

> ### THE *ROYAL OAK*
>
> Although direct conflict was intermittent and rare in Scapa Flow, some of the Royal Navy's greatest loss of lives took place here or in nearby waters. World War II saw the sinking of the *Royal Oak* by a German submarine. The deaths of 833 men constituted the Royal Navy's worst-ever disaster. On the night of 13–14 October 1939, the German submarine U-47 penetrated the defences at Kirk Sound, entered Scapa Flow and found HMS *Royal Oak* lying at anchor near the Holme shore. The first torpedoes hit glancing blows or missed altogether but a third salvo hit. The ship rolled over and sank within 15 minutes; many who died were trapped inside with no hope of escape. The submarine left the same way it came; its commander was personally awarded the Knight's Cross by Hitler. A buoy 2 miles south of Scapa Bay marks the official war grave where the ship sank. Every year, the anniversary is commemorated with a service over the wreck site during which the Royal Navy places a white ensign on her hull. The attack prompted the building of the concrete barriers to block the eastern approaches.

OTHER PRACTICALITIES

There's no **bank** anywhere on the Barrier Isles, but the **post office** in St Margaret's Hope (page 169) will issue cash against a debit card. For medical issues, try **Daisy Villa Surgery** in St Margaret's Hope (✆ 01856 831206).

There are no **petrol** pumps down this way: your nearest filling stations are in Kirkwall or at Deerness Stores (page 126).

LAMB HOLM

Less than half a mile long and scarcely any wider, Lamb Holm is a mere pebble at the foot of the mighty Mainland, yet it sees almost as many visitors as anywhere else on Orkney. This is, of course, because it is home to the ornate **Italian Chapel** (✆ 01856 781580; w tinyurl.com/italian-chapel; ⊕ Apr & Oct 10.00–16.00 daily; May & Sep 09.00–17.00 daily; Jun–Aug 09.00–18.30 daily; Nov–Mar 10.00–13.00 daily; £3), built by (Italian) prisoners of war in the early 1940s.

La Bella Cappella Italiana, to give the chapel its full name, is perched on a windswept mound overlooking Holm Sound. A visit to this minuscule building, which resonates with human emotion, is justifiably popular.

The chapel was built at Camp 60 in 1943–44 by covering two Nissen huts on the outside with concrete and coating them with bituminous felt. The artwork was completed by Domenico Chiocchetti; the wrought-iron work was undertaken by Giuseppe Palumbi, a trained blacksmith. They were joined by other felicitously named helpers – Bruttapasta, a cement worker, and Primavera, an electrician.

SMALL ATTRACTION MEETS MASS TOURISM

With more than 100,000 visitors a year, the Italian Chapel is among Orkney's biggest tourist attractions. As its popularity has risen in recent years, so has the issue of mitigating the pressures that come with such popularity. Concerns included the impact of coaches that each disgorged up to 100 cruise passengers, all eager to squeeze into the chapel. This has led to physical damage to the building from rucksacks banging against delicate paintwork. It became impossible to peaceably enjoy a place of serene beauty, to worship, or for families of POWs to honour their dead. In 2014 Orkney was shocked by the theft of three of the Stations of the Cross, which was felt to breach the sanctity not only of the chapel but more widely of Orcadians' strongly held belief that such things 'just do not happen' on their islands.

Although the Stations of the Cross have been replaced (the originals have not been found), the theft was the final straw. It triggered new entry arrangements, including CCTV, introduced during 2017. There are fixed visiting times and paid entry. Long gone are the days of informality, when you could turn up a little early or late and be given the run of the chapel for a few magical minutes by a friendly gatekeeper.

Coaches carrying cruise passengers must now make appointments to visit; chapel staff will advise individual travellers when such parties are likely to descend. These measures appear to have brought affairs under some degree of control, so you can now expect to visit the chapel without the intrusion of hassle. For many Orcadians, however, the fact that this has had to be done at all – combined with the breach of trust that presaged it – leave the world a poorer place.

THE MASTER OF THE ITALIAN CHAPEL

Born in Moena in 1910, Domenico Chiocchetti must have been struck by the contrast between the green pastoral valley in the Dolomites where he grew up and the windblown Scottish island where he was interred after being captured in North Africa. A professional artist, Chiocchetti turned to his skills to ease his homesickness. When the war ended and the time came for the Italian POWs to be repatriated, Chiocchetti stayed on for a few weeks to finish his work.

After he left, the chapel's fame grew but its condition quickly deteriorated and a preservation committee was formed. Chiocchetti was traced to Moena, where he was working as a painter and decorator. In March 1960, courtesy of the BBC, he was brought back to Lamb Holm for three weeks to restore his work. On his return home he wrote an open letter to the people of Orkney: 'Dear Orcadians, My work at the chapel is finished ... the chapel is yours – for you to love and preserve. I take with me to Italy the remembrance of your kindness and wonderful hospitality and ... the joy of seeing again the little chapel of Lamb Holm where I, in leaving, leave a part of my heart.' He returned again, with his wife, in 1964, bringing 14 Stations of the Cross hand-carved in Cirmo wood, a type of pine found in the Dolomites. When Chiocchetti died in Moena on 7 May 1999, his wife and daughter attended a memorial requiem mass at the Chapel in his honour. His daughter Letizia is the honorary president of the Italian Chapel Preservation Committee.

All four were among 1,300 Italian POWs brought to Orkney to work on the Churchill Barriers.

Outside the front door is a wooden carving of Christ on the Cross, gifted by the city of Moena, Chiocchetti's home town. Every so often, an expert delicately restores the blemishes that appear; most recently, in 2015, this was completed by Antonella Papa, an artist who has worked on the Sistine Chapel.

Chiocchetti began by hiding the interior of the corrugated iron of the hut behind a façade of plasterboard which he then painted with *trompe l'oeil* brickwork and carved stone to give the impression of tiles and stonework friezes. An altar, altar rail and holy-water stoop were moulded in cement by Bruttapasta.

A ceiling passage leads to the altar where an image of Madonna and Child, painted by Chiocchetti, gazes down at you. The infant Jesus holds an olive branch while an angel holds a shield from Chiocchetti's home town, depicting a ship passing from a dark storm of war to the light of peace. The painting was inspired by the same image by the artist Nicole Barabino, on a card given to Chiocchetti by his mother. On either side are paintings of St Catherine of Siena and St Francis of Assisi. Lanterns were made from bully-beef tins, and both a bell and candlesticks were taken from the rods of a stair on an old blockship.

Bruno Volpi, another POW at Camp 60, once explained why so many POWs invested time and emotion in the project: 'it was the wish to show, first oneself and then the world, that in spite of being trapped in a barbed-wire camp, with one's spirit physically and morally deprived of many things, one could still find something inside that could be set free'.

Perhaps less known is the fact the POWs built a second Italian chapel at Camp 34, just south of the Orkney Fossil and Heritage Centre on Burray, 2 miles to the south. Nothing now remains of this chapel, apart from pencil sketches that

5

Up to 1,300 Italian prisoners of war (POW) were moved to Orkney after being captured in North Africa in 1941. After being transported via the Cape of Good Hope and Liverpool, they were moved to Orkney specifically to work on the Churchill Barriers. Initially they refused to do so, pointing to the Geneva Convention, which forbade the labour of enemy prisoners for the war effort. Their deployment was controversial but ultimately justified on the grounds the barriers would benefit the community once the war was over (in terms of improved transport links). Between times, the POWs proved themselves a creative bunch, not just working on the barriers but manufacturing everything from furniture to jewellery and cigarette cases, often with elaborate detail. Islander visits were against the rules but the Italians nevertheless visited farms and villages. When the barriers were built, they hitched lifts to Kirkwall and sold their wares door to door. They staged concerts and played football, inevitably showing up local players with their superior ability in retaining possession.

suggest that it was almost as ambitious and impressive in execution as its more famous antecedent.

Just 200yds down the road from the chapel you will find the **Orkney Wine Company** (✆ 01856 781736; e info@orkneywine.co.uk; w orkneywine.co.uk; ◷ Apr–Sep 10.00–16.00 daily; other times, enquire ahead) which produces vegan-friendly liqueurs and fruit-based wines. Run by the enterprising van Schayk family who have risen from fermenting in demijohns bought from car-boot sales to the giddy heights of 1,100-litre stainless-steel tanks in a warehouse that stands, perhaps, from a commercial point of view, fortuitously, in the shadow of the Italian Chapel. Recently, the company has branched out and now also produces J Gow rum (w jgowrum.com) on the same site. If you are suffering whisky fatigue, or just curious about why someone would think of making wines this far north, the van Schayks will happily talk you through the process. They offer wine-tasting too, though if you are driving bear in mind that the innocuous-looking fruit wines that slide easily down the gullet kick in at 13.5% alcohol.

The 500yd-long Barrier 2 connects the south of Lamb Holm to Glimps Holm. The road skirts the eastern edge of this tiny uninhabited island before traversing Weddell Sound via Barrier 3 to make landfall on Burray.

BURRAY

Burray's name comes from a corruption of the Old Norse 'Borgarey', from 'borg' (broch) and 'oy' (island), thus meaning Broch Island. The brochs that so impressed the Vikings to give it this moniker have long since collapsed to ruinous states or disappeared altogether. At the height of the herring industry in the early 20th century, Burray was a major port with 25 boats docked here, supporting a population of 350 inhabitants. The island also has a long-standing tradition of boatbuilding.

Remarkably few visitors even give Burray the time of day – it can seem like just another small island to traverse while heading north or south – but it has one of Orkney's best museum type attractions and a couple of good places to stay and eat. The island's small dimensions (2 miles by 3) somehow also shoehorn in a decent beach and the island chain's 'fifth' causeway.

GETTING THERE AND AROUND Other than by private vehicle, transport is by bus. The X1 service (**w** orkney.gov.uk/transport) runs regularly from the bus shelter in Burray village to Kirkwall (◷ around 08.00–22.00 or later Mon–Fri; 22mins). Many services continue to Stromness, taking an hour.

 WHERE TO STAY, EAT AND DRINK *Map, page 158*

🏠 **Sands Hotel** (6 rooms) Burray village; ☎01856 731298; **e** info@thesandshotel.co.uk; **w** thesandshotel.co.uk. All on 1st floor, a mixture of refurbished dbls, suites & a family room (sleeps 4) all overlooking the bay. Set back from the village, the hotel strives for a nautical theme with porthole windows. In the large restaurant (◷ noon–14.00 & 17.00–20.45 daily; £££), some thought is put into meals, which include local scallops & an à la carte menu rising above the usual pub mains to include Cullen skink, 'blaggis

bonbons' (black pudding & haggis balls) & local salmon. Ask to dine in the conservatory, which has bay views. ££

🍽 **Orkney Fossil & Heritage Centre tearoom** Viewforth, Burray; ☎01856 731255; **e** info@orkneyfossilcentre.co.uk; **w** orkneyfossilcentre.co.uk; ◷ mid-Apr–Sep 10.00–17.00 daily. Fine home-baking with views over Echna Loch. Good range of toasties, soups & home-baked scones. £

SHOPPING Seaview Stores (Burray village; ☎01856 731209; ◷ 08.00–17.30 Mon–Fri, 10.00–17.30 Sat, noon–16.00 Sun) offers a range of groceries and alcohol. In a juxtaposition that doesn't cause an Orcadian to bat an eyelid, the shop also houses **Fluke Jewellery** (☎01856 731209; **w** flukejewellery.com; ◷ 08.00–17.30 Mon–Fri, 10.00–17.30 Sat, noon–16.00 Sun). Devotees of this distinctive jewellers (which, as the name suggests, specialises in creative designs of whales and dolphins), which was once based in Birsay on the Mainland, will be pleased to learn that it has been reincarnated. It is now run by local jeweller and farmer Bryce Wylie and Victoria Gardens.

WHAT TO SEE AND DO The excellent **Orkney Fossil and Heritage Centre** ✳ (contacts as per tearoom, see above) enjoys a delectable setting above Echna Loch. Ignore the pebble-dash exterior, as this is a gem. Pride of place goes to the outstanding fossil collection donated by the late Leslie Firth, a builder who quarried for stone at Sandwick, north of Skara Brae on the Mainland. The fossils emerged as Leslie was splitting stone in the quarry; they include impressive-looking specimens of lungfish, armoured fish and lobe-finned fish from a time when the area was submerged by Lake Orcadie.

Owned by the local community, the museum also offers fossils from further afield and a well-interpreted geological display. Upstairs lies a display of everyday objects assembled by Leslie's father, Ernest. There is an important genealogy section for visitors seeking to trace relatives. Finally, don't miss the excellent exhibition on the history of the Churchill Barriers.

The road running along the coast below the fossil centre looks like another Churchill Barrier but in fact is on the landward side of a narrow isthmus that forms **Echna Loch**. The name is Old Norse for 'giant's loch', so-called on account of the ayre (a lagoon-like stretch of water enclosed by a spit), which was said to have been put there by an Orcadian giant who disliked getting its feet wet. For such an idyllic spot, Echna Loch has a dark past. In the 17th century this is where female criminals were drowned while men were hanged on gallows positioned on the high ground above the water. More cheerfully, today the loch is a wonderful spot for birdwatching, with feathered rarities such as red-backed shrike occasionally spotted here.

As you travel through the Barrier Isles, you cannot fail to notice the remains of sunken ships poking out above the water. These are remains of the blockships, which preceded the Churchill Barriers. Many were ageing steamers deliberately sunk in World War I to block the entrances to Scapa Flow; more vessels were scuttled at the start of World War II to bolster defences while the Churchill Barriers were put being built. Over the years, some have been salvaged for scrap but those that remain provide a rather poignant spectacle. Next to Lamb Holm, the engine block of the *Lycia* can be seen by Barrier 2. The *Lycia* was driven ashore under her own steam in 1940; close by, the mast and hull of the *Emerald Wings*, sunk the same year, protrude above the waterline. Near Glimps Holm, the steam boiler of the *Argyle*, a World War I blockship, reveals itself at low tide. Further south, overlooking East Weddell Sound, Barrier 3 is fortified by the former Liverpool–Dublin steamer, the *Reginald*, its hull and bow marooned within a close distance of each other. On the Scapa Flow side of the Barrier are the remains of the captured German ship the *Empire Seaman*, which was sunk in 1940.

Burray village, half a mile south of the loch, is a low-key place, with playing fields and a hidden waterfront tucked down a quiet lane to the side of Seaview Stores. Burray is home to the workshop of Karen Duncan, the first Orcadian to be accepted into the Guild of Master Craftsmen. Karen specialises in modern design but does not have a studio/shop; instead her work can be seen in stores in Kirkwall and Stromness and at w karenduncanjewellery.com.

The east side of Burray is given over to the lonely, little-visited but beautiful **Bu Sand**. This is awkward to reach; the only access is down a lane that leads to South Links. As is often the case in Orkney, 'private' signs are dotted around the accesses to the beach; if you park back up the lane, walk east towards the shore and as a courtesy ask permission from anyone you see. The southern arm of Bu Sand is overlooked by a cemetery and the fragmented remains of St Lawrence Kirk, reached by the tiny access road just beyond the house at Leeth, off the minor road from Burray to Ness. An Inuit kayak bearing the date 1621 was preserved in the kirk around the year 1700, though it was later destroyed by fire; this is taken as evidence of a mini Ice Age during which the polar ice extended further south, enabling Inuit kayakers to explore Orkney waters.

As you cross from Burray to South Ronaldsay, look out for Orkney's second, less-heralded totem pole. A smaller cousin to the pole at St Mary's (page 131), the structure here was erected in 2002 by a local artist who fashioned it from a log of driftwood found floating nearby and christened it *The Viking*.

Two miles west of Burray village lies the small island of **Hunda**, reached by what is sometimes referred to as the fifth Churchill Barrier which runs east–west to connect Burray and Hunda. Its purpose is not entirely certain but may have been to prevent access to Scapa Flow by high-speed German E-boats. Hunda is usually reached by a fine, easy walk from Burray village along quiet lanes and the coast. At the time of writing, however, the island appeared off limits. Gates are padlocked amid a dispute between the landowner and the Orkney Islands Council. Ask locally to see if the situation has been resolved. If – when – this is the case, the barely hour-long walk around the island is worthwhile for the views of Scapa Flow and the barriers it provides.

Although it can seem small, at 7 miles by 3, South Ronaldsay is actually Orkney's fourth-largest island. In addition to the charming port of St Margaret's Hope at the north end of the island, it is home to two unusual burial chambers, the Tomb of the Eagles and the Tomb of the Otters. You can also tick off several standing stones across the island, as well as take in some outstanding clifftop scenery near Barth Head in the southwest corner. South Ronaldsay can seem a busy island, with a population of 850 people, many of whom work in Kirkwall. The name comes from the Old Norse 'Rognvaldsey', meaning 'Rognvald's Island'.

GETTING THERE AND AROUND The good news is that a fast and regular bus service runs between the Mainland and St Margaret's Hope. Frustratingly, that's where it stops. The X1 (w orkney.gov.uk/transport) runs regularly from the village pier to Kirkwall (30mins) from around 08.00–22.00 (at least) Monday–Friday. Many services continue to Stromness, taking just over an hour. Unless you've got a bicycle or are walking the coastline, getting any further south than St Margaret's Hope without a car is difficult.

ST MARGARET'S HOPE A strong case can be made for declaring St Margaret's Hope the most attractive of Orkney's villages. Tucked into the bowl of Water Sound, 'the Hope', as locals call it, exudes a distinct sense of yesteryear that echoes through its huddle of sandstone terraced houses amid the whiff of peat- and wood-burning stoves and the tang of seaweed that hangs in the air. Oystercatchers and gulls seem to peep and call around the clock amid the omnipresent soughing of a tide that bulges hard against the sea wall.

St Margaret's Hope is a fishing township, named for seven-year-old Margaret, the Maid of Norway, who died there on her way to marry the son of Edward I of England (the prearranged marriage was designed to defuse a succession crisis for her grandfather, Alexander III, King of Scots). At one time the town was also known as Ronaldsvoe.

Today it is a place packed with interest for its size (you can walk from one side to the other in 5 minutes) with two shops, two pubs and a café. And it was once busier still. Right up until World War I, the port boomed, feasting upon the herring catch. Among its famous citizens – depending on whether you are a fan or not – is William McGonagall, of doggerel-poetry fame, who rested his overworked quill here.

The village's compact, narrow streets take very little time to wander and sooner rather than later you will end up, variously and pleasingly, at a good café, pub, small museum or art gallery. Street names in St Margaret's Hope are impressively logical: Front Road, Back Road, Church Road … so no prizes for guessing where School Road leads. Here and there tiny alleyways, such as The Trance, thread their way between gardens linking one street to another.

Every few hours, the serenity of the village is interrupted for 15 slightly surreal minutes as the Pentland Ferry service from Gill's Bay arrives and departs. The ship disgorges its vehicles, which quickly disperse into the hinterland, allowing the village to return to its slumber.

🏠 **Where to stay** A handful of self-catering options are available around St Margaret's Hope and across South Ronaldsay – details at w orkney.com.

✳ 🏠 **Bankburn House** [map, page 158] (5 rooms) St Margaret's Hope; ☎ 01856 831310; w bankburnhouse.co.uk. Huge, mid-19th-century house oozing character. Stands high above St Margaret's Hope, on the A961 & 10-min walk from pubs & café. Front rooms have superb views right across to Hoy. 3 rooms en suite; all have fireplaces & sofas or *chaise-longue* & bay windows. Owner Mick Fraser is a former baker so be sure to ask for toast with the excellent b/fast. Staying here is a really different experience from the modern B&Bs that prevail across the Mainland. Also has 3 electric-vehicle charging points & an electric car for hire. Evening meals on request (2 courses £13; 3 courses £17.50). Recommended. **££**

🏠 **Bellevue Hotel** (3 rooms) Front Rd; 🌂 01856 831383; e info@thebellevueinn.com; w thebellevueinn.com. Rather gloomy as you enter but smart, well-appointed rooms, all on ground floor. Good-value family room sleeps 4 with space for sofa bed & cot. **££**

🏠 **The Creel B&B** (3 rooms) Front Rd; 🌂 01856 831311; e info@thecreel.co.uk; w thecreel. co.uk. Engaging B&B run by the gregarious David Loutit. All rooms en suite, with bay views & David's photography on the walls. Should you stay here, evening drinks with David may be among the memories you take home with you. 'I like to give my guests a pre-dinner drink & then kick them out to the pub,' he laughs. 'Our B&B is our home & you should expect to have some interaction with your host. People who have come to Orkney have, by definition, been pre-sorted from the run-of-the-mill traveller, so they are always a pleasure to talk to.' A born raconteur, David has enjoyed an interesting life's journey from Kazakhstan to

Orkney & is good company as he regales guests with tales of his time as a consultant to a company that printed money for the nascent central Asian nations that emerged from the collapse of the Soviet Union. Family roots in Orkney eventually brought him back home. 'I had been coming back for years. I'd brought all my wives here, & it was time to settle.' David cooks dinner for groups of around 10 but 'won't cook for 2 or 12'. Don't expect a Scottish fry-up for b/fast: 'I'm way too fussy,' he says. Guests will be served kedgeree with Westray-smoked salmon, or bubble & squeak. **££**

🏠 **Murray Arms** (6 rooms) Back Rd; 🌂 01856 831205; e info@themurrayarmshotel.com; w themurrayarmshotel.com. All rooms en suite; simply furnished but immaculately maintained. At the upper end of its official 3-star rating. **££**

🏠 **Richmond Villa** (5 rooms) Church Rd; 🌂 01856 831456; w richmond-villa.co.uk. 3 en-suite rooms, 2 on top floor with shared facilities including large family room. All attentively furnished. Owners Margaret & Duncan Cromarty are welcoming hosts. **££**

🏠 **St Margaret's Cottage B&B** (3 rooms) Church Rd; 🌂 01856 831637; e stmargaretscottage@hotmail.co.uk; w stmargaretscottage.info. Simply furnished rooms in a lovely traditional red sandstone house, once the home of a wealthy whaling captain. 2 rooms en suite, 1 with large bathroom. **££**

✖ Where to eat and drink

✖ **Murray Arms** Same contacts as hotel; 🕐 14.00–21.00 Mon–Fri, noon–21.00 Sat & Sun, bar 🕐 until late. Good food in a friendly pub. Highlight has to be the seafood platter (£35) which comfortably feeds 2, possibly 3. Puddings include rhubarb & gin crumble, & Orkney fudge cake. Perhaps wash it all down with a coffee laced with Highland Park whisky. **££**

✳ ✖ **Robertsons Coffee Hoose & Bar** Church Rd; 🌂 01856 831889; e jenna.simison@hotmail. com; 🕐 10.00–23.00 Mon–Thu, 10.00–01.00 Fri & Sat, 11.00–midnight Sun. Housed in a former grocer & coal merchants that dates to 1878, Robertsons moves seamlessly back &

forth between tearoom, bistro & bar, sometimes functioning as all 3 simultaneously. Mains range from toasties to chicken curry & quiche. Cakes include Dashing White Sergeant – a combo of biscuits, coconut & cherries. Good wine list, whiskies aplenty & local ales. If you're in the mood, order fizzy tea (£17.95 pp) which includes cakes & Prosecco or cocktails served in a teapot. All served among a setting of character, with original features such as the hardwood bar & high shelves. **£–££**

✖ **Bellevue Hotel** Same contacts as hotel; 🕐 noon–late daily. Small bar & billiards room. Limited range of the usual pie & chips variety. **£**

Shopping

B Doull & Son Church Rd; 🕐 08.00–18.00 Mon–Sat, also Jun–Aug 11.00–17.00 Sun. This is a useful store for picnic & self-catering fare; also sells

ice creams. The Doull family has a long-standing presence in the village, having been engaged in herring-curing in the early 20th century.

THE BOYS' PLOUGHING MATCH

Children's ploughing matches emerged in the 1860s on South Ronaldsay's potato fields. Competitions used simple ploughs that comprised a cow's hoof on a stick. Over time, this developed into a larger, annual event held using miniature ploughs with boys dressing up as horses. Today, the competitions also involve girls and the 'horses' continue to dress up in ornate costumes and harnesses. The matches take place on the Sand o' Wright in August, and visitors are welcome to observe.

The Old Trading Post Back Rd; ⊕ 08.00–20.00 Mon–Sat, 10.00–18.00 Sun. Another well-stocked store that also serves as a post office. Its eye-catching façade features a painting of a tracker, possibly from the Hudson's Bay Company.
The Workshop & Loft Gallery Front Rd; ✆ 01856 831587; w workshopandloftgallery.co.uk; ⊕ Feb 10.00–13.00 Mon–Sat; Mar–Dec 10.00–17.00 Mon–Sat; also Jan by prior arrangement. At the western end of Front Rd stands an impressive co-operative outlet that has been running for 40 years, selling mostly local & Orcadian clothing, jewellery, ceramics & paintings. Upstairs via a spiral staircase is an exhibition space that changes every couple of months. Knitwear is particularly striking with quirky & innovative jumpers (though at £195 these are more than just 'local' souvenirs to buy and leave at the back of the wardrobe).

What to see and do The Smiddy Museum (Cromarty Sq; ⊕ Apr–mid-Oct 14.00–16.30 daily; free) stands just back from the pier. It is the former blacksmith's shop of father and son William and Jock Hourston. Restored to how it would have looked in its early 20th-century heyday, the museum features anvils, ploughs and hearths. You are left with a strong impression of the importance of the parish blacksmith at a time when farming was becoming more mechanised and the use of heavy horses was growing. The smiddy also served as a social centre for the men of the village. There's a second room with archive photographs of St Margaret's Hope and you may with luck catch the engaging Johnny Tomatin, who acts as an informal but informed guide.

AROUND SOUTH RONALDSAY There's a good deal to see on South Ronaldsay beyond the Hope. To the west you'll find the peninsula of Hoxa Head, with fine beaches such as Sand o' Wright, important wartime ruins and excellent coastal walking. The east coast, meanwhile, appears to be all but entirely overlooked by visitors, but churches such as Peterkirk and the coast around Windwick Bay are well worth the journey. Further south, far from petering out, Orkney's most southeasterly landscapes rise to a crescendo with high cliff walking between Sand Wick and Burwick. And, right at the tip of the island, you will discover the Tomb of the Eagles, another of Orkney's most popular sites.

🏠 Where to stay *Map, page 158*

🏠 **Ayre of Cara B&B** (3 rooms) Grimness; ✆ 01856 831861; e ayre.cara@gmail.com; w ayreofcara.co.uk. Fine position at southern exit to Barrier 4 by eponymous Ayre of Cara. All rooms furnished to a high level with wood-framed beds & bright colour tones. **££**

⋏ **Wheems Bothies & Campsite** Wheems; ✆ 01856 831556; e wheemsbothy@gmail.com; w wheemsorganic.co.uk. Camping pods & tent pitches. Gorgeous location on the east side. Run by Mike Roberts, a tireless organic farmer & landscape architect. Based on a smallholding where some farm buildings are 200 years old. About 2 miles southeast of St Margaret's Hope. **£**

✕ Where to eat and drink   Map, page 158

Outside St Margaret's Hope there is just the one option for food.

✕ **Skerries Bistro** Banks; 📞 01856 831605;
w skerriesbistro.co.uk; 🕒 May–Sep noon–16.00
& 18.00–21.00 Mon, Wed, Fri & Sat, noon–16.00
Tue, Thu & Sun. Located at the southernmost tip
of the island, close to the Tomb of the Eagles,
this fine restaurant is heavily underpinned by
fish. The owner makes good use of contacts with

local fishermen, so crabs & lobsters from Burwick
harbour feature prominently. Housed in a glass-
frame building that offers superb views across
the Pentland Firth (normally, people relocate to
Orkney; in this case, the building has done so – in
a previous life it served as a marketing suite in
central Birmingham). ££

What to see and do

Hoxa Head The B9043 heads west from St Margaret's Hope to the peninsula of
Hoxa Head. Just a mile along here you reach a rectangular expanse of beach known
as **Sand o' Wright**, which is a remarkable dead ringer for Scapa Bay. Framed by cliffs
on either side, this is a shoreline of some beauty. Low tide exposes both red and
green seaweeds and the larger, ribbon-like brown wracks. The beach is backed by
an equally exquisite hinterland of wetlands and freshwater lochs created by a sandy
ridge, or ayre. From the car park a path leads north to the ayre; this enables a gentle
15-minute stroll with the chance to spot mute swan on the freshwater loch and reed

A WALK AROUND HOXA HEAD

Distance: 2 miles; time: 1½hrs
Start/finish: car park at road end beyond the B9043, 600yds west of Hoxa Gallery
⊕ *ND406934*
OS Map: Explorer 461 Orkney East Mainland

This short but glorious walk explores Hoxa Head. Perhaps surreally, it juxtaposes
stirring natural scenery with the clunking presence of some of Orkney's best-
preserved wartime batteries. From the car park head past the farmhouse and
take the clear path right towards the sea. The path is well trodden and the
walking should be easy. In spring, the air is full of Arctic terns, curlews, bonxies
and redshanks. Peer deep into the geos and, at their base, you should see black
guillemots (tysties), nesting on the lowest sandstone ledges.

You quickly reach the remains of Balfour Battery, where features include
observation posts and gun crew shelters. The battery was paired with the
similar Buchanan Battery on Flotta, directly across Hoy Sound. The original
armaments included two 12-pounder guns dating to 1894.

Beyond the Battery, the geos get wider, the ledge-like slabs ever more
dramatic; it can feel as though you are looking at a zoomed-in cross-
section of the Earth's early geology. At the headland of Hoxa Head you are
confronted with the fine panorama of Hoy to the west, John O'Groats to the
south and the southernmost extremity of South Ronaldsay rising up towards
the sea in the southeast. You are standing above the main entrance to Scapa
Flow: in wartime, it was a hugely significant location; today, oil tankers are
the main source of maritime activity. Turn left inland here, through a gate
(⊕ ND403927), following waymarkers through the former battery to meet a
clay track. Turn left and take the second turning on the right, with the fence
on your left as you return to the car park.

bunting teetering on fraying fronds amid a setting of meadowsweet and marsh cinquefoil. You will also find the remnants of the **Howe of Hoxa** (⊕ ND425939), a prominent Iron Age broch. Earl Thorfinn Skull-Splitter is said to have been buried here but as yet no remains have been found. The much-reconstructed inner wall is almost the sum of what has been left after bungled attempts at conservation in the 1850s.

Keep along the B9043 as it heads above the bay and you soon come to **Hoxa Tapestry Gallery** (✆ 01856 831395; e enquiries@hoxatapestrygallery.co.uk; w hoxatapestrygallery.co.uk; ⊕ Apr–Sep 10.00–17.30 Mon–Fri, 14.00–18.00 Sat & Sun). Located 3 miles west of St Margaret's Hope, this unusual gallery is further proof that Orcadians do their art a little differently. On display is the work of mother and daughter Leila and Jo Thomson, who both trained at Edinburgh College of Art. The tapestries are created by Leila whose larger works can be as big as 13ft by 7ft and take six months to complete. The tapestries hint at landscape features but the intention is more abstract, says Leila, and 'can be an expression of something that I had in my head. You are always thinking of ideas; I used to scribble them down in the middle of the night. Sometimes you need to make a tapestry just to get it out of your system.' Jo, meanwhile, is responsible for the striking landscape photographs and a technique known as monotype, where she paints with oil on glass, takes a single print and then adds detail and nuance with chalk.

For something different, **Gaira Driving Ponies** (Gaira; ✆ 01856 831523; m 07796 292507; e gairadrivingponies@btinternet.com) offers pony-driven tours and play sessions for children.

Hoxa Head forms the northern coastline of Widewall Bay; the southern, or lower 'jaw', of the bay is centred around the village of **Herston**, which is a pleasant cycle ride or short diversion along the B9042, which heads west off the main road a mile south of St Margaret's Hope. There's little to do as such but the grass that grows hard above the shore always seems freshly mown and the sturdy houses are embellished by attractive drystone walling.

Walking along the east coast

The eastern side of South Ronaldsay is largely given over to farming but funding has enabled a 9-mile-long path to be threaded along the coast from Kirkhouse, at the north end of Newark Bay, all the way south to Burwick. It's a delectable walk along a footpath that is, for the most part, clear if somewhat overgrown here and there. Reckon on 5 hours to complete the entire walk. Bear in mind, however, that there is no transport in this part of Orkney. Arrange a pick-up from a companion or enquire if your accommodation host is obliging enough to do the honours.

Before setting out south, explore **Peterkirk**, one of the oldest parish churches in Orkney. Dating to 1641, it is unusual in design, long and narrow with the pulpit tucked under a canopy in a recess on a side wall. The kirk overlooks a picturesque bay known as Pool of Cletts. The trail then climbs via Windwick (page 172) to the gloup, an inland hole set back from Halcro Head. The path also takes in the Tomb of the Eagles (page 173) before cutting inland during the breeding season to avoid the bird colonies of Old Head, where bonxies and Arctic skuas nest (they will mercilessly shoo you away should you ignore this seasonal diversion).

Windwick Bay and around

An unexpected sliver of sylvan joy awaits at **Olav's Wood** (w www.cs.man.ac.uk/~david/orkney/olavswood.html) a couple of miles north of Burwick, along Windwick (pronounced 'winnick') Road off the A961. A substantial woodland of native and exotic species, incorporating elements of heathland, radiates out from pools and a burn. The woodland was named for Olav Dennison, one of a group of islanders who planted the trees; as the first saplings were bedded in back in the 1970s, many trees are now quite mature. The wood should definitely be on your list for the island and repays a half-hour of exploration. A series of paths explores the top of the wood before converging on a track named 'Ian's Path', which leads to Olav's Wynd and Helen's Wynd, two coppices that tumble downhill by a burn. There's even a playful conifer-based maze to explore. There are dedicated parking spaces by the entrance (⊕ ND449869) between the settlements of Masseter and Linklater.

About half a mile further down the winding road from the wood you suddenly emerge above **Windwick Bay**, a superb stretch of coastline punctuated by two sea stacks, the Clett and the Clett of Crura. You will often see harbour and grey seals hauled out here; this is a popular pupping spot for both species. Peregrines nest in the cliffs below Nesta Head to the north. The bay is the war grave of 187 men who died when two Royal Navy destroyers, HMS *Opal* and HMS *Narborough*, foundered on the rocks of Hesta during a snowstorm on 12 January 1918. Just one man survived; William Sissons clung to a cliff edge for 36 hours until he was rescued. The headland is beautiful, so plans to erect a huge wind farm have not gone

A WALK ALONG THE EDGE OF ORKNEY FROM SAND WICK TO BURWICK

Distance: 4 miles (one way); time: 2½hrs
Start: Stensigar, Sand Wick Bay ⊕ ND432893; finish: Burwick ⊕ ND437840
OS Map: Explorer 461 Orkney East Mainland

The sloping southern half of South Ronaldsay feels as though it is racing towards the UK mainland: this walk applies the brakes and provides a fitting finale to the southernmost lands of Orkney. The route is waymarked from the township of Stensigar (which appears to comprise four houses, two long abandoned). To reach the start, take the signpost for Sandwick west off the A961 and follow the lane for half a mile. Just after you pass a standing stone, the road turns right; take the first left to reach a parking spot by an interpretation board. Follow the track downhill and walk along the beach for 100yds before going through a gate and up to the cliffs. The angular contours of Barth Head – a landmark visible from much of southern Orkney – are rarely out of sight. The path is always clear but often overgrown; the views are consistently outstanding. They reach new levels between Hoston Head and Barwick where sea stacks, sea arches and headlands connected by wafer-thin necks of land can halt you in your tracks. In spring and summer, the air is alive with nesting fulmars, curlews, oystercatchers and predatory bonxies and gulls. This is a good area for spotting orca offshore. Both sides of Barth Head reveal breathtaking views, with Orkney's Old Red Sandstone strata folded like plasticine under millions of years of intense geological pressure.

The last mile into Burwick is anything but low key as it involves an unrelenting stretch of cliff-edge walking that has occasionally prompted walkers to simply sidle under the barbed wire fence and continue inland. The final headland before you reach the jetty is a good spot to watch nesting guillemots; beyond, you are all but eyeballing John O'Groats and Duncansby Head. There is no public transport on this part of South Ronaldsay so you will either need to arrange a lift or just retrace your steps.

down well locally, with critics pointing not just to the visual intrusion but also to its proximity to the war grave.

Windwick Bay is also the location for the ongoing excavation of an **Iron Age broch** and adjacent cairns. The site is open (and tours available) when archaeologists are at work (tends to be mid-Jun–mid-Jul 10.30–16.30 Mon–Fri). Access to the site involves a short but steep unpaved road over a small bridge. The site has revealed startling treasures, including a marble-sized carving of a human head, an Iron Age bronze pin and a Roman bi-conical blue bead. The terracing of the site is of particular interest to researchers as it suggests that builders somehow shifted hundreds of tons of earth, rock and clay to create a level platform for the broch. You can keep up to date with developments at **w** archaeologyorkney.com.

An important area of **maritime heath** covers the southeast quarter of South Ronaldsay. A good way to appreciate this is to begin at the Olad Brae viewpoint (⊕ HY445878) on the main A961 road halfway down the island. This offers views back to the Mainland as well as south to the UK mainland. The adjacent island is Swona, known for its feral cattle (see box, page 153). A short walk from the viewpoint clambers up Ward Hill along an access path to the telecommunication mast. You can continue beyond should you wish, downhill to the clifftops. The area has been designated a Site of Special Scientific Interest on account of the number of lichen species found on the heathland. The landscape is tolerant of salt and wind and includes a mixture of grasses, sedges and dwarf shrubs.

The southern headlands This part of South Ronaldsay gives fine views over the UK mainland of Scotland. Firmly in the frame is Dunnet Head, its most northerly point, with cliffs dropping sheer into the sea; even more striking are the mountains of Assynt and Caithness, such as Suilven and Ben Royal, more than 80 miles away. Duncansby Head and the small community of John O'Groats are also clearly visible.

Sleepy **Burwick** harbour, tucked away in the southwest of the island, comes to life every few hours in spring and summer with the arrival of foot passengers on the service from John O'Groats. The vast majority are whisked away to the Mainland on tours, thereby immediately missing a strong contender for Orkney's spookiest church. **St Mary's**, 200yds east of the pier, was built in 1789 and is said to lie on the site of one of Scotland's earliest chapels. The graveyard is chocker with lichen-mantled tombstones, some with rather chilling epitaphs, such as 'here lies the dust of Elisabeth Budge'. Inside is a genuine curiosity in the form of a stone incised with footprints. Sober inspection suggests a Pictish coronation stone but legend insists the footprints belong to St Magnus: arriving at the northern shores of the Scottish mainland and with no boat available, he stood on the back of a sea creature that whisked him across to South Ronaldsay. When the animal touched the shore, it turned to stone, freezing the saint's footprints in time. The church key is available upon request (✆ 01856 831212).

A mile or so to the east, on the croft of Liddle, you will find one of Orkney's most extraordinary sites, the **Tomb of the Eagles** (✆ 01856 831339; **e** info@tomboftheeagles.co.uk; **w** tomboftheeagles.co.uk; ⊙ Mar & Oct 09.30–12.30 daily; Apr–Sep 09.30–17.30 daily; £7.50). Magnificently located on the elemental southeast cliff of the island, this Neolithic chambered tomb is among Orkney's most intriguing cairns.

Dating to 3000BC, the tomb was discovered by local farmer Ronnie Simison in 1958. Simison left the site relatively intact until the mid-1970s but, upon excavation, he found 16,000 human bones including 100 human skulls. These finds are barely half the story: he also uncovered a magnificently polished macehead, 70lb of pottery

5

and, most intriguing of all, the bones and talons of a white-tailed eagle. All the artefacts are on display at the site museum. The ticket includes a half-hour talk and the chance to examine some of the items. You are then left free to walk to the tomb, located a mile away along an easy grassy path. You pass Liddle Burnt Mound along the way, where pebbles were heated during the Bronze Age; whether this was for cooking or ceremony is unclear. You access the tomb through a passage entrance (pad through, wriggle on your tummy or yank yourself in on the trolley with a fixed rope). The experience is all the more stirring for being set among a brutally rocky and incised coastline. The return route offers the chance for a cliff-top walk above the deep Ham Geo, with nesting fulmars on view from May to July.

A mile west of the tomb, right on the southern tip of the island, the car park at Skerries restaurant at Banks was the scene of the 2010 discovery of a chambered cairn that has become known as the **Tomb of the Otters** (01856 831605; e banksoforkney@gmail.com; w bankschamberedtomb.co.uk; ⊕ Apr–Sep 11.00–17.00 daily, last entry 16.00; guided tours only, £6); you may also find it called Banks Chambered Cairn. The tomb was only partly excavated in 2010 but quickly yielded some astonishing finds, including 2,000 human bones laid down across seven distinct eras. Oddly, the excavators also recovered two wheelbarrow loads of otter spraint as well as otter bones. This has given rise to speculation about an otter cult, or even that otters were permitted into the tomb to aid the process of removing flesh from the dead. Amid other curiosities are the fact that the tomb was carved out of bedrock and that the entrance faces north, both rare occurrences in Orkney; one supposition is that the tomb belonged to a community separated or distinct from contemporary Orkney peoples. A visit involves a 30-minute talk and 10 minutes inside the tomb. The site is signposted from the A961. Just west of the restaurant and tomb, Liddle Loch attracts an abundance of birdlife and is a good place to spot short-eared owls quartering over the grasses.

6

Rousay, Egilsay and Wyre

While the crowds flock to Skara Brae, the islands of Rousay, Egilsay and Wyre lie just northwest of the Mainland, metaphorically twiddling their thumbs and waiting for the world to notice that between them they have 166 archaeological sites, as concentrated a compendium of ancient monuments as anywhere in northern Europe.

Rousay, Egilsay and Wyre are North Isles and form the northern and easterly fringes of Eynhallow Sound, a corridor of fast-running water that separates the islands from the Mainland. Apart from the abundance of archaeology, they are all supremely beautiful in very different ways. Rousay rises abruptly from the sea into distinctively conical hills. Egilsay and Wyre are, by contrast, low-lying, full of birdsong and given over to farming.

Even the journey to the islands is exhilarating, as Eynhallow Sound is a notoriously treacherous stretch of water where the tidal races, known locally as 'roosts', rush through at up to 9 knots. Taking such a journey makes the islands feel further away than the 2-mile girth of the sound.

GETTING THERE AND AWAY

Rousay, Egilsay and Wyre are reachable only by sea. Orkney Ferries services (return £8.50/27.50 passenger/standard car) depart from Tingwall, 12 miles west of Kirkwall on the Mainland. (Note that, unlike the other North Isles, the island is not served from Kirkwall.) You can also travel between the three islands: return fares from Rousay to either Wyre or Egilsay are £13.60 (standard car) and £4.30 (passenger). There are usually six departures a day from Tingwall. The ferry chugs back and forth between all three islands and the Mainland; you should, however, check timetables as not all departures take in both Egilsay and Wyre. While there is a theoretical risk of being marooned while on a day trip to Egilsay and Wyre, the ferry crew will make sure you don't commit yourself to an inadvertent overnight stay. As with many Orkney islands, if you just plan to make a day trip to one or more of these islands you should aim for the earliest crossings.

The crossing, meanwhile, is among the most lively of Orkney's ferry routes. Leaving Tingwall, the ferry master gives the Wyre skerries a wide birth in order to avoid the watery fate that has befallen so many ships in the sound. He ploughs due north, until you almost feel you can reach out and touch Rousay (this is a diverting experience in strong winds); he then takes a sharp turn to starboard. As you cross Eynhallow Sound you will see two uninhabited islands, Eynhallow to the west (see box, page 182) and the pudding-basin shape of Gairsay.

Tingwall lies just off the A966 and it will take you up to 30 minutes to drive there from Kirkwall. Bus 6 runs from Kirkwall travel centre to Tingwall and is integrated

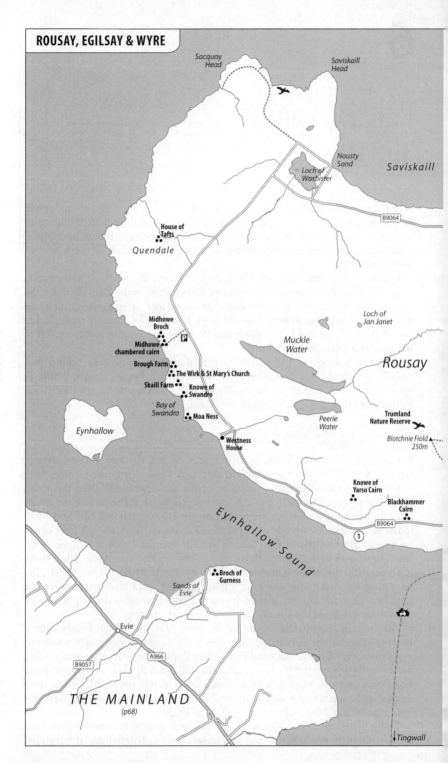

Sacquoy Head

Saviskaill Head

Loch of Wasbister

Nousty Sand

Saviskaill

B9064

House of Tafts

Quendale

Loch of Jan Janet

Midhowe Broch

P

Muckle Water

Midhowe chambered cairn

Rousay

Brough Farm

The Wirk & St Mary's Church

Skaill Farm

Knowe of Swandro

Bay of Swandro

Moa Ness

Eynhallow

Peerie Water

Trumland Nature Reserve

Blotchnie Fiold 250m

Westness House

Knowe of Yarso Cairn

Blackhammer Cairn

B9064

Eynhallow Sound

1

Broch of Gurness

Sands of Evie

Evie

A966

THE MAINLAND

(p68)

B9057

↓Tingwall

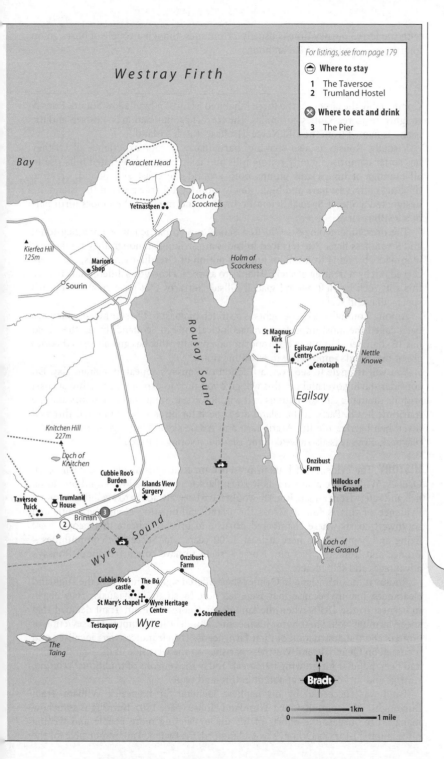

Westray Firth

Bay

Faraclett Head

Loch of Scockness

Yetnasteen

▲ Kierfea Hill 125m

Marion's Shop

Sourin

Holm of Scockness

Rousay Sound

St Magnus Kirk ✝

Egilsay Community Centre

Cenotaph

Nettle Knowe

Egilsay

Knitchen Hill 227m

Loch of Knitchen

Cubbie Roo's Burden

Islands View Surgery ✚

Onzibust Farm

Hillocks of the Graand

Taversoe Tuick

Trumland House

Brinian ③

②

Wyre Sound

Loch of the Graand

Onzibust Farm

Cubbie Roo's castle

The Bú

St Mary's chapel ✝ Wyre Heritage Centre

Stormieclett

Testaquoy

Wyre

The Taing

For listings, see from page 179

⌂ **Where to stay**
1 The Taversoe
2 Trumland Hostel

✖ **Where to eat and drink**
3 The Pier

N

Bradt

0 —————— 1km
0 —————— 1 mile

with the ferry. Journey time is usually 27 minutes, though a couple of buses go on longer routes and take up to an hour.

ROUSAY

Comfortably the largest of the three inhabited islands in Eynhallow Sound, Rousay roughly measures 5 miles by 5 miles. The correct pronunciation is 'Rowsee' and the island is named from the Old Norse 'Hrolfsay' ('Rolf's island').

Visually, Rousay is also striking, particularly if your experience of Orkney has so far comprised gently rolling hills and lush farmland. Serrated hills rise in all manner of lumps and bumps both around the coast and inland, creating thrilling cliffs, vast bays and high, lonely moorland. Large parts of the island are designated a Site of Special Scientific Interest and much of the moors form part of a RSPB reserve.

The prevailing geology is Old Red Sandstone, in particular, Rousay flagstones and Stromness flags. The terraced hillsides are striking; although they might look manmade, bringing to mind an unlikely notion of Orcadian vineyards, they were carved out by retreating glaciers. Thanks to a process known as differential erosion, this soft rock has left behind glacial hillside terraces that have created Rousay's spectacular cliff scenery.

Among Rousay's must-see sights is a stretch of coast to the southwest which has been called the most important archaeological mile in Scotland. In all, the island has 15 chambered tombs, a disproportionate number that has given rise to theories about the island's importance in Neolithic times.

You will struggle to see even a fraction of Rousay's appeal in a single day. Do consider staying overnight as this will give you time to explore the northwest coast with its dramatic cliff formations and wildflowers, to frequent both moors and the maritime heath. Parts of the island are superb for birds – including red-throated diver, hen harrier, merlin, Arctic tern and Arctic skua. With a good beach and a playpark, Rousay is also a welcoming island for young children.

HISTORY The evidence of human presence on Rousay is as old as anywhere on Orkney. With fertile plains on its western flanks, and Eynhallow Sound providing fish and safety from attack, Rousay would have been attractive to Neolithic peoples. Evidence of this is found across the island, culminating along the south and southwest coasts where chambered cairns and brochs indicate that people were living and being buried here at least 5,200 years ago. Successive communities – Bronze and Iron Age, Pict and Norse – seem to have concurred about Rousay's advantages and settled here.

Rousay is the only island in Orkney that suffered significantly from the Highland clearances, mainly because they were led here by single individuals. They began in earnest in the 1830s when the landowner George William Traill decided that sheep farming would best boost his income. This decision prompted the eviction of crofters and the destruction of their farmsteads. The clearances were localised and focussed on Quandale and Westness parishes on the west side of the island, which had been popular for growing beremeal. Today the remains of traditional crofting, runrigs and turf dykes are apparent in this landscape.

Traill was succeeded by his nephew, General Sir Frederick William Traill Burroughs, who commissioned Trumland House (page 180). Burroughs somehow managed to surpass the efforts of his uncle, evicting more people and writing himself into history as Orkney's worst landlord; the two men are responsible for the two-step decline in Rousay's population, from the maximum of 1,000 at the start of the 19th century to just over 200 today.

A lot of the archaeology exposed today was uncovered in the 1930s at the behest of another Trumland House occupant, Walter Grant, who invested wealth garnered from whisky by inviting some of the period's most influential archaeologists to excavate main sites. Most are now in the care of Historic Environment Scotland.

Visitors with ancestral ties to the island can look at Rousay Roots (w rousayroots. com) and Rousay Remembered (w rousayremembered.com); enquire at The Pier café and Crafthub (page 180) by the ferry jetty or Rousay Tours (see below) to contact local genealogists.

GETTING AROUND Trumland Pier (though everyone just calls it 'the pier') is located in the southeast of the island and is the point of arrival and departure for the ferry to the Mainland and Egilsay and Wyre. Rousay is larger than many people think, with its coast and moorland fringes circumnavigated by a 13-mile single-track circular road. This happens to be the highest road in Orkney – the most elevated stretch is around Sourin Brae – and offers monumental views that will make you catch your breath with a perspective unique to the North Isles. There is no bus service, so if you are planning only a day trip, walking will limit you to little more than Trumland House and the Taversoe Tuick cairn (page 181), which are close to the pier. (If you want to head west to the Midhowe Broch you're looking at a 10-mile return walk.) Most likely you will need to bring a car. Cycling is a pleasure on Rousay's quiet roads but the climb from sea level through the parish of Sourin in the northeast will certainly test your fitness. Bike hire is available at Trumland Hostel (page 180). Thanks to the peat tracks that cut deep into its moorland heart, and a handful of waymarked footpaths, Rousay is as geared up for walking as any Orkney island.

TOURIST INFORMATION AND TOUR OPERATORS The waiting room (the formal name is the Trumland Visitor Centre and Waiting Room) at the ferry pier hosts an unexpectedly exhaustive collection of information on the history, wildlife and geology of Rousay. It is open at all times. The latest news about the island can be found on the website of the Rousay, Egilsay and Wyre Development Trust (w rewdt.org).

Paddy Maguire of **Rousay Tours** ✳ (☏ 01856 821234; e patrick_maguire@ hotmailco.uk; w rousaytours.co.uk; £35/12 adult/child) offers entertaining and insightful tours. Paddy doesn't miss much – expect to see the major sites and be regaled with tales of island life, most of them repeatable. He is also good and engaging company: as well as showing you Rousay's key (mainly archaeological) sites, he will simply chew the cud with you and allow you glimpses of what makes island life in the north of the UK tick.

WHERE TO STAY, EAT AND DRINK As with many islands in Orkney, sleeping and eating options are limited. The success of those that do it well suggests there is space for new ventures here. For the limited range of self-catering, visit w aroundrousay.co.uk.

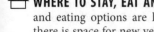 **The Taversoe** [map, page 176] (4 rooms) Breckan; ☏ 01856 821325; e taversoe@ hotmail.com; w taversoehotel.co.uk. En-suite rooms are dbls or twins – modern, extremely comfortable with view over Eynhallow Sound. The restaurant (☉ noon–17.00 Mon, noon–21.00 Tue–Sat, noon–19.30 Sun; open to non-guests, book in advance; £) has same views & is 1 of

surprisingly few places in Orkney where you can simultaneously dine & admire the landscape. Meals well priced for their quality. Among a mix of classics, Orcadian specialities & Indian fare, try mushroom pakora followed by a Westray crab salad; puddings include St Clement's sponge, a concoction of orange sponge & lemon zest. There's also a convivial bar (⊕ May–Sep 11.00–17.00 Mon, 11.00–23.00 Tue–Sat, 11.00–22.30 Sun; shorter hours in winter) serving all the local whiskies & ales & international wines you might desire. It's a wonder no-one has tried the Taversoe

business model on any of the other North Isles: it's hard to see how it wouldn't work. **££**

🏠 **Trumland Hostel** [map, page 177] (11 beds) Trumland Organic Farm; ☎ 01856 821252; e trumland@btopenworld.com. Individual & family room available. Also a campsite. **£**

🍴 **The Pier** [map, page 177] Trumland Pier; ☎ 01856 821359; ⊕ Apr–Sep 11.00–17.30 daily. Located in the same building as the Crafthub, this friendly café – the island's social hub – boasts a modest range of warming food including soup. Fine views over Eynhallow Sound. **£**

SHOPPING   Rousay has a couple of rather charming places to browse and pass the time with the islanders.

The Crafthub ☎ 01856 821455; e crafthub@ btconnect.com; w crafthuborkney.co.uk; ⊕ Apr– Sep 11.00–17.30 daily. Located immediately above the pier, this is a good-quality retail outlet for local craftspeople & artists. It offers a chance to pick up a memento or 2 such as a bobble hat or knitted cowl. Useful small bookshop, too.

Marion's Shop Essaquoy, Sourin; ☎ 01856 821365; ⊕ noon–13.00 & 14.00–17.30 Mon & Wed, 11.00–13.00 & 14.00–17.30 Thu, 14.00–17.30 Fri. Just 3 miles from the pier on the northeast of the island, this is the only store on Rousay & is a useful place to stock up or buy bits and pieces for a picnic. You could even enjoy that picnic in the sheltered garden across the drive, sitting on chairs fashioned from flagstone & under

the gaze of exotic-looking shrubbery. 'I put the garden together because I once saw some students just eating their lunch by the side of road,' says Marion. Having spent a great deal of her life in Australasia & the South Pacific, Marion has brought back several floral species from the region that grow vigorously in the grounds of the shop, such as a tall Australasian pine. A scientist rather than a horticulturalist by training, Marion has also found Rousay ideal for growing strawberries. 'We had the ex-ambassador to Sweden living on the island & we ended up providing strawberries for the Queen's birthday in Norway. We were producing seven tonnes year.' The shop opening hours are just a guide: Marion is usually around & will always open up if you are in need of supplies.

OTHER PRACTICALITIES   There is no **bank** on the island so best to bring some cash with you, although the shop, Crafthub and the Taversoe all take cards. **Islands View Surgery** (☎ 01856 821265) is located half a mile east of the pier and immediately south of the B9064. **Petrol** is available from Marion's Shop (see above).

WHAT TO SEE AND DO   Just about all of Rousay's sites are accessible from the island 'ring road'. The points of interest below are described in a clockwise direction but can easily be visited in reverse.

Southern Rousay   Just across the road from the pier you cannot miss the Baronial splendour of **Trumland House** (☎ 01856 821322; e info@trumlandhouse; ⊕ Jun–Aug 10.00–17.00 daily; £2.50), built in 1872 to a design by David Bryce, the exponent of Scottish Victorian Baronial architecture who also designed Balfour Castle on Shapinsay (page 197). The house was to be the home of Frederick William Burroughs, who inherited much of Rousay, and his wife Eliza D'Oyley Geddes. Burroughs was known as the 'Little General' due to his short stature. A fire in 1985 badly damaged the building; it was inadvertently caused by workmen, although an alternative version of the story suggests that Burroughs' ghost was responsible.

The current owners, Annelliey and Craig Gregg, have spent several years painstakingly restoring the building with a view to opening it as a local museum and wedding venue, possibly in 2019. Their commendable attitude towards openness could not be in greater contrast to that experienced at Balfour Castle. Visitors are welcome to explore the beautifully tended gardens, walk woodland trails and cross the front lawn. There is even a 'vole trail' behind the house where you might just see the adorable furry mammals. Look out for great yellow bumblebee plus birds such as greenfinch and siskin, which thrive in the sheltered, walled environment of the gardens. Trumland is also home to many species of moth and several butterflies. Even otters make it this far from the shore to wash their fur in the freshwater pools.

If you expect the Greggs to be stiff-upper-lip types in formal wear, brusquely directing servants, you could not be more wrong. You are more likely to mistake Annelliey for a gardener as she pushes a wheelbarrow around the grounds, a hoe dangling over her shoulder. 'I first saw the house when I came here on an archaeological dig,' she recalls. 'It just looked so sad, with broken windows. Then the sun shone on it and it was simply beautiful. We just couldn't bear the idea of it falling down.'

Continuing west, after 500yds you come to **Taversoe Tuick,** a rare two-storey chambered cairn. This is one of only two tombs in Orkney to feature two burial chambers set one above the other; the second, Huntersquoy, is almost within sight – over on Eday. Taversoe was discovered in 1898, and, just for once, this is a chambered cairn easily entered with barely a crouch. A small stepladder enables you to clamber down to the bottom bunk, so to speak.

Less than a mile further down the road is **Blackhammer Cairn.** Set back from the road, this is a stalled cairn (a Neolithic tomb divided by upright slabs into stalls on either side) where excavations uncovered the remains of two men, along with the bones of cormorants, gannets, geese, oxen, red deer and sheep.

Close by is **Knowe of Yarso Cairn.** At nearly 200ft above sea level, this is the highest of Orkney's tombs. It offers superb views across Eynhallow Sound and Orkney Mainland. It will take 10–15 minutes to reach it from the road. Start from the small car park (✛ HY407275) above the Taversoe hotel. A clear track leads up a lane and signposts nudge you left on to a moorland path. Inside, the flagstones and ledges have turned an eerie mossy green. An excavation in 1934 uncovered the remains of at least 29 adults (disconcertingly, only the skulls were found for 17 of these), most of which were in the inner chamber. The skulls were positioned face-up and side-by-side along the bottom of the wall. The rest of the bodies were found disarticulated and broken.

Westness walk
The Westness coast, nearly 5 miles from the pier, is not to be missed. Many archaeologists consider this dramatic route of cairns and brochs to be the most important archaeological mile (although actually closer to 1½ miles) in Scotland. The slightly hyperbolic rhetoric associated with this stretch of coastline – the phrase 'a walk from the dawn of human time' occasionally appears in tourist literature – is actually, for once, not too far off the mark. Every important element of Orkney's timeline is squeezed into this stretch of coast: from the first Stone Age settlers to Pictish tribes, Vikings (with Norse antiquities including a cemetery and longhouse), the earls and the crofting era. Perhaps best of all, the entire ensemble is free: there's no timed-ticket entry and no queues. Indeed, you may have the whole slice of coastline to yourself. The best way to experience this special area is on foot.

The walk described here (you may also see it referred to as the 'Westness heritage walk') is circular, just over 3 miles in length and will take most people around 2 hours to complete. The coastal stretch is a mixture of footpaths (some overgrown), open ground and rocky foreshore. Begin from the car park (✪ HY376307) from where Midhowe Broch and what looks like a large aircraft hanger (housing Midhowe chambered cairn) are visible far below, by the shoreline.

A clear path leads downhill to the 'hanger' and the broch, which is perched on Curly Geo. Head for the broch first. The broch is one of Scotland's best-preserved examples of these enigmatic Iron Age structures and dates to from 200BC–200AD. Wonderfully, you can walk right into it and examine the substantial living quarters. The occupants were known to be wealthy, for dark orange Samian pottery from the Roman Empire was recovered from the broch. Made from local flagstones, the remaining wall of this broch extends to 14ft high.

The setting is nothing less than sensational, surrounded by vast, wave-pounded slabs and ledges, and by narrow geos. Out to sea, the spectacle is magnificent, with water racing into Eynhallow Sound at startling speed and hurtling over unseen

EYNHALLOW

Sitting near the mouth of Eynhallow Sound, Eynhallow is clearly visible from the Westness walk. The island is uninhabited thanks to a combination of clearances (by the Balfour family, who also owned Shapinsay) and an outbreak of fever. Eynhallow is ringed by shingle and sandy beaches, outcrops of flagstones and in some places a shoreline that rises abruptly 7ft (2.1m) from the sea. There's a smattering of prehistoric houses.

The name means 'holy isle' in Old Norse and Eynhallow was certainly once occupied by monks. Before that, legend says it was inhabited by the magical and enigmatic finfolk (page 36). By the southwest shores of the island lie the well-preserved remains of a Romanesque 12th-century church. This had been adapted and served as a series of dwellings for centuries. What's left today stands to roof height, and includes a nave, a porch, an arch and a chancel.

The church was only discovered during the clearances: to ensure those evicted did not get any fancy notions of returning, the Balfours had the roofs of all the houses torn off. During this act of vindictiveness the church emerged. Several houses had been formed from the skeleton of the church.

Wildlife is very rich here. A long-term fulmar-study project is based on the island and there are sizeable populations of Arctic and great skuas, and an Arctic tern colony. Eynhallow is one of Orkney's most important sites for harbour seals; as many as 900 adults have been counted during aerial surveys. The rare hart's-tongue fern forms a colony on a rocky outcrop in the ravine that cuts across the island.

The good news is that Eynhallow has a regular ferry; the bad news is that it runs just once a year. Every July, the Orkney Heritage Society (w orkneycommunities.co.uk/ohs) organises a trip to the island, accompanied by guides. Book ahead as it is extremely popular with locals. There are no roads on Eynhallow so you'll need good footwear. Even if you don't manage to visit, the island has a spectral presence, a sensation enhanced when the *haar* descends, cloaking and revealing the island perhaps four times in a single hour. The atmosphere is captured in *The Malevolent Mists of Eynhallow*, a Stephen King-like horror novel by John Edward Radcliffe, in which bells are rung by the dead buried in the island church.

shallows and skerries. As the name suggests, Midhowe is the middle of three brochs; the third is just to the west under the conspicuous grassy hillock; the first is sufficiently modest that you may have passed over it without noticing.

The western cliffs near here are fantastic for seabird colonies comprising guillemot, kittiwake and fulmar. Gaze across from here to the Mainland and you can pick out the Brough of Gurness. Magnificent when visited, from this vantage point the settlement of Gurness can look minuscule and timeless: the mind's eye can easily envisage smoke emerging from it or humans in animal skins endeavouring to spear fish by the coast.

Retrace your steps (heading east) along the coast to the adjacent **Midhowe chambered cairn**. About 5,000 years old, this huge communal burial chamber is known as the Great Ship of Death, on account of the 25 human bodies that were found when the site was excavated in the 1930s. The site was subsequently fortified by the stone-and-corrugated-iron building that now encases it; you walk above the site along a walkway and gantry. Archaeologists still cannot say for certain why the cairn is so big, nor why so many such cairns were built in Orkney. The Midhowe cairn would have been an imposing sight – visible from the Orkney mainland – so might have had special significance. Alternatively, it could just be that every family or community had such tombs and that this is simply how all of Orkney once looked.

The path continues east just above the coast, though from now on it is often faint, neglected and overgrown. (This is a surprising state of affairs, given the enthusiasm with which this route is promoted by tourism authorities.) You first reach the forlorn-looking gable-ends of the deserted 18th-century farmstead, **Brough Farm**. This has been uninhabited since 1845 but the site was occupied by the same family and their descendants from the 14th to the 19th centuries.

Close by is **the Wirk,** the remains of a late medieval ceremonial hall belonging to Sigurd of Westness. It was hereabouts that Earl Paul the Silent was abducted by Swein Asleifsson while hunting for otters, whereupon Rognvald was recognised by Sigurd as Earl of Orkney. Notwithstanding Paul's misfortune, this is still a good place to see otters – at the very least you are likely to see fresh spraint. Adjacent to the Wirk is the roofless **St Mary's Church**, which dates to the early 17th century but stands on the site of a previous church. The path here may be very overgrown: walk behind the church and make for the cairn on the large ridge of rocks above the shoreline, then continue east. The next site along the coast is **Skaill Farm**, a ruined 18th-century farmstead with a circular kiln for drying corn. The inhabitants were evicted in the early 19th century: in 1841, 118 people were recorded as living close by; by 2004 this had fallen to just eight.

Try and keep close to the shoreline as you continue to work your way around the **Bay of Swandro**. On the north side of the bay is the **Knowe of Swandro** (✛ HY375296). This unique archaeological site includes a 5,000-year-old Neolithic chambered tomb, the concentric outer walls of which survive underneath the storm beach and are thus only exposed in summer (see box, page 184). Initially, it can be hard to pick out but the site includes Iron Age roundhouses, Pictish buildings, a Viking settlement and a Norse long hall. Results so far suggest that Swandro was a high-status settlement in the Pictish period and that this importance continued into the Viking/Norse era when it was part of the estate of Sigurd of Westness. In this area two boat graves have been excavated, each containing the remains of men, as well as weapons and tools. One man had four arrowheads in his body. The boats were constructed using a Viking technique known as 'clinker building', with oak and iron nails.

6

SAVING SWANDRO

Excavation at the Knowe of Swandro began in 2010 and continues every summer. For many years it was assumed that the knowe was 'merely' a broch. Excavations, however, have identified an extraordinarily diverse site with occupations spanning several distinct eras – from a Stone Age chambered cairn through to remains from Viking times.

Having been around for the best part of 5,000 years, the knowe is now in imminent danger of being destroyed by coastal erosion. In response, the Swandro-Orkney Coastal Archaeological Trust (w swandro.co.uk) is crowdfunding to excavate and record the site before its inevitable destruction. Excavations should continue in July 2019 and again in 2020; visitors are welcome at the site, which will be open daily apart from weekends.

The Knowe of Swandro represents an important opportunity to totally excavate a Neolithic chambered tomb using modern scientific techniques – a first for Orkney. The immediate priority is the chambered tomb, the entrance passageway of which was uncovered during a trial excavation in 2017. The burial chamber is currently undisturbed by the sea and is likely to hold Neolithic burials, but the outer walls of the tomb are being steadily eroded so limited time remains before the chamber is destroyed.

The final site you pass is **Moa Ness**, a former Viking graveyard, though there is little to see today. One grave comprised the resting place of a Viking woman who wore a brooch thought to be Celtic in origin and 'obtained' in a raid around AD750. Made from silver-gilt and featuring gold filigree and inlaid amber, this has become known as the 'Westness brooch' (now in the National Museum in Edinburgh). This and other discoveries were fortuitous as they were uncovered only when a farmer dug a hole to bury a cow. The walk ends just before **Westness House**. After the first farm outhouse bear left up the track between farm buildings with a quarry on your left. Walk up to the circular island road and turn left. A pleasant mile along this quiet road leads back to the start point.

Quendale, Sacquoy Head and the north coast

A mile or so north of Midhowe Broch the road turns sharp right and climbs high above the lush and vast plains of **Quendale**. This is an empty landscape, left unchanged from the time of the clearances in 1846. You can pick out distinctive runrig farming lines and the features of cleared crofts. In the far distance, at the base of Horse Brae, is the House of Tafts, the oldest two-storey house in Orkney, dating to at least the 16th century. The house was abandoned rather than cleared.

As the road descends you pass the **Loch of Wasbister**, which features two crannogs or Iron Age fortified settlements built on artificial islands. One is connected by a stone causeway that lies 3ft under water.

There's a fine walk to **Sacquoy Head** that begins from the northwest corner of the loch (⊕ HY391333). Do not attempt this walk in fog as there are a couple of extremely narrow and deep geos that cut a long way inland (at least one walk map you may come across plots a course right across a geo!). If driving, park with care on the verge as no vehicles are permitted on the access track to Sacquoy Farm. The walk is linear, so including the return you are looking at just over 4 miles (2hrs).

Waymarkers direct you past Sacquoy Farm and through a gate where a thin path soon peters out. The best approach is to turn immediately left and keep close to the wall until it becomes low enough to clamber over. Then head north-northwest, keeping as close to the cliff edge as you are able, in order to avoid disturbing nesting birds. Views are sensational, with overhanging cliffs vying for your attention with the outline of Westray. Look back east to observe sea arches beginning to form at the base of Saviskaill Head. During the breeding season you will see great and Arctic skuas, ringed plover, fulmar, black guillemot and a handful of puffin. Walk west with the coast and after 600yds you come to the Loch of Sacquoy, from where there are fine views towards the Mainland. The huge sea stack visible below Costa Head on the latter has the rather mundane name of Standard Rock. Return the same way.

The north coast of Rousay continues eastward with high cliffs swooping down to the vast Saviskaill Bay. By the road at the northeast corner of the Loch of Wasbister, you'll find **Nousty Sand**, a small beach with a couple of picnic tables. You are likely to see both harbour and grey seals hauled out here. The highest point of Orkney's highest road – 410ft – is found just below Kierfea Hill.

A WALK THROUGH TRUMLAND NATURE RESERVE

Distance: 4 miles; time: 2½hrs
Start/finish: Taversoe Tuick cairn, half a mile along the circular road west of the pier ✪ HY427275
OS Map: Explorer 464 Westray, Papa Westray, Rousay, Egilsay & Wyre

The brooding moors and hills of the RSPB Trumland reserve overshadow the smattering of human activity around the pier. This a wonderful place for eye-catching bird activity, including hen harriers sky-dancing in spring and short-eared owls on the hunt. Meanwhile, that flash of gold may be reflecting sunlight or it could be a golden plover, a bird whose haunting whistle can make these moors seem eerie. In May and June you are very likely to hear the more lullaby-like song of the cuckoo.

A good way to explore the reserve is to walk up to Blotchnie Fiold and Knitchen Hill from Taversoe Tuick cairn. From the car park, walk up the farm track towards the quarry and turn right following the footpath signs through a field, crossing lumpy and open ground to a stile. From now on, the walking is much easier, involving waymarked peat tracks and paths. After 400yds you reach a T-junction of paths: turn left, following the sign 'long path 5km'. The route slowly climbs uphill past the Loch of Knitchen where you may well see red-throated diver. The trail winds its way up to the summit of Blotchnie Fiold (at 820ft/250m, Rousay's highest point). From here, you can see all the North Isles, as well as Fair Isle (on a clear day and with binoculars). The craggy mountainous outline to the south is provided by Cuilags and Ward Hill on Hoy. To the east, if you scan the hinterland of Rousay, you can pick out the intriguingly named Loch of Jan Janet.

The return follows a different route but take care to follow the right waymarkers as they sometimes nearly converge, like ski-slalom poles, with the ones you followed on the way up. The correct ones lead you in a direct line along the spine of Rousay to the cairn and trig point on Knitchen Hill (774ft/227m). The path then descends sharply to the east of the pier – keep left where another trail joins from the right. When you reach the circular island road, turn right to return to the starting point.

Rousay was briefly home to the poet, writer, visual and conceptual artist, and gardener Ian Hamilton Finlay (1925–2006). Finlay become known for his innovative compositions, known as 'concrete poetry', in which layout and typography are as important as the words themselves. His first published work in this form, *Rapel*, appeared in 1963. An appropriate memorial – a concrete rectangular block etched with words – to the man can be found overlooking Saviskaill Bay on the north side of Rousay. It reads: '*Gods of the Earth, Gods of the Sea*'.

Rousay's moorland Rousay's substantial moorland kicks in at around 200ft above sea level and is dominated by gorse, blanket bog and wet heath. These support around 3% of the UK Arctic skua population as well as a pair or two of hen harrier. You can obtain an easy taster of this overlooked landscape by walking up to the lochs of **Peerie** and **Muckle Water**. Starting above Westness House (there is a small car park (✜ HY384292) by an abandoned house on the side of the island road), the walk is uphill along an easy track (2 miles return). 'Peerie', curiously, is the Shetland word for 'small', as opposed to 'peedie', the Orcadian word. In spring and summer you may well see red-throated diver on the waters.

Faraclett Head The northeast corner of Rousay is dominated by Faraclett Head, which bulges out into Westray Firth. The headland is a swirling compôte of grazing farmland, sweeping flanks of grassland and overhanging cliffs, known as hags. The spectacular view of distant Noup Head lighthouse on Westray adds a frisson to a truly superb geological slice of Orkney. In clear weather you may also be able to make out the whirlpools that lurk between the headland and Westray and which form yet another hazard for the unwary sailor in already tempestuous waters.

EGILSAY AND WYRE

The two other inhabited islands of Eynhallow Sound are easily visited from either Tingwall or Rousay. Both Egilsay and Wyre played extremely important roles in Orkney history and each has enough appeal to merit exploration. The summer ferry timetable allows you to visit both in a day, taking the 09.10 from Rousay to Egilsay (journey time 20mins); then the 13.35 on to Wyre (journey time 15mins); and finally the 17.15 from Wyre back to Rousay (5mins) and then the Mainland.

In good weather this little-advertised itinerary is surely one of the world's most charming ferry routes and makes for a wonderful day of walking, birdwatching and visiting some substantial archaeological sites. Even on a warm summer's day you may be the only passenger (though you must book the day before), making the £2.20 journey between each island remarkably good value for effectively procuring your own personal ferry service.

Keep an eye out for dolphins, whales and porpoises as well as basking sharks, which occasionally float through the sound. In between Rousay and Egilsay is Holm of Scockness, a tiny island that is uninhabited and used for grazing livestock. 'Scockness' is an Old Norse name and equates to something like 'little island of the crooked headland'. Recent years have heard talk of construction of a bridge

Distance: 2½ miles; time: 2hrs
Start/finish: car park below Faraclett Farm ✪ HY447325
OS Map: Explorer 464: Westray, Papa Westray, Rousay, Egilsay & Wyre

This short but excellent 2-mile circular walk explores the coast around Faraclett Head. From the informal car park below the farm, follow waymarkers uphill and over two stiles. After this, signs temporarily disappear as you continue upwards under telephone wires and through a gate, whereafter they reappear. Walk clockwise along a clear path with Faraclett Head flanking upward to your right. Views open up across the vast Saviskaill Bay; with Kierfea Hill's conical contours glowering down at you, Rousay seems much more substantial than its modest dimensions suggest. West, off trail, is Rinyo (✪ HY439322), a Neolithic settlement of seven-plus houses. The site has now been backfilled but excavations (1939 and 1946) suggested a Neolithic village even larger than Skara Brae; houses had beds, boxes and fireplaces. Sadly, funding, weather and location have apparently left Rinyo languishing at the bottom of the archaeological to-do list.

The path sweeps around the front of the headland. Keep to the track as it runs between waymarkers; the land on the lower seaward side is eroding and has created hags. In spring and summer, bonxies keep an eye on you, providing a menacing, if feathered, escort should you stray nestwards.

On the east of the headland, the path fades and reappears as it descends and circles back to its start. As you drop to the first kissing gate, an exquisite view emerges, with Westray to the east, the Loch of Scockness to the fore and Eday's moorland framing the skyline. After crossing a stile, turn right to follow the drystone wall until you see a gate and stile down to the left. Follow waymarkers across fields – keep an eye out down towards the coast for the Yetnasteen standing stone – until you reach a farm track. Here, cross the field under the telephone wires to return to the first two stiles of the walk and the car park.

The Yetnasteen stone is worth an aside. Given the cast of characters who feature in the annals of Orkney folklore, a stone that walks to a loch on New Year's Eve fits comfortably into the oeuvre. Yetnasteen is a standing stone nearly 7ft high that sits in the landscape (✪ HY447327) just to the west of the Loch of Scockness. The name comes from the Old Norse, 'jotunna-steinn' ('giant stone'); the story is that this was once a giant who was turned to stone by the warm rays of the morning sun. Each New Year as the clock strikes midnight, the giant takes just two steps to stride the few hundred yards to the Loch of Scockness, takes a drink of water, then returns to his usual position. The more prosaic explanation is that, on the rare occasions that the sun shines in late December in Orkney, the shadow of the stone can seem to 'walk' across the landscape.

between Egilsay and Rousay; should this ever come to fruition, the ferry link would be consigned to history. Note that both islands only have self-service tea and coffee (with an invitation to pay or make a donation), so you'll need to bring food with you. Public toilets are located by both island piers. Neither island has B&B or hostel options.

EGILSAY Shaped like a teardrop, Egilsay (pronounced 'Aygilsee', with the stress on the 'Ay') dangles in Rousay Sound, just over a mile to the east of Rousay. The name is generally assumed to come from the Old Norse for Egil's Island. Another theory is that 'Egils' was perhaps an early corruption of the Gaelic word 'eaglais' meaning 'church', although this would be an extremely rare example of a Gaelic place name in Orkney.

Egilsay is historically hugely important, for this is where Earl Magnus Erlendsson was executed in 1117. He had met his cousin Earl Haakon to discuss peace terms, but it transpired that Haakon's attendance had a murderous subtext. The act triggered a cult around the deceased earl, the island became an important medieval pilgrimage site and the cathedral in his name was built in Kirkwall. As well as history, the island also offers superb walking (it marks the end of the St Magnus Way long-distance trail; see box, page 100) and birdwatching. On the downside, Egilsay is undergoing a sharp population decline (33% in a decade), now leaving just 26 residents. The school closed in 2011. Depopulation, incidentally, affects Rousay and Wyre too: as beautiful and fascinating as they are, all three islands face demographic and economic challenges. A recent report by the Orkney Islands Council defined them as 'becoming threatened' by population decline, below-average economic activity, an ageing population, and a reliance on inward migration.

What to see and do The ro-ro ferry arrives at the pier on the west side of the island. The prime point of interest, the 12th-century **St Magnus Kirk**, stands just 600yds uphill, near to where Magnus was murdered. To reach it, climb over the signposted stile on the left (to the north) above the pier and walk through the fields; the side gate to the graveyard is usually locked. The low wall, oddly, has no stile on its outward site, so you must clamber your way on to the wall and use the stone steps on the church side to get back on to terra firma. Alternatively, you can reach the church by ignoring the signposted stile, walking up the lane to the crossroads and turning left to reach the church. This adds only half a mile to the route.

THE LIFE, TIMES AND MARTYRDOM OF MAGNUS

Magnus Erlendsson was born in 1080 and was the son of Erlend, who shared the earldom of Orkney with Paul, whose son, Haakon, was Magnus's cousin. After Paul and Erlend were displaced by Magnus Barelegs, the younger Magnus (Erlendsson) was forced to accompany the Norwegian king on a raiding expedition along the west coast of Britain as far south as Anglesey.

Much of what is known from this time is drawn from the *Orkneyinga Saga* and far from universally agreed upon. The popular version is that Magnus's piety soon came to the fore, as he refused to take part in the pillaging on offer; instead, to the fury of the king, he stayed put and sang psalms on the ship. Magnus later slipped away and swam (this is the *Orkneyinga Saga*) to Scotland where he jointly ruled Orkney with his cousin Haakon. Magnus married a Scottish aristocrat and his piety extended, reportedly, to taking a cold bath whenever he felt earthly temptation.

According to the *Orkneyinga Saga*, Magnus's popularity with his subjects left Haakon jealous, and hostility between the two emerged. A potential battle at Tingwall (near the jetty for the Rousay ferry) was averted but the decisive action soon followed. Sometime between the years 1115 and 1118 an attempt to make peace was arranged: Haakon and Magnus would meet on Egilsay, each with two

Standing on a brow with a backdrop of sea and the island of Westray, the church enjoys a magnificent position. It has an unusual design, with a rectangular sanctuary to the east and a tall round tower (originally 70ft high) to the west, while the extravagance of the stonework reflects the wealth of Orkney at the time. The roof was stripped away in the 19th century and the building is open to the elements. This Norse church is one of only two remaining distinctive round-towered Viking churches in Europe and has drawn parallels with Irish churches and contemporaneous churches in East Anglia and north Germany.

Continuing to the crossroads above the church you reach **Egilsay Community Centre**, which was once the school. The doors are always open and there's a modest interpretation centre here, along with facilities for hot drinks, an honesty box and a toilet. In sunshine the outside tables are perfect for a picnic.

Visible from the centre, a cenotaph 400yds southeast marks the spot where Magnus is said to have been executed. You can reach it by taking the track that heads east from the community centre and turning right through a kissing gate.

There's little other historical interest on Egilsay but the island makes for some glorious walking. From the cenotaph you can continue down the track as it winds its way east for half a mile through grazing fields to a gate located hard above a small but delightful beach at **Nettle Knowe**. Here, you look directly across at Eday; in summer, you will often see gannets plunging into the water for fish.

A longer walk, taking up to 2 hours there and back, follows the 'main' road on the island due south from the crossroads into the heart of the RSPB reserve of Onziebust (pronounced 'onny-bust'). Egilsay has some superb wetlands – along with Shapinsay, it is the most important Orkney island for a habitat that is rare in Britain.

The road leads south to Onziebust Farm, a good mile from the cenotaph. It's worth continuing through the farmyard where you should go through the gate and along the path between two fences. Head directly for the conspicuous Lumps to the southeast – the Hillocks of the Graand. Beyond here, Egilsay tapers to a watery

ships and an equal number of men. Haakon turned up with eight ships, leaving Magnus to conclude that any deal was off.

Magnus was seized. His offers to go into exile or on a pilgrimage to save his cousin's soul were turned down but Haakon was agreeable to Magnus's third suggestion, that Haakon mutilate or blind Magnus. However, the attendant chieftains wanted a death and an end to the joint earldom. As for the method of execution, the *Saga* records that Magnus declared 'it is not seemly to behead chiefs like thieves.' After Haakon's banner-bearer Ofeig refused to slay him, Magnus's head was cleaved by Lifolf, Haakon's cook, and buried where he fell, initially denied a Christian burial.

Magnus's body was moved to Christchurch in Birsay, a cult emerged dedicated to his memory and, soon enough, miracles attributed to him were occurring all over the place. The mossy ground where he was killed almost immediately turned to lush, rich grass. A further 'miracle' involving William the Old, the Bishop of Orkney, appears to have cemented Magnus's power beyond the grave. William had tried to play down the miracles but one day he was struck blind in Birsay Cathedral only to recover his sight after stumbling upon Magnus's grave. Sure enough, Magnus was canonised in 1135. He remains one of the most renowned saints in Scandinavia.

point around the Loch of the Graand. If you go through the gate by the hillocks you can edge your way along the coast by the dense iris beds to the side of the loch. From late April to July you should *not* do this however, as you will be walking right above nesting fulmars. Out of season, it's easiest to return the same way.

WYRE As with Egilsay, Wyre's modest dimensions – just 2 miles long by a mile wide – belie the interest to be found here. Local people are traditionally referred to as 'wyre wilks', or whelks. The name 'wyre' comes from the Viking 'vigr', or 'spearhead', and refers to the island's distinctive shape.

Human occupation on Wyre goes way back: recent discoveries at Ha' Breck in the southwest of the island have remains of wood dating to 3300BC. Apart from its natural beauty and superb setting between the proverbial rock (Rousay) and a hard place (the Mainland), Wyre has several attractions that repay a visit, including the impressive remains of a castle built for a 12th-century Norse chieftain and wealthy landowner, Kolbein Hrúga.

Wyre is easily explored by foot on a day trip from either the Mainland or Rousay. Good paths in the form of a cross cover the heart and top half of the island.

Wyre's population – 29 at the last census – has long had a reputation for innovation and taking a stand; the island was Orkney's first to introduce mechanised farming in the 1950s. More recently, when the Dounreay nuclear power plant was proposed on the Scottish mainland across the Pentland Firth, local people were closely involved in what became known as the Declaration of Wyre, a petition opposing its construction that even sought the endorsement of the royal families of Demark and Norway.

What to see and do Wyre's pier is located on the west side of the island, directly opposite the Rousay Pier, and the main sites of interest are all located a good mile to the south. Walk up the winding track from the pier to the brow of the island and follow the road as it bears right. Half a mile from the pier you reach the **Wyre Heritage Centre** (⊕ always open) where there is plenty of information on the history of the island and the chance to make yourself a hot drink (there's an adjacent honesty box).

Along the way, and set back from the road on the right, is **The Bú**, former home of the Scottish poet Edwin Muir. The farmstead (still privately occupied) is where

Muir spent his childhood before an increase in rents forced his family to relocate to Orkney's Mainland. The name Bú (Old Norse for 'great hall') raises the possibility that it was once at the heart of a Norse estate, perhaps that of Hrúga.

A signposted path from the heritage centre directs you towards Cubbie Roo's castle. Before you reach it, you come to the 12th-century kirk of **St Mary's chapel**. Enter the churchyard – which is often overgrown – via the rusty iron gates. The small Romanesque chapel exudes a great deal of charm: a round-arched doorway leads into the nave and the brickwork is still in good condition. During restoration work in the 19th century, a grave in the chapel was found to contain the remains of a tall, well-built man: according to conjecture, it may have been the Norse chieftain Kolbein Hrúga. What is certain is that some iron-mail armour richly decorated with brass rings was discovered in 1933; it is now in the National Museum of Scotland. The chapel was built either by Hrúga or his son, Bjarni, who was Bishop of Orkney (Bjarni was an enlightened fellow for his times, reinvigorating the construction of St Magnus Cathedral and establishing a foundation for the teaching of Latin there; he was also an accomplished poet).

The substantial remains of **Cubbie Roo's castle** stand high behind the chapel. The castle was built for Hrúga, whose name glissades into the giant Cubbie Roo of legend. To reach the castle, climb up and down the unusually wide steps at the back of the chapel and make your way up the small hill to the castle. This stands on a low hill surrounded by marshland and was originally reached by a flagstone bridge from the east. Surrounded by ditches and ramparts and centred on a former three-storey tower, the castle was built under the auspices of Hrúga in the early 12th century. Still visible today are the stepped window sills, the rock-cut water tank in

EDWIN MUIR

One of Scotland's most important poets – albeit perhaps nowadays overlooked – Edwin Muir was born in Deerness in 1887. His family moved to Egilsay two years later where they lived in Bú farm for six years. While it is widely reported that they were forced off the island after the beastly William Burroughs (of Trumland House notoriety) put the rent up after spotting an extra haystack in the farmyard – and this is true – locals noted that matters were made worse by Muir's father's lack of competence as a farmer.

The Muirs moved to Kirkwall and then Glasgow. Muir's parents and two brothers died in quick succession. To survive, Muir took up a succession of exacting jobs in factories, including one where charcoal was produced from bones. He then taught himself German and, with his wife, Willa Anderson, a classicist, travelled in central and eastern Europe, worked for the British Council and taught English at Harvard.

Muir wrote poetry for much his life and would often speak fondly of childhood on Egilsay and how it influenced both his outlook and writing. He described Scotland, from the perspective of Wyre, as 'my second country' – with Wyre as the 'country' closest to his heart. His best-known poem, *The Horses*, was published in 1956. Alluding to the Cold War, it depicts the emergence of horses into a post-apocalyptic world. Muir was rated highly enough among peers to have T S Eliot as his publisher: Eliot wrote of Muir that, 'under the pressure of emotional intensity, and possessed by his vision, he found, almost unconsciously, the right, the inevitable, way of saying what he wanted to say'. Muir died in Cambridgeshire in 1959.

6

the centre and a stone oven. Contemporary access to the tower was via wooden ladder. The castle was constructed during turbulent times, when a stronghold surrounded by marshy land and commanding far-reaching views would have been a sensible survival strategy.

According to the *Orkneyinga Saga*, Kolbein Hrúga was 'the most outstanding of men. He had a fine stone castle built there. It was a safe stronghold.' In reality, it is more likely that Hrúga lived in the more comfortable farmstead at The Bú and only used the castle as an observation post and a defensive retreat. Hrúga never had to defend his castle but a hundred years after his death a descendant fled there and withstood a long siege. By 1500 the castle was already abandoned.

A couple of other pleasant walking options lie south of the castle, off the main road. The first option is to make for the **Taing** (5 miles return, nearly 3hrs), the inlet located at the tapering tail of the island (a spit). Keep on the road until it ends at the farm at Testaquoy. Where the road splits, bear left and strike out over the fields through a series of gates to reach the spit. You should not do this walk in the breeding season as you will disturb nesting Arctic terns: the birds will in any case bombard you and make it impossible to proceed. Outside this period, this is a good place to see harbour and grey seals and you may be able to pick out the kelp pits at the extreme point of the spit.

Halfway between the heritage centre and Testaquoy, a shorter walk along a dedicated footpath leads to the small bay at **Cavit** (3 miles; 1½hrs). From the main road, 600yds south of the heritage centre, look out for the gate (⊕ HY441258) leading to Cavit farm: follow the track as it passes the farmhouse and heads south to the coast with fine views of the Mainland amid a landscape full of birdsong in spring and summer.

Before you return to the pier, there's a pleasant walk to be had on the east coast of the island that leads to an unusual ensemble of stones at **Stormieclett**. Where the spinal road turns sharp left towards the pier, keep on through the gate and along the farm track as it bears right past the front door of Onziebust Farm (unrelated to the farm of the same name on Egilsay). Head east on the track for 400yds beyond the farm and follow it as it bears right. You should now be able to see the stones down to the southeast about 400yds away. Follow the grassy track that forks left to reach the shore and stones. The stone enclosures here have no parallel in Scotland: one school of thought places them in the Bronze Age; another points to their similarity to Norse sheep enclosures in Iceland.

7

Shapinsay

Just 3 miles north of Kirkwall, Shapinsay is, according to Orkney Ferries, the most popular of the North Isles for a day visit. Proximity to Kirkwall is, however, only one reason to visit. The island is home to the most unusual 'village' on all the isles, has an impressive broch, a surprisingly remote stretch of moorland and plenty of wildlife.

Shapinsay is separated from the Mainland by a deep-water channel called, variously, Wide Firth to the west, The String to the south and Shapinsay Sound to the southeast. Measuring just 4 miles east–west and the same north–south, the island topography – green and lush with distinctive square 10-acre fields and straight roads – creates an easy symmetry that lends itself to exploration on foot or by bicycle. The island is low lying, the highest point, Ward Hill, rising to the Mighty Mouse height of 210ft (64m). The island name comes from the Norse 'hjalpandisey', which may possibly mean 'helping', in that the island had a safe harbour that provided shelter in bad weather.

For a small island, Shapinsay's population comes across as extremely dynamic, perhaps providing proof of the adage that, when it comes to seeking opportunities for external funding and grants, 'if you don't ask, you don't get'. The Shapinsay Development Trust is active, organising everything from night classes to ballet workshops for islanders held by touring arts groups.

HISTORY

A curiosity is that the *Orkneyinga Saga* and other Icelandic tales make no mention of Shapinsay. While this suggests that the island may have been unimportant to the Norse earls, it has certainly been inhabited for thousands of years and there is evidence across the island of Neolithic, Bronze Age and Pictish occupation. The sub-peat dykes in the southeast of the island around Purtaquoy suggest that early peoples made full use of the island's agricultural potential. At least seven brochs dating from 500BC–AD500 have been identified. Elwick Bay, location of the island's pier, was where King Haakon IV of Norway sought to compose his 100-strong fleet before setting off for the Battle of Largs in 1263 (to no avail, he was defeated; page 18).

Island life radically changed in the 16th century when the Balfour estate was created and a succession of lairds stamped their vision on Shapinsay. Hailing from Fife, the Balfour family was gifted church land on the island in a 1560 charter from the Bishop of Orkney. Thomas Balfour, a former tenant farmer who acquired a private income by marrying a rich French Huguenot, imposed the distinctive design on the island's only village that remains in place today.

The settlement, known as Shoreside, was renamed, rather predictably, Balfour; another legacy of this megalomania is that, in the eyes of the Post Office, Shapinsay

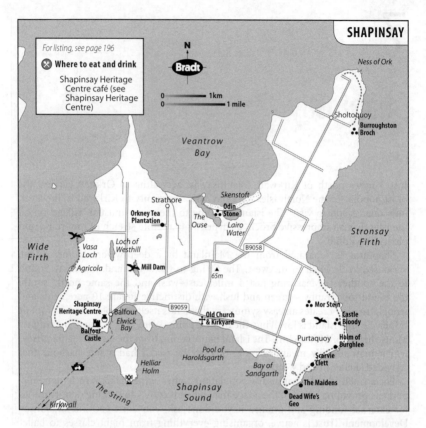

For listing, see page 196

⊗ **Where to eat and drink**
Shapinsay Heritage
Centre café (see
Shapinsay Heritage
Centre)

SHAPINSAY

N

Bradt

0 ——— 1km
0 ——— 1 mile

Ness of Ork

Sholtoquoy

Burroughston
Broch

*Veantrow
Bay*

Skenstoft

Strathore

**Odin
Stone**

Orkney Tea
Plantation

*The
Ouse*

*Lairo
Water*

*Stronsay
Firth*

*Wide
Firth*

Vasa
Loch

Loch of
Westhill

B9058

Agricola

Mill Dam

▲
65m

Shapinsay
Heritage Centre

Balfour

B9059

Mor Stein

Elwick
Bay

**Old Church
† & Kirkyard**

Castle
Bloody

**Balfour
Castle**

Purtaquoy

Holm of
Burghlee

*Pool of
Haroldsgarth*

Scarvie
Clett

*Helliar
Holm*

*Bay of
Sandgarth*

The Maidens

The String

*Shapinsay
Sound*

**Dead Wife's
Geo**

Kirkwall

is still considered to be 'Balfour' so letters sent from the island will be franked 'Balfour', rather than Shapinsay. This is thought to be the only such UK instance of a person being a postal address. Elsewhere, distinctly un-Norse place names with colonial and Great Powers connotations (eg: Inkermann and Balaclava) are less than subtle nods to the Balfours' legacy.

Meanwhile, under the supervision of Colonel David Balfour, the distinctively symmetrical farm layout of Shapinsay emerged in the 1850s through a process known as 'the improvements' (those who implemented them are referred to as 'the improvers'). Before this time, people farmed under the runrig system, where everyone had a strip of land and shared common grazings. Under the Balfours they were instead given consolidated units of 10 acres. The result was that farming production stepped up dramatically in the course of the mid-19th century: cultivation had previously covered just 700 acres but now rose to more than 6,000 acres. In essence, what you see today is a Victorian landscape superimposed on ancient plots.

The island remains heavily farmed: cattle and sheep prevail and the cattle population of 3,000 far exceeds the human equivalent of just 320. Nevertheless, there is a primary school (see box, page 198), many people commute to the Mainland and there is reckoned to be a 50:50 split between long-term islanders and incomers.

Twenty-first-century Shapinsay seems a surprisingly bustling place – every hour or so the ferry seems to unload and take on board a full quota of vehicles – but the infrastructure taken for granted elsewhere is a fairly recent phenomenon here: only in the past 40 years has the island had mains water and electricity. More recently, the island has embraced the newest green technology: a trial energy scheme (w bighit.eu) is powering the school by converting electricity from the community wind turbine into hydrogen.

A project to establish an oral-history archive (w shapinsayspeaks.com) has been set up, documenting tales and memories of islanders who have lived here for generations. These range from harrowing accounts of epic snowstorms to entertainment in the era before TV or gadgets. 'Islanders would just visit people,' says Lynne Collinson of Shapinsay Development Trust. The project is also recording the experiences of recent incomers. 'Theirs are the memories of the future,' says Lynne.

GETTING THERE AND AWAY

Shapinsay is only accessible by ferry; there is no air service. Orkney Ferries runs from Kirkwall to Shapinsay five times daily from May to September (25mins; return fares £27.20/9.50 standard car/passenger); in winter the Sunday service drops to just two crossings. On the journey look out for the uninhabited island of Helliar Holm and its automatic lighthouse. Shapinsay offers its own out-of-hours evening passenger ferry service. This is designed to offer islanders a chance to eat out on Kirkwall or to accommodate those working shifts on the Mainland but visitors can also make use of it if they want to leave Shapinsay after the last scheduled ferry. This must be booked in advance (m 07901 575161; departs Balfour around 19.00; £7 single).

Another reason you might consider travelling to Shapinsay as a foot passenger is that drivers must reverse on to the ferry. This is manageable for most people at the Kirkwall terminal but the Shapinsay slipway is much steeper and at low tide (when the ship sits even lower in the water) the point at which the slipway and ferry ramp meet can resemble a steep-sided valley. The crew have seen many a smoking clutch over the years and will happily drive your car on if you wish.

GETTING AROUND

A modest network of roads reaches most points of Shapinsay. The B9058 traverses the island from the ferry port at Balfour to the Hillock of Burroughston Broch in the northeast, while the B9059 heads east above the Bay of Scandgarth. There is no bus service, but contact the Shapinsay Development Trust (m 07901 575162) in advance and they will pick you up from the pier and even offer, for a donation, to give you an informal tour of the island before you take the return boat back.

The island has some gentle hills but nothing to deter even the casual cyclist. With no bike hire, however, you'll need to bring your own wheels.

TOURIST INFORMATION

The island has no tourist information centre; for now, you only have annotated island maps on boards around the island and a leaflet available at the heritage centre (page 197).

⌂ WHERE TO STAY, EAT AND DRINK *Map, opposite*

At the time of writing there was nowhere to stay on the island, a state of affairs frustrating to islanders and visitors in equal measure. Recent closures of B&Bs has been caused by retirement and island departures rather than lack of demand. It's worth noting that from October to April there is nowhere to eat and drink on the island either, though the Shapinsay Development Trust will always offer you shelter in its converted boathouse headquarters on the eastern edge of Balfour village. If you feel a day is not enough to explore Shapinsay, you can avoid paying twice to take a vehicle over by leaving it at the pier in Balfour overnight, returning to the Mainland as a foot passenger, and staying in or close to Kirkwall.

✳ 💻 **Shapinsay Heritage Centre**
café ⊕ May–Sep noon–16.30 daily. Toasties, soups, cakes & hot drinks, all well priced & served

in the atmospheric former smithy. Original fireplace remains in place. Recommended. £

SHOPPING

While most people will make just a day trip to Shapinsay, you won't need to bring provisions with you. The excellent island shop, **Thomas Sinclair** (❄ 01856 711300; ⊕ 09.00–17.00 & 18.00–18.30 Mon–Fri, 09.45–10.45 & noon–17.00 Sat, 14.00–16.00 Sun), is located 100yds up the road from the pier. It is well stocked, sells locally made preserves and serves hot pies to take away (see box, below). Balfour Bakery operates in a tiny backroom of the shop, baking three days a week and selling in the shop every day, producing bannocks, honey and spelt bread and 'fatty cutties' (a homemade calorific sultana delicacy).

Look out here (and in shops on the Mainland) for **Orkney Isles Preserves** (e orkneyislespreserves@orknet.co.uk), made by Shapinsay islander Glynis Leslie, which include chutneys made with mango and green tomato. These are sold in the heritage centre, island shop and on the Mainland.

ISLAND SHOPPING

A striking feature of Orkney is that the well-run shops on the outer islands lie at the heart of the community. If your long journey up to the islands has been punctuated by deflating pit stops at dreary national chains, you are in for a pleasant surprise. The Thomas Sinclair shop on Shapinsay is no exception. More than other Orkney islands, the shop must feel the heat from supermarket competition on the Mainland but co-owner Sheena Sinclair sees things differently. 'We are not in any way competing with the supermarkets; we are providing a completely different service,' she says. 'There's that little else on the island, so the shop is highly social.' Established in 1920, the shop is the only survivor of five present at that time. It is housed in the old boatyard, and a replica model of the *Iona*, the steamship that used to do the Kirkwall run, stands proudly in window. Today, the shop employs seven part-time staff, making it an important employer.

Separation from the Mainland brings it challenges. 'We use wholesalers in Kirkwall to supply us and there are several times a year when the weather kicks in and they call up to tell us we won't be getting the chilled stuff that day,' says Sheena. 'It's all part of the beauty of it.' If you are in any doubt about the importance of the tourist shilling to such outlets, Sheena points out that 'business over the summer months is an added bonus for us with people coming in.' Sheena has plans for a café attached to the shop which may well be in place by the time you visit.

OTHER PRACTICALITIES

There are no **banks** on Shapinsay but you can draw money with a debit card from the **post office** (located in Thomas Sinclair; ⊕ 09.00–11.30 Mon–Wed & Fri, 09.00–11.30 & 12.30–17.00 Thu, 09.45–10.45 Sat) or use cashback at the shop.

The **surgery** (✆ 01856 711284) keeps very short hours, so consider contacting the Visit Scotland travel centre for current surgery details. The island's only **petrol** pumps are located by the shop and keep the same hours.

WHAT TO SEE AND DO

BALFOUR The village is one of the most picturesque of the North Isles' townships, overlooking Elwick Bay. It is laid out in a distinctively linear design, and its single street runs so straight that it would have the Romans purring. Stretching for 400yds at right angles to the pier, the village is lined with attractive grey stone houses.

The just-so appearance of the village is the late 18th-century handiwork of Thomas Balfour and represents a fine example of a planned settlement. The village housed the cotters (farm labourers who were given cottages in return for their labour) that had been cleared from the southwest corner of Shapinsay as well as the blacksmiths, masons and carpenters employed on the Balfour estate. Today the line of houses along the main street is a mixed bag: some are occupied on long-term rents, others are let for self-catering while still more are unoccupied.

Shapinsay Heritage Centre ✱ (⊕ May–Sep noon–16.30 daily; free) is well worth visiting. Based on the upper floor of the smithy, halfway through the village, it houses yesteryear artefacts that are a cut above the memorabilia such places usually offer. Among the most diverting features are a 120-year-old pram, poems by island poets such as John Skea (whose compendium *Verses from Ostaft* recalls a way of island life now past), and a tribute to the island's rich musical tradition. The interpretation of island wildlife is excellent and there is a good gift shop offering locally made goods, including tasteful knitwear by Jean Coomber of Thyme Crafts.

Balfour's other attractions lie south of the heritage centre. Not many islands would be happy for a toilet to be the first eye-catching structure that visitors set their eyes upon as the ship docks, but look out for the low stone structure built into the right-hand side of the shore. This is a **sea-washed toilet** that was (and presumably still could be) flushed twice daily by the tides. The toilet has a counterpart: the high stone feature known as Dishan Tower, which was designed in the mid-19th century as a saltwater shower. Perhaps even more contrarily, it is topped with a dovecote.

Immediately behind Balfour village is the castle. Outriders of the castle estate bookend the village. At the far, north end of the street, you will see the Round Tower, which represents the remnants of the gasworks for the castle. Built into it is a stone marked with the date 1725 and taken from Noltland Castle on Westray. Just across the road you will see the northern road that leads into the estate, flanked by two ashlar pillars and two stone houses with fine gables. All the way down the other end of the street by the pier is the high castellated lodge, part of the mock defences around the harbour. The Balfour crest stands at its peak.

Balfour Castle is a striking sight, resembling a Highland castle and looking out of all proportion to the small island on which it stands. Built in the Scottish Baronial style, it is a riot of crow-stepped gables and conical towers. The castle itself has worn many guises over the years. The Balfours occupied the castle as recently as 1961 when David Hubert Ligonier Balfour died heirless. Until recently it was an exclusive hotel; now it is privately owned and there is no public access. This is

Nearly all the outer Orkney islands have a primary school that is not only key to the community but also central to its island's future. The population of a school is a pretty good indicator of the state of the island's economy, reflecting the desire of people to raise a family while in meaningful local employment. At the time of writing, Shapinsay primary school has 28 pupils: three in nursery and the remainder divided into two classes that broadly reflect infant (ages 4–7) and junior levels (ages 7–11). The smallest year group had one child (in P3, the equivalent of Year 2 in England) and the largest, P5 (Year 4) had six children. (High-school-age children commute to the Mainland every day.)

One of the wonders of such schools is how teachers manage with such a wide age group. 'We find the younger ones get stretched and pick up things more quickly and the older ones get more responsibility,' says Shapinsay's head teacher Emma Clements. 'In any big school you will have abilities in a year group that range over three or four years, so this is no different. And we are teaching much smaller classes, so the pupils get more attention.'

The small size also helps pupils develop people skills, says Emma. 'The children don't tend to play in the same age group, but all play together. And if you don't get on with someone you have to work it out because the school isn't big enough to go off with another group.' Emma also personally feels her job is rewarding. Whereas most head teachers are effectively administrators nowadays, she gets to teach classes three days a week.

There are downsides: Emma would like to have full sports teams and a cohort to form a school orchestra. The benefits outweigh this, she feels. 'We know the children from when they are born; their parents are our friends, and the school and staff are very much part of the community.'

a pity as, remarkably, the building internally accommodates much of the original Georgian house over which it was built. Activity today appears to centre upon the hosting of shooting parties in winter.

A WEST COAST WALK The coast west of Balfour Castle is easy to explore and takes in fine seascapes as well as a couple of fetching lochs. A circular route, mixing paths, lanes and open ground, follows the coast west of Balfour up to Vasa Loch before turning inland and heading south back to the village (4½ miles; 2–3hrs).

To reach the coast take the stone stile just above the pier, to the right of the telephone box by the gate to the castle. Essentially, you now just hug the coastline all the way to Vasa Loch. Walking south of the pier, you pass Dishan Tower (also referred to locally as 'The Douche') and get a frontal view of the castle: the more you stare at it the more it resembles the building equivalent of Gulliver in Lilliput. Pass through three gates along the way; after the third, keep left of the shoreline fence.

Just across the water is the small island of Helliar Holm, a real bird haven but uninhabited (due, legend says, to a curse thrown upon the island by two brothers who were banished by the bishop). You then reach a magical hidden lake known as **Agricola**, where mute swans often nest on islets. Cross a stone stile in a wall to reach **Vasa Loch**, another gorgeous birding location. The loch is barred from the sea by a mixture of shingle and concrete. Bear right at the end of the loch and head uphill to the junction. Here, you feel as though you are on the 'backbone' of Shapinsay. Turn right and return downhill to Balfour. Down to the left is **Mill Dam** RSPB reserve, where there is a hide. This dam is a little gem and an important habitat, as wetlands are poorly represented in Orkney. The water here was a natural marsh that was dammed in the 1880s to provide water for the mill. The loch is favoured by 25 species of bird, including many waders, as well as black-headed gull and water rail. Winter sees whooper swans and greylag geese gather here in their hundreds. Just as easy on the eye is the Loch of Westhill down to the west.

THE NORTHEAST The northeast corner of Shapinsay is home to the island's prime archaeological draw. Follow the B9058 almost to its end at Sholtoquoy and you will see a signpost for **Burroughston Broch**, located by a car park 400yds along a farm track (✛ HY537213). Dating to the Iron Age and surrounded by the faint remains of two houses, this substantial broch is smothered with grass that leaves an unprettified and impressively authentic appearance. You are free to enter underneath the huge lintel and nose around as you wish; you'll find some excellent interpretation at the broch's heart. Look out for the spyhole by the cell at the entrance, a gentle reminder that Iron Age people were just as curious as we are to know who has come to visit. Even from inside the broch, you may well hear harbour seals calling; to see them, stroll a few yards south to the ledges where they haul out.

From the broch car park, you can follow a delightful 2-mile coastal loop. This should be done either side of high tide as field fences have been laid to the high-water mark and you will need to step down on to the flat shoreline rocks on at least three occasions. The route itself is easy: you simply head north and stay outside the fields. There are fine views across to Sanday, with its conspicuous wind turbines and low-lying eastern seaboard. In spring keep as close to the shore as possible to avoid disturbing nesting oystercatcher and snipe.

After a mile the coast turns left at the Ness of Ork and you reach a car park above the small but delightful beach at Sandy Geo. There's an unexcavated broch here. Follow the paved road back for a mile to the starting point.

THE CENTRE The heart of Shapinsay is dominated by the vast **Veantrow Bay**, a collage of beaches, rocky promontories, ayres, lochs and ever-shifting tidal sands, all strung in a mile-long arc along the north coast of the island. The most attractive stretch of beach is **Skenstoft**, which can be explored from the end of the lane that heads west from Inkerman. You need to walk along the rocky shoreline for a couple of hundred yards to reach the sands. Alternatively, you can access them along the signed footpath to the Odin Stone from the B9058 (✛ HY508178) which leads down to The Ouse, a sandy lagoon that fills at high tide. At low tide look out for the **Odin Stone** (✛ HY506191), a large (6ft by 4ft), black and shiny erratic boulder. Some accounts say that it served as a sacrificial altar to Norse gods, though this is contested; more likely, it served as a marker for delimiting foreshore rights under Udal Law (see box, page 19). The promontory immediately northwest of The Ouse gives fine views; or you can walk around the edge of Lairo Water, a brackish lagoon, then explore the eastern side of the bay.

Along the B9058 just north of its junction with the B9059, a turning north towards Strathore leads after half a mile to Parkhall, where you can take a peek at Orkney's embryonic tea industry. At the **Orkney Tea Plantation** (✆ 01856 711755), islander Lynne Collinson is growing white tea on a 1ha 'micro-plantation'. She has planted 1,000 seedlings of white tea, imported from Nepal and selected for their

EXPLORING SHAPINSAY'S MOORLAND

Distance: 4 miles (circular) or 5 miles (there and back); time: 2½–3hrs
Start/finish: the Mor Stein ⊕ HY526168
OS Map: Explorer 461 East Mainland
(Note that the second section of this walk is difficult to negotiate and can, depending on local land management, be impassable. If this is the case, be prepared to turn back and retrace your steps.)

This sensational hike takes in Castle Bloody, the Mor Stein and striking coastal scenery; it is also the proverbial walk of two halves. The first section, from the Mor Stein to Castle Bloody, can take as little as half an hour; the second leg around the coast requires up to 2½ hours and has some tough walking as you approach the Pool of Haroldsgarth.

Head north from the lay-by by the stone along the road to the T-junction and turn right (southeast) to follow a lane. This soon becomes a farm track that winds its way right up to Castle Bloody. In spring the air will be filled with bonxies, Arctic skuas, oystercatchers and geese.

From the 'castle', follow the narrow track east to the coast, keeping the fence on your right, then turn south. The path comes and goes, but it is best to keep close to the coast to avoid both marshier parts and disturbing nesting birds. You'll squeeze your way between some delightful ponds and mires as you cross the moor. The path drops down to a crumbling stone grouse-butt above the boulder-strewn shoreline. Look back uphill and you will see the Holm of Burghlee, a huge sea stack separated from Shapinsay by the narrowest of chasms. The path now edges its way along the shore; the geos often have seals hauled out at their bases at low tide. The coastline here is different from anything else in Orkney, being characterised by geos at the base of which are singular and low-lying slabs of rock. These serve as a platform from which emerge pillars and squat sea stacks of black rock that resemble Dalí-esque chess pieces. Among the highlights are the miniature sea stacks known as The Maidens (⊕ HY525138) and, close to the southern headland of this walk, the violent incision into the coast that goes by the suitably bleak name of Dead Wife's Geo. How this landscape does not feature in any tourist brochures is a mystery. Around the geos are a couple of narrow points where the path runs right along the cliff edge: take care or scramble over the adjacent wall for the few yards involved.

After passing a deserted stone building you reach a sprawling chambered cairn (⊕ HY522149). At this point the walking becomes extremely tough and slow-going: the grass is high, the divots huge and you will essentially be wading through awkward ground. You may decide that the best option is to retrace your steps from here.

If you continue, walk ahead with the sea on your left and, as soon as possible, step down on to the rocky foreshore around Broad Geo, where things are easier. Continue around the Bay of Sandgarth. Just over halfway around, turn right up the grassy track (⊕ HY519158) to the crossroads and go straight uphill back to the lay-by.

tolerance of the cold. Lynne has plans to open a visitor centre in 2020, which will offer tasting sessions and serve tea. In the meantime, she is happy to talk about the project and show visitors around. Drop in or contact her ahead of your trip.

THE SOUTHEAST Two miles east of Balfour, along the B9059, you find the remains of the lonely **Old Church and Kirkyard**. The original church was built here in 1559 and its successor, built in 1802 but now also derelict and disused, still hosts the Balfour family tombs along its burial aisle.

The southeast corner of Shapinsay, beyond the end of the B9059 at Purtaquoy, has a different feel from the rest of the island. The lush green grass has disappeared, replaced by Shapinsay's modest parcel of heather-dominated moorland. Perhaps the brooding atmosphere is created by the rugged landscape of marshes in which stones push their way out of the ground, or maybe it is down to the name of **Castle Bloody** that is given to the ruins of the chambered cairn that lie at the heart of the landscape (and gets its gruesome moniker from the human remains that were found here). At 6ft in height and 40ft in diameter, the Neolithic mound of Castle Bloody is a conspicuous sight on the landscape. An excavation of the site in the 1980s left archaeologists puzzled: there was no sign of an entrance passage, nor of any stall slabs. Yet its location and other elements strongly suggested a Maeshowe-type cairn. The original chambered cairn is topped with a more recent cairn, intended, rather mundanely, to help fishing boats navigate.

Along the approach road to Castle Bloody stands the **Mor Stein** or Mora Stane (✛ HY526168). This high stone is thought to have been placed here during the Neolithic. Sometime within the past few hundred years it was knocked down and broken; it has since been reinstalled, though now stands 3ft shorter.

UPDATES WEBSITE

You can post your comments and recommendations, and read feedback and updates from other readers online at **w** bradtupdates.com/orkney.

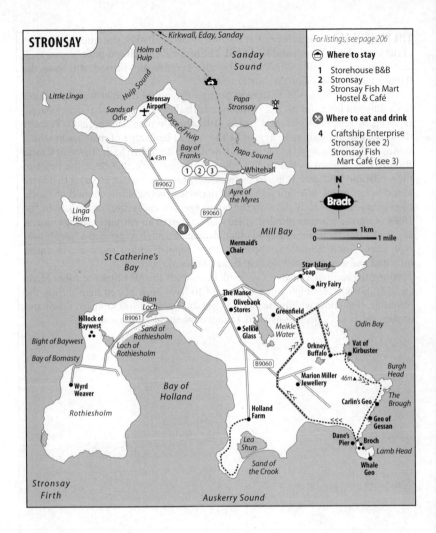

STRONSAY

Kirkwall, Eday, Sanday

Holm of Huip

Sanday Sound

For listings, see page 206

Where to stay
1 Storehouse B&B
2 Stronsay
3 Stronsay Fish Mart Hostel & Café

Where to eat and drink
4 Craftship Enterprise Stronsay (see 2)
Stronsay Fish Mart Café (see 3)

Little Linga

Huip Sound

Sands of Odie

Stronsay Airport

Oyce of Huip

Papa Stronsay

Bay of Franks

Papa Sound

Whitehall

1 2 3

B9062

Ayre of the Myres

N

Bradt

Linga Holm

B9060

Mill Bay

0 1km
0 1 mile

▲43m

Mermaid's Chair

St Catherine's Bay

Star Island Soap

Airy Fairy

Blan Loch

The Manse
Olivebank
Stores

Greenfield

Odin Bay

Hillock of Baywest

B9061

Sand of Rothiesholm

Selkie Glass

Meikle Water

Vat of Kirbuster

Bight of Baywest

Loch of Rothiesholm

Orkney Buffalo

Burgh Head

Bay of Bomasty

B9060

46m ▲

Wyrd Weaver

Bay of Holland

Marion Miller Jewellery

Carlin's Geo

The Brough

Rothiesholm

Holland Farm

Geo of Gessan

Dane's Pier

Broch

Lamb Head

Lea Shun

Whale Geo

Stronsay Firth

Sand of the Crook

Auskerry Sound

8

Stronsay

Wherever you go on Stronsay, you can see and hear the sea. Indented with crescent-shaped beaches that nibble into just about nook and cranny of its coastline, Stronsay (7 miles north–south, 5 miles west–east) also boasts an elevated spine that traverses the island from northwest to southeast: the result is that you are always less than a mile from the sea.

The island name has been translated in several ways from Old Norse and could mean either 'good fishing land', 'profit island', 'beach island' or 'star island'. The last of these doubtless refers to Stronsay's shape: all arms and legs, with headlands and promontories cutting into the water.

Sitting on the eastern fringe of the Orkney archipelago, Stronsay lies northeast of Shapinsay, south of Sanday and east of Eday, all of which are visible from the island. Stronsay's eastern flanks front the North Sea. Despite being low lying – with a maximum altitude of just 154ft (45m) at Burgh Hill – this beguiling island manages to offer extremes of landscape. Travel around the lush, grassy interior, where sheep and cattle graze their days away and you'll wonder what all the fuss is about. Until, that is, you reach the coast where Stronsay explodes into a landscape of great drama, from the best natural arch in Orkney to rugged moorlands.

HISTORY

Stronsay is thought to have been inhabited as far back as 10,000 years ago; a site with worked flint dated to the Mesolithic has been found close to Mill Bay. Five Iron Age brochs have been identified on the island. Fishing has always been important and the Vikings certainly used island waters and harbours; later the Dutch did the same until the 17th century. Kelp production was a key industry during the 18th century and Orkney's first factory was set up in 1722 on Stronsay by James Fea of Whitehall (of Stronsay, not London).

You're sure to come across reports on the island of the sea monster that washed up in 1805, said to be 55ft in length. In all probability this was a basking shark (although the reported length is more than twice that of a typical adult 'basker', others suggest this was in fact a rorqual whale); the 'bristles' (most likely baleen) were kept as a curiosity by the Romantic poet Lord Byron.

The herring catch also began to sustain the island in the early 19th century: migrating herring passed some 10 miles east of the island on their way south to spawn. The industry really took off in 1816 when the local Laing brothers backed a hunch and offered to pay five fishing boats for five years, whether or not they caught any fish. Seven years later there were 400 boats fishing for herring out of Whitehall, Stronsay's main settlement. Thousands of men, women and children were employed at curing stations – most famously the 'herring girls', itinerant young women from the Outer Hebrides and the Moray Firth. The industry was so huge that it was said to be possible to scramble from boat to boat between Whitehall and Papa Stronsay without getting your feet wet. Around this time, Stronsay's population peaked at more than 4,000. In the 1920s and 1930s, herring migration patterns changed, throwing the industry into crisis. Appeals for government support were rejected and the sector collapsed.

With a flat and fertile coast, Stronsay has long been the ideal landscape for farming, and the island is still punctuated by 25 beef and sheep farms. Nowadays, in summer, as many as 6,000 cows and 4,000 sheep graze on the island, which is so lush that most farmers are able to grow their own winter feed. Accordingly, farming is a key employer, along with inshore fishing (largely of green, velvet and brown crabs, the latter known as 'partens'), the school and health services.

AUSKERRY

Clearly visible 3 miles from the south coast of Stronsay and 15 miles from the Mainland lies the lonely island of Auskerry. Less than a mile wide and long, Auskerry is punctuated by a striking lighthouse that guards the north entrance to Stronsay Sound. Auskerry is phenomenally rich in wildlife, being an internationally important breeding ground for British storm-petrels, which nest in old rabbit burrows, and Arctic terns. As for flora, the rare Iceland yellowcress grows here along with a nationally scarce fern, small adder's-tongue.

Historically, Auskerry is thought to have been home to a large Bronze Age community but then uninhabited from the 12th until the mid-19th centuries (when lighthouse keepers took up residence). For the past 40 years, the island has been home to Simon Brogan and Teresa Probert, who converted a one-room stone bothy into a four-bedroom house. The couple also established Isle of Auskerry (w isleofauskerry.com), producing hand-dyed yarns and high-quality materials, such as sheepskin rugs and knitting kits, from their flock of North Ronaldsay sheep (or 'rollies', as Teresa refers to them). The couple cure their own sheepskins and hand-clip fleeces before the wool is spun offshore.

In a previous life, Simon was manager of the prog-rock group Jethro Tull before buying the island in 1973. 'Simon loved rock music but didn't like the things that went with it – the travel, the international hotels,' says Teresa. A few years after buying the island, Simon met Teresa – who was working on farms during her gap year – on a ferry to Stronsay. Day-to-day management of the sheep is rarely dull. 'You can't use a sheepdog on the "rollies"', says Teresa, 'as they won't be intimidated.'

The couple home-educated their three boys. 'It was really hard but the right thing to do. We became a very close-knit family,' she says. Every day continues to be different. 'The light and landscape are always changing,' says Teresa. 'I came back to Auskerry once on a very low tide and the sheep were right out, beyond the end of the pier, eating seaweed. I'd never seen that before.'

The journey to the island is arduous and takes up to 2 hours across strong tides. 'Auskerry Sound is one of the nastiest pieces of water in Orkney,' says Teresa. The turbulent waters mean Stronsay fishermen will be reluctant to take you in their small vessels, so to visit the island you need to contact a Kirkwall-based boat operator (page 74).

Today the human population stands at 370, enough to sustain a school that teaches pupils all the way through to the age of 16 (to study Scottish Highers, they must board in Kirkwall on a weekly basis). The island attracted international headlines in 2018 when, in an attempt to guard against a slow population decline, the development trust advertised for people to relocate here. As the advert put it: 'Stronsay has a sense of place, freedom and self-sufficiency that city dwellers frustrated with the frenetic pace of modern life can only dream about.' Having received several hundred enquiries, the policy appears to have paid off, with up to half a dozen families poised to move in.

GETTING THERE AND AWAY

BY AIR Loganair flies from Kirkwall twice daily Monday to Friday and once on Saturday, but has no flights on Sunday (8mins; £37/45 single/return if you stay at least one night on the island). Stronsay's airfield is located 2 miles north of Whitehall Pier in a rather elemental location, squeezed between the Sands of Odie and a sea loch, the Oyce of Huip. Depending on how busy they are, your accommodation may arrange a lift or you should call Don Peace (✆ 01857 616335) for a taxi.

BY FERRY Orkney Ferries ships arrive at the village of Whitehall on the shores of Mill Bay in the northeast of the island. Journey time is 1 hour 25 minutes for direct services from Kirkwall or a little over 2 hours for those services stopping at Eday or Sanday (return fares £39.40/16.70 standard car/passenger). As with many of the North Isles, if you plan to day trip on Stronsay you need to take the first ferry of the day in order to have enough time before the afternoon return sailing, and you'll also need to bring a vehicle. If travelling from Eday on the triangular route that runs between Kirkwall, Eday, Stronsay and Sanday, the journey to Whitehall takes half an hour with one-way costs of £10/4 standard car/passenger.

GETTING AROUND

The ferry docks at Whitehall Pier, which is connected to the rest of Stronsay by the B9060. The B9062, known locally as 'the top road', passes for a spinal route on Stronsay and runs northwest–southeast along much of the island. Most roads are either narrow two-way lanes or single tracks with passing places. There is no bus service, so you are going to need a car to see much beyond Whitehall. Alternatively (and fortunately), Stronsay lends itself to easy cycling; even better, you can use bikes for free from Ebenezer Stores (✆ 01857 616339). If you need a taxi, contact Don Peace (✆ 01857 6163350).

TOURIST INFORMATION AND TOUR OPERATORS

There is no tourist office or information point on the island, just the usual boards with annotated maps located at the pier and airport. Up-to-date information on events and opening times can be found in the local newsletter, the *Stronsay Limpet* (w stronsaylimpet.co.uk) as well as the useful island website w visitstronsay.com and the Stronsay Development Trust website (w orkneycommunities.co.uk/SDT). The **Stronsay Ranger** is Charlie Richings (m 07922711525; e stronsayranger@ gmail.com), who leads wildlife and historical tours around the island and can provide good suggestions for places to walk. Finally, for young children, there is a good play park at the community centre by the school on the top road.

Stronsay has limited options for sleeping, but fortunately they are all good and make staying on the island – something that is really recommended – a viable option. At the time of writing Stronsay has no self-catering options.

🏠 **Storehouse B&B** (5 rooms) Whitehall; 🕿 01857 616263; e annemaree.carter@btinternet. com; w tinyurl.com/storehouse-b-b. A good choice: spacious, modernised & en-suite rooms. Downstairs room can accommodate family of 4, has a wet room & is suitable for guests with limited mobility. Upstairs the 2 front rooms overlook the harbour. Living room with wood-burning stove exclusive to guests. **££**

🏠 ✳ **Stronsay Fish Mart Hostel** (5 rooms) Whitehall; 🕿 01857 616401; m 07789 104861; e fishmartstronsay@gmail.com; w stronsayfishmart.uk. Excellent, recently renovated hostel with 4 en-suite rooms (3 dbls & a 4-bed) & 1 with wet room suitable for travellers with limited mobility. Room 2 has one of Orkney's finest views, looking out across harbour & sound to Sanday. Run by friendly & tireless Evelyn & Richard Seeber. Located, as name suggests, in the old Stronsay fish market. **£**

🏠 **Stronsay Hotel** (4 rooms) Whitehall; 🕿 01857 616213; e cjdbuk@gmail.com; w stronsayhotelorkney.com. Run by the welcoming Chris & Debbie Allen. Neat, tidy & well-maintained rooms including 3 twins, 1 dbl; room 5 has a sofa & is more like a small flat. 1 room suitable for travellers with limited mobility. **££**

🍴 **Craftship Enterprise** Mallett; 🕿 01857 616249; e dianne@craftshipenterprise.co.uk; w craftshipenterprise.co.uk; ⏰ Apr–Sep 11.00–16.00 daily. Café located upstairs above the craft shop (see box, opposite). Serves filling meals including lasagne, sausage casserole & home-baked goods. **£**

✳ 🍴 **Stronsay Fish Mart Café** Same contacts as hostel; ⏰ 11.00–15.00 Mon–Wed & Fri–Sun. Run by hostel owners & just as good. Food ranges from scampi & chips to paninis, soups, excellent home-baked cakes & a filling all-day b/fast. Strongly recommended. **£**

✗ **Stronsay Hotel** Same contacts as hotel; ⏰ May–Sep 17.00–23.00 Tue, Wed & Sun, 17.00– midnight Thu, 17.00–01.00 Fri & Sat; winter closed Tue. Hotel bar serves filling pub fare, ranging from Orkney steaks to scampi. **£**

ENTERTAINMENT

The island has a strong music scene, led by Stronsay's Silver Darlings, a local group of adults and younger musicians who play traditional dances and have produced several CDs (w stronsayssilverdarlings.co.uk). The Community Centre hosts three major craft fairs each year. You'll find details of events posted at the Fish Mart and in the *Stronsay Limpet*.

SHOPPING

Stronsay sustains two excellent stores, both with long opening hours, so there's no need to stock up in Kirkwall.

Ebenezer Stores Whitehall; 🕿 01857 616339; ⏰ 07.30–19.30 Mon–Sat, 10.00–13.00 Sun. Well stocked & convenient for the ferry. The Dickensian-sounding name harks back to a boat belonging to the original owners.

Olivebank Stores Millbank; 🕿 01857 616255; ⏰ 08.30–18.30 Mon–Sat. Standing on the mid-point of the island spinal road, this is one of those little gems that make travel worthwhile. While no architectural beauty from the outside, it is packed to the rafters inside with everything from food to DIY materials. Maurice & Sheila Williamson, owners for the past 50 years, even cut & package the meat they sell. 'There's a saying that if you want something a little bit different go to your local shop, not a supermarket,' says Sheila. 'People want to buy things they want, they don't want shops to provide them with standardised things they can buy anywhere.'

STRONSAY CRAFTS

The island's craft movement has gained momentum in recent years to the point where a 'craft trail' has recently been established. From textiles and painting to soap, glass-making and weaving, there are several outlets where you can browse for locally made souvenirs, or simply enjoy an insight into island art. 'The island has some fantastic artists and there are a lot of hobbyists – woodworkers, weavers – who are equally talented,' says Dianne Riley who runs **Craftship Enterprise** (✆ 01857 616249; e dianne@craftshipenterprise. co.uk; w craftshipenterprise.co.uk; ⊕ 11.00–16.00 Mon–Wed, Sat & Sun) based in a restored chapel at Mallett, overlooking St Catherine's Bay halfway down the B9060. 'The building looked so sad when we bought it; it was totally ruined,' she says. 'There was no glass in the some of the windows, so we felt we had to put its eyes back in.'

Dianne's own enterprise features papercrafts and unique decorations based on shells found from beachcombing. She is not short of inspiration to draw upon. 'Partly it must be in the blood of the islanders but you have such wonderful light and space here. It's much harder to be creative in a city.' Visitors wishing to join one of the workshops organised by Dianne should contact her; she also offers week-long craft 'retreats', offering the chance to learn a skill in depth.

Probably the most distinctive artwork on the island is produced at New Biggin on the western edge of Rothiesholm by Eunice Bourn, who operates as **The Wyrd Weaver** (✆ 01857 616230; e thewyrdweaver@btinternet.com). Eunice produces hand-appliqué textiles from her own looms; with a unique, elemental appearance, these combine folk art and island themes. Her cushions with prints of the outline of Stronsay are strikingly earthy and rustic; each differs from the next. It's fair to say that Eunice, who studied archaeology before training as a weaver, puts her heart and soul into work. 'I've always been interested in prehistoric textiles,' she says. 'It wasn't a decision to come and live and work in Orkney, it was more like a calling. When I work I feel I'm re-awakening ancestral memories of an ancient craft. When you create something, your essence goes into it.' Bourn welcomes visitors to her studio though she asks that you call in advance.

Other craft-based outlets worth investigating include **Star Island Soap** (Stronsay Isle View; ✆ 01857 616281; e info@orkneystarislandsoap. co.uk; w orkneystarislandsoap.co.uk), which sells soaps with fragrances of lemongrass and ylang ylang; **Selkie Glass** (Sunnybank, next door to Olivebank Stores; ✆ 01857 616228; e selkieglass@gmail.com), which features fused and stained glass produced by the island doctor Rosalind Neville-Smith; **Marion Miller Jewellery** (Blinkbonny, just south of the end of the B9060; ✆ 01857 616354; w marionmillerjewellery.com); and personalised textiles by Hazel Shearer of **Airy Fairy** (Airy, a mile northeast of Meikle Water; ✆ 01857 616231; w airyfairyonline.co.uk).

$ **Royal Bank of Scotland** Whitehall; ⊕ 09.00–15.00 Tue. Also, post office gives cash back.

✚ **Geramount Surgery** ☎ 01857 616321

✉ **Post office** Ebenezer Stores, Whitehall; ⊕ 08.30–17.00 Mon–Sat

Petrol The only pumps are located at Olivebank Stores (page 206) & keep the same hours.

WHAT TO SEE AND DO

WHITEHALL Whitehall village lies right on the northeast coast of Stronsay, overlooking Papa Sound and Papa Stronsay. It is that rare thing on Orkney's Outer Isles – a community big enough to justify being called a village. A long row of houses lines the main street overlooking the harbour, and there is a shop, post office, excellent café and pub. At high tide, the sea laps against the stone wall lining the exceedingly fetching harbour, swamping the bay like a bathtub on the verge of overflowing. Whitehall also faces northwest and, from May to September, sunsets can fill the bay with a stunning collage of burning reds and yellows.

Whitehall is as quiet as you would expect a small village to be; even the bustle of cars arriving and departing from the ferry takes just a couple of minutes. The days when Whitehall was one of Scotland's largest herring ports is now just a memory. That activity is recorded in thoughtful fashion at the Fish Mart, the renovated fish market, whose walls exhibit contemporary accounts and photographs.

For a pleasant stroll, head west along the shore for half a mile to the Bay of Franks. You'll pass a ruined chapel along the way, while in the sheltered bay an old stone barge pokes above the water. At first glance the barge passes for a skerry but was used until the 1930s to provide coal to fuel the herring boats. As it sank, islanders altruistically 'salvaged' the coal before it got a soaking.

If you walk east along the road out of Whitehall you soon come to a small row of houses known as Lower Whitehall, which was built during the herring heyday. A walk out here – barely half a mile – provides fine views of the barracks-like monks' quarters on Papa Stronsay. A short walk immediately south of the village leads to the Ayre of the Myres, a picturesque spot with a picnic table. The water here is good for swimming.

THE NORTH OF STRONSAY The northern flank of Stronsay is incised by the romantically named Sands of Odie, which are as attractive as the name suggests. They are a couple of miles from Whitehall, so to reach them involves a decent walk or a quick cycle or drive. To get there, follow the B9062 north and then take the unclassified road to the northeast towards the airport; just as this turns sharp right you'll see a gate. Go through this for 500yds to reach the beach. The rock ledges exposed at low tide are smothered in seaweed and, combined with the backdrop of neighbouring islands and sea, create a striking colour scheme. The small island visible here is the Holm of Huip, an important breeding ground for grey seals in autumn (and you may also see harbour seals hauled out here).

THE ISTHMUS Stronsay is pinched at the waist by the incursion of two magnificent bays, Mill Bay to the east and the stunning **St Catherine's Bay** dominating the west side of Stronsay. St Catherine's is easy to reach – just follow signposts off the B9060 to the parking place 400yds downhill. Walk up through the dunes to take in one of Stronsay's finest views: high tide sees waves muscle right up on to the dunes; at low tide the beach is vast, with delightful rivulets, different with every tide, draining the water away at a fearsome rate of knots. The backdrop is glorious, with the Mainland framing the view and Hoy's hills peeking out on the skyline. At low spring tides you will see locals out collecting razor clams ('spoots').

On the east side, access to Mill Bay requires a little more effort ('to the beach' signs are in short supply on the island). Take the turning left off the B9060 just north of the Manse (✛ HY654254) and follow this downhill for 600yds. Park by the old mill in the long lay-by then walk across the road and down the grassy track on to the beach. You can stroll right along the sands – scrambling over the rocks at the midway point if the tide is up.

A couple of classic Stronsay legends are attached to **Mill Bay**. Halfway across is a rock formation at the back of the bay known as the Mermaid's Chair; sit in it and you will apparently be able to see the future. Somewhere at the far western end of the bay lurks the Well of Kildinguie. Drink its waters and you will be immune from every disease except the Black Death. You'll have the devil's own job to find the well though, as it has thwarted many over the years and has attained the elusive stature of the Holy Grail. 'We think we found it once … maybe,' says Charlie Richings, the Stronsay Ranger (page 205). Another striking feature of Mill Bay is how you rarely see any plastic washed up here. An offshore sand bar nudges the world's flotsam further south; locals claim that for this reason the bay is among the most pristine in the UK.

Marooned in the middle of Stronsay is the freshwater loch of **Meikle Water**, a restful place where you can simply gaze at the comings and goings of wild creatures. Ducks such as red-breasted merganser and shoveler are often spotted here. The track to the house and small farm at Greenfield on the northeast side of

STRONSAY: A HAVEN FOR RARE BIRDS

An island on the edge of the North Sea, such as Stronsay, makes an inviting resting place for rare migrant birds that get blown off course. The island's resident bird expert, John Holloway, lives by Mill Bay and has counted more than 300 species of bird on Stronsay, including unusual ones such as icterine warbler, parrot crossbill and bee-eater. Anyone who guesses the rarest bird spotted on Stronsay deserves a prize, however. 'It's the magpie,' says John. 'We've had just one sighting, in the 1990s. It just goes to show that what people define as a rarity is all relative to where you see it.'

Stronsay's appeal for lost birds lies not just in its location but also in its habitat, particularly its gardens. These are crucial for the smaller migrants. 'Many of these birds just follow a band of warm air, get here and find it's a bit colder than they expected,' John says. They thus hunker down in whatever shelter they can find – among them the hedges adorning Stronsay's gardens.

John is also a highly competent artist who has illustrated several books on the island's birds and from his time working on Fair Isle. Now retired, John used to run a B&B for bird lovers known as Stronsay Bird Reserve; he is still more than happy to chat and advise visitors on what to see and where to go (☏ 01857 616363; e johnfholloway363@btinternet.com). Above all, stresses John, you don't need to be a birder to enjoy Stronsay's flutterers. 'If you try and compete on birdwatching you are just never going to win,' he says. 'The people who enjoy birdwatching look to have a nice day and even if they don't see anything they still feel they had a special time.' Try and get hold of John's superbly engaging book on birdwatching on Stronsay, *To Fair Isle and Back* (page 286).

the loch makes the best approach. Access stops about 150yds short of the loch, but this provides an ideal distance from which to view the birds (through binoculars) without disturbing them. It is not possible to walk around the edge of the loch and, due to the extremely swampy ground, this is in fact quite dangerous.

ROTHIESHOLM The peninsula of Rothiesholm (pronounced 'Rouse-um') extends for 4 miles in the southwest of the island, is accessed by the B9061 and is worth exploring for its fine beaches. The pick of the bays is the Sand of Rothiesholm, which outlines the coastline for more than a mile until a bleak backstop of moorland intervenes. The easiest access is from the small car park at the northeastern edge of the bay (⊕ HY637247). This bay is backed by lovely dunes and is good for beachcombing. In spring the skies are full of Arctic terns and patrolling bonxies. **Blan Loch**, just by the car park, is an important wintering site for great northern divers.

The lovely walk along the beach can be extended into a loop of 3 miles that takes in the northern coastline of the peninsula. It's best to do this as the tide starts to retreat because beach walking here at that time is gorgeous and means you do not have to hurry to avoid getting your boots wet on either side of the peninsula. At the far (southwest) end of the bay, cross the stile on to the road and turn left for 200yds. Go through the stile on the right side of the road and follow the faint track though the fields, with the Loch of Rothiesholm on your right and a deep ditch to your left. Cross two small footbridges and a farm track, then bear half-left, making for the conspicuous green mound. This is the **Hillock of Baywest**, an unexcavated 3,000-year-old burial mound. Head for the stile in the corner of the field to reach the beach at the Bight of Baywest. This attractive beach is layered with large, smooth stones. Bear right and follow the coast, either squeezing along the grassy fringe or walking on the beach and pebbles. After a mile, just before you reach some houses, take the fenced path that runs inland to the road. Turn left to return to the car park.

Half a mile further west of the Loch of Rothiesholm is another gorgeous beach – facing northwest this time – at the Bay of Bomasty. High above to the south lies the moorland peninsula of Rothiesholm, which is cloaked in heather and turns a magnificent purple in summer. Peat tracks lead into the moors and are the easiest way to explore and avoid disturbing breeding birds. The best place to start is where the Rothiesholm road turns sharp west, about 400yds east of the Bay of Bomasty. The tracks fork and either route gives fine views before petering out after half a mile.

THE VAT OF KIRBUSTER Stronsay's premier attraction is the dramatic arch and gloup (or blowhole) known as the Vat of Kirbuster. Located in the southeast corner of the island, this natural arch represents a shockingly elemental slice of geology and deserves its place in Orkney's sizeable pantheon of startling clifftop architecture. To reach the Vat, you must drive or cycle to Kirbuster (the destination is well signposted) some 3 miles from Whitehall. Park in the lay-by (⊕ HY682241) just south of Kirbuster Farm. Walk along the narrow path through the field to the coast and turn right; within 10 minutes you'll be at the Vat.

A WALK FROM THE VAT

Distance: 6½ miles (circular); time: 3–4hrs
Start/finish: lay-by at Kirbuster Farm (⊕ HY682241)
OS Map: Explorer 465 Sanday, Eday, North Ronaldsay & Stronsay

Dominated by the Vat of Kirbuster and the huge sweeps of Odin Bay and Lamb Bay, this is a stunning walk, wonderful year-round but perhaps best in spring when birdlife and flowers are abundant. It's not, however, a walk for young children or those who dislike cliff edges. From the lay-by, head east for the Vat of Kirbuster and then keep along the coast. There is a path of sorts (sometimes clear, sometimes a faint sheep track) that contours the cliffs. The scenery is breathtaking: geos slice inland while elsewhere the coast simply falls into the sea, or demands attention through its vast slab-like ledges. Several sea stacks have already broken free from Stronsay; just south of the Vat of Kirbuster, you'll see two such columns, known as Two Castles and Tam's Castle. On the summit of the latter stand the remains of an early Christian hermitage. In spring the cliff ledges are packed with birds: guillemots at the base, then kittiwakes, plus fulmars near the top. You should also see puffins between late April and August. The coast is dominated by maritime heath and grassland; the salt spray makes life difficult for most plants, with the exception of the salt-tolerant white flowers of grass-of-Parnassus and scurvy grass.

The path winds its way up to Burgh Head from where you can peer across to another dislocated headland, The Brough, which also harbours early Christian remains. Follow the coast as the headland turns southwest. A couple more deep geos line up for inspection here – Carlin Geo and the Geo of Gessan – before you reach Lamb Head. At the southern end of Lamb Bay, a fence runs at right angles to Lamb Head. Turn left in front of it and walk 200yds up to the conspicuous archaeological mound; as yet unexcavated, this was originally thought to be the remains of Pictish houses but is now reckoned to be a broch. If you have the energy, it is worth pushing on to Whale Geo, perhaps the deepest of all the geos on this walk, at the pinnacle of Lamb Head. Afterwards, return downhill to cross the stile and turn right (north). Just to the left, at the neck of the isthmus, lies a rocky ledge known as Dane's Pier. You will almost always see grey seals hauled out here. Continue along the coast for 1 mile. Where the grass finally meets a track, turn right uphill and inland (⊕ HY677220). Bear right at the junction with the B9060 and keep on the road. Turn sharp left with the road and, after 300yds, sharp right along another road (signposted for the Vat of Kirbuster). Finally, turn right again after 400yds to return to the lay-by.

You know you've reached the right place as the cliff edge suddenly curves deep inland in a broad arc and – just – completes a full circle. The result is the creation of a gloup measuring 150ft in diameter and dropping for 60ft to the sea. On its seaward side the gloup has partially collapsed, allowing the sea to rush in. (This may be the origin of the name, as 'vat' is Old Norse for water or lake; that said, 'kirbuster' translates as 'church farmstead' and there is a farm but no church nearby.) The rim above the collapsed cliff is supported by a single ridge of sandstone, which functions as a natural lintel or capstone, keeping the structure from collapse. A couple of fences and boardwalks allow you to walk around the Vat in relative safety. Exposed ridges and rocks add to the drama, as do the huge fronds of tussock grass that drape down the Vat's sides, resembling a frozen green waterfall. Just as impressive is the birdlife – fulmars and ravens – that tend to nest on these vertical grasses. You can return the same way or consider a circular walk that continues via Burgh Head and Lamb Head (see box, page 211). Some tourist literature mistakenly recommends Bluthers Geo (✪ HY687243), along the route to the Vat, as a good place for swimming: ignore this advice as it is a dangerously steep geo. To make matters worse, most tourist literature locates the geo a little further north, so you can waste time looking for a safe place to reach the shore here: there isn't one.

HOLLAND AND SAND OF THE CROOK The southerly parts of Stronsay have other areas of interest, including the intriguingly named Sand of the Crook. Getting to this pretty, crescent-shaped bay is not easy, involving a significant element of plodding over rough tussock grass, but is worth the effort. Although it is less than 2 miles away, you should reckon on taking an hour to get there on foot. Start from the cemetery at Holland (✪ HY661223). Go through the gate that is signed for the bird hide but keep straight ahead (due west), through another gate, until you reach the coast. Cross the stile and work your way south along the grassy coastal strip (there is not really any path). If the tide is out it can be easier to walk across the stones, sand and seaweed. The drystone wall here looks like it could stretch on to infinity but you finally reach the beach. While it looks inviting to return by a more direct route via the bird hide, in reality this is impractical as electric fences, marshes and livestock will combine to thwart you. The hide is reached more easily from the cemetery: just follow the sign south, then walk along the top of the loch. The hide overlooks the delectable loch of Lea Shun, which is home to birds such as pintail and (in summer) greenshank.

PAPA STRONSAY Barely half a mile across the water from Whitehall lies the tiny island of Papa Stronsay (w papastronsay.com; e contact@thesons.org), which is home to a community of Transalpine Redemptive monks (a traditionalist religious community founded in 1988), known locally as 'the brothers'. The island was first settled by the Papari, the monks of St Columba, in around AD600 when it became known as Papey Minni, or Little Priests' Island. Life on the island has not always been tranquil. In 1046 it bore witness to the murder of Earl Rognvald Brusason by supporters of Thorfinn the Mighty (Rognvald had been imbibing the malt produced by the monks). Records of the presence of the monks since that time are vague and it is possible they were absent for up to 700 years before returning in 1999 when the order bought the island.

It is possible to visit Papa Stronsay on a boat provided by the brothers. However, access is informal and can be hit and miss: sometimes the monks respond to visitor requests and sometimes they don't. It's certainly worth asking the Stronsay Fishmart or Stronsay Hotel to help break the ice. The brothers also offer silent religious retreats for laymen and priests alike. Informal exploration of the island is permitted but not actively promoted. The modest sites include a chambered cairn known as Earl's Knowle, remnant drystone chimneys from early kelp-burning kilns; and the 11th-century St Nicholas chapel, which is thought to sit atop an earlier Pictish church. In spring and summer, the spectacle of nesting Arctic terns is a delight, though you should bring a hat to thwart their territorial instinct to divebomb intruders. Sometimes you may be accompanied by a brother as you explore. If your visit coincides with the monks being busy in their greenhouse, you may even be able to go home with a bag of Papa cherries.

Even if you don't visit the island, consider purchasing the magnificent calendar produced by the monks, which lists the religious feasts and the liturgical colours related to the days of the year and astronomical information. These are truly works of art.

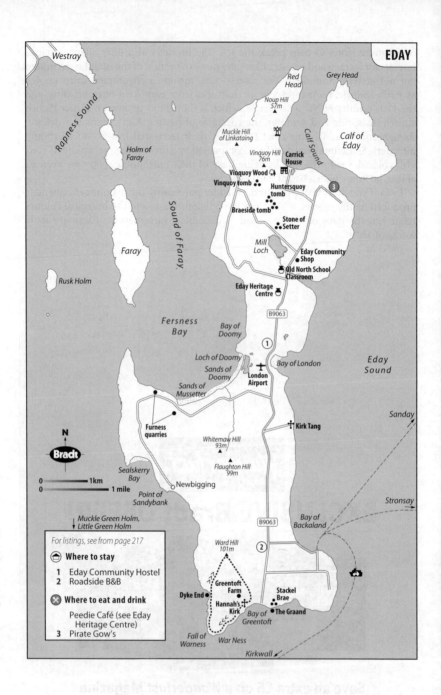

9

Eday

Eday is located slap bang in the middle of the waters north of Kirkwall, surrounded on all sides by its neighbouring North Isles, with ferries sailing up and down the sounds and firths on either side, and frequently traversed by inter-island flights. It sounds like a busy place – and it even has a London Airport. Yet Eday has a different ambience from all its peers. This is actually the quietest of the populated islands and feels, even more than the others, like a *real* island – one geared up almost entirely for residents, a place where people live and work the land. As a tourist you are made welcome but you are not the main event. Little visited, Eday is comfortably Orkney's most underrated and overlooked island.

Eday is shaped vaguely like an hourglass, with headlands at either end and an isthmus in the middle (the name comes from the Old Norse for 'isthmus isle' and is pronounced 'eedee'), and lies 14 miles northeast of Kirkwall. Distinctly hilly, Eday is 8 miles long and barely 2 miles wide and all but over-washed by the sea at that mid-point. Offshore but tucked into the contours of Eday's northeast coast is the Calf of Eday.

From every part of Eday you can see land: Sanday to the east, the Westrays to the north, Stronsay to the southeast, Shapinsay to the south and Rousay to the west. Geographically, Eday offers the visitor a slice of most of the other islands: it has hills and moors to rival Hoy, a couple of gorgeous beaches that might have been imported from Sanday and cliffs that resemble those of Papa Westray.

Here you will discover a landscape of moorland and grassland, with the north and south of the isle dominated by peat. Meanwhile, dune heath prevails at the isthmus where sandy soil overlays the peat. The cliffs comprise the red and yellow rocks of Middle Old Red Sandstone; you may well have already seen a slice of the island, for stone quarried on Eday was used to build St Magnus Cathedral in Kirkwall.

HISTORY

Eday was first settled around 5,000 years ago by farmers whose greatest legacy and imprint was their chambered tombs. In use from around 3000–2000BC, these tombs probably served as communal burial places as there appears to have been one tomb for each small community.

From the 16th century onwards, Eday was governed by lairds, several of whom introduced various industries, such as kelp-burning and saltworks. As you walk along the Eday shoreline, you will spot old stone walls and other structures that were once used to store and harvest kelp.

Eday is the only Orkney island that has substantial quantities of peat. From 1926 to 1945, Eday Peat Company provided summer employment to 11 men who cut 900 tons of peat every year – using a traditional tusker tool (a spade with a sharp-

Eday's bucolic landscape provides perfect habitats for a range of wildlife. Year-round you will see oystercatcher, lapwing and curlew in the fields. Autumn and spring witness great migrations, with birds passing through on their journeys to their Arctic breeding grounds, or indeed settling on Eday; in autumn, the direction of travel is firmly set southwards. Winter sees redwing, fieldfare, waxwing and snow bunting taking advantage of the island's shelter. In spring, guillemot, razorbill and puffin dive into waters below the sea cliffs of the Red and Grey Heads.

The moors are a fine place to spot short-eared owl, hen harrier and the tiny merlin on the hunt. Whitemaw Hill and adjacent Flaughton Hill, a mile north of the ferry port towards the southern end of the B9063, are among the very few breeding sites on Orkney for the whimbrel, a rare relative of the curlew. Mill Loch is home to one of the UK's densest concentrations of red-throated diver.

Eday has a substantial resident population of otter: as well as along the shoreline you may see them wherever there is fresh water, such as sand dunes and quarries, to where water trickles down from the hills, or simply collects during heavy rain. It is not uncommon to even see them on the flanks of the moors, seeking a break from saline waters. Substantial populations of both harbour and grey seal can be found around the coasts while the west coast and Calf Sound are places where orca can be spotted.

Less obvious places are also treasure troves: surveys have identified 120 wildflower species on Eday. Accordingly, an anthology of roadside-verge flora on Eday would be quite lengthy but would include autumn gentian near the airport and devil's-bit scabious elsewhere. Meanwhile, ditches and fields are home to yellow flag iris and marsh marigold. As you'll soon discover when you strike out over the moors, the highly absorbent sphagnum moss thrives in damp areas. Unsurprisingly, Eday is also the only island in Orkney where you will find bog myrtle.

bladed 'wing' just below the head) – mainly for export to distilleries on the British mainland where it was used to dry malted barley before fermentation.

The population of 150 includes a boost from recent incomers. Farms are found along the fertile coastal strip while fishing and shellfishing continue. Peat remains a major fuel. Despite its small size, there is a school with around ten children of nursery and primary age. However, it has been more than 30 years since the island had a senior school, since when older children have had to board in Kirkwall. Recently, modern technology has offered an alternative with a proposal that for two days a week, children in S1 and S2 (aged 11–13) study at Sanday's high school, while on the other three days they follow an e-learning curriculum on Eday, allowing them to stay on the island.

GETTING THERE AND AWAY

BY AIR The name of Eday's airport is beloved by pub-quiz fans who enjoy any opportunity to point out that there is more than one London Airport in the UK. Named for its location by the Bay of London at the pinch point of the island, it lies 4 miles north of the ferry port at the Bay of Backaland. Loganair flies from Kirkwall only on Wednesday, when there are two flights. Fares are £37 single; a return 'sightseer' fare of £45 applies if you stay at least one night.

BY FERRY Orkney Ferries operates a service from Kirkwall to the port in the Bay of Backaland in the southeast corner of the island. It runs two to three sailings daily from May to September. Direct services take 1¼ hours; those that travel via Sanday take the best part of 2 hours; via Stronsay the journey time is 2 hours 35 minutes (return fares are £39.40/16.70 standard car/passenger). A slightly reduced service operates in winter.

With a little planning it is possible to put together an itinerary that allows you to spend a few days travelling between Eday, Sanday and Stronsay without returning to Kirkwall (Eday–Sanday takes 20mins; Eday–Stronsay is 30mins).

GETTING AROUND

The B9063 runs the length of the island from the ferry pier to Calf Sound in the north. An impressive network of unclassified roads penetrates Eday's decidedly modest interior. Cycling is a good option along the island's extremely quiet roads. An informal taxi service seems to come and go; enquire ahead to Roadside B&B (see below) to see if it is running.

TOURIST INFORMATION

The only source of events and activity is the **Eday Heritage Centre** (⊕ Apr–Sep 10.00–17.00 daily; page 218). Sadly, the **Eday Ranger Service** was not in operation at the time of writing. When a new ranger is appointed, the service will offer a series of guided walks and other activities during the summer months. Ask at the shop or heritage centre for updates.

 ## WHERE TO STAY *Map, page 214*

Eday has just two places to stay, a good B&B and an independent hostel. For details of self-catering options visit **w** orkney.com.

Eday Community Hostel (5 rooms)
Located by the fire station, 1 mile south of the shop; ☎01857 622283; **e** hostel@eca.islands.scot; **w** eca. islands.scot. Unstaffed but affiliated to the Scottish Youth Hostel Association network. Mix of shared & private rooms are well maintained; facilities include good kitchen, laundry, living room & hot showers. **£**

✳ **Roadside B&B** (3 rooms); ☎01857 622203; **e** anne.cant_eday@hotmail.co.uk. En-suite, thoughtfully decorated & cosy rooms in former island pub. Characterful building with exposed stone walls & huge welcoming lounge. Run by extremely friendly & kind Anne Cant. Located by the ferry port. **££**

 ## WHERE TO EAT AND DRINK *Map, page 214*

There's just the one place to sit down and eat on Eday – and it's rarely open; it is, however, absolutely brilliant. You can also order bread from **Peedie Bakehouse** (see box, page 218).

✳ **Peedie Café** Eday Heritage Centre; ⊕ Apr–Sep 11.00–16.00 Sat & Sun (10.00–17.00 Mon–Fri self-service tea, coffee & biscuits only). The only option for eating out on the island but, perhaps unexpectedly, given Eday is such a quiet

place, the café is one of the very best in Orkney. Located in a back room of the heritage centre & overlooked by impressive friezes of island themes, it serves excellent food & proper coffee. Soup of the day will fuel your walks or you can opt

Order lunch in the heritage centre and you may get a choice of focaccia or sourdough; travel around the island and you will notice adverts for the Peedie Bakehouse and its range of slow-risen organic white, brown and wholemeal breads, ciabatta and Moroccan flatbreads. But you'll search in vain for a store. So far, so intriguing. The riddle of the elusive bakery is that it does not exist in the form of a shop; it does though have a mission control in the form of the home of Maggie Brown (✆ 01857 622214; e bakehouse@cormoss.me.uk) one of the best artisan bakers in Orkney.

Maggie is self-taught, and gave up a university job to move to Orkney from Aberdeenshire. 'Baking bread came out of sheer exasperation. I ran a couple of cafés and the cooking was great but I got fed up with only being able to source local white rolls. Bread always challenges you', she says. 'It's a joy.' She uses organic flour mainly because it is stone-ground 'and so is not milled to death to look like talcum powder'.

Maggie bakes all year round but runs a pop-up honesty shop in the summer months. She sees her role as more about serving the community and visitors than making a profit. 'We sell the organic products at much lower prices than we should because we want them to be accessible to everybody', she says. Maggie bakes on Friday and Saturday and welcomes orders from day visitors and those who are self-catering on the island. She's happy to drop the bread off wherever visitors find it convenient. Don't forget to order scones, too, made by her husband Angus and which she asserts are the best on Orkney.

for specials such as salmon with locally baked rye bread & really fine puddings such as spiced sponge with ice cream. Strongly recommended. £

⌨ Pirate Gow's Furrowend, at the north end of the island, overlooking Calf Sound; ✆ 01857 622270; m 07432 008431; ◷ 17.00–20.00 Fri, plus some Sats in summer. Take-away fish & burgers. £

SHOPPING

The island shop, **Eday Community Shop** (Hammarhill; ◷ 10.00–14.00 Mon & Sat, 09.00–13.00 Tue & Wed, 09.00–13.00 & 18.00–19.30 Thu, 13.00–17.00 Fri, 14.00–16.00 Sun) is located 5 miles north of the ferry port. It is impressively well stocked with everything you need if you are walking or self-catering.

OTHER PRACTICALITIES

There is no **bank** on Eday but the **post office** located in the village shop (◷ 10.00–14.00 Mon & Sat, 09.00–13.00 Tue–Thu, 13.00–17.00 Fri) issues money on debit cards and the shop gives cashback. **Petrol** pumps are located at shop; credit-card payment is possible 24/7.

WHAT TO SEE AND DO

The excellent **Eday Heritage Centre** (◷ Apr–Sep 09.00–17.00 daily; free, donations welcome) is housed in a converted Baptist chapel, two-thirds of the way north up the island. Various displays offer a useful introduction to the island economy (peat features heavily) as well as archaeology, wildlife and Eday's role in tidal energy. The upper floor houses an archive where any descendants of Eday residents may research their family history. In a nice touch, from May to August local residents are on hand to talk about island life. Another thoughtful quarter of the centre is devoted to the lives, times and deaths of Eday men who died during World War I.

If you have ever wanted to inspect a life-size replica of a submarine, you have the chance at **Old North School Classroom**, located on the main road just south of the shop; you'll find it on the west side of the road, opposite a conspicuous shed with a corrugated iron roof. The old classroom contains a private collection run by Mike Illett (✆ 01857 622225), a former submarine mechanic who relocated to Orkney after working at a special-needs school in Norfolk. The house somehow accommodates the replica components of the submarine HMS *Otter*, including the control room, motor room and living space. 'I collected a few bits from the submarine and put them on the mantlepiece,' Mike says. 'Then as I got more, I put them in a shed; as it grew I needed a bigger shed.' Mike is always happy to show visitors around on an informal basis and there is no charge. Call ahead or just knock on the door.

EDAY HERITAGE TRAIL Most points of interest in Eday can be seen by walking the island's Heritage Trail (you can pick up a leaflet for this at the Visit Scotland centre in Kirkwall). This is quite a tough circular walk of nearly 6 miles (3–4hrs). Parts of the route are over path, but others are on open ground where, for the most part, posts guide you across heather-rich moors. The trail starts and finishes by the shop at Mill Bay (✛ HY568365); stock up before you go as there is no other food option along the way.

From the shop, cross the road and take the minor road signposted for Cusbay along the shore of **Mill Loch**, which is 400yds along the road. This 25-acre loch is one of the best places in Britain to enjoy the sight and sound of breeding red-throated divers, supporting perhaps the country's most densely packed breeding population of the bird, with eight to ten pairs nesting each year. The loch fringes feature mosses and taller vegetation, making it an ideal nesting site for the divers. Snipe also nest in the wet margins of the loch. The rest of the site is a mosaic of moorland vegetation that includes blanket bog, marshland, wet heath and acidic grassland. To avoid disturbance, you are asked to observe the birds and other wildlife here from the roadside hide.

Continue for another 400yds along the road then turn right through the kissing gate (✛ HY565369) to reach the unmissable **Stone of Setter**, one of the most iconic – and certainly largest – standing stones on Orkney, dominating the surrounding landscape. Reaching 15ft and mantled in lichens, the monolith resembles three fingers raised in salute. Its provenance is uncertain but a ghoulish element may be introduced by the surrounding mounds and bumps that are thought to be the remains of de-fleshing chambers, suggesting that the stone may have been part of a site where the dead were ritualistically cleansed before burial.

Head to the northwest corner of the field with the stone and continue on a boardwalk to pass the old school. Close by in the same field – look due north in the direction of Carrick House – are the indistinct remnants of the Fold of Setter, a Bronze Age enclosure most probably used for livestock but now all but enveloped by peat. Continue northwest to get a fine view of Red Head, which comprises both Middle Old Red Sandstone and Eday Marl. Follow a combination of boardwalks and posts to reach the **Braeside tomb**. This large Neolithic example is known as a 'stalled' tomb on account of its likeness to a byre (cattle shed): its internal layout

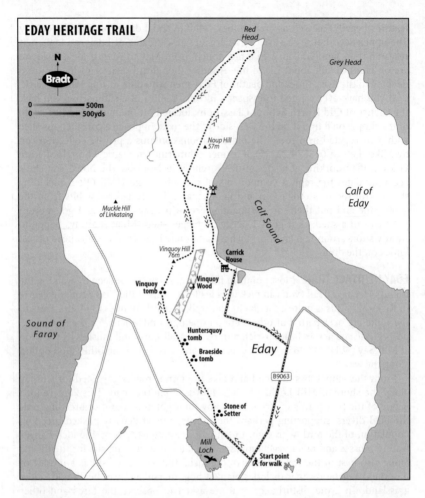

EDAY HERITAGE TRAIL

Red Head

Grey Head

N

Bradt

0 ——— 500m
0 ——— 500yds

Noup Hill
▲57m

Calf of
Eday

Muckle Hill
of Linkataing ▲

Calf Sound

Vinquoy Hill
▲76m

Carrick
House

Vinquoy
tomb

Vinquoy
Wood

Sound of
Faray

Huntersquoy
tomb

Braeside
tomb

Eday

B9063

Stone of
Setter

Mill
Loch

Start point
for walk

comprises a chamber divided by upright slabs. The line of the entrance passage points directly at the Stone of Setter. Follow the poles for a further 200yds to reach the **Huntersquoy tomb**, which was unusual in that it had two tombs, one on top of the other, reached by separate passages. Little remains of the upper tomb; the lower is usually flooded and inaccessible.

After Huntersquoy, the route heads uphill on a narrow path to a distinct mound on the skyline, **Vinquoy tomb** (⊕ HY562384). You can enter the tomb, which is cut into the sloping hillside, through a gate (bring a torch). Inside this is a Maeshowe-style tomb with four side cells leading from the central chamber; the appearance looks coarser and less refined than other such tombs, though this may be a result of the rougher texture of Eday sandstone that was used to build it.

From Vinquoy, head due north along the ridgeline for half a mile to the distinctive cairn on **Vinquoy Hill**, where a handmade mirador points out Fair Isle and surrounding islands. Continue north to the drystone dyke, in front of which turn right downhill to reach a kissing gate just above **Vinquoy Wood**. The wood is interesting, not just because woodlands are uncommon on Orkney but because, planted in 1833, it is one of the earliest attempts at re-wooding the island after it had been conquered by peat. Trees comprise larch, ash, rowan and hornbeam. Their contorted limbs, shaped by salt-laden gales, are an arresting sight. They attract birds such as wren, chaffinch and migrant warblers and flycatchers; in winter they harbour a long-eared owl roost. Just as striking, in season, is the vivid yellow of gorse that carpets hill flanks.

Keep heading north and contour around the flanks of Muckle Hill of Linkataing, past a crumbling drystone dyke. Keep the fenced enclosure to your left and head for the gate in the drystone dyke at the base of **Noup Hill** (❂ HY564394). The path is almost always under water: after you have manoeuvred your way over the mini-lake bear half-right uphill along the track past the stone sheepfold. The path over Noup Hill becomes easier for a while and before long you reach the trig point of Red Head. You can get that edge-of-the-Earth feeling here: within view, only Papa Westray (to the west) and Sanday (east) poke further north; closer by and to the east is the parallel headland of Grey Head on the Calf of Eday.

Bear southwest, following the fence line for a mile through the vast peatscape that accounts for this part of Eday. Much of the walking is over open ground, although the occasional peat-cutter track makes things easier. When you finally reach a gate and signpost (❂ HY558398), don't go through the gate, but instead turn left over open ground with the fence now on your right. The track isn't easy to find: continue for 400yds until the fence meets a stone wall. Here, turn sharp left for 100yds over the peat and you come to the track; turn right along the path, which becomes increasingly distinct and drops you back down to the boggy meeting of trails at the bottom of Noup Hill. Go through the gate and bear half-left across open ground to reach the small lighthouse by the shore (❂ HY565393). Head south along the shoreline (where the rails you see were from tramways that took peat from the hills to be ferried to the Calf of Eday and then on to the Mainland) and pass through a gate into a field; follow posts to bear left and skirt around Carrick House. Until recently, the house was open by appointment but is currently closed. This may change, so ask at the heritage centre. The dark stain on the drawing room

JOHN GOW

It's hard to think of a more clichéd profile of a pirate than John Gow, the last such privateer to be hanged in the UK. Born around 1698 in Wick in Caithness, Gow moved with his family to Stromness. Gow took part in a mutiny at the age of 26 on the trading vessel the *Caroline* and assumed the title of captain. He renamed the ship *Revenge*, a more appropriate title for what he had in mind. After wreaking havoc and committing various acts of perfidy around France, Spain and Portugal, he fled to Orkney in an effort to give the authorities the slip. There, Gow affected the air of a respectable trader but old habits died hard: before long he attempted a raid on the House of Clestrain in Orphir. He then turned to Carrick House, the home of the laird of Eday (James Fea, an old school friend). Unfortunately for Gow, he was caught out by the strong tides and foundered on the Calf of Eday. Needing assistance to refloat, he sent five heavily armed pirates to shore. They were taken for a drink and overpowered. He was taken prisoner and held at Carrick House before being sent for trial in London. He was hanged (twice – the first time, the rope broke) then his body was tarred, chained and hung over the Thames. Sir Walter Scott visited Orkney in 1814 and collected tales about Gow for his 1821 novel, *The Pirate*.

floor in the house is claimed to be the blood spilled by pirate John Gow during a failed escape in 1725 (see box, page 221).

Go through the gate on to the small lane and turn right. Follow this road up to Carrick Farm and turn right to rejoin the B9063. Walk three quarters of a mile back to the shop.

THE ISTHMUS OF EDAY The isthmus of the island is punctuated by two wonderful sights. On the west coast lies the magnificent sweeping conjoined bay of the **Sands of Doomy** and the **Sands of Mussetter** on the west coast, which is backed by spectacular dunes. Little more than a stone's throw in the opposite direction lies the **Bay of London**. To reach the sands you can walk through the airfield and pass the Loch of Doomy to your left. This is a wonderfully unheralded beach – very much in keeping with Eday – where you can stroll for hours with little prospect of encountering anyone other than the occasional dog walker. For even more seclusion, clamber over the small promontory at the northern end of the sands past Doomy cairn and drop down by the **Bay of Doomy**, an exquisite little beach. When the strong and chilly easterly winds blow, this is a welcome sheltered spot. Looking out across the Bay of Doomy you see two uninhabited islands – **Rusk Holm** and the larger **Faray** – which are grazed by sheep and also popular with grey seals.

Ruined churches are quite a feature of Eday, with a handful sprinkled along and off the main road, some more decayed than others. The starkest can be found on the coast at **Kirk Tang**, a mile south of the airport. To reach it, take the road turning from the B9063, which is, coincidentally, by the island's (still operational) church (⊕ HY562327). All that is left of the small chapel are two walls and a lintel that stare out across Eday Sound. The cemetery here houses the oldest graves on the island and is also home to Commonwealth War Graves.

WAR NESS The southern tip of Eday is centred around the low-lying point of War Ness. This area is much softer and lusher than the north, so much so that the southwestern cliffs are known as the Greeny Faces. The best way to explore War Ness is on a fairly easy waymarked route of 3 miles that also takes in **Ward Hill**, Eday's highest point (310ft/101m). You should expect to take 2–3 hours to complete the walk, including stops.

GREEN ENERGY

Eday's fast-flowing offshore waters have made it attractive to test tidal energy, in particular creating hydrogen from marine power. The Fall of War Ness, a mile or so off the southwest coast of Eday, has a strong current of 7.8 knots on a spring tide. For this reason it was chosen as the site of a European Marine Energy Tidal Test Facility run by the European Marine Energy Centre (EMEC; w emec.org.uk). This was the world's first marine-energy test centre and remains a focus of activity. Turbines trialled here come in all shapes and sizes but successful works have included the first tidal-energy machine to feed electricity into the national grid (in 2008); the test rig that achieved this, operated by OpenHydro's Open Centre turbine, remains off the Fall of War Ness. In 2018 a tidal energy turbine generated three gigawatt hours of electricity. Other infrastructure you might see includes a yellow floating tidal turbine, operated by Scot Renewables, which divides its time between Eday and Lyness on Hoy. Many other devices are based on the seabed.

Begin from the small parking area overlooking the Bay of Greentoft (⊕ HY560288) at the road's end beyond the B9050. Look out over **The Graand**, a long seaweed-splattered outcrop, where dozens of seals routinely haul out. Cross a stile and follow the arrows along a path just above the shoreline, passing a series of stone ledges that jut out into the sea. After 600yds you cross a burn through which gurgle 60 gallons of fresh water every hour from a spring uphill known as Lady's Well. Close by, albeit indistinct, are the remnant stones of **Hannah's Kirk**, once thought to be a place of worship. Burnt mounds have been identified here too, where people once heated stones in water, perhaps for cooking food. Nowadays, the stones are useful for skipping over the boggy waters from Lady Well.

The path curls around above War Ness, where at low tide, slab-like stones stretch far out into the sea. Go over a stile and follow the path as it curls gently uphill. Be mindful here, as the geos cut inland quite subtly and the drops are significant. Offshore are the islands of **Muckle Green Holm** and **Little Green Holm**; both have been designated Sites of Special Scientific Interest (SSSIs) and more than 650 seals – both harbour and grey – pup here each year.

Edge your way above the largest geo, Dyke End, and go through the gate above the cliffs. Head across the field uphill to the water tank on the skyline. A collection of fingerpost signs here points to the other North Isles. From here, continue north for a further 600yds to the post on the horizon. Only when you reach this can you finally see the summit cairn and trig point of **Ward Hill**. In clear weather, the view is exceptional: all the North Isles and the Mainland are lined up for inspection.

Return to the water tank and bear half-left down towards Greentoft Farm. Go through the gate and keep the wonderful stone sheepfold to your left. The old house here in the shape of a Norse longship dates from the 16th century; it now serves as a byre. Even the 'new' farmhouse dates to 1895. Go through another gate into the farmyard and follow the drive out of the farm, bearing right to head back downhill to the starting point. A little further east, by the next house along the shoreline, look out for **Stackel Brae**, a fortified Norse house on the south coast. Much of it has been reclaimed by the sea but elements of it are still visible.

The southwest corner of Eday is served by an unclassified single-track road that runs all the way down to **Newbigging** and is well worth exploring. The road heads west at the turning by the surgery on B9063 and then threads behind the Sands of Mussetter with fine views of the dunes backed by marram grass. There's easy access to the dunes and beach from their western end via a small parking place (⊕ HY542333). Half a mile or so further along the road around Furness, look out on either side for disused quarries that were once dug to yield the yellow stone that formed St Magnus Cathedral in Kirkwall. Now reclaimed by nature, the most appealing of these is the U-shaped dale that leads down to the sea. The road turns south, passing through a small woodland before arriving above the white sands of Sealskerry Bay, with Seal Skerry poking out above the water a few hundred yards offshore. This protrusion is aptly named, for both harbour and grey seals haul out here at low tide.

To reach the bay, park by the ruined croft houses that are almost parallel with the eastern edge of the beach (⊕ HY534323). Go through a gate and then look for the buoy on the fence that denotes a gate. From here you are almost upon the dunes. If you're in need of a short walk, continue above the bay to the west coast where you are confronted by an extraordinary jumble of giant rock slabs pointing upwards; it's as if an earthquake has been frozen in mid-upheaval. Half a mile further, at the road's end, you'll find the EMEC research offices and hub. Immediately south of their buildings you can walk across the grass and work your way down to the Point of Sandybank, a tiny beach with skerries exposed at low tide.

THE CALF OF EDAY Less than half a mile off the northwest coast of Eday is the Calf of Eday, an island that is both a birdwatcher's paradise and home to a cluster of archaeological sites. Both a SSSI and a Special Protection Area, the island is just 1 mile wide and 1½ miles north–south yet supports around 30,000 breeding birds from 12 species. Its dry heath and grassland are home to Britain's largest colony of great black-backed gull (938 pairs at the last count). Other species include shag, Arctic and great skuas and kittiwakes. The northern tip of the Calf is capped by the spectacular Grey Head, which mirrors the larger Red Head on Eday. Along the west coast of the island, facing Eday, are the remains of saltworks. These began operation in the 1630s and are one of Britain's best surviving examples of the industry.

Elsewhere are prehistoric houses, chambered tombs and traces of field boundaries. Most archaeological sites are located around the south side of the island. While walking inland is largely easy – thanks to sheep nibbling the grass to within an inch of its life – to walk up from the shore involves wading through heather that can be 3ft deep.

Transport to the Calf is offered by Hamish Thomson (\ 01857 622322; m 07780 819132; e calfsound@gmail.com), who grew up overlooking the Calf and makes the short trip across Calf Sound in 10 minutes. The landing is hard against the southeast rocky foreshore of the Calf: there is no pier, so the trip is not suitable for those with limited mobility. The cost is £50, which can be divided between up to five passengers. Access is dependent on permission from the landowners, which is arranged by Hamish, and also on the farming year: no access is allowed during lambing in spring.

10

Sanday

Narrow your eyes and Sanday becomes a passable doppelgänger for any of the Isles of Scilly, all of 800 miles to the south off the coast of Cornwall. Pronounced 'sandy' and, indeed, meaning 'sandy island' in Old Norse, the island is appropriately defined by more than 25 strikingly white beaches and bays. Set within a magnificent landscape of sand dunes, machair – coastal meadows that are rarely found outside the Outer Hebrides – tombolos (back-to-back beaches), spits and shingle ridges, Sanday has plenty to attract you. It's not just people who are drawn here, however: these gorgeous shores enjoyed a flicker of national media attention in March 2018 when a young male walrus turned up – an extremely unusual sighting of this massive pinniped.

Located 15 miles north of Kirkwall as the oystercatcher flies, Sanday is the largest of the North Isles, stretching for 16 miles from west to east and measuring 7 miles from north to south at its widest point, although its girth tapers to a single mile at either end. Romantic types perceive the island to resemble a sea dragon floating in the Sanday Sound. Three near-island neighbours keep Sanday company: Eday, 1½ miles to the west; North Ronaldsay, 4 miles northeast; and Stronsay, 3 miles south across Spurness Sound.

To the first-time visitor, Sanday can seem a contrary place, as it combines the faint air of a rugged frontier community with the landscape of an idyllic seaside holiday destination; occasionally, a delightful vista of shell-sand beaches is interrupted by an abandoned car in the middle of an adjacent field (you'll be told they function as scarecrows), and so quiet is the island that it can sometimes come as a surprise when a human figure emerges into view on a misty morning. Most of the population is scattered across the island's farmsteads, and consequently there is no real hub. Although there are tiny communities at Kettletoft and Lady Village, in the south and centre respectively, to describe either as even a hamlet is possibly to overstate matters.

It will, however, be the memory of a graceful landscape that you take away with you. Sanday's beaches and low-lying grassy meadows allow huge skies to dominate, creating a magical light at all times of day. On a clear night, few places in Britain can boast a sky so filled with stars. From autumn through to March you also have a good chance of seeing the northern lights or the 'Merrie Dancers' as they are sometimes affectionately called on Orkney. Conversely, now and then the thick North Sea mist, known as *haar*, descends to remind you just how far north you are.

HISTORY

People are believed to have lived more or less continually on Sanday since Neolithic times, resulting in the island's extraordinary profusion of prehistoric and Viking sites. Sanday's appeal to Neolithic peoples was based on its low-lying and straggling terrain, with light, sandy and fertile soils that, even today, remain easy to cultivate. The same soil that attracted farmers at least 6,000 years ago also helped preserve

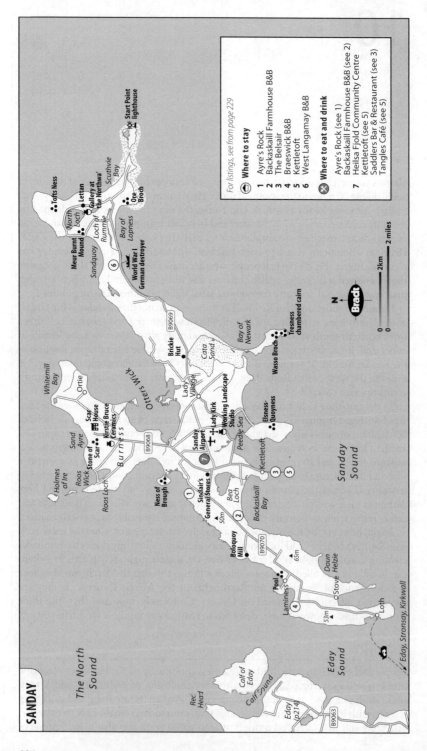

SANDAY

The North Sound

Red Heart

Calf of Eday

Calf Sound

Eday Sound

Eday (p214)

B9063

B9070

B9068

Whitemill Bay

Holmes of Ire

Roos Wick

Roos Loch

Sand Ayre

Stone of Scar

Ortie

Scay House

Kirstie Bruce Ceramics

Burness

Ness of Brough

Sinclair's General Stores

50m

Backaskaill Bay

Bea Loch

65m

Doun Helzie

Stove Helzie

53m

Boloquoy Mill

Pool

Laminess

Loth

Eday, Stronsay, Kirkwall

Sanday Airport

Lady Kirk

Working Landscape Studio

Elsness-Quoyness

Peedie Sea

Lady Village

Cata Sand

Bay of Newark

Wasso Broch

Tresness chambered cairn

Otters Wick

Brickie Hut

B9069

Sanday Sound

Kettletoft

Sandquoy

Loch of Rummie

World War I German destroyer

Meur Burnt Mound

North Loch

Lettan

Gallery at the Northwa'

Tofts Ness

Scuthvie Bay

Bay of Lopness

Ore Broch

Start Point lighthouse

N

Bradt

0   2km
0   2 miles

For listings, see from page 229

Where to stay
1 Ayre's Rock
2 Backaskaill Farmhouse B&B
3 The Belsair
4 Braeswick B&B
5 Kettletoft
6 West Langamay B&B

Where to eat and drink
   Ayre's Rock (see 1)
   Backaskaill Farmhouse B&B (see 2)
7 Heilsa Fjold Community Centre
   Kettletoft (see 5)
   Saddlers Bar & Restaurant (see 3)
   Tangles Café (see 5)

Sanday has always been a popular island with artists. Its light and sands attracted the composer Peter Maxwell Davies who moved here from Hoy (see box, page 143) in 1988, staying until his death in 2016. In recognition of his new home, Davies wrote the music for the *Songs of Sanday* (the words were written by Roderick Thorne), many of which were originally performed by children's choirs on the island. The songs include the lamenting tone of *Whales* and *The Raft Race*, which has an eerily supernatural conclusion.

their dwellings, tools and food. Medieval taxation rolls show that Sanday's land was valued more highly than other islands on account of its fertile soil.

One consequence of sites being popular for thousands of years is the gradual creation of 'farm mounds,' which are everywhere on Sanday. Each generation built upon its predecessors' foundations, gradually raising the land. Consequently, many of Sanday's modest hills are far from natural but rather augmented by the accumulation of manmade deposits discarded or abandoned over millennia.

More than most of Orkney's islands, Sanday offers a very real chance of coming across hitherto unknown archaeological sites. Sandy soil is wonderful for covering and engulfing the largely coastal settlements for thousands of years, revealing them only when erosion, shifting sands and the fiercest of storms combine. Up to 100 sites are currently being eroded. Excavations at Pool, just north of the Loth ferry port, have revealed a large settlement that was occupied for thousands of years and yielded Neolithic, Pictish and Viking remains; 10,000 shards of Neolithic pottery were found there, a majority of it of distinctive design.

History on Sanday is still being pieced together. In 2011, the renovation of an old farmhouse in the centre of the island, Appiehouse cottage, led to the discovery of a cross on a flagstone under the flooring. Now on display at the Sanday Heritage Centre, this became known as the Appiehouse Stone, identified as the earliest Pictish Christian symbol stone on Orkney (dating to the 7th or 8th century). On one side the stone was carved with a cross and a beast resembling a seahorse; the opposite side shows a large disc with a swirl. Much of what is known about Sanday's peoples is taken from various finds across the island: Tofts Ness was once a huge burial site that served peoples from the Neolithic to the Iron Age, while a Viking burial grave uncovered in the north of the island points to a meaningful Norse community that existed here.

Today, Sanday's population stands at around 500, well down on the peak of 2,500 in the 18th century. Nevertheless, the island feels buoyant: the school teaches more than 60 pupils up to the age of 16; this and NHS services each account for 30% of island employment. The Sanday Development Trust is active, securing funding for restoration, grassroots projects and training, all of which is helping Sanday to buck the wider trend of small-island depopulation. Farming contributes another 30% to the local economy.

GETTING THERE AND AWAY

BY AIR Loganair flies from Kirkwall to Sanday twice daily between Monday and Friday, and once on Saturday (12mins; £37/74 single/return). The airfield is in the centre of the island; get your B&B to organise a transfer or contact Ayres Rock taxi (✆ 01857 600410).

Sanday's isolation and rich vegetation make it appealing to a wide range of animals, and spotting them can really enhance your time here. You don't even have to be a birder to enjoy the natural spectacle. On the avian front, every species of bird that nests on Orkney can be seen on Sanday. Around 20 pairs of swallow make it this far north every year along with Arctic and Sandwich terns. In winter you can see bar-tailed godwit on the wetlands around Cata Sand while whooper swans join resident mute swans in fields behind Backaskaill Bay and Sand Ayre. Lapwings, oystercatchers, curlews and (except in midsummer) sanderlings are everywhere. In 2018, Sanday was lucky enough to host six calling male corncrakes, an uplifting boost for efforts to conserve this nationally rare bird. Surprises sometimes crop up including hoopoe, red-breasted flycatcher and ortolan bunting, which invariably attract the attention of birdwatchers from further afield. Otters are numerous here, though, as ever, patience is required to see them: Tresness beyond Cata Sand is a good spot. Harbour and grey seals seem to bob up all over the place; they are the one animal you are just about guaranteed to see, from the high tide mark behind the pubs in Kettletoft to Cata Sand and the Holms of Ire. Finally, beachcombing for seashells is a delight and among those to be found on the shores at Cata Sand, for example, are Faroese sunset, pelican's foot and Hungarian cap.

BY SEA The MV *Earl Thorvinn*, MV *Varagan* and MV *Earl Sigurd* run from Kirkwall (return fares £40/16 standard vehicle/passenger), docking at Loth in the southwest of Sanday. Direct services take 90 minutes, but services via Eday or Stronsay take a further 30–60 minutes. The schedule varies during the week, although there are always two services each day in summer. A Sail & Ride minibus service (m 07513 084777) connects the ferry port to anywhere on the island, but must be booked the previous day.

GETTING AROUND

To best see most of what Sanday has to offer, come by car or bicycle, as the island has no bus service. Bear in mind if you're **on foot** that Sanday is bigger than many people expect, meaning that you will struggle to see much of the island unless you pay for taxis (contact Ayre's Rock: ☏ 01857 600410) or take a tour (see opposite). The distances from Loth to Kettletoft and Lady Village are 8 and 9 miles respectively, while from Lady Village to Start Point lighthouse is a further 12 miles. The single option for 'public' transport is the Tuesday shopping service offered by the **Sail & Ride** Minibus service (m 07513 084777) that runs around the island and ends up in Lady Village. There is no car hire on the island.

Sanday's **roads** are good: the B9070 from Loth to Bea Loch is two-way, but elsewhere it's mainly single-track roads with passing places. The B9068 runs north to south from Kettletoft to Burness, and the B9069 runs from just north of Kettletoft all the way past the Bay of Lopness to the eastern end of the island.

The island is broadly flat which lends itself to **cycling**. You can easily spend days biking from one beach to another, perhaps meandering between rarely visited ancient tombs. Ayre's Rock campsite and hostel (see opposite) near the ferry port offers a helpful pick-up and drop-off service to save you from hitching or taking a taxi across the island when you're done cycling. For bike hire (£20 first day, £12/day thereafter) contact Dave Pendlebury (☎ 01857 600237; m 07717 059583; e peands@ aol.com), based by the heritage centre in Lady Village.

For **walking tours**, contact island ranger Emma Neave-Webb (☎ 01857 600359; e ranger@sanday.co.uk), who is employed by the development trust and leads guided walks throughout the summer. Island Tours (☎ 01857 600410; £17/hr for one person; £3/hr for each additional person) is another good choice, run by the very knowledgeable Paul Allan of Ayre's Rock hostel (see below).

TOURIST INFORMATION

In the absence of a Visit Scotland or other official information point, **Sanday Heritage Centre** (☎ 01857 600359; w sanday.co.uk, click on 'heritage centre'; ⊕ Apr–Oct 09.30–17.00 daily; Nov–Mar 09.30–17.00 Sat & Sun) in Lady Village is the best source of visitor information. The **Sanday Development Trust** (w sanday. co.uk, click on 'community groups') also keeps up to date with activities such as ranger walks and tours. You'll find further information at **Heilsa Fjold**, the trust's community centre (⊕ Tue–Sun, times vary, check development trust website), opposite Sanday School a mile west of the heritage centre.

 ## WHERE TO STAY   *Map, page 226*

There's not a great deal of accommodation on Sanday. The few hotel rooms are adequate, but the B&Bs very good. Just about all options are near the ferry port. For self-catering accommodation, go to w sanday.co.uk and click on 'visitors'.

⌂ **Backaskaill Farmhouse B&B** (3 rooms) Backaskaill; ☎ 01857 600305; e janey4geoff@ btinternet.com; w bedandbreakfastsandayorkney. com. Charming & characterful B&B run by Jane Taylor & Geoff Betts in an original 165-year-old farmhouse. One each of dbl en suite, twin & sgl. Comfortable, eclectic but stylish décor & furnishings (think suit of armour, mosaic table); upstairs lounge has plush sofas in which to sink & watch the waters of Backaskaill Bay. **££**

⌂ **The Belsair Hotel** (3 rooms) Kettletoft; ☎ 01857 600206. Simply furnished rooms, all en suite with family room facing the sea. **££**

⌂ **Braeswick B&B** (3 rooms) Braeswick; ☎ 01857 600708; e jon@braeswick.com; w braeswick.com. Modernised bungalow with a fine location close to ferry port & overlooking Braeswick Bay. 3 well-appointed dbls; Room 3 is the one with the views. Access ramp for wheelchair users but rooms not adapted. Guest wing has conservatory with views across the bay towards the Holms of Ire, Papa Westray & the Calf of Eday. Evening meals on request. **££**

⌂ **Kettletoft Hotel** (7 rooms) Kettletoft; ☎ 01857 600217; e marktlawlor@btopenworld.

com. Two dbls & 4 sgls with shared bathroom & 1 dbl en suite. Simply furnished but clean. **££**

⌂ **West Langamay B&B** (1 room) West Langamay; ☎ 01857 600756; e robin@rogartcroft. co.uk. The only accommodation option in the north or east of the island. Robin & Penny Calvert are friendly hosts. Lovely setting looking down to Lopness dunes; direct access to the beach. Ground-floor room but unsuitable for large wheelchairs. Evening meals on request. **££**

✳ ⌂ **Ayre's Rock** (8 rooms) Broughtown; ☎ 01857 600410; e sandayhostel@gmail.com; w ayres-rock-hostel-orkney.com. Expect a warm welcome from this friendly hostel & campsite run by Paul & Julie Allan. On the site of an old mill, the old byre has been converted into a hostel with simply furnished but neat rooms inc an en-suite family option. Separate cottage sleeps 4, & there is also a campsite, camping pods & a caravan with superb sunset views in summer. In between being a firefighter & a teacher, this energetic couple run a taxi service & offer tours of the island. 'I used to work on autopilot in a retail job,' says Paul, who relocated from the West Country with his family 12 years ago. 'I just felt there had to be more to life.' Recommended. **£**

The choice for food on Sanday boils down to pub food or home dining. With no standalone restaurants, you must turn to the hotels or the extremely good fare offered by other accommodation providers.

Ayre's Rock This hostel (page 229) also offers take-away fish & chips on Sat (⏱ 16.30–19.00). £

✕ **Backaskaill Farmhouse B&B** Same contacts as B&B; ⏱ 17.00–20.00 daily, Sun lunch by appointment, advance booking necessary. Geoff is a chef with 40 years' experience, rustling up fine dishes – 'food that you can taste & plenty of it' – ranging from Asian to continental & vegan. Menu is a mix of advance requests (inc gourmet menus) & what Geoff has in his larder. ££

Heilsa Fjold Community Centre Lady Village; w sanday.co.uk; ⏱ May–Sep 11.30–14.30 Tue & Wed; Oct–Apr Tue only. Small café inside the community centre serving hot drinks & toasties. When the centre is open (⏱ Tue–Sun, times vary, see website), visitors are welcome to use the centre to shelter from the weather or eat packed lunches. £

✕ **Kettletoft Hotel** Same contacts as hotel; ⏱ restaurant: 17.00–20.00 Tue–Sat, noon–15.00 Sun (for carvery); bar: 17.00–midnight Tue, 11.00–midnight Wed–Sat, 11.00–18.00 Sun. Standard but filling pub fare, with a 'chip night' on Wed &

Sat (⏱ 16.30–20.00) with fish, curry & burgers, all served with chips. Eat in the bar (complete with pool table, dartboard and parrot) or the dining room; although the former can get noisy & is more cramped, it does offer views over Kettletoft Bay so you can watch the tide lap up. The seals seem so close you feel you could almost pat them. It gets busy in summer months, so booking is advised. £

✕ **Saddlers Bar & Restaurant** Same contacts as Belsair Hotel; ⏱ May–Sep 17.30–19.30 Mon–Sat, noon–14.00 Sun (buffet only); shorter hours in winter, enquire ahead. Pub standards – fish, burgers – prevail at this eatery in the Belsair Hotel, but it occasionally offers tapas & other themed foodie evenings, as well as take-aways on 'chip night' (⏱ 16.30–19.00 Wed & Sat). Run by the tireless Kaye Towrie, who also manages the post office downstairs, it also has plans for a café (⏱ 10.00–14.00 Tue & Fri). £

Tangles Café Same contacts as Kettletoft Hotel; ⏱ 11.00–17.00 Wed–Sat. Located in the front dining room of the Kettletoft Hotel, this serves coffee, cakes & toasties. £

ENTERTAINMENT

The highlight of the social year is the **Sanday Show**, usually held over the first weekend in August at the showground next to Sanday School, when livestock is paraded and judged, and visitors can munch on homemade baking. There's a community feel to the event, making it well worth visiting the island at this time. The **Sanday Soulka** (w sandaysoulka.org), a combination of festival and themed events ranging from sea angling to traditional dance, is held across three separate weekends during the summer at various locations.

SHOPPING

SUPPLIES

Sinclair's General Stores ☎ 01857 600312; ⏱ 09.00–20.00 Mon–Sat, noon–16.00 Sun. For self-caterers, this is located just above Bea Loch, at the junction of the B9070 & B9068. It serves as a general store for the island & is well stocked – you can pick up anything from a towel rail to a roof bolt.

Sanday Community Shop Lady Village; ☎ 01857 600483; e sandaycommunityshop@gmail.com;

w sandaycommunityshop.com; ⏱ 09.00–20.00 Mon, Wed & Thu, 09.00–17.30 Tue, Fri & Sat, 13.00–16.00 Sun. Serves a similar purpose as Sinclair's but has more of a deli ambience.

ART

A number of excellent artists are active on Sanday are worth seeking out. Some of the following also sell their wares at the **Sanday Community Crafthub** in Kettletoft (⏰ 11.00–15.00 Wed, Sat & Sun), where, despite the unprepossessing exterior of the building, you can pick up ultra-local arts & crafts such as woollen necklaces & angora wool.

Gallery at the Northwa' 📞01857 600381; e billtoon3@btinternet.com; w seascape-art-orkney.co.uk; ⏰ 10.00–17.00 daily. Over at Tofts Ness you will find this excellent studio, home to seascape paintings by Bill McArthur (see box, page 240).
Kirstie Bruce Ceramics 📞01857 600799; e kirstiebruce496@yahoo.com; w kirstiebruceceramics.com; ⏰ 11.00–14.00

Mon–Fri. Operating her studio & Sound of the Sea at Stumpo, Burness, Kirstie displays her handmade ceramics here, inspired by Sanday's textures, patterns & shapes. 'The coastline has a strong spiritual & visual connection for me,' she says. 'It's a place I turn to, in order to clear my mind & get inspiration for my work.'
Working Landscape Studio 📞01857 600282; e carolyn574@btinternet.com; w working-landscape.co.uk; ⏰ times vary, call ahead. Carolyn Dixon has her studio at Kirkha', 600yds west of Lady Kirk on the B9069, & her work includes pen-and-ink & watercolour landscapes of Orkney & further afield.

OTHER PRACTICALITIES

Sanday has neither **banks** nor cashpoints but both shops and the Kettletoft Hotel will give you cashback. Most accommodation takes cards, but always check.

✚ **Sanday surgery** 📞01857 600221
✉ **Kettletoft post office** ⏰ 09.00–12.30 Mon, Tue & Thu, 14.00–16.00 Wed, 14.00–17.30 Fri

Petrol Pumps available at both Sinclair's General Stores & Sanday Community Shop.

WHAT TO SEE AND DO

A good number of visitors make the mistake of coming to Sanday for just one night or even – given there is just a handful of hours between the ferry's arrival and its last departure – an extremely short day. Do this and you will struggle to see much at all: instead, the island is worth at least three days of your time, though you could easily spend a fortnight here and not run out of beaches to walk upon nor archaeological sites to nose around.

THE SOUTHWEST Running from the Loth ferry terminal to Bea Loch, the southwest peninsula of Sanday is well worth exploring. Otters can often be seen around the terminal early in the morning – or at other times when the ferry's away.

Stove and around About 2 miles from the port take the turning south for Stove down a minor track. Park by the electricity station and walk to the exquisite hidden beach of **Doun Helzie** (pronounced 'Doon Hellie'). Tucked away beneath cliffs carpeted with flowers and busy with nesting fulmars in spring, the beach is barely a mile's walk from the car park. To get there, walk back up the road from the car park for 300yds and turn right along the farm track. At the brow, turn right before the

A WORD OF CAUTION

On Sanday, always keep an eye on tide times when venturing along the coast. The proliferation of beaches on the island means that east and west tides come into play. There's not that much in it, usually 30 minutes or so, but bear this in mind to avoid getting your feet wet or marooned at locations such as the Holms of Ire. For tide times, ask at either island shop (see opposite).

gate and walk between the fence and the wall. This path heads towards the sea and bears left across an exposed clifftop (be careful with children here). Keep ahead for 400yds or until you can slither down the dunes on to the beach. Low tide reveals a delightful sliver of sand and a handful of caves at the southern end of the beach where there is also a modest arch. Return the same way.

At the road end in Stove is a collection of buildings you won't find in the tourist brochures. The collapsed boiler and steam engine houses and red-brick chimney might seem more at home in 19th-century industrial Lancashire, but in fact they represent a 19th-century attempt at a model industrial farm. Surrounded by long-deserted caravans, the site is rather eerie.

Pool Travelling north from Stove, the coastline around the settlement of Pool offers a pleasant combination of beach strolling and informal archaeology, where you may simply stumble upon something old and interesting. Turn down the lane to **Laminess** and park on the right just before the first houses. In the 1990s the bay at Pool was subject to major excavation, with archaeologists uncovering not just Neolithic but also Pictish and Viking remains. Findings included a 6th-century stone slab carved with graffiti and a Pictish symbol stone, both of which are now in the Orkney Museum in Kirkwall (page 123).

To visit these excavations is to induct yourself into thousands of years of history, with findings from Neolithic periods lying below those from medieval times in the upper layers of soil. The black, scarred part of the coast – the most eroded section – is where you can view the lowest levels of the site. Stand on the shore facing the sea and you can see the stripes of red peat ash, dark cultivation soils and light sand blows, all built up, one layer after another. Stonework and artefacts are falling out of

A WALK ALONG BACKASKAILL BAY

Distance: 4 miles; time: 2hrs
Start/finish: parking space at Backaskaill Bay ✦ HY646394
OS Map: Explorer 465 Sanday, Eday, North Ronaldsay & Stronsay

In this corner of Sanday, the east coast is dominated by Backaskaill Bay. This walk explores its shores, takes in a romantically ruined church and offers the chance of a hot drink and cakes in Kettletoft.

Begin at the car park by the shore in Backaskaill and walk east along the beach. This is a beautiful spot: rich with flowers in July and August, the machair is also a fine location for birdwatching. At the far end you come to the ruins of the 16th-century Cross Kirk, one of Sanday's two dilapidated churches. Sanday folklorist and antiquarian Walter Traill Dennison is buried here. Follow the lane above the church to reach the ruined corn mill; just a low wall now survives. The path reaches the B9068 where you turn right into Kettletoft; here you can visit the Crafthub (page 230), or choose between the two hotels for sustenance.

From here on, the walk follows paved roads. Head north along the B9068, past the lane to Cross Kirk, noting Bea Loch on your left. At the junction by Sinclair's Stores, turn left along the B9070. After 600yds it's worth the small diversion to the left to the pier and loch shore for views of the birdlife. Returning to the B9070, head west then follow the road as it bears sharp left and heads southwest. After 1,000yds turn left, following the sign back to the car park.

the shoreline at different levels: root around and you may find sheep's bones eaten thousands of years ago or perhaps something more exciting, such as a bone needle. If you do, contact the Orkney Museum (✆ 01856 873535).

If the tide at Pool is going out, you can turn your exploration into a gorgeous walk north across the sands and around to the **Noust of Boloquoy**, where you will find the rather mournful 19th-century **Boloquoy Mill**, a derelict but reasonably substantial meal mill staring out to sea. It can also be reached down a track off the B9070, but bear in mind there is nowhere there to park your car without blocking field gates.

Two miles further up the west coast from Boloquoy, take the minor road towards **Ayre** and follow this above the coast until it nearly returns to the B9070 (⊕ HY662416). Park with care nearby and walk down the grassy track towards the coast for the best part of a mile and you'll reach the substantial **Ness of Brough**, the location of a Channel 4 TV Time Team excavation that found pagan Viking graves. Four conspicuous circular mounds rise up on the headland here, each 50–100ft in diameter and 7ft high. A 19th-century excavation turned up some Viking artefacts here, but in 1997 island schoolgirl Shona Grieve wrote to Time Team asking them to see if there was also a Viking grave to be uncovered. On the last day of a three-day dig, they turned up a curve of stones that is thought to be part of a stone grave boat, of which fragments were removed for further study.

THE NORTHWEST PENINSULA

Burness The centre and north of Sanday are characterised by large farm holdings, their isolated houses punctuating the skyline as a consequence of being built on farm mounds (page 227). Easily the most striking building in the parish of Burness is the now-derelict **Scar House**, located at the northern end of the B9068. This former laird's house is a daunting place. Built in the early 19th century, it is surrounded by an imposing wall and old garden. An austere façade of a grey, sheer cliff face is augmented by a dormered attic. 'Scar', incidentally, comes from the Old Norse *skar* – normally a rim or edge, but in this case, a shore. In the field between the cemetery and Scar House – and best seen from the main road – is the 16-tonne **Stone of Scar**. Legend says that this vast lump had been cast on to the island by a witch from Eday, furious at her daughter for eloping with a lover to Sanday. The truth is just as impressive: not only did the stone journey all the way from Norway during the last Ice Age, embedded within a glacier, but it also now lies a mile from where nature left it. In 1880 the rock was moved from Coos Moo towards Scar with a view to positioning it as a landscape feature. In a scene that would not look out of place in *Only Fools and Horses*, the cart transporting it collapsed under the load and the stone was abandoned, to this day remaining where it fell.

From the cemetery at Scar, a waymarked walk of about a mile leads straight ahead and along the shore of **Sand Ayre**. Don't get too excited by the conical, broch-like structure in the field to the east; this is in fact an early 19th-century windmill. The shoreline route leads to the site where a Viking boat burial was found in 1991. The discovery of the site, its excavation and its findings were all dramatic: a visiting archaeologist happened to notice a human leg bone protruding from eroded dunes, leading to an emergency excavation that took place amid wintry conditions and under floodlights. This revealed three human skeletons: a young man, a child and an old lady. Among the items buried with them were an exquisitely carved whalebone plaque, a gilded bronze brooch, a sheathed sword and a quiver of arrows. As the site has been thoroughly excavated – the key items are displayed at the Orkney Museum – there is essentially nothing to see here now, but the walk is an attractive one in its own right as it takes in fine coastal views, particularly west towards Westray and Eday.

Whitemill Bay On the peninsula immediately east of the Holms of Ire, Whitemill Bay is another vast, sweeping crescent of sand, its eastern tip pointing to North Ronaldsay, just 4 miles to the northeast. As you approach, you will see to the east a row of derelict houses standing cheek by jowl. This is the abandoned 19th-century village of **Ortie**, a doomed crofting township designed by the laird of Scar. At its height 70 people lived here in 14 crofts, many of whom were engaged in the kelp trade, whose collapse is thought to have prompted the community's decline.

It's an uplifting stroll along the headland from the car park behind the dunes at Whitemill Bay: simply head east along the bay, follow the coast round and walk on the grass or beach to Whitemill Point ('mill', in this instance, originates from the Old Norse *meir* meaning bay). Should you want a closer look at the abandoned village, extend your walk from Whitemill Bay a little further south and walk up through the dunes (✪ HY688454). Access to the site from the road has been roped off by occupants of the nearby houses making it clear they don't welcome inspection.

Travelling south from Ortie you are greeted by the expanse of **Otters Wick**. This is one of Sanday's – and Orkney's – great bays, and every bit as romantic and beautiful as its name might suggest. The easiest access is from the road that skirts the bay's edge

TIDAL WALK FROM SCAR TO THE HOLMS OF IRE

Distance: 5 miles; time: 3hrs
Start/finish: lay-by by the cemetery (✪ HY673451)
OS Map: Explorer 465 Sanday, Eday, North Ronaldsay & Stronsay

This is a superbly elemental walk across a gorgeous bay that takes in two islets accessible only at low tide (so check tide times before you go). Start from the same location as the Scar Viking walk (page 233) and head west along the lane towards Scar House, navigating three gates as you walk through a farm. Follow the grassy track straight ahead between two stone walls. Where a fence replaces the stone wall, keep ahead through two gates to reach a cairn by the shores of Roos Wick bay. Turn left along the top of the bay, passing a farm and on to a grassy track, with the bay on your right and Roos Loch to your left. This makes for gorgeous walking, with neat birds too. In winter, resident mute swans are joined by whooper swans and you may well see great northern divers in the bay. Follow the track uphill to the cairn then walk across the grassy soils to Whale Point on the coast above the causeway to the two islets, collectively known as the Holms of Ire. Assuming that the tide is low, walk the mile from here to the northern end of the Outer Holm. Take your time, as the going is extremely slippery. The landscape is extraordinary: rocks seem to have been utterly shredded by the fierce seas and the ever-changing, always piercingly sharp light on this tapering point verges on the ethereal. It's quite something to stand here with the tide menacingly muscling up on either side and know there is nothing further north in a straight line until the North Pole. The Inner Holm has the remnants of an old chapel as well as six 'planti-creus', shelters used for growing cabbage seedlings. At the far end of the Outer Holm, low tide exposes the wreck of a trawler that ran aground in 1940. When you've finished exploring the holms, return the same way.

between Burness and the community of Otterswick. Other than at high tide, the sands unequivocally lend themselves to clearing the mind through unfettered roaming. In June, harbour seals pup nearby and you may well see them swimming here.

LADY VILLAGE AND VICINITY At the heart of the island is **Lady Village**, home to the heritage centre, community shop, a sobering memorial to both World Wars, and little else. The village's slightly unusual name is believed to originate from 'Our Lady of the Kirk', ie: the Virgin Mary. It exudes a disarticulated air; located at a discrete settlement a mile away are the airfield, school, swimming pool, doctors' surgery and community centre.

Start exploring by visiting the **Sanday Heritage Centre** (⊕ Apr–Oct 09.30–17.00 daily; Nov–Mar 09.30–17.00 Sat & Sun; free). Housed in a former temperance hall, this fine little centre gives an insight into what has made Sanday tick over the centuries. Pride of place goes to the remarkable Appiehouse Stone (page 227) but there is also a modest collection of worked bone objects and maceheads. Wartime and natural history are documented, as is the unsettling tale of the 11 sperm whales that died after beaching on Bea Sand in December 1994; the cause remains unknown but one theory is that they were disorientated by the noise of a jackhammer being used to build a water treatment plant nearby. The whales were buried in a mass albeit unmarked grave in fields behind the beach. The centre also has a small but good souvenir shop.

Just behind the centre stands a partial reconstruction of one of Orkney's more unusual open-air archaeological sites, the **Meur Burnt Mound**. The real thing is located close to North Loch at Tofts Ness (page 239) but this structure is nevertheless impressive. The centrepiece is a stone water-storage tank thought to be 3,000 years

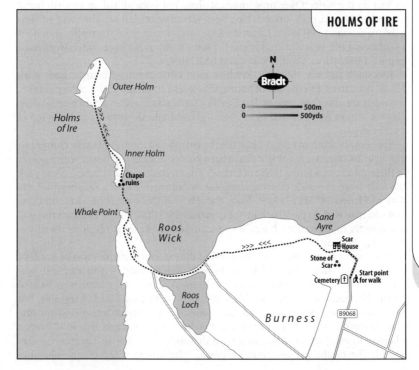

Distance: 7 miles; time: 2½ –3½hrs
Start/finish: car park by Brickie Hut, ✪ HY702414
OS Map: Explorer 465 Sanday, Eday, North Ronaldsay & Stronsay

Quite simply, this walk is right up there with the best of the UK's wild and elemental hikes. Not only can you take in the wonderful dunes and lagoon-like bay of Cata Sand, but also you can enjoy the mesmerising experience of reaching an exposed chambered cairn right on the southern tip of the Tresness peninsula. Bear in mind that, at high tide, you should be prepared to either get your feet wet or to plough through the dunes. Although fun and safe (you won't get stranded), the latter is tough going.

From the car park head southeast along the track towards the dunes. The walk to the headland is reasonably demanding so resist the temptation to walk on the dunes until your return. The wildlife provides magnificent accompaniment, from nesting fulmars to bar-tailed godwits probing the sands, plus attractive plants such as sea aster on the saltmarsh, marram grass wafting in the wind on the dunes and northern marsh orchid emerging in damper areas.

When you reach the dunes bear right and walk along the shoreline. Vehicle tracks here lead to Tresness farm. Whatever the weather, the interplay of light is remarkable, and colours rise through the spectrum from shades of green, yellow and blue to

old. People would heat beach pebbles in a peat fire and then throw them in the tank to heat up the water. Over time, the heat-shattered stones piled up to form burnt mounds. So far, 21 such mounds have been identified on Sanday. The meur site was used for around 1,000 years. Located a little further back from the replica mound is a traditional 100-year-old croft house (⊕ same hours as heritage centre; free), lived in until 1966 by Jock Scott, a joiner and boat builder.

Just south of Lady Village is Sanday's most curious ruined church, **Lady Kirk** (⊕ all year; free). On the site of both a Viking-era site and a 17th-century church, the ruins are also the home of The Devil's Clawmarks, a rather spooky set of deep grooves – most likely caused by erosion – gouged into the balustrade at the top of a set of steps.

Three miles south of Lady Village lies the chambered tomb at **Elsness-Quoyness**, dating to 2000BC. Archaeologists have been known to mention the site with a quiver in their voice, considering it one of Orkney's masterpieces. The closest you can park is a mile away, at a wide clearing along the minor road from the cemetery at Lady Kirk to Elsness (✪ HY676388). Note, though, that this road is in poor condition and you may wish to park back by the cemetery (✪ HY675399). Although this will add another mile's walk each way, it's a picturesque and easy stroll along the shores of the Peedie Sea.

Thanks to a thoughtful reconstruction of the exterior – unlike most of Sanday's archaeological treasures, which are buried underground – you can see how Elsness-Quoyness looked when it was, so to speak, in use. If the tomb were located on the UK mainland, entry would doubtless be both timed and chargeable, but here you can wander at leisure at any time of day without intrusion from the outside world. The setting is dramatic, perched on a headland that is all but an island of its own, tethered by a small spit that shelters the Peedie Sea from Sanday Sound. The tomb's narrow entrance passage, leading to a rectangular chamber

white. Where the dunes fizzle out, follow the track left of the farm and go on to the headland. Keep on the farm track on the east (left) side of the peninsula. At one point the track disappears into a loch and you must tramp around this before rejoining it. This spot can feel very isolated, with drystone dykes gently sinking into the loch and seabirds cackling overhead. Eventually the track bends round to the headland by a trig point. Hard on the low cliff edge here (⊕ HY712375) is the chambered cairn of **Tresness**, thought to be similar to that at Elsness-Quoyness (see opposite). While you cannot enter, if you scramble down the ledges to the beach (it's only 6ft or so) you can stare into its entrance, a low passageway flanked by stones. Sites such as this can really bring home to you how and why people may have chosen particular places to live and to be buried; isolated and free of modern-day signage and interpretation, Tresness is a purer experience than many archaeological sites.

Continue in a clockwise direction around the headland. The terrain becomes stodgier through the grassy hillocks. After 600yds you reach **Wasso Broch**, a 12ft-high green mound with a protrusion of rocks on its cap. As with Tresness, you cannot enter, but you can inspect it closely by walking beyond the broch, turning right and skipping over a drystone wall. As with the chambered cairn, the setting is elemental. From here, cut across the field to rejoin the track that heads north past the farm and the dunes. If you have the energy, the dunes are great fun to yomp up; in a westerly wind, the beach on their eastern side is a wonderful spot for a picnic.

with side cells, has drawn comparisons to Maeshowe (page 108). The remains of 12–15 people were found in pits beneath the floor while two carved stones and a bone pin resemble finds at Skara Brae (page 98). The passageway is low and usually muddy; a torch is supposed to be in the box by the entrance but it's best to bring your own. If all else fails, a frosted skylight allows just enough natural light in. As you approach the tomb, expect to be inspected by nesting fulmars and be mindful of cows with calves between May and September.

Where the B9069 skirts Cata Sand you will see a small, squat building by the car park. This is known as the **Brickie Hut**, a former control room for a dummy airfield that was set up during World War II in the fields behind, complete with runway lights. This was one of eight decoy airfields for Scapa Flow, but, as it turned out, it never saw any action. The hut is currently a shell, though there are plans to convert it into a small interpretation centre detailing both the island's military history and surrounding landscape.

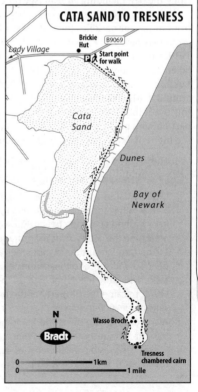

CATA SAND TO TRESNESS

10

237

The Brickie Hut stands at the head of the magnificent **Cata Sand**, a vast tidal sandy bay stretching for 2 miles and flanked by 30ft-high dunes of glittering white sand that nature has sculpted into extremely fetching triangular shapes. One after another, the dunes dance their way down the eastern flanks of the bay among a collage of spits, bars and flats. The interchange of light and water here is utterly astonishing. When the tide ebbs, it is as though the proverbial plug has been pulled, and the converse is true as well; the waterless bay can suddenly flood with a sheet of water so thin at first that the aquamarine colours resemble a photo montage of the Caribbean. Even more remarkably, the dunes do not represent the end of the bay: where they finally collapse, the firm headland of Tresness emerges to nudge for a further mile out into Sanday Sound. Here, you will find two extraordinary archaeological sites, Wasso Broch and Tresness chambered cairn (see box, page 236).

THE NORTH END Confusingly, the area any visitor would reasonably describe as the eastern end of the island is known locally as the 'North End'. Whatever compass point you use, it is a hauntingly magical, sometimes eerie landscape; deeply ancient, here as much as anywhere on Orkney, you get a palpable sense of the land in which our distant ancestors lived. If anything, the North End is even more rural than the rest of the island.

Heading east from Lady Village, high sand dunes initially shield you from the **Bay of Lopness**, but you soon come to a small car park with the best viewpoint and starting place for a beach walk. The bay is gorgeous and stretches for 2½ miles between the headlands of Newark and Lopness. At least 14 archaeological sites have been found along the bay, including an Iron Age broch at **Ore Ledge** at the easternmost point.

The most diverting sight at Lopness is a little more contemporary. Right in front of the car park lies the watery remains of a **World War I German destroyer**, grounded here in February 1920. The B98 had arrived in Scapa Flow on 22 June 1919, the day after the German fleet was scuttled there. The destroyer was being taken to the breaker's yard at Forsyth when it slipped its tow and drifted into Lopness. You can catch glimpses at high tide, while at low tide you can explore around it. Most of the ship was cut up for scrap but substantial parts remain. Oddly, this is not the only inadvertent German wartime maritime visitor to make it to this part of Sanday. A German U-boat, U70, ran aground further east at Tofts Ness on the night of 7–8 April 1918. The crew furiously tried to jettison weight to re-float,

THE GERMAN SUBMARINE, THE WHALE AND UDAL LAW

Under Udal Law (see box, page 19), the Bay of Lopness has been owned by a local family for generations. Initially they drew an income from processing kelp washed up on the beach. Known as the tangling industry, this involved bleaching the heads of the long strands and storks of kelp before selling them to the farming and food industries as fertiliser. Just occasionally, however, beach ownership and the responsibilities this brings throw up more diverting tasks. When the B98 foundered on the rocks in 1920 (see above), under Udal Law it became the property of the owners, the Tulloch family. 'This involved salvaging 4,000 tonnes of brass, so it was quite a catch for granddad,' recalls Alan Tulloch, who owns the Standing Stones Hotel on the Mainland (page 90). The flipside, notes Alan, is that if a whale gets beached or washed up, he is now responsible for the cost of its removal. 'You need to get the army to tow it out to sea and blow it up,' he points out.

There's more to explore around Northwall and Tofts Ness than just archaeological sites. The area is a muddle of mires and wetlands and forms the heart of the East Sanday Coast Ramsar Site, which embraces a 30-mile stretch of coast and, together with Cata Sand, is also presently designated as a (European Union) Special Protection Area. The alternately rocky and sandy coastline is notable for the presence of sand dune and machair habitats, as well as extensive inter-tidal flats and saltmarsh. The site is further characterised by blown sand, plus a series of tombolos, bars, spits and shingle ridges. In winter, accumulations of rotting kelp harbour large numbers of sandhoppers and other invertebrates, providing a plentiful food supply for internationally important populations of waders including purple sandpiper and turnstone. Northwall is also a particularly good place for ducks such as goldeneye.

hefting the torpedoes out of their vessel. Finally, after 7 hours, they slipped back into the water and escaped. The remarkable thing is that the event was witnessed by a resident at Tofts Ness who assumed the coastal watch would have seen events unfold, so did not bother to report it.

As you head further east, Sanday begins to narrow and the huge white dunes on the far side of the coast emerge looking like waves about to crash on to land. The shores of **Sandquoy** on the north coast is where the walrus turned up in 2018 (page 12).

Enjoying a remote location at the northeast protrusion of the island is **Tofts Ness**, a place of remote farms that is home to a prehistoric funerary complex of possibly hundreds of burial mounds. Tofts Ness is not a single site but an entire landscape with remnants uncovered from the Neolithic period through to the Iron Age. Almost everything you look at here has strong prehistoric influences. The location also prompts contemplation: it not only forms the edge of Sanday, but also one of the outer edges of Orkney. As such Tofts Ness feels like it is on the margins of two worlds: ours and the prehistoric. Tellingly, it is thought that inhabitants here may have been of lower social standing than others on Sanday.

One of the most important sites of its kind in Britain, Tofts Ness was the scene of an extraordinary find in 2015 when the skeleton of a ten-year-old child, thought to be up to 4,000 years old, was uncovered by a beachcomber. The remains had been exposed by a winter storm and they are now being studied by experts from Historic Environment Scotland.

Tofts Ness is not laid out or interpreted for the visitor; instead it is up to you to wander across a landscape scattered with burial mounds, cairns and ancient field walls. One of the best ways to experience the landscape is to walk the minor road that encircles much of the area, perhaps starting from Northwall to the south. This 3½-mile loop along a very quiet road is hugely enjoyable as everywhere you look you will see some remnant of the past. The route also passes two lochs: the Loch of Rummie in the south and the larger North Loch. Both are full of bird activity and you may well see otters here, too. You can take a short diversion on the loop around the shores of the Loch of Rummie (look for the stile at ✪ HY759447; the track follows a signposted path clockwise around the top of the loch and brings you out by The Gallery at the Northwa').

On the north side of the loop in the settlement of **Meur** (✪ HY746457), you will find the surprisingly substantial remains of the **Meur Burnt Mound**, located at the western end of a drystone dyke. While the tank was transported to the Sanday Heritage Centre, the well and fire remain in situ (removing them would have led the road above to collapse). Locals may well approach you to talk about their involvement in the excavation of 2005. This was considered an emergency dig as the tank was at first mistaken for a burial cist.

Further south of Meur, in an area referred to as Northwall, you find the remains of the radar station at **Lettan**, part of the chain of World War II radar operations along the east coast of Britain. If you want to explore deeper into Northwall and Tofts Ness, take the path that runs due east from The Gallery at the Northwa' (see box, above) and drop down on to the magnificent dunes at Scuthvie for a change of colour and light. You can walk right up the coast to the headland at Tofts Ness if you wish, a distance of some 2½ miles, and a good hour or more, one way

Sanday's eastern extremity is marked by **Start Point lighthouse** (w sandayranger. org; ◷ guided tour only with Sanday Ranger; free). To reach it, follow the B9069 to its end, where it becomes a sandy track. Park in the small lay-by 600yds down this lane; heed the signs to drive no further, as the road literally collapses into the sea. From here it's a mile walk to the lighthouse. As lighthouses go, Sanday's is quite unusual, with black-and-white vertical stripes, and the sloping roofs of the keeper's cottage combine from a distance to give the impression of a child's fold-out rocket. At just 75ft, it is also squatter than most and, as with many lighthouses, it's a Robert Stevenson design; in 1806, it even boasted the first revolving light in Scotland. The final part of the walk requires the crossing of a watery causeway, which is only safe to do for 2 hours before low tide and one hour after. You'll need stout walking boots or wellies. Inside the lighthouse, the staircase is unusual in that it curls upwards in an anticlockwise direction.

11

Westray

If you were designing an ideal island on the northern edge of Britain, you might opt for thrillingly steep cliffs that get smashed on a daily basis by the elements and wonderful wildlife that is as easy to observe as anywhere in the country. You might place a lighthouse for dramatic effect at its northern tip; and, for contrast, adroitly position some secluded lochs. Then perhaps you would throw in a dynamic population, good shops, a pub, creative types, high-quality food producers and good transport links. And you would end up with something very much like Westray.

Travel around the isolated and often-empty North Isles for any length of time and Westray can come to resemble the bright lights of the city. With nearly 600 human residents, this is easily the most populated outer island – and with that comes a proactive and tight-knit community. Named from the Old Norse 'vestry' (meaning 'west island'), Westray lies 24 miles northeast of Kirkwall and 6 miles north of Rousay. Meanwhile its protruding southeasterly skerries seem to reach out like bony fingers, all but clutching at the island of Eday.

The island is made up of Rousay flagstone, with rocks piled on top of one another, sometimes gently tilted this way and that. This helps to create a heavily indented coastline that reaches 50 miles in length – and this on an island measuring only 8 miles by 2. Indeed, so crenulated is this shoreline that it served as an architectural template for the new V&A museum in Dundee.

Whereas scattered communities prevail on most of Orkney's North Isles, Westray has the only village of any size, Pierowall. An extremely attractive place it is too, running around the edge of a horseshoe bay; perhaps it is this embracing topographical arm that has historically engendered such a strong sense of community. One of the most striking aspects of Westray is that this is a true working landscape. Homes are intended to be lived in rather than win architectural awards, while the fertile land is geared up to be farmed and has been worked by farmsteads for many centuries. This is one of Orkney's most productive agricultural islands, with beef cattle key to its economy.

Orcadian is spoken widely; indeed, the Westray version of it includes some words of its own, such as 'dubter' (a light shower). You will also hear 'thine' used for 'your'. Islanders are known traditionally as 'aaks', the Orcadian name for the guillemot, a bird you will see here in abundance, along with fulmar, kittiwake, puffin and, most magnificently of all, gannet.

While farming rather than fishing is the mainstay of the economy, harvesting white fish, crab and lobster remains important and, combined with those cows plus local bread and cheese, Westray exports more than all the other North Isles put together.

Westray has achieved Fairtrade status, which means that a majority of outlets sell a significant range of 'fairly traded' goods. This is no mean feat, given the particular challenges of island life – higher transportation costs and lower turnover – which

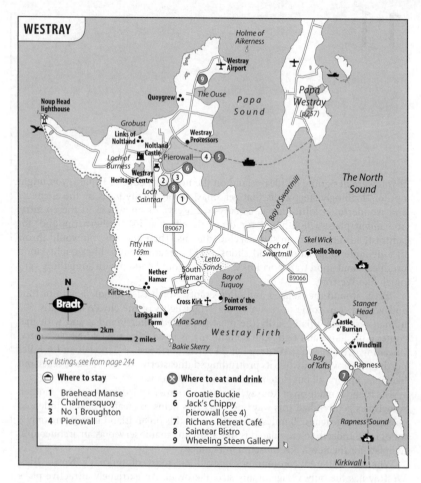

WESTRAY

Holme of
Aikerness

Westray
Airport

Quoygrew The Ouse

Papa
Sound

Papa
Westray
(p257)

Noup Head
lighthouse

Grobust

Links of
Noltland

Noltland
Castle Westray
Processors

Pierowall 4 5

Loch of
Burness

Westray
Heritage Centre 2 3

6

The North
Sound

8

Loch
Saintear 1

B9067

Bay of Swartmill

Fitty Hill
169m ▲

Letto
Sands

Loch of
Swartmill

Skel Wick

Skello Shop

N

Bradt

Nether
Hamar

Kirbest

South
Hamar

Tuffer

Cross Kirk ✝

Bay of
Tuquoy

Point o' the
Scurroes

B9066

Stanger
Head

Langskaill
Farm

Mae Sand

Castle
o' Burrian

Windmill

0   2km
0   2 miles

Westray Firth

Bakie Skerry

Bay
of Tafts

Rapness

Rapness Sound

Kirkwall ↓

For listings, see from page 244

🛌 **Where to stay**

1 Braehead Manse
2 Chalmersquoy
3 No 1 Broughton
4 Pierowall

❌ **Where to eat and drink**

5 Groatie Buckie
6 Jack's Chippy
   Pierowall (see 4)
7 Richans Retreat Café
8 Saintear Bistro
9 Wheeling Steen Gallery

begs a question as to why, if Westray can manage to do this, the concept is not ubiquitous across the UK.

HISTORY

As the Ice Age ended, Westray and Papa Westray (see *Chapter 12*) may have still been connected by land, which would have enabled early dwellers to move easily between the two through a landscape thought to have been distinguished by tundra-like grass and small trees. Westray is saturated with ancient settlements and monuments dating to the Neolithic, testifying to enduring human presence here. Sites such as the Links of Noltland point to a sizeable community already present during the Neolithic and still during the Bronze Age (the cemetery is one of Orkney's largest such sites). Pottery and vessels made of Shetland soapstone indicate early established links between the two island groups. Westray is thought to be unique in having cemeteries that date to the same time as Iron Age brochs, such as that at Knowe of Queena Howe.

The first Christian monks arrived around AD500, and elements of early settlements can be unpicked from the rock-stack and island hermitages such as

Holm of Aikerness and Castle o' Burrain, as well as on Papa Westray. Westray is thought to have been among the earliest islands to have been settled by the Vikings, who favoured Pierowall as they could moor their shallow-draught longboats there. They named it Hofn (meaning harbour). At the time this was the only Norse village in Orkney and the nearby links (a landscape term for a coastal area of sandy soils, dunes and undulating topography; not to be confused with golf courses that bear this name) at Noltland is known to have been home to Britain's largest Viking cemetery.

During Norse times, Pierowall swiftly gained a reputation as the best harbour for trading in either Orkney or Shetland. The *Orkneyinga Saga* (see box, page 35) paints a striking picture of a vibrant, wild 12th-century Westray with local families holding sway from power bases at Rapness, Pierowall and Tuqouy. Those Norse ancestors left a strong fishing tradition which continues to this day, and dried fish in particular was exported.

The defeat of the Spanish Armada in 1588 had demographic consequences for Westray. One ship from the fleet is said to have been wrecked off the island with several survivors settling on Westray and marrying local women. Their descendants are still here today. The kelp boom that brought work and money to many Orcadian islands also swept Westray from 1780 to 1825 and then again in the latter half of the 19th century (in truth, kelp-collecting was harsh work with poor pay, the profits creamed off by the lairds).

In the early 19th century, crofters were kicked out of their homes in the settlement of Broughton on the southeastern arm of the Bay of Pierowall, and left to eke out a living along the shoreline. Sometimes, these events are referred to as being part of the notorious 'clearances' but they seem to have had more to do with economic readjustments rather than Crown-imposed diktats. Their homes were replaced by cottages; while these have also since long gone, modern houses now follow the same detached layout above the shore.

By the mid-19th century, Westray's population stood at 2,032, with 940 males and 1,092 females. Gill Pier was expanded in 1883 and the Spanish demand for dried fish drove the industry, attracting migrant labour from Fair Isle and Shetland. The first steamer to connect the island (and other North Isles) to Kirkwall arrived in 1885. While the focus of war in 20th-century Orkney centres upon Scapa Flow, Westray played a key role too, with naval staff stationed here to search for U-boats. World War I claimed 38 Westray men.

Fishing continued to expand and, by the 1960s, large creel boats, crewed by the island's first full-time fishermen, had been adapted to catch white fish with nets. At its height, seven white-fish boats sailed from Pierowall in the 1980s–1990s. The fleet dwindled subsequently, with just one boat left nowadays, and the emphasis has turned strongly to crab-processing, lobsters and fish farms.

GETTING THERE AND AWAY

BY AIR Westray Airport is located on the northeastern tip of the island, 2 miles north of Pierowall. Loganair (page 45) flies its doughty eight-seater Islander aircraft from Kirkwall two times daily (but one on Sunday), with fewer flights in winter. Flights cost £18 single, £36 return. As with other North Isles, 'excursion fares' encourage you to spend a night on-island; should you do so, the fare drops to £21 return. Most famously, Westray airfield is known throughout the world as one point on the world's shortest scheduled flight – to its neighbour Papa Westray (see box, page 258).

BY SEA Because of high demand for flights, most visitors travel from Kirkwall to Westray by sea. The port is at Rapness, in the south of the island. The spectacular journey follows a Viking sea route, weaving past Egilsay and Eday and through waters that can perform a passable impression of high seas in bad weather. Just before making landfall at Rapness, the ferry squeezes into Rapness Sound between the skerries of Rusk Holm and the Holm of Farray – both are good for hauled out grey seals, which also pup here in October. Expect to enjoy close views of gannets plunging into the sea for fish. Orkney Ferries (page 50) operates two or three sailings daily (one on Sunday) direct from Kirkwall to Rapness. Journey time is 1 hour 25 minutes. The Friday sailing returns via Papa Westray, adding 1 hour 20 minutes to the journey.

A separate ferry, the *Golden Mariana*, shuttles back and forward between Westray and Papa Westray, a journey that takes 30 minutes (page 257). This leaves from Gill Pier, on the northeast side of Pierowall, a mile or so from the heritage centre and hotel.

During high season (late June to late August), Orkney Ferries runs a Sunday Special excursion from Kirkwall to Westray. This enables visitors to spend a few hours on an island where normal schedules would either render a visit meaningless or require an overnight stop.

GETTING AROUND

Westray is busy enough to boast two B roads. The B9066 runs north–south from Rapness to Pierowall, finally coming to a halt at the airfield. The B9067 connects Pierowall to the west side of the island (known, logically enough, as Westside).

The useful Westray Bus Service bus (m 07789 034289; May–Sep, other times on request) is integrated with both Kirkwall and Papa Westray ferries. Tickets from Pierowall to Rapness cost £2.10.

If you want to hire a car or bike, contact W I Rendall (page 248), who offers vehicles for £45 per day and bicycles for £15 per day. If you need a taxi, Graham Maben (\ 01857 677777; m 07766 073088) is useful for pick-up and drop-off at airfield or if doing lengthy linear walks, eg: West Westray Walk.

TOURIST INFORMATION AND TOUR OPERATORS

The island's tourist information centre is housed at **Westray Heritage Centre** ✳ (\ 01857 677414; e westrayheritagecentre@gmail.com; w westrayheritage.co.uk; ⊕ May–Sep 11.30–17.00 Mon, 09.00–noon & 14.00 & 17.00 Tue–Sat, 13.30–17.00 Sun; Oct–Apr by appointment). The monthly island newspaper *Auk Talk* always covers what's on and offers insights into local life.

Informative (and recommended) island tours are conducted by local couple Andy and Keren Penn who operate **Westraak Tours** (\ 01857 677777; m 07793 216922; e info@westraak.co.uk; w westraak.co.uk; £42 half-day, £60 full day including lunch at the Penns' home). More specialist tours are offered by the aptly named Don and Sandra Otter of **Westray Wildlife** (\ 01857 677846; m 07938 814403; e info@westraywildlife.co.uk; w westraywildlife.co.uk; £38/50 half/full day), who also sell excellent photographic prints of island landscapes and wildlife.

 ## WHERE TO STAY *Map, page 242*

Westray has one rather tired-looking hotel, a handful of good B&Bs and an excellent hostel so hanging your hat on the island is certainly viable. For self-catering options visit w westraypapawestray.co.uk.

🏠 Breahead Manse (2 rooms) ✆01857 677861; e info@braeheadmanse.co.uk; w braeheadmanse.co.uk. Located 1 mile south of Pierowall on the B9066, tucked away behind the huge, decaying manse. Rooms located in 1863 village hall, which has been thoughtfully restored with wooden flooring & panelling. Both rooms en suite; 1dbl, 1 sleeping 3. Owners will convert into self-catering should you require (£50/night). **££**

🏠 Chalmersquoy (3 rooms in B&B, 5 in hostel) ✆01857 677214; e enquiries@chalmersquoywestray.co.uk; w chalmersquoywestray.co.uk. Exquisitely decorated en-suite rooms have warm touches throughout, eg: Shetland(!) bed covers, wrought-iron banisters & wooden shutters. Rooms named after grandparents of current owners Teenie & Michael Harcus. Room 'Annie' has a 4-poster & honeysuckle wallpaper ('that's the flower that granny liked,' says Teenie). Snug hostel has 12 beds in 5 rooms, including a family room that sleeps 4 tucked away upstairs. Hostel's 1st-floor lounge is 1 of the comfiest places to enjoy 1 of Orkney's best views – sink in huge sofas to look out over Pierowall Bay. One room suitable for travellers with limited mobility. The Harcus empire also includes a campsite with hook-ups and 2 self-catering units furnished to same high standards (£300–350/week). **£–££**

✳ 🏠 No 1 Broughton (4 rooms) Pierowall; ✆01857 677726; e enquiries@no1broughton. co.uk; w no1broughton.co.uk. Beautiful location by Pierowall Bay: serene views of harbour, with seals often lazing on skerries just yards from house. Four dbls: 3 en suite, 1 with private facilities. Tastefully decorated with velvet curtains & stylish recesses. Mighty fine b/fast offers choice of Skipper's Brekka (hot-smoked salmon) or the Orkney Omnibus (bacon, haggis & beans). Run by Jerry Wood, a friendly local artist who paints landscapes & figures in oils. A former sheep-farm manager in Cumbria, Jerry also builds & restores drystone dykes on the island. **££**

🏠 Pierowall Hotel (6 rooms) Pierowall; ✆01857 677472; e pierowallhotel@gmail.com; w pierowallhotel.co.uk. Simply furnished but comfortable rooms – ask for 1 with a harbour view. Dated décor offset by friendly staff. Mix of dbls & twins, 4 en suite, 2 with shared facilities. **££**

✖ WHERE TO EAT AND DRINK Map, page 242

Aside from the Pierowall Hotel, there has long been nowhere on the island where you could sit down for a formal meal, although you can enjoy substantial portions at a couple of the cafés. That should change in 2019 with the planned opening of Saintear Bistro. From autumn to spring, keep an eye out for the pop-up restaurant operated by Adam and Lin Sharp, the owners of Braehead Manse (same contact details; see above), whereby they turn their B&B – if unoccupied – into a buffet-style restaurant serving anything from single dishes (£15) to five-course blowouts that include lobster (£60).

✖ Pierowall Hotel Same contacts as hotel; ⊕ May–Sep noon–14.00 daily & 17.00–20.30 Wed–Mon, also Tue for hotel guests & Tue 17.00–19.30 take-away; Oct–Apr noon–13.30 & 18.00–20.00 days vary, check ahead. Basic menu but hearty portions of cod, pies & quiche; vegan & gluten-free options. Pick is the Westray seafood platter of crab, smoked mussels & salmon (£15.50). Also friendly bar with fire & sofas (⊕ 11.00–midnight, sometimes later). **££**

✖ Saintear Bistro Saintear; m 07825 017124; e saintearwestray@gmail.com; ⊕ check but expected to be 09.00–20.30 daily. At the time of writing the intention was to open this new bistro just south of Pierowall in spring 2019 but weather & logistics may intervene – this often happens in Orkney – so call in to see the state of play. Owners Rebekah & Andrew Wilson aim to emphasise local food such as Cullen skink, Westray cheeseboards & Orkney beef in a 20-cover building with views across the island. Interesting winter-time plans include storytelling & community-prepared dishes. **££**

✳ ☕ Groatie Buckie Inside W I Rendall, Pierowall; ✆01857 677389; ⊕ Jun–Sep 10.00–16.00 Mon–Sat, & also Jun–Aug 14.00–16.30 Sun; Oct–May 10.00–16.00 Thu–Sat. Tucked away at the back of the store, this delightful & gaily decorated café offers toasties, soup & proper coffee. If you're hungry, opt for the Westray platter of cheeses, chutneys & biscuits (£4.50). **£**

⌨ **Jack's Chippy** Broughton; ☏01857 677471; ⊕ Jun–Sep 17.00–21.00 Wed, Fri & Sat; Oct–May 17.00–20.00 Wed & Sat. In the same building as Pierowall Fish (see opposite), on the south side of the harbour. Usually at least 8 different fish on menu, including haddock supper £6.90, scallop supper £9.30 & squid supper £7.30. When available menu extends further to feature John Dory, halibut & even catfish. Free delivery within Pierowall. £

⌨ **Richans Retreat Café** Rapness Pier; ☏01857 677877; ⊕ 08.00–18.30 daily. Snug, welcoming café albeit with just a handful of seats. No menu: owners Paul Booth and Linda Drever offer whatever they have to hand, ranging from sandwiches to spaghetti bolognese, cakes & hot drinks. Outside front door, don't miss beautifully carved wooden frame from captain's cabin of a Norwegian vessel shipwrecked in 1723. Craft shop sells almost exclusively Westray products. This café is very much what Orkney is about: externally nothing to write home about but inside offers an informal, quirky & innovative experience. £

⌨ **Wheeling Steen Gallery** Buckleberry; ⊕ Mar–May, Sep, Oct & Dec 13.00–17.00; Jun–Aug 11.00–17.00 Mon–Sat. Fairtrade organic teas, fresh coffee, biscuits & frozen yoghurt – the latter may be unexpected but proves hugely popular. £

ENTERTAINMENT

The **Graand Owld Byre** (same details as Chalmersquoy; page 245) stages regular music concerts in summer, usually on Tuesday nights, which provide a good opportunity for locals and tourists to meet one another. In alternate years (2019, 2021, etc), a long weekend of music and entertainment known as the **Westray Connections** is staged in summer. In July, a modest bustle is generated in Pierowall harbour by the **Westray Regatta**.

SHOPPING

FOOD AND DRINK Westray has an excellent baker and a fine artisan cheesemaker, neither of whom has a shopfront; instead their products can be bought in the island's

AN ISLAND DOCTOR

A network of GPs looks after the population of Orkney. As you might expect, they have historically been at the heart of their local community with most of the outer islands having a resident GP. In recent times this has begun to change. Recruitment in general practice has become more difficult across the UK and Orkney is no exception: fewer doctors appear willing to live full-time on an island, on call 24/7 for six weeks at a time and living in communities where everyone is their patient. In addition, they face risks that come with professional isolation from their peers.

In Orkney, a pool of experienced GPs provides 24/7 primary and emergency care for the remote island communities on a part-time basis. The Westray team comprises three GPs who each works for three weeks then, after a 24-hour handover, passes the baton to a colleague. A similar system operates with four GPs on Sanday, while the Stronsay and Hoy communities are served by resident GPs. Other islands have care provided by advanced nurse practitioners with GP support.

'A typical day involves surgeries in the morning and afternoon, house calls – sometimes up challenging farm tracks – and phone calls,' says Dr David Mazza, who works on Westray. Blood samples, flown to Kirkwall's Balfour Hospital twice weekly, are at the mercy of the mists. If the aircraft is grounded the bloods must be retaken another day. 'This usually happens on a particularly busy blood-taking day,' says Mazza.

three shops and across the Mainland. **Wilsons of Westray**, based at Noltland Farm, is a family enterprise, run by Jason and Nina Wilson. They produce three distinctive cheeses from their own herd of Ayrshire cows: the washed-rind Westray Wife; the creamy Noltland Castle; and the Cannonball, a small round cloth-hung cheese. The Wilsons started their business in 2012, converting a beef farm to dairy and installing a milking parlour. W F M Brown is ubiquitously known as the **Westray Baker**. Although they have no retail premises of their own, their bakes are sold at all island shops (as well as on the Orkney Mainland) and your eye is likely to fall upon their distinctive flaky biscuits – rather like a millefeuille without the custard – and the ginger-flavoured parkin biscuits.

For an island group that has no fish market, Orkney sells and processes a good deal of what gets hauled out of the sea. Though much diminished from its heyday, Westray remains the centre of the islands' industry. **Pierowall Fish Ltd** (Broughton; ✆ 018587 677471; w pierowall-fish.co.uk; ⏱ 09.00–17.00 Mon–Fri, also May–Sep 09.00–13.00 Sat) sells delicious salmon (reared in Papay Sound and smoked on the premises), mackerel and scallops (gathered by the local boat *Maggie J*). White fish is brought in on the island's sole remaining deep-sea vessel, the *Keila*, and topped up with fish from the Shetland and Scrabster markets. You'll find their products in Kirkwall, Stromness and Dounby. A major shellfish company, **Westray Processors**, works out of the large building at Gill Pier and produces brown crab in fresh, frozen and pasteurised forms. They don't have a shopfront but again you will see their products in shops and restaurants across the islands.

Also on sale across the island (and wider Orkney) are the varied flavours produced by **Westray Chutney** (✆ 01857 677471; e enquiries@westraychutneys. co.uk; w westraychutney.co.uk). Ann Rendall (who co-manages Pierowall Fish) has produced 20 different chutneys, using dates, cranberries, mango, onion and pineapple, many either Fairtrade or sourced from Westray vegetables. For supplies, check out the following:

The GP and nurse team also deal with accidents and emergencies, which, being unpredictable, can range from a minor laceration needing stitches to a significant road traffic accident. Emergency cases are evacuated and depending on their condition, patients may be transferred to Kirkwall, Aberdeen or Edinburgh. Every Wednesday the Westray GP takes the ferry to Papa Westray to hold a surgery there. This, perhaps not coincidentally, happens at the same time as the weekly island coffee morning. Outside observers may see this as a means of tackling isolation on a remote island but David's perspective is instructive: 'We do have to think practically about a person's social situation and environment but there is amazing informal support from the community. In my experience, isolation is much less of an issue here than in a city.'

The emergency-care element of being an island GP is stretching, David admits, but the work has compensations. Not long after I started, I walked into the shop when it was busy and, looking around, I realised I knew everyone there.' The job allows me to work holistically as a GP in the way that I have been trained to do but which had become more challenging in busy urban general practice. The community I see in Westray is remarkable in its can-do attitude, inclusivity, links with the past and its readiness to adapt for the future. Westray is a beautiful place but it is the community that makes it a remarkable place to work.'

J C Tulloch Pierowall; ✆01857 677373; ⏰ 09.00–
19.30 Mon–Sat, 12.30–14.30 Sun (all year). This
licensed grocers is located diagonally opposite
Rendall's & operates to the same high standards.

Skello Shop Skelwick; ✆01857 677351;
e skelloshop@gmail.com; ⏰ 09.00–18.00
Mon–Sat, also summer 14.00–17.00 Sun; see
ad, page 255. The most southerly of this island's
unlikely trio of busy & well-stocked grocery shops
sells meat, vegetables, chilled food, alcohol &
homewares. There's even a self-service coffee
machine. You may still hear it referred to as Peter
Miller's Merchants, after the man who established
the business in 1912. Run by his descendants until
2015, it is now managed by Uka & Ken Summers.
Located 5 miles south of Pierowall, right by the
coast at Skelwick, south of the Loch of Swartmill.
Worth checking out & handy if you are walking
along the east coast. Will take advance orders for
arrivals who are self-catering.

W I Rendall Pierowall; ✆01857 677389;
⏰ 08.30–18.00 Mon–Fri, 09.00–18.00 Sat, &
Jun–Aug 14.00–16.30 Sun. This well-stocked
general store is particularly strong on local
vegetables, eg: chillis & cucumbers, grown in
polycrubs (wind-resistant greenhouses) behind
the village.

HANDICRAFTS

Hume Sweet Hume Pierowall; ✆01857
677259; e info@humesweethume.co.uk;
w humesweethume.co.uk; ⏰ 10.00–17.00
Mon–Sat, also May–Sep 14.30–16.30 Sun. This is
a great place to buy distinctive & sometimes quirky
knitwear, from jumpers that can be worn upside
down – known as ladder tunics – to ponchos
with cuffs. Items are hand sewn, a process known
as grafting, which means they have no seams.
All clothing is designed by Jenna & Lizza Hume,
local sisters who, despite significant international
acclaim, have chosen to stay on their home island.
'We started out with cushions & throws & then
decided to do something a little different,' says
Lizza. 'That is how we approach our designs. We
do pay attention to colour forecasting but the
most exciting thing is just how ideas pop into your
head. You have to be inventive here, nothing is as
immediate as it is in a city.'

OTHER PRACTICALITIES

There are no ATMs, but you can withdraw cash from the **post offices**, located at
Skello Shop (⏰ 09.00–18.00 Mon–Sat, also summer noon–14.30 Sun) and J C
Tulloch (same hours as shop; see above), and shops give cashback. **Petrol** pumps
are available at W I Rendall. **Westray Surgery** is located at Gill Pier (✆ 01857
677309; w tinyurl.com/westray-surgery).

WHAT TO SEE AND DO

PIEROWALL The houses and shops of Pierowall are attractively sprinkled around
the Bay of Pierowall. The village is surprisingly elongated; from Gill Pier in the
north to Pierowall Fish in the south is 1¾ miles. On the north side of the bay, the
skerries of the harbour give way to the Sands o' Gill, a small beach of golden sand.
Apart from inspecting a handful of 'sights' in the village, Pierowall Bay is simply
a pleasant place to walk along, stopping for a coffee, nosing around a gallery or
watching the Papa Westray ferry come and go.

Immediately above the shore, roughly halfway round the village, the ruined
Lady Kirk stands slightly aside from a graveyard whose headstones stare out to
sea. The church dates to the late 17th century although it stands on foundations
laid down in the 13th century. The sizeable remains reflect how the church has
expanded to accommodate a larger congregation, something that points not only
to the God-fearing sensibilities of 17th-century Westray folk but also to the island's
ability to support and encourage people who could make a living here. A couple of
imposing tombstones, placed upright and protected by a Perspex cabinet, reinforce
this impression.

Secluded Rackwick Bay on the west coast of Hoy is a stunning place to explore, whether on foot or two wheels (O) page 141

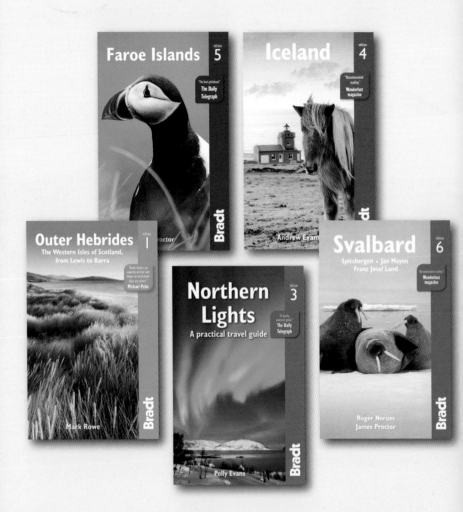

The excellent **Westray Heritage Centre** ✳ (📞 01857 677414; e office@ westrayheritage.co.uk; w westrayheritage.co.uk; ⊕ May–Sep 11.30–17.00 Mon, 09.00–noon & 14.00–17.00 Tue–Sat, 13.30–17.00 Sun, other times call ahead; £3/2.50 adult/child) provides a detailed history of the islands and has a handful of signature attractions that offer insights into Westray's deep Neolithic past. The enigmatic stone-carved Westray Wife, also known as the Orkney Venus (see box, page 251) shares pride of place with the Westray Stone, a rock carving discovered by a digger driver in 1981 in a tomb next to the Pierowall Hotel. The Stone lies in two lozenge-shaped parts some 4ft long, and has been dated to around 2000BC. The surface is intricately carved with spirals. It is believed to have been part of a chambered cairn similar to Maeshowe and is striking for its similarities to a stone found at the Newgrange Megalithic tomb in Ireland. The discovery at Newgrange of a mace head made from Orkney flint has strengthened the theory that there were connections between the two places. The centre also has a fine fossil collection, including a rare placoderm (armoured fish), while visitors with historical ties to the island can make use of the excellent genealogy section, where knowledgeable staff are willing to help. The other wing of the centre sells locally made knitwear and other souvenirs. Outside – you can't miss it – is a vast skeleton of a sperm whale that washed up at Tuquoy in 2007.

A few yards from the centre is **The Gallery** (📞 01867 677770; e peter@ westrayartgallery.co.uk; w westrayartgallery.co.uk; ⊕ times vary, enquire ahead) where artist Peter Brown is happy to talk about his work – paintings, sculptures and

ACCURSED KELP AND TANGLE DYKES

Mention the word 'kelp' and people tend to think of large fronds of seaweed. In Orkney, it means something rather different and refers to the product created by a gruellingly intensive process of gathering, burning and cooling seaweed. Kelp was a key industry across Orkney in the 18th and 19th centuries (good news for lairds such as George Traill), sometimes accounting for two-thirds of the islands' exports; it was used in the production of soap and glass.

The work was arduous: wet seaweed had to be cut from rocks, gathered from the shore and lugged away for drying. The seaweed was then lit in a kelp kiln, little more than a shallow stone pit, and heated until it became a boiling liquid. When it cooled, it solidified into kelp 'slag', which was broken into chunks and stored. The smell is said to have been unspeakable and the acrid fumes were blamed for the island crop failures. All too soon the boom turned to bust as in 1830 a Spanish alternative to kelp caused the Scottish market to crash.

Nevertheless, right up until the second half of the 20th century, the processing of 'tangles' (kelp stalks) provided some Westray residents with an income. After being hauled up the beach, the tangles were 'klokked' – twisted and snapped to break off the fronds. As you walk around the island, eg: at the Links of Noltland, you will see 'tangle dykes', low walls covered in lichens where the tangles were kept while they dried. For every tonne of dried tangle, four tonnes of wet material had to be dragged off the beach. In early summer, these were tied in bundles and piled up at Gill Pier to be shipped for processing as everything from ice-cream stabilisers to material for denture imprints. When the industry finally closed in 1998, the going rate was £176 a tonne.

driftwood creations – and island life. Peter describes his work as 'atmospheric and abstract landscapes and seascapes' and they certainly capture the varying weather that sweeps through the islands. 'People are always surprised that artists here don't just paint puffins,' he adds gently.

NORTH OF PIEROWALL Just a mile north of Pierowall lies the ruined 10th-century settlement of **Quoygrew**. To reach it, take Rackwick Road north from the Sand o' Gill and park with care by the settlement of North Haven. From here, it is a short walk across the fields to the site (✪ HY444506), which is clearly visible for afar. Quoygrew is a classic Orcadian example of how a building can be adapted, built upon and its purpose altered time and time again. Though it was originally a turf-built farm, excavations have uncovered layers of human history up until the 1930s, including a building resembling a Norse hall and a medieval farmstead. Quoygrew is thought to have been a wealthy farm for much of its time, with a nearby midden revealing that the occupants enjoyed a diet of saithe and cod. Soapstone pots from Shetland have also been found. The last tenants moved out in 1937.

Back in Pierowall, a signposted road by the school leads three quarters of a mile to **Noltland Castle** (⊕ 08.00–20.00 daily; free). Standing defiant on the brae above Pierowall, the castle oozes drama and looks exactly the sort of place a notorious ne'er-do-well would call home – which is indeed the case. Built around 1560 and with a name derived from the Norse for 'cattle land', the castle was owned by the notorious Gilbert Balfour, master of the household for Mary Queen of Scots and sheriff of Orkney. He was described as a man motivated by 'neither fear of God nor love of virtue'.

Just staring at the exterior can induce a shudder or two. The castle comprises a main rectangle of 6ft-thick defensive blocks, with square wings at diagonally opposite corners creating a classic Z-plan appearance. Above, it is the 71 narrow shot holes, from which muskets could be fired while affording castle occupants protection from retaliation, that really strike you. These, and the absence of ground-floor windows, tell you that Balfour habitually expected trouble.

The interior is well worth exploring. The ground floor is given over to kitchens and includes a slender service staircase that was used to take food and ale up to the feasting Balfour. The main route to the great hall on the first floor was a huge spiral staircase with a carved newel post (central supporting pillar). The great hall – now open to the elements – was where Balfour dispensed justice to the people of Westray in between Bacchanalian evenings of wine and meat. An adjacent four-storey tower provided family accommodation. What remains is hugely atmospheric, with green lichens mantling much of the masonry adding to the sinister gloom. There are light switches on the stairways but a torch will be helpful. Balfour was destined to never put down roots here. Implicated in the murder of Lord Darnley, Mary's second husband, he was forced to flee the country. Unable to kick his inclination for intrigue and villainy, he was executed in 1576 in Stockholm for plotting to kill the king of Sweden.

Some 500yds north of the castle lies the graceful beach of **Grobust** whose appealing dunes conspire to produce a landscape of stirring beauty. The grasses that back on to the beach here are one of Orkney's rare slivers of machair, the coastal sea meadows more usually associated with the Outer Hebrides. In summer they transform from a sandy green into vast splashes of colour produced by eyebright, felwort, cowslip, sandwort and many other plants. Down to the left above the sea – but with no access – is an obvious mound, the **Knowe of Queena Howe**, thought to contain a broch tower.

Among the dunes you will find the **Links of Noltland**, a multi-phase settlement that features both Neolithic and Bronze Age elements. The site originated around 3000BC but was subsequently abandoned and later reoccupied. The site is open to the public in July and August when archaeologists continue their excavations. For the rest of the year, everything is covered with sheeting to see it through another Orcadian winter. Neolithic remains comprise the stone footings and semblances of hearths and furnishings of at least six houses, similar to those at Skara Brae. Among the discoveries are bone pins, beads and grooved pottery. The presence of animal remains in tombs and settlements across Orkney is substantial, from dog skulls at Cuween Hill on the Mainland to sea-eagle bones on South Ronaldsay. Yet the Links of Noltland have revealed something just as extraordinary in the form of 30 cattle skulls that encircled a building now known as 'structure 9'. This was something far more profound than merely the discarded bones of animals that had been eaten for survival; instead all had been placed upside down with their horns sticking into the ground, some interlocked. They were uncovered in a cavity wall, so would not have been visible to the contemporary occupants. Though clearly a ritual of some kind, archaeologists are as yet unable to shed any further light on why a community may have chosen to kill 30 animals that would have been so important to continued survival. Efforts being made to stabilise the dunes, which are continually eroding (rabbit warrens adding to the problem) have included importing sand. The local community and Heritage Environment Scotland are working together to safeguard the Links' future.

The beach of **Grobust** is one of the most attractive on Westray. The gentle crescent of sand is broken by a series of wave-smoothed flagstone ridges where

THE ORKNEY VENUS

Cattle skulls were not the only eye-popping discovery yielded by the Links of Noltland. In 2009, an excavation of a midden at 'structure 8' uncovered a Neolithic carved-sandstone figurine just 1½in high. Known as both the Orkney Venus and the Westray Wife, the figure is believed to be the earliest representation of a human on Orkney. It is one of only four such figures found in the British Isles. With a small head on its bell-shaped body, the figurine can bring to mind a Christmas-tree decoration. Human features incised on the object include an 'M'-shaped etching that could be a brow and two parallel lines that appear to depict a nose. Two round dots are suggestive of eyes. The 'torso' is etched with what may be breast or dress fastenings (one of these is squarer, the other more diamond-shaped). The back of the figure is grooved with fine lines that may represent hair on the 'head' and textile designs on the torso, suggesting that the larger, lower part of the figure may be a dress. The figure remains an enigma, its purpose uncertain. One theory is that, as the figure is intact and the etchings prominent, it was not handled often so was perhaps an object of veneration or held some other symbolic purpose. Alternatively, it may simply have been a decorative pendant or even the product of idle work carried out to while away the day – certainly, the soft sandstone could easily have been carved by a bone tool and the decoration etched quite swiftly. You can make up your own mind easily enough as this remarkable object is displayed in the Westray Heritage Centre in Pierowall. Two similar figurines have been found on Westray at other sites. Both are displayed here too: one, uncovered in 2016, has deep decoration marks but is missing a head; the other is more eroded and formless.

11

a brief perusal may reveal fish fossils. As you stroll to its eastern end, look back and Noup Head lighthouse reveals itself. The combination of sandy machair soils, blue-green sloping rocks, verdant grasses, a glassy sea and yellow-white dunes all combine to create a colour scheme of great symmetry that is aesthetically easy on the eye.

While you can drive or cycle to Noltland Castle, the Links and Quoygrew, you can also visit them on a 4-mile circular walk. From Pierowall, walk up School Brae and turn right at the top. Follow the road as it bends left to reach Noltland Castle. Keep ahead on the road for a further 600yds then turn right, following the sign for Links of Noltland. The road gives up just above the dunes of Grobust. Walk along the beach, over the grass at the far side and through the gate. Follow the winding grassy track as it contours by the sea for three quarters of a mile, then continue along the paved road that joins from the right to reach Quoygrew. To return to Pierowall, return to the road at North Haven, turn right and then left on to Rackwick Road.

Just under 2 miles north of Pierowall, along the airport road, you will find one of Orkney's most beautiful art galleries, the **Wheeling Steen Gallery** (✆ 01857 677292; e wheelingsteen@gmail.com; w wheeling-steen.co.uk; ☉ Mar–May, Sep, Oct & Dec 13.00–17.00 Mon–Sat; Jun–Aug 11.00–17.00 Mon–Sat). The workshop of Edwin Rendall and his daughter Rosemary, the building space (the name comes from the Norse for 'resting stone') is spectacular, with a vaulted ceiling and mezzanine. Just as striking is the restored cabin of a 19th-century shipwreck, the Norwegian barque *Emerald*, which serves both as gallery and Edwin's studio. Displays feature Edwin's acrylic seascape and landscape paintings plus photography by both father and daughter. The latter is frequently outstanding, with stirring shots of cliffs or hills infused with wild Orkney weather and close-up details of flowers and grasses. The whole business has come some way since Edwin started out selling photographs along with traybakes at car boot sales in the 1990s. Edwin's paintings are impressionistic. 'Some are abstract – I'm trying to catch a feeling of the experience of living on an island,' he says. 'Every year, every season, things on Westray look a little different and perhaps I pick up on those things subconsciously.'

The gallery overlooks the Ouse, a graceful area of saltmarsh where the sea retracts at low tide to reveal a pond-shaped beach. This is a restful place to watch ducks and waders come and go. The airfield is just half a mile further north along the road. Even if you're not flying this is a good place to watch the aircraft take off and land. Just offshore is the Holm of Aikerness, where you can often see harbour seals on the rocks.

NOUP HEAD Even amid an archipelago of fractured and dramatic cliffs, the northwest coast of Westray can lay rightful claim to being the wildest and most elemental landscape of all. While not quite the northernmost point on either Westray or Orkney, Noup Head offers Orkney's definitive geological crescendo before the empty waters that separate the islands from the Arctic take over.

To insinuate yourself in the elements, you can walk all the way from Pierowall (8 miles there and back). If you do not feel confident of walking in such primal conditions, or prefer not to ascend the steep, stone track to the lighthouse, then you should contact one of the island's two tour operators; it does seem unfair that one of Orkney's most magnificent spectacles is only visible to the fully able-bodied.

To walk from Pierowall, follow road signs for the Noup up past the school and Noltland Castle. By the farm at Backaras, take the left-hand path downhill between fields to the coast, over a couple of stiles and turn right (ignoring the signpost, which unhelpfully points left). At this point, the scenery really kicks in and you soon pass two natural arches. The cliff-walking is just that; there are stiles that offer a slightly more inland route if you don't wish to stride right by the edge. Look back south and Westray's coastline continues in the same hair-raising vein.

The walk begins to gently climb uphill past deep geos that incise their way inland (this is another of those Orkney hikes you know better than to walk in mist). Soon enough Noup Head lighthouse – another Stevenson family creation, 79ft high – fills the frame (as it does on the cover of this book). Looking north and south, the scenery here is simply so wild that the lighthouse can resemble an architectural exclamation mark, as though expressing astonishment at its own location. If the cliffs around Yesnaby and the West Mainland appear to have been hacked away with a fretsaw, Noup Head and its approaches have simply been guillotined.

Just below the last ridge on the south side of the lighthouse there is a series of ledges where you can sit and watch the seabirds on the cliffs. Just about everyone wants to see puffins here, and you're sure to see some from May to July, but the showstoppers are gannets, a relatively recent arrival to Westray. From May to late September you will see adults returning to their nest, beaks full of fish. If you have seen them diving from afar all over Orkney this can make for a pleasing closing of the circle. Gannets are kept company by kittiwakes, razorbills, guillemots and fulmars. Just occasionally, a peregrine puts the wind up everything; come the winter you may even spot a flurry of snow buntings. To return to Pierowall, pick up the track that runs from the lighthouse; after a couple of miles this joins the paved road at Backaras, from where you retrace your steps.

A longer version of this walk is perfectly plausible. You can walk all the way from Kirbest, just above Mae Sand in the southwest, to Noup Head, a distance of 5½ miles. Expect to take up to 3 hours to complete this stretch. This is truly magnificent, with unending views along cliffs of great drama, where the description 'vertical' really doesn't do justice to just how precipitous the landscape is. The walk is over what is a frequently boggy landscape so can be arduous; in windy weather, the pay-off is the spectacle of reverse waterfalls, whereby water is blown back up the cliffs, sometimes right over your head. Bear in mind you need to either return to Kirbest the same way (if you left your car there), walk into Pierowall (a further 4 miles) or call the island taxi.

WESTRAY'S WESTSIDE After the drama of Noup Head, the scenery around the southern half of Westray begins to calm down. All the time, the faintly terraced outline of **Fitty Hill** (554ft/169m) stands brooding above you. Fitty Hill is an easy climb, most simply accomplished by the waymarked path off the B9067 near Heatherbank. Only the last stages verge on the steep side and the 2-mile return walk should take most people under 2 hours. Orkney's summits usually repay the effort of the climb with views of other islands in the archipelago but Fitty Hill offers the chance to look north to Shetland where you will see not just Fair Isle but the huge ski-slope outline of Foula, 45 miles away.

The other major landscape feature is the cavernous bay of **Letto Sands**, almost a mile in length and with a beach that extends just as far at low tide. The beach is rich in mussels and cockles, so you will share the retreating tide with avian foragers such as great black-backed gull and oystercatcher. The best access to the bay is from the minor road that connects the B9066 and B9067; drivers will find a couple of informal parking places where it's possible to pull up and wander on to the beach.

The key site, however, is the stirring spectacle of the tombstone-encircled **Cross Kirk**, which stands lonely as it juts out to sea to the west of Letto Sands and Bay of Tuquoy (pronounced 'too-kwoi'). This Romanesque medieval parish church is considered to be one of the best-constructed churches in Orkney. It was built in 1140 for the Westray Norseman Thorkel Flettir (Thorkel Flayer) on his return from the crusades and later held by his heir Haflidi; both were supporters of Earl Rognvald. A surprising amount of the church survives, including the original doorway, along with an arched window and the chancel arch. A slab incised with Norse runes was found inside the church. The remains poking out of the cliff west of the church are thought to be those of Thorkel's house and farmstead. The setting is elemental, the church tottering in the heart of an ancient graveyard still used by islanders, right next to a sea that muscles up against the cemetery and withdraws at low tide to expose vast, polished rock slabs.

To reach Cross Kirk, continue down the B9067 and turn hard left at the crossroads of Tufter and South Hamar. About 200yds along on the left is South Hamar (✪ HY449439), a rare example of an Orkney 'steading' or 'but and ben' croft, complete with outbuildings and barley-drying kiln; this is currently being restored. Continue for a mile to the small parking area by the Point o' the Scurroes. The kirk is signposted and lies a further 800yds along a rather overgrown coastal path. Don't try and walk further west towards Mae Sand as the path is overgrown and impassable. To reach Mae Sand, return to Tufter and continue ahead on the B9067. After half a mile, the B road peters out at a T-junction. You need to bear left here along the road.

Then keep straight along the lane and look for the small signposted parking place close to Langskaill Farm. Behind the modern-day farm at Langskaill, archaeological work has uncovered a Norse longhouse behind the present-day farm. Below the longhouse lies an Iron Age 'souterrain' (earth house); nothing, however, is visible to the casual visitor. Walk south along the lane and downhill through a stile with fields on either side to Mae Sand (where the beach's soft sand is far more amenable to hanging around in fine weather than the coarse and gritty constitution of Letto Sands). Turn right and with the sea to your left make your way up the far end of the beach, following the grassy flanks to where they peter out at the skerries. This has fine views of Bakie Skerry, where harbour seals often lounge. The grassy mound here, Knowe o' Skerrie, contains a prehistoric cemetery and shrine.

On your return towards Tufter, look up the lane to the left signposted for Kirbest (the start of the walk up the west coast to Noup Head) and you can see the line of abandoned farmhouses of Nether Hamar running up the hill.

THE SOUTH OF WESTRAY Back on the B9066, head south and follow a signposted turning for Swartmill east down a road that for a mile or so skirts the shores of the Loch of Swartmill. If you head down the east side of the loch, you will see a small parking area with a picnic table that offers views both of the loch and the Bay of Swartmill, where a narrow beach reveals itself at low tide.

A mile or so further south on the B9066, look for another turning east for the Castle o' Burrian, a rock stack that is one of Orkney's best sites for puffin from April to July. The rock stack is barely half a mile along the coast but you have the option of extending this into a circular walk of 3 miles, which will take most people about 90 minutes (this also allows you to say you have walked from the North Sea to the Atlantic). If you have young children desperate to see the birds, keep them close as the path runs adjacent to the edge of high cliffs.

The walk starts at the small lay-by (✪ HY500425) by an 1850s mill that ground bere and barley. The mill has long been taken over by birds but the wheel remains in place. Go through a kissing gate and follow the cliff-edge path, sometimes along boardwalks, until you reach **Castle o' Burrian**. This lozenge-shaped sea stack is covered with tufted grass; if you stare hard you may pick out remnant stones that are thought to have been the site of an early Christian hermitage.

The path continues, still enthusiastically edging close to the cliffs; in places the cliffs are in the process of collapsing into embryonic sea stacks. At Stangar Head, the sea has hollowed out rocks to create a cave-like amphitheatre. Given a decent swell, the sea can rise up and squirt through two small windows in the rocks, tumbling out like waterfalls.

The seascape now shifts, with the hilly dunes of Sanday replaced by the bulkhead silhouette of Eday's northerly moors. At a stile, a waymarker points you inland up a grassy path. This becomes a track and as you head downhill towards the B9066 look out for the remains of the windmill at Sangar. Cross the road and head downhill along a track to the beach. Views of Rousay fill the frame here, with the western cliffs of the Mainland behind and St Magnus Kirk on Egilsay to the south. The beach is laid out for inspection as an arc of clear white sand. As you walk, look out for the path (a rickety waymarker may still be in place; ✪ HY497416) halfway along that points you uphill past the graveyard. Turn left on to the B9066 and after 400yds turn right to return to the start of the walk.

12

Papa Westray

Known as 'Papay' to its inhabitants and everyone else on Orkney, Papa Westray is one of those resonant names that brings to mind a far-flung location on the periphery of everyday life. Perched at the north of the Orkney archipelago, 20 miles north of Kirkwall, and lying more or less on the same latitude as Stavanger in Norway, Papay certainly ticks the geographical box for remoteness. Gaze north from the appropriately named North Hill and you're looking at water unbroken until you reach the Arctic. This is an island where mains electricity only arrived in 1980. There is, though, a certain irony in the fact that an island so cherished for being 'away from it all' is so well connected to the outside world, with its prime attraction being the blink-and-you-miss-it flight from neighbouring Westray (see box, page 258).

Papay is tiny, just 4 miles long by a mile wide, yet there is plenty to keep you here for considerably longer than it takes the aircraft to fly here. The island has important Neolithic sites, viewed in the extraordinary light that you only really experience on small islands: fine, delicate sky blues that blur with sandy beaches and dark green moorlands. All this is framed and infilled by a fabulously indented coastline of cliffs, bays and farmland.

Like its neighbour Westray, Papay simply feels like a place that has been lived in by real people for centuries: nothing is manufactured for show. Walk around the southern coasts and you will see the 'nausts' (artificial slipways) where, in the absence of a natural harbour, boats had to be dragged up above the high-tide mark. Some date to Viking times.

Papay life is centred on Beltane, in mid-island, where you will find the hostel and from where the key attractions radiate out west and east. The island shop and hostel are the social hubs of today's vibrant community.

HISTORY

The island is named for the Papae, the Celtic priests who lived here, possibly from as early as the 5th century. Positioned on the safer west-coast passage to the north, Papay was considered a good springboard for missionaries who had been dispatched across Dark Age Europe. Yet Papay was considered a good place to live long before that. The major Neolithic settlements at the Knap of Howar and on the Holm of Papay indicate settled communities were in place at that time (around 3600–2500BC) and the island is home to 60 identified archaeological sites.

Remains of Iron Age brochs have been uncovered and the island may have even been the seat of the Pictish bishopric of Orkney, though any remains that might strengthen this theory are now submerged below St Boniface Kirk.

The medieval landscape of Papay was very different from today, being distinguished by irregular rigs (parcels of arable land divided by unploughed ridges called baulks). Water would have lain on the undrained fields and low turf-roofed houses would have been all but camouflaged into the fields.

From the 17th century onwards, the island was owned by the Traill family, who proved efficient at exploiting island resources (eg: kelp) to their benefit, if less so to the advantage of islanders. Kelp-processing was a huge employer at this time (see box, page 249) but when the industry collapsed, the Traills turned to livestock production. The introduction of the North Isles steamer service in 1885 meant that animals could be shipped south from Kirkwall to the UK mainland. This resulted in a dramatic transformation of the Papay landscape. The Traills squared off and drained the fields then built stone dykes (and roads) in a process referred to as 'improvements'.

Papay's population has dropped significantly since the 1831 census recorded 392 people; by the late 1990s fewer than 60 residents remained. In response, the Papa Westray Development Trust was established to steer the island away from depopulation. The figure has since risen to around 95 and is now considered not only stable but slowly creeping upwards. The primary school has seven children (junior high children must take the daily boat to Westray) and several families have relocated here in recent years. In addition to health, airport and council-related jobs, construction is a big employer. There's certainly a vibrancy here that is missing on some other islands, and an enlightened, progressive attitude that manifests itself in many ways, such as pursuing the status of a Fairtrade island as well as a strong artistic streak. 'Papay's an active island,' says Jonathan Ford, the island ranger. 'It's somewhere you can make things happen and you have room to do things.'

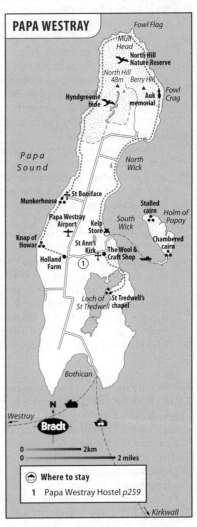

GETTING THERE AND AWAY

BY AIR Loganair flies from Kirkwall to Papa Westray twice on Monday, three times Tuesday to Saturday and once on Sunday, with an additional seasonal flight (mid-June to August) on Tuesday, Thursday and Saturday. Flights are usually via Westray, some via North Ronaldsay. Fares are £18 single, £36 return and £21 'excursion fare' return, which is conditional on staying at least one night. The airfield is located in the centre of the island, half a mile's walk from the hostel.

BY SEA The most common way to reach Papa Westray is to take the seasonal passenger ferry (May–September) from

THE WORLD'S SHORTEST FLIGHT

We live in a world where you can now fly non-stop for 9,000 miles from the UK to Australia in 17 hours. Fortunately, for romantics everywhere, you can also fly non-stop for just 1.7 miles and a minute or two in the airspace that separates the airfields of Westray and Papa Westray.

With the right tailwinds, the flight can take less than a minute. 'I've read somewhere that the record is 48 seconds but I find that hard to believe,' says Captain Colin McAllister, who has flown the sector some 4,000 times. 'It is more likely to be around 55 seconds. It depends which heading you have as we generally try to take off and land into the wind.'

The distance is shorter than the runway at Heathrow Airport and both taxiing and the safety briefing can take longer than the flight itself. Like everything else involved with the flight, the aircraft, an eight-seater Britten-Norman Islander, is different to anything you have probably experienced before. The formalities of check-in are remarkably relaxed and convivial.

The novelty aside – you go up, you go down – the flight is extremely beautiful and offers fine views of both islands as well as Sanday distantly to the south and Fair Isle to the north. 'Sometimes I have to shake myself and remember that this is quite something,' says McAllister.

The service was launched in 1967 and certainly sped up contact with the outside world: until then, islanders' only interaction with the Mainland was the thrice-weekly ferry journey, which took 6–9 hours and visited all the North Isles on its route.

Perhaps the most impressive element of the flight is that it is not a gimmick. In other parts of the world, such a flight might be marketed and branded – and punters charged accordingly. Some of your fellow passengers may also be flying for the unique experience but you may sit next to a doctor or an archaeologist – not that you have much time to strike up a conversation. 'It's simply a sector we fly as part of our daily services,' says McAllister. 'It is not designed for any market other than the locals. It's just a happy coincidence that it has this special significance.'

Flights can be booked up to three months in advance but short-notice seats are released the day before if they have not been taken up by islanders. The cost is £17 single. Don't forget you can fly in both directions, though flights do not go back and forward between the two islands: after the short hop, the pilot heads back to Kirkwall, sometimes via North Ronaldsay. Don't forget to arrange your official certificate, which you can pick up from the inter-island departures office at Kirkwall Airport.

Gill Pier in Pierowall on Westray to New Pier at the southern end of Papa Westray, 2 miles from the hostel. The service is operated by Orkney Island Ferries (⊕ May–Sep 6 services daily Mon–Wed, 5 Thu, 4 Fri & Sat, 3 Sun; £4.30/2.15 single adult/child; 25mins). In other months, only the school boat runs between the two islands. You can use this but need to arrange it in advance through Orkney Islands Ferries. The journey is beautiful, with fine views of both islands and Eday's high cliffs as well as gannets crashing into the sea. In an ideal world, you might fly to Papay and take this ferry back to Westray.

Orkney Ferries also operates a weekly service from Kirkwall to New Pier on Tuesdays. This takes 1 hour 50 minutes direct, 4½ hours if sailing via North

Ronaldsay (summer) or 2¼ hours if via Westray (winter). Single fares £20/8 standard car/passenger.

GETTING AROUND

Papay is small, so there is no real need for a car (and you would have to come on the Kirkwall ferry as the Westray service is for foot-passengers only). Cycling and walking are a delight; contact the Papay Ranger (see below) to arrange pick-up and drop-off of rental bikes (£10/day). Neither car hire nor taxi is an option on Papay but folks at the hostel offer a pick-up service to the airfield or ferry for £6.

TOURIST INFORMATION AND TOUR OPERATORS

As with most of the Outer Isles, there is no visitor centre in the conventional sense. The shop at Beltane (page 260) has leaflets on sites and walks around the island. The island website w papawestray.co.uk has useful details of what to see and what's on. A decent booklet on island history and life, *Exploring Papay*, is on sale at the shop and the Kelp Store (page 262).

One of the best ways to explore the island is to take a guided tour led by Jonathan Ford, the Papa Ranger (℡ 07931 235213; m 07931 235213; e papayranger@gmail.com; w papawestray.co.uk; Apr–Sep). He offers an excellent Papay Peedie Tour lasting 7 hours (£50/25 inc lunch & tea) which explores most of the island. He's also one of three skippers licensed to run boat trips to the Holm of Papay (3hrs; £25). During summer months, the RSPB also offers walks exploring North Hill reserve (e orkney@rspb.org.uk; Wed & Sun).

WHERE TO STAY, EAT AND DRINK   *Map, page 257*

At the time of writing, there are neither B&Bs nor cafés on Papay. The island development trust is actively seeking to address this. Fortunately, the single place to stay is, thanks to a recent renovation, the best hostel in Orkney. A list of Papay's smattering of self-catering options can be found at w papawestray.co.uk.

✳ 🏠 **Papa Westray Hostel** (6 rooms) Beltane House, Beltane; ℡01857 622244; e beltanepapay@aol.co.uk; w papawestray.co.uk/beltane-house.html. Well-run, snug & friendly, this hostel features ample mod cons, including 2 new kitchens. 5 dbl bedrooms (£30pp, £50 for 2) & a family room sleeping 5 (£60), all en suite. 1 room suitable for travellers with limited mobility. 2 2-person wooden bothies in grounds (£25/40) with use of new toilet block in hostel. Large dining room plus snug conservatory-style lounge with TV. All tastefully decorated with local artwork & prints from the island camera club. Hostel is very much the social centre of the island (see below). You'll find the island 'pub' in the corner of the residents' lounge: a store cupboard stocked with ales, wines & spirits, which is unlocked every Sat & drinks served from the extremely modest bar counter (non-residents welcome). Highly recommended. **£**

ENTERTAINMENT

Papa Westray Hostel regularly hosts film nights with a drop-down screen, as well as dances and bands, including the island's own group, Poor Man's Corner, playing Scottish folk music with accordion, guitars and fiddles – and even a washboard.

Autumn sees the Øy Festival, also known as the Papay Arts Festival (w papawestray.co.uk/events.html) while plans are being drawn up for an annual beachcombing festival to begin in 2019. While the island has no café, if you want an insight into Papay life visitors are welcome to attend the coffee mornings (⊕ 10.30–11.45 Wed) at St Ann's Kirk. The weekly doctor's surgery is held at the same time; the two combine to create an unlikely social event.

SHOPPING

The Papay Shop Beltane; \01857 644321; w papawestray.co.uk/papay-shop.html; ⊕ 10.00–noon & 15.30–17.30 Mon & Wed–Fri, 10.00–noon Tue, 10.00–noon & 18.00–19.00 Sat. Attached to the hostel & among the UK's top 200 Fairtrade outlets, this is unexpectedly one of the best-stocked & varied stores on all of Orkney, particularly given Papay's small population. Sells fruit & vegetables from the island's community market garden, alongside a wide range of wines, beer & spirits, plus quinoa chips & wholemeal pasta.

The Wool and Craft Shop Daybreak; \01857 644275; e margitdaybreak@gmail.com; ⊕ 10.00–14.00 Tue–Thu, other times ring bell. Some 400yds downhill from the hostel & shop, this is a small gem. Run by Margit Fassbender, it is almost literally packed to the rafters with yarns & woollen knick-knacks. You can pick up knitted goods or rough fleeces for spinning or felting. A wall map of the world has pins stuck in every location that buyers of Margit's Papay socks (75% merino; £25 a pair) have come from. Ask to see the old-fashioned post stamp still in use behind the counter; the tiny numbers of the month are manually inserted into the stamp.

OTHER PRACTICALITIES

The island is one of the few to use a '**flying bank**', whereby a Royal Bank of Scotland (RBS) employee arrives by air once a month to deal with islanders' financial matters. More practically, you can get cashback at The Papay Shop and withdraw money at the **post office** located within The Wool and Craft Shop. **Petrol** pumps are found at The Papay Shop; for **medical** issues, call the island nurse (\01857 644227).

WHAT TO SEE AND DO

KNAP OF HOWAR ✳ This is Papa Westray's prime attraction, the oldest preserved stone house in northern Europe and consequently the earliest example of a Neolithic settlement in Orkney, predating Skara Brae. The Knap, which has origins as far back as 3600BC, is a prehistoric two-roomed farmhouse, its walls standing to their original height. This reason alone makes it one of Orkney's must-sees. Combined with its superb setting, right on the west coast, it is simply spectacular; only its distance from Kirkwall keeps the Knap from being deluged by visitors.

The Knap is not a village like Skara Brae but seems to have been the home of a single, virtually self-sufficient family unit. The two surviving buildings both have an entrance at one end and are linked by a cross-passage. The farmhouse is the larger of the two buildings and is subdivided by stone slabs into an outer living/sleeping room and an inner (more inland) cooking/work room. Each room is 'furnished' with a bench; the inner room has a stone hearth. The smaller building was built later and may have been a store, workshop or byre. This is divided into three, also has a hearth and is internally furnished with recesses that served as wall cupboards and shelves.

The substantial remains have been preserved under an overlay of shell sand. Excavations have found tools made from stone and bone as well as early Unstan ware pottery, while studies of midden deposits show that the early inhabitants grew barley, reared cattle, sheep and pigs, and harvested fish, seabirds and shellfish, including oysters, which are no longer found in the area. Like Skara Brae, the Knap would originally have been located some distance inland. The Knap of Howar's eventual decline is thought to have been caused by similar factors to those that affected Skara Brae. The climate had been warmer when the Knap was established; and strengthening winds, combined with woodland clearance, may have contributed to the site's eventual abandonment. To reach the Knap, follow the signposted path just south of Holland Farm, then cross fields for 400yds until you see the settlement surrounded by a metal fence.

HOLLAND FARM AND AROUND Located on the north side of the junction of the main island road and the lane to the hostel, locally this is known as Poor Man's Corner, as it was where the farm servants of the Traills would hang out in between their toil. Although still a working farm, this is the former home of the Traills and remains the most extensive traditional steading in Orkney, with buildings dating to the 17–19th centuries. You can explore the outbuildings by yourself – just look for someone to ask out of courtesy – but the best way to visit is on the island tour led by the Papay Ranger (page 259), partly because there is little or no signage.

A good place to start on the farm is **John o' Holland's Museum** ✳ (⊕ always; donation invited), identified by the harness hanging from the gable end and based in the bothy where the eponymous John lived until 1922. As your eyes adjust to the gloom, what emerges resembles a prop room for a theatre with giant mallets and scythes to inspect. The jumble of machinery and artefacts is captivating; eye-catchers include vicious-looking codfish baits with hooks, known as 'murderers', and a fine pair of handcuffs that brought errant islanders to heel. Outside, and tucked away on the north side of the farm, is the horse-driven threshing mill dating to 1823. A rakishly ruined doocot (or dovecote) stands left of the track leading down to the Knap of Howar. In the fields, look for the stone cairns or 'stack-steethes'; these flat platforms raised stacks of crops off the wet ground.

Elsewhere in the UK, this rich heritage would have been monetised and sanitised into a 'visitor experience'; the fact that this is not the case here tells you a good deal about the Orcadian approach to life.

THE TRAILL FAMILY

Travel around the North Isles for any length of time and you will notice how often the Traill family pops up. Their origins lie in the 16th century when George Traill, a companion of Earl Robert Stewart, came to Orkney from Fife. Thanks to a combination of lucrative business deals and – just as important – marriages to heiresses, the Traills prospered and accumulated estates. These included parts of Rousay, Sanday and Westray as well as the entirety of Papa Westray and North Ronaldsay. They also owned parcels of the Mainland, including Skaill House, overlooking Skara Brae. The Traills of Holland, on Papay, were the most influential branch of this powerful family.

In 1637 Thomas Traill, George's oldest son, bought the House of Holland, which today stands close to the island's memorial to the world wars. The family was to rule as lairds over the island for the next 250 years. Not all the Traills have gone down in history as bad eggs, however. In the late 19th century William Traill emerged as a keen and knowledgeable antiquarian and excavated the Knap of Howar.

12

A mile or so north of Holland, again on the west coast, stands lonely **St Boniface** (⊕ always open), a pre-Reformation kirk and one of the oldest Christian sites in northern Scotland. The 12th-century church was built by the Norse, possibly on an earlier Pictish structure. At that time it would not have appeared so isolated but instead commanded a strategic location for missionaries en route to Shetland. Inside is a small rectangular chapel with recently restored box-pews. The nave was enlarged in the 17th century.

Two Pictish symbol stones were discovered here (one is in the Orkney Museum, the other in the National Museum of Scotland) along with fragments from a Pictish reliquary shrine which suggests a church was present here from at least the 8th century. The grand tomb of the Traill family also stands to the rear of the church.

West of the church, a settlement all but reclaimed by the sea indicates that others have also considered this site to be important. The site is called **Munkerhoose**, suggesting that a monastery was also once here. Intriguingly, excavations uncovered the remains of a large broch and Viking weaving sword as well as funerary monuments dating to the Bronze Age. You can see – just – traces of the site if you walk towards the shore behind the church. Look for a little tract of a wall heading out to sea and an adjacent midden that continues to yield fishbones and shells.

KELP STORE ✳ (⊕ always; donation requested) Whatever else you do on Papay, do not miss this beautifully restored gem just east of Beltane, standing by the shores of South Wick. This was the fulcrum of the island's lucrative trade in processed seaweed (see box, page 249). You can read an informed account of the importance and impact of the kelp industry on the island and browse the many books on everything from great auks to island history. The building is a place of great charm; nice touches include the three seats neatly positioned in front of a wide-screen television on which you can watch a DVD of Papay residents talking about life and times in a way that is informative rather than twee. If you hit bad weather while walking around the island, it's a great place to shelter and dry off.

PAPAY WILDLIFE

For such a small island, Papa Westray certainly packs in the wildlife. Clearly, you are 200 years too late to see great auk. More positively, curlew, redshank and oystercatcher can be found across the island and the drumming of snipe is a sure sign of spring. The RSPB has a management agreement with North Islands graziers which sees cattle grazed at low levels to avoid disturbance to nesting waders. The maritime heath of the RSPB reserve at North Hill supports huge colonies of wildflowers, notably Scottish primrose. North Hill is also a major nesting area for seabirds (including great and Arctic skuas), gulls and ravens. View them from the hide at Hyndgreenie (best accessed along the track that leads off the end of the central road). The cliffs, ledges and geos at Fowl Crag are good places to see kittiwakes, fulmars and puffins. Tysties nest on the lower ledges, while the dainty Arctic tern is a regular sight overhead. Migrant songbirds such as whitethroat and spotted flycatcher gravitate to the island's extremely modest tree specimens, such as a stand of sycamore behind the school and the fuchsia that runs along the wall of St Boniface. Autumnal fungi are quite noticeable on Papay and cowpats are fertile sources of growth for inkcaps.

THE SOUTH The **Loch of St Tredwell** dominates the south of the island. Fringed with reeds and irises, it is popular with ducks. A pleasant one-way walk of a mile or so (20–30mins from the hostel) along the east side of the loch leads to a **chapel**. From the hostel, head downhill and turn right at the junction, following the lane past the houses. The lane becomes a grassy track. As you near a drystone wall on the right, take the clear grassy tractor track that veers right. Shortly after, take the narrow path through the grass. Cross two stiles to reach the chapel, which is dedicated to St Tredwell and lies by the remains of a broch on a conspicuous promontory poking out into the loch. You can just about see the broch wall in the undergrowth and the pile of stones that marks the chapel. Otters are often seen around here.

The chapel is named for a woman who may or may not actually have been a saint and may not even have been buried there. Triduana (or Tredwell) was admired by King Nechtan of the Picts, who particularly complimented her eyes. A holy virgin, Triduana responded by gouging out her eyes and offering them, skewered on a stick, to the king. The *Orkneyinga Saga* names her as Trollhoena, which sounds decidedly less Christian, and ascribed healing powers to her and the loch. Either way, in medieval times, pilgrims who were blind or suffered other eye afflictions would visit the waters in the hope of a cure from its magical waters.

The tale inspired a poem by George Mackay Brown, which includes the lines:

> Then, whoever had bruised or blinded eye
> Walked round the shore of Tredwell Loch
> Seven times, sunward,
> And, for the gift of sight
> left a small coin on the chapel step

George Mackay Brown, Orkney Pictures and Poems

The south of the island gets very few visitors indeed but has a rather delightful appeal. The gorgeous sands of **Bothican**, immediately west of New Pier, are fringed by machair. Meanwhile, a short walk east – no more than 15 minutes – along the coast from the pier brings you good views of puffins from May to July either side of a small quarry.

THE HOLM OF PAPAY An island off an island off another island, the Holm of Papay forms a protective arm around the northern cusp of South Wick. Barely half a mile long and even more slender in width, the Holm is easily explored in a couple of hours. The sites to gravitate to are both large Neolithic burial cairns, one located at either end of the Holm. At the southern end of the island lies a **chambered cairn**, dating to around 2000BC (the mound is visible from Papay). You enter through a hatch in the roof. The lengthy entrance passage leads to a central chamber with ten single and two double-side cells. With your torch you can pick out striking Neolithic art of a staccato, or 'pecked' appearance, which includes a carved 'eyebrow' design on top of a lintel which recalls the eyebrow features on the Orkney Venus. One theory suggests that the Holm is linked to the Knap of Howar and that its tombs may have been where the occupants of the Knap would have been laid to rest after death. At the north end of the Holm is a **stalled cairn** that dates to around 3500BC. The latter tomb was more carefully excavated than its southern counterpart; four compartments were identified and contained the remains of eight individuals.

To reach the island, contact the Papay Ranger (page 259) to arrange a boat from the old pier by the Kelp Store. You are usually dropped off and left to explore

12

Distance: 7 miles; time: 3–4hrs
Start/finish: Hostel, Beltane ⊕ HY492516
OS Map: Explorer 464 Westray, Papa Westray, Rousay, Egilsay & Wyre

Papay's small size means that exploring its coastline on foot is a viable option. An added bonus is that the island is one of Orkney's easiest to walk around, thanks to an extensive coastal trail, sheep-nibbled grasses, and plentiful stiles and gates. A good circular option exploring the northern two-thirds heads clockwise from Beltane via North Hill, calling at the Knap of Howar, St Boniface Kirk and the Kelp Store.

From Beltane, head uphill to the central island road and dogleg left following signs to the Knap of Howar. Beyond the Knap, head a mile north to reach St Boniface, then ascend gently to North Hill. Hug the coast where vast, smooth ledges and slabs keep you company. A stone stile grants access over a drystone dyke into the RSPB North Hill reserve. From May to September keep to the coast to avoid disturbing nesting birds including the grumpy bonxie.

Papay's northernmost point exudes an elemental feel; sizeable cliffs flanking Mull Head and the adjacent Fowl Flag drop seawards via further flagstone ledges that resemble giant staircases. Immediately north of Mull Head is the Bore, a strong tidal race where the Atlantic elbows into the North Sea. At times the sea bubbles as if boiled by a huge underwater fire. Cairns here warn you away from cliff edge. Apparent craters are precisely that: hollows created by Royal Navy target practice during World War II.

The route, now over open ground, sweeps clockwise around the headland and turns south. North Hill, surrounded by fiercely contouring and featureless moorland, looks far taller than its modest measurement (157ft/48m). Between North Hill and Berry Hill (to the east) is a small, hidden valley from where you cannot see the sea. One local story tells that Spanish Armada treasure is buried here.

Clambering over a step-stile at Fowl Crag, you reach a cairn and a claret-coloured carving of a great auk – the 'penguin of the northern hemisphere' – staring mournfully out to sea. This represents a moving dedication to the UK's last-known example of this flightless bird, shot nearby in 1813; its mate had been stoned to death on her nest a year earlier. (A few years ago islanders installed a remote-controlled great auk nearby and announced that the species had come back from the brink, triggering newspapers and television crews to book flights to Papay. When the joke unfolded, there was a collective sense of humour failure among the media and several vitriolic and patronising columns about communities on remote islands.) Take care as the Holm of Papay comes into view; smothered with thrift and sea pink in spring, the cliff edges are just rocky, overhanging hags.

Shortly afterwards you encounter two stiles. Take the left-hand one and drop to the shoreline. Follow the path as it comes and goes, then dips to the vast crescent-shaped sands of North Wick. Just before the farm at the far end of the beach, walk up to the road and follow this to South Wick and the Kelp Store. From here, walk uphill along the road then turn right to reach Beltane.

by yourself in the company of sheep from Holland Farm which are left to their own devices (to the extent that they mostly lamb themselves in spring). The open ground is generally pretty rough, particularly over stones from the landing site at South Cruive that lead on to the main part of the Holm. Storm petrels come in to roost and nest at night, and you may catch sight of them departing in the early morning if you stand on the shores of South Wick.

12

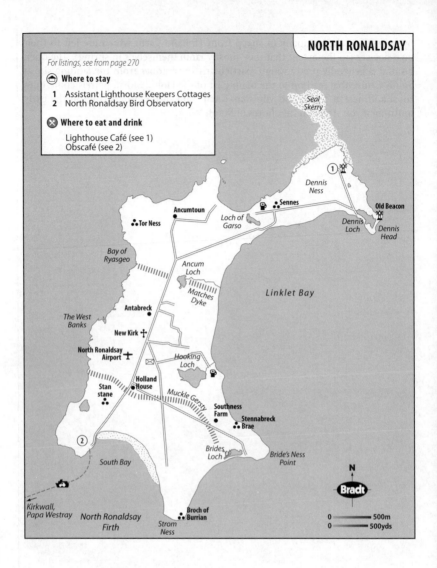

NORTH RONALDSAY

For listings, see from page 270

🛏 **Where to stay**

1 Assistant Lighthouse Keepers Cottages
2 North Ronaldsay Bird Observatory

❌ **Where to eat and drink**

Lighthouse Café (see 1)
Obscafé (see 2)

Seal Skerry

Dennis Ness

① 🗼

Old Beacon

Ancumtoun

Loch of Garso

Sennes

Dennis Loch

Dennis Head

Tor Ness

Bay of Ryasgeo

Ancum Loch

Linklet Bay

Matches Dyke

The West Banks

Antabreck

New Kirk ✝

North Ronaldsay Airport ✈

Hooking Loch

Stan stane

Holland House

Muckle Gersty

Southness Farm

Stennabreck Brae

②

South Bay

Brides Loch

Bride's Ness Point

N

Bradt

Kirkwall, Papa Westray

North Ronaldsay Firth

North Ronaldsay

Strom Ness

Broch of Burrian

0 —— 500m
0 —— 500yds

13

North Ronaldsay

More than anything, it is the silence that strikes you on arrival upon North Ronaldsay. In spring the air may be full of birdsong while autumn brings the cackling of geese. But it is fundamentally the absence of manmade noise that announces to the newly arrived, whether they step off an aircraft or walk away from the ferry pier, that they are on the most remote outpost of an already remote group of islands. Just 3 miles long and 2 miles wide, North Ronaldsay is a pebble on the periphery of Orkney – and one located 34 miles northeast of Kirkwall, 28 miles south of Fair Isle and 50 miles from Shetland. The island may be further north than the southernmost tip of Norway, but thanks to the Gulf Stream, it enjoys a milder climate – windy and wild at times, for sure, but rarely freezing.

A distinct culture has survived here because of this remoteness. You will notice more obviously Orcadian surnames than elsewhere – Cutt, Tulloch, Muir, Scott and so on. The island outline reinforces this feeling of a place apart, with a delectable coast comprising shapely bays that gently evoke islands half a world away in the South Pacific. North Ronaldsay's small size and modest stature – its highest point rises to just 70ft (21m) – means that its light can be particularly striking, bouncing between shallow seas, sandy shores and sky. On sunny days the sand is a brilliant, Caribbean white but even on wet days it is mournfully beautiful. Nights can be equally stirring. With no light pollution the *aurora borealis* puts in regular appearances in late autumn and winter, while the island is awaiting a decision on its application for Dark Skies status.

While the cachet of making it this far is reason enough to visit North Ronaldsay, the island punches above its weight when it comes to attractions. This is the land of the North Ronaldsay sheep, sometimes locally called 'rollies', famous for living almost entirely on the beaches, nourished by a diet of seaweed. They are kept off the heart of the island by a sturdy 13-mile-long, 19th-century stone dyke, thought to be the only structure of such stature in the world.

For wildlife lovers, North Ronaldsay has few equals. Located as the first and last staging post for birds flittering between Arctic breeding grounds and the shelter of more southerly climes, the island bursts with avian activity during spring and summer migration.

HISTORY

The origins of the island's name is a mystery, lost in the North Sea *haar*. It could originate from the Old Norse 'Rinansey'; 'Ringan' was a name by which 'Ninian' was often known, hence the name could mean Ninian's Isle. There is, however, no evidence that St Ninian ever visited, so many historians dismiss the link as guesswork. The present name of North Ronaldsay is quite possibly merely a corruption or misunderstood parallel to South Ronaldsay.

NORTH RONALDSAY'S BIRDS

North Ronaldsay is widely regarded as one of the UK's best places to watch migratory birds, which is why there is a bird observatory stationed here (page 270). The reasons are simple: location and habitat. Positioned in the far north of the Orkney archipelago, the island is firmly on migration routes and landfall here acts as a vital staging post in spring for birds heading north to Iceland, Greenland and Scandinavia; in autumn, there is an astonishing change of shift as these birds all head south to escape the Arctic winter or are shunted westwards by winds emanating from Asia. In between, the island plays host to many species embarking on the race to breed. Similar places are found all along the coasts of Britain but there the birds have a greater choice of locations into which to disperse or disappear: here, there is only North Ronaldsay, surrounded by the open sea, so what drops in will be more concentrated and visible.

Herons and whooper swan can be spotted as well as more than a thousand wintering greylag geese. Wrens thrive in the drystone walls, while rock pipit, wheatear and starling breed in gaps between the dyke's stones. Corncrake is a passage migrant so only rarely can it be heard calling for a mate; the dominance of farming for silage means that crops are cut too soon for the bird to breed. Raptors include kestrel, hen harrier and buzzard, while short-eared and long-eared owls prey on wood mice. Perhaps surprisingly, the island also plays temporary host to many African migrants, from pied flycatcher to garden warbler. Some stay to breed: swallows are doing increasingly well here, with 25 pairs typically nesting. The island also routinely plays host to the occasional avian showstopper: in spring 2017 the first UK sighting of red-winged blackbird occurred here, while a strikingly beautiful Siberian blue robin (only the fourth ever seen in the UK) dropped by that autumn.

The diverse habitats are key: shore and shingle support colonies of breeding Arctic tern and provide good foraging for sanderling and ringed plover. At low tide a large area of rock, seaweed and rock pools is exposed, which provides feeding for further waders such as purple sandpiper, turnstone and redshank.

North Ronaldsay was certainly occupied from Neolithic times but little remains or has been uncovered from that era. Several stone burial cists have been identified, which clearly point to occupation going back several thousand years. These are dotted around the island but none are particularly remarkable; in most cases they are identified as mounds in the ground or a modest higgledy-piggledy jumble of stones, as is the case at Senness (✛ HY775554) at the northern end of Linklet Bay, where a cist containing human remains was excavated in 1872. Other evidence of occupation from prehistoric times include the striking standing stone, Stane Stone, in the south of the island and the landscape of Tor Noss, thought to have once housed a substantial stone circle.

North Ronaldsay was certainly on the radar of the Orkney earls. One harrowing tale recorded by the *Orkneyinga Saga* is of the grisly demise of Halfdan Longlegs, a bit-part player in the Orkney earldoms of the late 9th century. According to the *Saga*, Halfdan killed his father's right-hand man but was subsequently defeated in battle in nearby waters by his victim's son, who happened to be governing Orkney for the Norse king Rognvald Eysteinsson. In retribution, Halfdan was killed by having his ribs cut from his spine and his lungs pulled out though slits cut into his back.

Two large earthen dykes, Matches Dyke and Muckle Gersty, cross the island from west to east. They are unrelated to the drystone sheep dyke, predating it by 800 years. Some archaeologists think that Matches and Muckle were constructed by three brothers who sought to divide the island up between them.

The island was bought by the Traill family in 1727. Their descendants, who still own the island, often spend summers here in the ancestral Holland House.

Kelp-burning was a major industry on the island, beginning in the 1720s before collapsing in the late 19th century and eventually expiring in 1930. An old island saying has it that fishermen could smell North Ronaldsay kelp 'half roads to Foula', the westernmost Shetland island. In the absence of coal and peat on the island, seaweed was burned to heat houses. An unfortunate by-product was arsenic, which found its way into watercourses and food; the resulting poisoning is thought to have been responsible for the island's unusually high historical rates of miscarriage. Today, this 'crop' is still used on the island, applied untreated to the land as a fertiliser, though the arsenic concerns have long since dissipated.

The collapse of the kelp industry triggered an exodus, with people leaving for the Orkney Mainland as well as Canada, the US, Australia and New Zealand. Demographically, North Ronaldsay has never really recovered. In the late 19th century more than 500 people were recorded as living on the island. Today, that figure hovers between 50 and 60.

Before the advent of giant trawlers in the 1970s, cod, ling, saithe and halibut could all be caught offshore by local boats. Today the remnants of this industry survive in small-scale inshore fishing of lobster and crabs. Electricity only arrived on the island in 1983. North Ronaldsay is no island idyll. Living here has always been hard, a fact of economic life demonstrated by plummeting demographics and the startling number of collapsed and abandoned farmsteads that dot the landscape (see box, page 271).

GETTING THERE AND AWAY

BY AIR The Kirkwall–North Ronaldsay route is operated by Loganair and flown in an eight-seater Islander that takes just 21 minutes to make the hop from Kirkwall (three times daily Mon–Sat, twice Sun; £18/36/21 single/day return/excursion fare if you spend at least one night here). The airfield is located to the south of the island, near the west coast. Most passengers walk from the airfield to their accommodation (if it's the bird observatory, the walk takes 25 minutes). If you're travelling light, or at least without a suitcase, you can pick up a bicycle at the airfield to get to your accommodation (page 270).

BY SEA Orkney Ferries runs from Kirkwall to North Ronaldsay (Tue, Fri; takes up to 2hrs 40mins, although add 2hrs for Tue return sailing, which stops at Papa Westray; return fares £39.40/16.40 standard car/passenger). Note that, unless you fly one way, the timetable commits you to three or four nights on the island. Ferries dock at Nouster Pier, in the southwest of the island, a 5-minute walk from the bird observatory.

During high season (late Jun–late Aug) Orkney Ferries runs **Sunday Special Excursions** to North Ronaldsay, allowing the day tripper to spend 4 hours on the island – enough time to visit the bird observatory and perhaps stretch your legs with a brisk walk across the island to the lighthouse.

GETTING AROUND

Given North Ronaldsay's toy-town size and broadly flat topography, most visitors walk or cycle around the island. If you have travelled to Orkney by car, consider leaving it in Kirkwall while you visit the island. A network of single-track lanes – with passing places – runs up and down North Ronaldsay and from east to west, which, along with a handful of farm and field tracks, give access to all points of interest. The walk from the bird observatory to the lighthouse is 2½ miles, which will take most people just over an hour. You can hire bikes from the observatory or just pick one up from the airfield and pay at the observatory. Most of the time there is no need to book these. However, to be sure of a bicycle in July and August you can reserve one (☏ 01857 633297; e bikehire@northronaldsay.co.uk; £8/day, family hire – 4 bikes – £25/day, electric trike £15/day).

There's no island bus but Tommy Muir (☏ 01857 633244) runs an island taxi and hire-car service. A taxi from the airfield to the observatory will cost around £7–8. Car hire usually works out at about £40–50 per day.

TOURIST INFORMATION

There is no tourist information centre, but North Ronaldsay Trust operates a useful website (w northronaldsaytrust.com) and the island website (w northronaldsay.co.uk) covers the latest developments. You can also pick up leaflets at the Bird Observatory (see below).

 ## WHERE TO STAY *Map, page 266*

North Ronaldsay Bird Observatory (10 rooms) Twingness; ☏ 01857 633200; e warden@nrbo.prestel.co.uk; w nrbo.co.uk; ⊕ all year. Privately run operation monitoring the island's avian comings & goings that combines B&B (7 rooms) & hostel (dbl, 2 4-bed; shared facilities & self-catering option). Good levels of comfort, hearty food. B&B rooms all en suite & simply furnished. Terrific views from upstairs, taking in vast seascapes, neighbouring islands & Fair Isle. Sole room on ground floor adapted for travellers with limited mobility. Adjacent space for camping & electric hook-up for vehicles. While the observatory attracts a fair number of hardcore birders, it is not exclusively tailored to them. Warden Alison Duncan & team (a cheery ensemble of assistant wardens & graduate volunteers gaining ornithology experience) make everyone welcome. DBB option available: communal dinner usually a choice of fish or meat (generally North Ronaldsay mutton), though you can order from a wider menu in advance. **££**

Assistant Lighthouse Keepers Cottages (2 properties, sleeping 4/5 people) ☏ 01857 633257; e lighthousecottages@northronaldsay.co.uk; w northronaldsaylighthousecottages.co.uk. One of Orkney's most stunning self-catering. Both cottages beautifully restored with period-piece fittings including open-hearth fires, recessed shelving & tartan furnishings. Only downside is proximity to the foghorn. £600/week in high season. For other self-catering options, visit w northronaldsay.co.uk. **£**

✕ WHERE TO EAT AND DRINK *Map, page 266*

✳ 🖵 **Lighthouse Café** 📞01857 633297; m 07526 629654; e cafe@northronaldsay.co.uk; 🕐 May–Aug 10.30–16.00 daily, 17.00–19.00 Thu–Sat take-aways & home delivery; Sep–Apr times vary, enquire in advance, though usually open Fri. Housed in the Old Principal Lighthouse Keeper's cottage (the second set of buildings in the complex – you need to walk past the first block to reach the café). Excellent café serving homemade bread & toasties, with strong emphasis on local food including North Ronaldsay mutton & Orkney cheeses & breads. Save room for waffles for pudding. Beer & wine list makes good use of Orkney's most northerly licensed premises. **£–££**

🖵 **Obscafé** Same contacts as bird observatory. By day this is a café open to non-residents of the observatory (🕐 noon–14.00 daily) serving soup & sandwiches. In the evening, it becomes a good, invariably sociable bar (the only one on the island; unlike other Orkney isles, North Ronaldsay is not thought historically to have had a pub culture). **£**

REVIVING A COMMUNITY ON THE EDGE OF THE BRITISH ISLES

Many Scottish islands have suffered from depopulation and North Ronaldsay is no exception. The school is currently closed, though it was due to reopen in August 2019 for a single pupil who had reached school age. Yet rather than sit back and watch the community dwindle, islanders have formed the North Ronaldsay Trust with a view to rejuvenating the local economy and attracting incomers to stay.

'It's chicken and egg,' says Alison Duncan, who sits on the trust board. 'We need to provide places to live for people who move here with jobs; but we need jobs for people to come in the first place.' The trust has advertised a full-time role restoring the stone dyke, and other possible developments include a small business park in the old lighthouse buildings that could house a tannery for sheepskins, a chocolate maker and a unit producing sea salt from seaweed. The long-term aim is to restore and reoccupy one house every year for the next 30 years. While this ambition may seem limited, each incremental addition will make a huge difference to the island, says Alison. 'Even if the school has one child, it employs a teacher, classroom assistant and a janitor. That's three jobs.'

In 2018 a BBC television documentary, *The Island That Saved My Life*, focussed on Sarah Moore, who, shy and suffering from depression, moved to North Ronaldsay and swiftly became involved in the island to the extent that she holds down several jobs, including working at the airfield and post office. While the film concentrated on Sarah's story, it perhaps glossed over the point that Sarah's multitasking is far from unique: just about everyone on the island has more than one job. 'Incomes are small, so one job doesn't always make for a viable income,' says Alison.

Alison moved to North Ronaldsay 30 years ago. 'I first came here on holiday by plane. At that time, there wouldn't be another plane for two days, which I loved. We were on our own. There's something magical about the island. I'm optimistic about the future. Living on a small island is not everyone's cup of tea, but there is so much here if you are the right person.'

North Ronaldsay WHERE TO EAT AND DRINK

13

North Ronaldsay offers you some splendid walking; in particular it is possible to walk right around the island, a distance of 13 miles. The terrain along this coastal route is a mixed bag: most of the west coast is reasonably easy to negotiate as are the flatlands around Tor Ness in the northwest. Also straightforward are the long stretches of beach. The pick is probably Linklet Bay on the east coast and its attendant greensward, which is best accessed from the lane heading east from Antabreck in the middle of the island. On the other hand, the southeast corner, around Strom Ness and Bride's Ness Point, requires a little more effort in the form of clambering over rocks and slabs that can be slippery after rain.

You could complete a circuit of the island in 3–4 hours, though to do so would arguably be to miss the point of doing such a walk. Instead, an easy stroll of 6–8 hours would allow you time to perhaps pause for a picnic overlooking the Bay of Ryasgeo, to sit on the sands overlooking Linklet Bay watching eider ducks feeding in the sheltered shallows or gannets diving further offshore, or to choose a spot near the lighthouse to watch the seals come and go as Seal Skerry, mostly submerged at high tide, reveals itself on the ebb. Alternatively, you can walk part of the coast and then use the many lanes and tracks to zigzag your way back to either the pier or the observatory, as the mood takes you.

SHOPPING

ObShop North Ronaldsay Bird Observatory; 01857 633200; ⊕ noon–14.00 Mon & Wed–Sun, noon–16.00 Tue, shorter hours in winter. Well stocked with everything for the larder from milk to tinned vegetables and ice cream. Also has a wide choice of branded observatory clothing, including polo shirts, hoodies & toys. In practice opening hours are flexible & should you arrive late someone at the observatory will open up for you to buy milk & basics.

OTHER PRACTICALITIES

There's no bank on the island but the observatory shop gives cashback.

✚ **Doctor** Linklet House 01857 633226
✉ **Post office** Roadside; ⊕ 10.00–noon Mon & Wed–Fri, 14.00–16.00 Tue

Petrol Hooking Loch & Garso. Few visitors bring a car to the island. but if you do need fuel contact Tommy Muir (01857 633244) to arrange topping up the tank.

WHAT TO SEE AND DO

North Ronaldsay's most conspicuous sight will track your every move on the island – the drystone wall that runs just inland from almost the entire North Ronaldsay coastline and thus frames the horizon. Made from local stone, the wall was built in 1832, at a time of considerable economic downturn after the collapse of the kelp industry, to confine the sheep to foreshore. Its height of up to 6ft is enough to deter even the most energetic 'louper' (jumping sheep). Historic Environment Scotland has described the dyke as 'probably the longest drystone construction conceived of as a single entity in the world.'

Procedures for maintaining the integrity of the dyke were laid down by the North Ronaldsay Sheep Court, established in 1839. The court remains the regulatory body to this day and maintenance continues to be undertaken communally by those whose farmland abuts the wall.

THE SOUTH Positioned among the crofts of Twingness and Lurand in the southwest of the island, conveniently close to Nouster Pier (where the Kirkwall ferry arrives), the North Ronaldsay Bird Observatory (page 270) is worth visiting for updates on what species are passing through. It is a good place to break any walking tour you may be making of the island.

The observatory is positioned on the western edge of **South Bay**, a gorgeous stretch of sand curving in a crescent for half a mile along the southern tip of the island. You will almost certainly see both harbour and grey seals hauled out here. The beach is also popular as a 'run' for the sheep, which dash past you as the tide retreats in pursuit of freshly exposed seaweed to nibble. (Sheep are not the only herbivores here: look inland at the eastern end of the bay and you will see, a little surreally perhaps, an alpaca farm.) The eastern end of the bay is capped by Strom Ness Point, where you will find the Broch of Burrian. This tower was excavated in the 1880s and identified as a centrepiece of an extensive Iron Age settlement complete with underground chambers. What remains of the broch has its back to the interior of the island, protected by earthworks and a grassy mound; from the seaward side, it is more substantial and impressive, rising in a semicircle with stonework up to 10ft in height.

North Ronaldsay was occupied by the Picts and distinctively Christian objects were found here, foremost among them the Burrian Cross, just over 2ft long, with a cross carved to one side, whose location appears to accommodate the accompanying Ogham script (an early medieval alphabet used to write early Irish language). While the cross is now housed in the National Museum of Scotland it has left an indelible imprint on Orkney where it has inspired 1,001 jewellery designs.

SAVING THE WALL

Much of the island population helped in the arduous task of building the drystone dyke but over the years maintaining it has proved even more exacting. The future of the wall is uncertain. Climate change, with its attendant fiercer storms and higher seas, is making maintenance of the dyke ever harder. Recent tempests have greatly damaged the dyke along the east coast – and not all of it has been restored to robust health. Although the wall is listed Grade A (a local authority-level listing system of a building's historical, cultural or architectural importance) by Historic Environment Scotland, it is highlighted in Scotland's 'Buildings At Risk Register'. In 2015, the Orkney Sheep Foundation (w theorkneysheepfoundation.org.uk) was established with the aim of securing the future of both the dyke and sheep. While the sheep remain in high demand for their USP of a seaweed diet, this status could be jeopardised if the wall were to crumble. A festival (w nrsheepfestival.com) was held for the first time in 2016 and was so successful that it has been held every year since, usually in late July and early August. Volunteers help restore sections of the drystone dyke, and other activities include wool workshops and traditional island dancing. Visitors are welcome to attend.

13

A mile or so north of the broch – but best reached via the island road network rather than the coast – is the modest rise of **Stennabreck Brae** (✛ HY770527), whose lumpy summit is peppered with a cluster of small stone huts. The hill itself is thought to be at least partly manmade, arising from centuries of accumulated settlement deposits. An excavation in 1883 rummaged around the mound, identifying it as 'prehistoric', but yielding few particularly useful clues. You can reach the brae along the lane that runs southeast of Hooking Loch. Pass the collapsed windmill and Southness Farm and, 100yds after the turfed house on the left, the brae is visible to the left; take the clear grassy track here north to reach it.

Just south of the airfield, in a field west of the road to the bird observatory, you cannot miss the striking monolith known as the '**stan stane**', or standing stone. Rising 13ft high, this slender stone – just 3ft wide – is perforated with a hole in its 'midriff'.

Theories abound as to the provenance and original purpose of the stone. The hole may have been a sighting hole for another stone or a celestial event, or the stone itself an outlier for a stone circle that stood on Tor Ness in the northeast of the island. A further theory suggests that the stone and the now-invisible Tor Ness complex somehow combined to make a primitive calendar. Dip into Orkney's vast compendium of folktales, however, and the stane was made by a giant woman who found the stone on the beach, stuck her finger through it, went on to the land and planted it in the ground. Whatever the provenance, the stone has for centuries been part of a local tradition whereby islanders gathered round it on New Year's Day and sang songs.

A short dogleg north up the central island road from the stane is **Holland House**. This is still owned by the direct descendants of the Traill family, and was used by RAF personnel during World War II. From the road you can see three cannons, retrieved from a 1744 shipwreck, pointing south towards the sea. The house and gardens are not open to the public but the grounds represent North Ronaldsay's only (modest) woodland and despite its small size the trees here are a magnet for birds. In spring and autumn you are likely to see ringers from the observatory here seeking to monitor avian arrivals and departures.

BIRD NETS

The observatory is surrounded by what, to the non-birder, appear to be mysterious nets, as if someone has half-assembled a garden trampoline. These are in fact mist-nets, which play a key role in the collection of information on the numbers, health and direction of passage birds. The birds fall harmlessly into pockets in the nets, from which they are extracted for 'ringing', whereby individually numbered lightweight metal bands are placed around a bird's leg. Should a ringed bird be retrapped, its movements can be tracked. The observatory has used such methods to record data on weight, physical condition, age and sex of more than 75,000 birds of more than 200 species since 1987. Put all this together and you have an invaluable insight into the state of the birds that come to the UK. This is all the more important given the pressures that birds face from habitat loss, hunting and climate change around the UK and far beyond. It's worth mentioning that not every naturalist agrees with ringing. Some argue that the practice impairs and delays the ability of a tired migrant bird to rest and refuel after an arduous journey. Moreover, capture-related deaths and injuries do occur, though they are very uncommon.

North Ronaldsay is one of two sets of Scottish islands (the other is the Uists) to have endured intense conflict between conservationists and everybody's favourite bundle of animal magnetism – the hedgehog.

In 1972, a postman brought two hedgehogs to North Ronaldsay, releasing them in an attempt to control slugs; by 1986, surveys suggested that the population might be as many as 400–600 animals. Hedgehogs were put firmly in the frame, suspected of causing the failure of the island's colony of Arctic terns and ringed plovers, so the decision was taken by islanders to capture North Ronaldsay's hedgehogs and move them to the Mainland. Over a few years, around 180 animals were translocated. Although the hedgehogs were certainly implicated in munching birds' eggs, it seems they were not the only factor. Conservationists concluded that a dramatic shortage of sand eels, in the case of the terns, was primarily responsible for the birds' decline. The hedgehogs' impact, while not negligible, was secondary.

Some 600yds north of Holland House, just north of the war memorial, the **New Kirk** functions as a heritage archive. The emphasis is less on a chronological narrative of island history but rather on a moving and sizeable collection of photographs of island life: families cycling up lanes, fishermen hauling up their boats, horses ploughing fields. Many of the images date to the 1940s and 1950s but look as though they could have been taken a century earlier.

THE NORTH Located at the northeast extremity of Orkney (making it the first land sighted by seafarers headed from Shetland, Fair Isle and Norway), North Ronaldsay has offered a welcoming beacon in the form of a lighthouse since 1789. The Stevenson family had a hand in both the original 18th-century beacon and its 19th-century successor, which remains in place today.

The modern lighthouse was built in 1854 at Dennis Head, 3 miles from the observatory (an hour's walk or 20-minute cycle). This is a beacon of no little stature and, at 109ft, is the UK's tallest land-based lighthouse. Tours (m 07703 112224; e lighthousetours@northronaldsay.co.uk; ⊕ times vary, call ahead or email; £6/3, £2 if combined with a wool mill tour) are conducted by Billy Muir, who has been the lighthouse keeper for 50 years. On a busy day he will hail you from the top of the tower to climb up and meet him. As you wheeze your way up the 176 steps and past seven windows, you appreciate that Billy is understandably reluctant to meet and greet every visitor at ground level.

You are paying for the view, which is among the best Orkney has to offer. On a clear day with binoculars you can pick out the hills of Hoy and, closer by, all the North Isles. On a cloudless night, the light, which flashes every 10 seconds, can be seen from Wideford Hill to the west of Kirkwall. To the north, in line with the foghorn, Fair Isle lies 28 miles distant, with Sumburgh Head on Shetland beyond. Informally, upon request, Billy will also open up the lighthouse at night: on a clear night, this is an astonishing experience as every few seconds the perfect darkness is scattered by light thrown across what feels like the whole of Orkney.

The former engine room at the new lighthouse complex has been redecorated and converted into a working **woollen mill**, operated by A Yarn from North Ronaldsay (m 07768 201651; e woolmilltours@northronaldsay.co.uk; w northronaldsayyarn. co.uk; 20-min tours cost £6/3 or £2 when combined with a lighthouse tour).

13

The powerful waters and notorious, hidden reefs of North Ronaldsay Firth have claimed many ships, particularly around Seal Skerry to the north, where at least five wrecks lurk. Among the earliest recorded wreck was the *Svecia*, a Swedish East Indiaman that grounded on the Reef Dyke, just south of the island, in 1740. Ninety hands were lost along with a cargo of gold coins, porcelain and sandalwood. The tragedy almost bankrupted the Swedish East India Company.

Operational in 1789, the Old Beacon was one of the first four lighthouses commissioned in Scotland. The need for it was driven in part by the island's position on the Far East shipping route from northern Europe (Britain's wars with France meant that the English Channel was a place to be avoided at that time). Built to a height of 65ft, it was constructed under the supervision of engineer Thomas Smith, who was assisted by his stepson, one Robert Stevenson, who subsequently founded the family dynasty of lighthouse builders. This was, perhaps, not his finest hour. Ships still kept being wrecked, partly because in poor visibility captains would mistake the beacon for the light of a ship in safe harbour. The decision to decommission was made in 1806 and, to avoid confusion with a new lighthouse at Start Point on Sanday, the original oil lamps and copper reflectors were replaced by a stone ball, which is still in place today.

You can follow the process from finessing the raw material through to the finished yarn, ready to be turned into everything from ornamental toys to tasteful sweaters. The natural colours of the sheep range from white to ash-grey, and brown to black, so the raw material can be mixed to produce variegated yarns.

Adjacent to the woollen mill, the **North Ronaldsay Visitor Centre** (housed in the same building as the Lighthouse Café; ⊕ same hours) has two rooms dedicated to excellent accounts of island life and the history of the lighthouses. A small shop sells cups, T-shirts, woollen goods and other souvenirs.

Some 600yds south of this complex lies the **Old Beacon**, the predecessor to the modern lighthouse. Made from undressed stone, it is a Grade-A-listed building, located at the end of a gracious curve of shingle and foreshore. The Old Beacon is closed: the staircase was taken out in the 19th century to prevent people entering and has never been replaced. The land in between the two lighthouses is visually striking, with the remains of several kelp pits hugging the shoreline. This area is the only chunk of common land on North Ronaldsay and you can see the remnants here of small, square enclosures known as crues, which served as miniature walled gardens, allowing islanders to grow cabbages and other vegetables. This is also one of the few parts of the island where the dyke cuts inland and, accordingly, the grass here is nibbled to resemble a billiard table. Somewhere here, though never identified with certainty, are said to lie the remains in a Norse Grave of Halfdan Longlegs (page 268).

On the shore by the Old Beacon you will usually see a slender boat, which is the only existing example of a North Ronaldsay *praam* (a small fishing boat). The *praam* was adapted from a Norwegian design and favoured because its long bow and small keel made it manoeuvrable and easy to haul out.

Head a little under 2 miles west along the island road from the lighthouse and you reach Tor Ness, North Ronaldsay's northwest corner. This can be a hauntingly beautiful place, a stark plateau painted in green and grey tones that drops down

SHEEP AND THE SEASHORE

The spectacle of sheep foraging on the beach is probably the single most vibrant image you will take away from a visit to North Ronaldsay. On most beaches, the retreating tide signals the arrival of wading birds such as sanderling and redshank. On North Ronaldsay they are joined by the sheep.

They are classified as a rare breed, and exhibit small upright ears, short tails and concave or 'dished' noses. Their remarkable longevity is attributed to the many antioxidants found in their preferred diet of seaweed. Red dulce is their favoured foodstuff, but they will graze grass at high tide. They are also known to scavenge the feet of washed-up seabirds.

The sheep's precise origins are much debated. They may have arrived during the Iron Age, with Vikings subsequently replenishing the stock. However, recent DNA tests suggest a close match with the primordial north European short-tailed sheep (excavated at Skara Brae); might an almost pure lineage be on display here?

Originally the sheep were kept on grass inland and provided meat for islanders to eat rather than to sell offshore. All this changed during the 19th century when crofters considered grazing cattle to be more profitable. The sheep rebelled at their subsequent confinement to small fields, leaping barriers to rejoin the promised land of grasses that lay beyond. In response, they were banished to the shoreline and the drystone dyke (see box, page 273) built around the island.

At their peak 2,500 sheep inhabited the island; following recent sales, the number has dropped to 2,000. Both meat and fleeces are highly prized (so much so that flocks are managed off-island, including on Auskerry and Linga Holm, to enable restocking should disease ravage the North Ronaldsay sheep). Their diet produces a distinctive 'gamey' flavour – from the iodine contained in seaweed – and a lean carcass. The fleece, meanwhile, is double coated, with soft insulating hair close to the skin and longer coarse hair layered on top. This means that clipping must wait for the lith (the gap between the old and new fleece) to rise.

In perhaps one of the last remaining examples of communal farming in western Europe, husbandry is an undertaking shared by all sheep-owning islanders in return for their sheep being allowed to graze the beach. The sheep resolutely refuse to be herded by sheepdogs, simply scattering instead. Instead they are 'pounded', being pursued at high tide along the shoreline and corralled into stone-built pens, or punds. This happens three or four times a year (usually April, early July, September and October) for lambing, shearing, castrating and, in autumn, for slaughter. If you're on the island around these times, the spectacle is definitely worth taking in – you may even be invited to help by closing a pen or two.

In 2018, the closure of Kirkwall abattoir briefly threatened the flock's existence, as it was uneconomic (as well as stressful for the sheep) to send them to slaughter in Caithness (northern Scotland). Fortunately, a financially viable arrangement was made to transport sheep to a Shetland abattoir, although some may be uncomfortable at transporting sheep overnight across open seas.

13

NORTH RONALDSAY ROCK POOLS

If you haven't explored a tidal rock pool lately, head to the North Ronaldsay beaches, which boast many hundreds of marine and littoral plants and animals. The West Banks, South Bay, Tor Ness and Linklet Bay all offer fine rock-pooling. While limpets, whelks and *spoot* shells (razorshells) are washed up by the tide, you may find brittle stars and starfish if you lift up a rock or two. The tide also strands small jellyfish on the shore in late summer while pipefish are sometimes thrown on to shore by rough weather.

on to vast slab-like and wave-pummelled Rousay flagstones. The best way to access Tor Ness is from the farm track (⊕ HY763554), which leaves the single-track paved road at Ancumtoun. The landscape is interspersed with the occasional boulder and, as you turn south along the west coast at Tor Ness, you pass some 15 circular depressions, up to 30ft in diameter. These are believed to be either barrow mounds or kelp-burning pits. It's thought a stone circle once stood here, though little evidence remains today.

ORKNEY ONLINE

For additional online content, articles, photos and more on Orkney, why not visit **w** bradtguides.com/orkney?

Appendix 1

LANGUAGE

While everyone in Orkney speaks English, a few words of Orcadian will go down extremely well locally and may even lead to you being sat down in a pub or passing a whole ferry journey while learning different words and expressions. The nature and origins of Orcadian mean that it is not a formal language. As Dr Simon Hall, author of *The Orkney Gruffalo*, points out: 'you can't teach Orcadian the way you can teach French'. Nevertheless, a few words and phrases will come in handy. As good an insight into Orcadian as anything can be gained from getting hold of Dr Hall's book, in which the ways in which Orcadian differs from English – at a basic level – become immediately apparent. Translated by Dr Hall, this charming children's classic opens with the lines: 'A moose teuk a dander through the grimly trees/A fox saa the moose, an thowt You'll feed me!'

GUIDE TO PRONUNCIATION Many words in Orcadian are entirely different from English, eg: 'tirrie' ('petulant'), 'pivver' ('to vibrate', or 'to shake') and 'fuffle' ('to work clumsily'); meanwhile words that are the same or similar are pronounced differently: 'bread', 'head' and 'dead' become 'breid', 'heid' and 'deid' and 'arm' becomes 'erm'; 'over' becomes 'ower'. Meanwhile 'tall' is pronounced 'taal', 'wall' becomes 'waal' or 'wa', 'neither' becomes 'nither', 'mother' is pronounced 'mither' (and 'father', 'faether'). And 'mouth' and 'town' become 'mooth' and 'toon', respectively.

A FEW BASICS Plurals can occasionally differ from English: the Orcadian plural for 'horses' is 'horse'; but the plural of 'peat' is 'peats'.

When it comes to grammar, it will help to understand a few words that you will recognise but which have a different function in Orcadian. For example, it can help to know how to conjugate the verb 'to be': 'I'm' is 'Ah'm'; 'you're', 'thoo're'; 'he's', 'he's' (ie: the same); 'we're', 'wir'; 'you're', 'yir'; 'they're', 'thir'. The last is also used to mean 'there is' and 'there are'. An elementary understanding of the Orcadian language (or dialect) will also shed light on the landscape you are looking at, as about 99% of place names are of Norse origin, as are topographical features.

SOME USEFUL WORDS The following is merely a handful of words that can come in handy together with others that are unique to Orcadian and which, as language so often does, provide insights into the sorts of things that require expression in any given culture.

Pronouns

me	me, my	thur	their
mesael	myself	ye	you
thoo	you	dae	do
thee	your	na	no

o	of	whit	what
ither	other	wur	our
tae	to		

Orkney life

andoo	row a boat against the wind or tide so that it retains its position	muckle	big
		neep	turnip
		nuik	small enclosed place or nook
auld, owld	old	peedie	small
bairn	child	pund	enclosure for holding
besmilk	the milk of a cow newly calved		animals, eg: North Ronaldsay sheep
		reel	dance
cleg	horsefly	rudge	the rattle of pebbles on a
closs	narrow passage between two buildings (a particular feature of Stromness)		beach (less enchantingly, of mucus in the throat)
		servant	farm labourer
coo	cow (plural: kye)	sharn	cow dung that sticks to
cubbie	straw basket		trousers, field gates or shovels
flattie	a small, flat-bottomed boat	skreever	howling gale
frootery	witchcraft	sookan	straw rope twisted in a
furtiver	whatever, in any case		single strand
gaan	going	spoot	razor clam
gablo	crawling insect	stook	set of six sheaves of wheat
gimmer	a young ewe		left in a field to dry
gowster	gale, strong wind	tattie	potato
gyte	crazy	tattie-bogle	scarecrow (in the North
hashie	choppy (as in sea)		Isles, this role is invariably
hoose	house		performed by a collapsed
ladeberry	rocky shelf functioning as a pier, often seen, sometimes incorporated in place names		car)
		teebro	heat haze on a warm day
		trimse	agitated, moving from one
lowse	unsettled (weather)		leg to another, as though
louper	North Ronaldsay sheep that has jumped over the wall from the beach back into fields		needing the toilet
		tusker	peat-cutting tool
		whamsy	seasick
		wheou	sound of wind rushing
maagse	to walk with some difficulty through thick mud		through gaps in the door
		yole	a traditional Orkney fishing
mairch stone	boundary stone		boat, with twin masts but
manse	dwelling house of the minister of the church		with no deck
merrie-dancers	northern lights		

Geographical terms

ass	ridge (eg: Backarass on Westray)	ayre	strip of seawater almost completely cut off from ocean by narrow neck of land
ay	island, suffix attached to most Orkney islands, in the form of 'ay' (eg: Eday) and 'a' (eg: Flotta); from Old Norse 'ey'		
		berry	rock (from 'berg')
		bister	dwelling place
		bratta, bratt	steep

bú	Old Norse for great hall	oyce	saltwater lagoon enclosed by a shingle spit, eg: Tankerness; from the Old Norse 'oss'
burn	a stream		
calf	refers to small islands next to larger ones (rather than any reference to livestock on them), eg: Calf of Eday; from Old Norse 'kalf-ey'		
		quoy (sometimes queena)	an area of enclosed and cultivated common pasture; one of the most common appendages to place names in Orkney. Pronounced 'kwee' on the Mainland, 'kwoi' in some other places, eg: Westray
clett	rock		
dalr	dale (eg: Rendall)		
detter	stream, running water		
evie	backwater or eddy, from Old Norse 'efja'		
fea, fell, fiold	hill, from Old Norse 'fjall'	rost, or roost	a treacherous tide, or meeting of currents, such as off the north coast of Papa Westray
firth	fjord, sea loch		
fors, furs	waterfall		
geo	narrow incision into coastline		
		scalp, scap	ship, from Old Norse 'skalp'
gill	stream or valley	setter	dwelling place, house
gloup	deep hole to the sea near cliffs, from Old Norse 'glufr'	skaill	hall-house; important Norse building, which served both a residential and an administrative purpose
hafn, hamn, haven	harbour		
hamar	rock or crag	skal, skel	soft rock
haugr, howe	mound (eg: Maeshowe)	sker, skerry	rocky islet, outcrop
hesta, hesti	horse or stallion	string	strong current (the water between the Mainland and Shapinsay is called The String)
holm	small, flat island, eg: Lamb Holm (home to the Italian Chapel)		
hoolie	gale or high winds	swilkie	whirlpool. You will sail over a swilkie if you cross the Pentland Firth from Gill's Bay to St Margaret's Hope
hop, hope	shallow bay		
housa	house		
howe	barrow, from Old Norse 'haugr'		
		taing	tongue, or spit of land
kampr, kame	ridge or crest	toft, taft	abandoned site of house, from Old Norse 'topt'
knap	knob or bump, often used with place names, eg: Knap of Howar		
		ton, town	hedge creating an enclosure, from Old Norse 'tun'
kuml	burial mound	toumal	field belonging to a dwelling
lang	long	twatt	piece of land, clearing
links	sandy ridges near sea	vardi	beacon, watchtower, now 'ward' (eg: Ward Hill), the name given to (usually) the highest hills on Orkney islands
mae	sand dune, stretch of sand		
mire, myrr	marsh or bog		
mullar	gravel beach		
ness	point of land		
noup	peak	vat	lake
noust	a scooped-out hollow near the shore (usually banked up with stones) where a boat can be safely hauled out above the high-tide mark	voe	small bay, sheltered inlet of the sea, from Old Norse 'vagr'
		wick	bay, from the Old Norse 'vik'

Appendix 2

GLOSSARY OF ARCHAEOLOGICAL TERMS

broch	Iron Age tower made from stone. Purpose was unclear but may have served as food stores or even simply as statements of power.
brough	naturally defensive headland
but and ben	typical Orcadian dwelling, usually dating from the 17th century onwards. Outer room/kitchen served as the 'but', the living quarters as the 'ben'; 'ben-end' is also a general term for the best room of a house.
burnt mounds	small structures with mounds of burnt stone, usually adjacent to running water. Purposes may have included heating food and perhaps serving as saunas.
burial mound (also barrow, tumulus)	mound of earth covering grave, resembling a hillock. Usually relates to Bronze Age sites.
cairn	a heap of stones
chambered cairn	a Neolithic, single, large burial chamber, reached by a low, long entrance passage. Several side chambers branch off from the central chamber. Usually covered with a cairn. Also called Maeshowe-type cairns.
cist	stone coffin or burial chamber, pronounced 'kist'
crannog	Iron Age fortified settlement, built on artificial islands
gavel-end	Orcadian term for the gable of a house
grooved ware	one of two distinct styles of Neolithic pottery (the other is Unstan ware, qv). Distinctively flat-bottomed and highly decorated; created by grooves scoured using stone implements.
henge	a level circular platform of earth defined by a ditch and usually with an external bank. There can be one or two entrances, and many (but not all) have been embellished with circles of standing stones.
megalith	huge, single standing stone, possibly also a component of a tomb. You also hear talk of 'megalithic' tombs or circles, which means they are composed of large stones.
midden	an area used for rubbish disposal. Yields from mounds of such decomposed refuse provide important clues as to diet of prehistoric peoples.
ogham	a form of writing known to be used by the Picts and dating to the 1st century AD to inscribe stone slabs and personal objects
passage grave	as the name suggests, a stone tomb entered by a low passageway that leads to one or several chambers where bodies were placed
ragstones	stones set on edge on top of a wall
runes	angular lettering in the form of scratched symbols on stone, bone and wood. Introduced by the Vikings.

stalled cairn	Neolithic tomb typically comprising a single entrance chamber divided by upright slabs into stalls on either side. You will sometimes hear these referred to as Orkney-Cromarty cairns.
steeden	Orcadian term for farm buildings/steadings
Unstan ware	Neolithic style of pottery, typically shaped with rounded bottoms and decoration around the rim. Takes its name from the stalled cairn at Unstan, south of Maeshowe and Stenness.

SEND US YOUR SNAPS!

We'd love to follow your adventures using our *Orkney* guide – why not tag us in your photos and stories via Twitter (🐦 @BradtGuides) and Instagram (📷 @bradtguides)? Alternatively, you can upload your photos directly to the gallery on the Orkney destination page via our website (w bradtguides.com/orkney).

Appendix 3

FURTHER READING

BOOKS Orkney boasts a rich literary heritage that dates back to the *Orkneyinga Saga* (see box, page 35), circa early 13th century. The following list of recommended titles is far from exhaustive but all have been personally read by the author. They will hopefully give insights into the breadth of subjects covered by Orcadian writers as well as those from beyond the islands' shores.

The best place for book browsing is The Orcadian Bookshop on Albert Street in Kirkwall (page 119). The bookshop is owned by the Orkney Media Group, which regularly publishes a wide range of uniformly excellent books on history, wildlife, island life and culture as well as local fiction. Stromness Books and Prints (page 81) on Graham Place in Stromness is another excellent outlet. The specialist publisher Birlinn (w birlinn.co.uk) also boasts a broad range of Orkney-themed literature.

Archaeology

Barnes, Michael *The Norn Language of Orkney and Shetland* Shetland Times, 1998 and Barnes, Michael *The Runic Inscriptions of Maeshowe, Orkney* Uppsala Universitet, 1994. Two works by the world's leading expert on Norse runes, remarkably accessible given the depth and complexity of the subject matter.

Dowswell, Paul & Fleming, Fergus *Stone Age Sentinel* Usborne, 2005. *Horrible Histories*–style stampede through the Stone Age. Good one for children.

Orkneyinga Saga: The History of the Earls of Orkney. Translated by Herman Palsson. Penguin Classics, 1981.

Wickham-Jones, Caroline *Monuments of Orkney* Historic Environment Scotland, 2014. The best basic pre-reading to enlighten you about both the main and less-heralded sites on Orkney.

Wickham-Jones, Caroline *Orkney: A Historical Guide* Birlinn, 2015. More in-depth title but still extremely accessible and lucid.

Wickham-Jones, Caroline *Between the Wind and the Water: World Heritage Orkney* Windgather Press, 2015. More discursive approach to archaeological themes, placing sites in historical and social context.

Fiction

Bailey, Sara *Dark Water* Blackbird, 2016. Moving tale of a woman whose return to her native Orkney to care for an ailing father rakes up forgotten memories.

Barnby, Gabrielle *The Oystercatcher Girl* Thunderpoint, 2017. Tracks the relationships in Kirkwall between a recently deceased man and three women.

Bryce, B K *Maeshowe Murders* Neverton Publishing, 2017. A Neolithic whodunnit by a local author.

Hall, Simon *The Orkney Gruffalo* Itchy Coo, 2015. Children's classic recounted in Orcadian. Also *The Orkney Gruffalo's Bairn*.

Mackay Brown, George *Beside the Ocean of Time* John Murray, 1994. Fantastical novel set in 1930s Orkney, shortlisted for the Booker Prize.

Mackay Brown, George *Six Lives of Frankie the Cat* Floris Books, 2002. Children's classic that shows the breadth of Mackay Brown's writings.

Scott, Sir Walter *The Pirate* Elibron Classics, 1822. Inspired by the author's visit to Orkney and the villainous actions of Eday pirate John Gow.

History

McGoogan, Ken *Fatal Passage: The story of John Rae, the Arctic Hero that Time Forgot* Bantam, 2002. Detailed account of Rae's dramatic expeditions.

Thomson, William P L *Orkney Land and People* Orcadian Ltd, 2008. In-depth social and historical account by an acclaimed historian.

Thomson, William P L *The New History of* Orkney Birlinn, 2008. The definitive history, once reviewed as 'the book of the century so far as Orkney is concerned'.

Tulloch, Peter *A Window on North Ronaldsay* Orcadian Ltd, 1995. Definitive account of life and times on Orkney's northernmost isle.

Wilson, Bryce *Graemsay: A History* Orcadian Ltd, 2015. Riveting tales of lairds, fishermen and gold-diggers on a small Orkney island with a big history.

Wilson, Bryce *Stromness: A History* Orcadian Ltd, 2013. Account of the town from its 16th-century origins.

Island life

Allardyce, Keith *Silent I & Silent II* Orcadian Ltd, 2016–17. Two fine photographic and slightly dystopian records of Orkney's deserted buildings.

Flanagan, Dave *Board* Fledgling Press, 2015. Engaging true account of an Orcadian overcoming his fear of the sea by learning to surf.

Hebden, Rosemary *Eday, Orkney's Best Kept Secret* Carrick Press, 2008. Lovingly written and passionate account of this much-overlooked island.

Hewitson, Jim *Clinging to the Edge, Journals from an Orkney Island* Mainstream, 1996. Entertaining and insightful vignettes of life on Papay.

Liptrot, Amy *The Outrun* Canongate, 2018. Uncompromising account by an Orcadian who returns to her roots to address her alcoholism.

Long, Patricia *The Heart of Stromness: Stories My Mother Told Me* Self-published, 2017. Engaging narrative of early 20th-century stories handed down through a family.

Mackay Brown, George *For the Islands I Sing* Polygon, 2008. Insightful memoir, published posthumously, according to the great man's instructions.

Mackay Brown, George *Letters from Hamnavoe* Savage Publishers, 2013. Lively, sometimes spiky, compendium of 25 years' worth of Mackay Brown's weekly column for *The Orcadian*.

Mackintosh W R *Around the Orkney Peat Fires* Orcadian Ltd, 1999. Short stories of press gangs, smugglers and witches.

Molberg, Gunnie *A Swedish Orcadian* Orcadian Ltd, 2016. Anthology of striking images by an adopted Orcadian photographer.

Muir, Tom *The Mermaid Bride and other Orkney Folk Tales* Orcadian Ltd, 1998; also *Orkney Folk Tales*, History Press, 2014. Recounting of a mixture of engaging and edgy folk tales, only some of which you'd read to the kids.

Muir, Tom & Irvine, James *George Marwick: Yesnaby's Master Storyteller* Orcadian Ltd, 2014. Captivating and sometimes rum anthology of late 19th-century tales and traditions.

Park, Janette A *Simmans, Sookins and Straw-Backed Chairs: Orkney Arts and Crafts* Orkney Arts, Museums and Heritage, 2017. More of a booklet but excellent, offering a fascinating insight into Orkney's relationship with the Arts and Crafts movement.

Language

Flaws, Margaret & Lamb, Gregor *The Orkney Dictionary* Orkney Language & Culture Group, 2005. Essential guide for those seeking to decode – or deploy – a smattering of the Orcadian dialect.

Hall, Simon *The History of Orkney Literature* Birlinn, 2010. Excellent and accessible guide to Orkney's substantial canon of literature.

Natural history

Dean, Tim & Bignall, Anne *The Orkney Book of Wildflowers* Orcadian Ltd, 2014. Definitive guide to Orcadian fauna and flora, with incisive text by Dean and eye-catching illustrations by Bignall.

Flowers, Margaret & Woodford, Bridget *Teoos and Tea Flooers* Beautifully illustrated book on the provenance of Orcadian names for local birds and plants. Out of print but worth enquiring at secondhand bookshops.

Holloway, John *To Fair Isle and Back* Piggott Printers, 1990. Wonderful book about birdwatching on Stronsay, beautifully illustrated by the author.

Other Bradt titles For a full list of Bradt's UK guides, see w bradtguides.com/shop.

Greig, Donald & Flint, Darren *Dumfries and Galloway* 2015.

Rowe, Mark *Outer Hebrides* 2017.

Poetry

Ferguson, Maggie *George Mackay Brown, The Life* John Murray, 2006. Comprehensive biography of one of Scotland's – and Orkney's – finest 20th-century poets.

Mackay Brown, George *Collected Poems* John Murray, 2006. Edited by Archie Bevan and Brian Murray. Definitive anthology.

Muir, Edwin *Selected Poems* Faber & Faber, 2008. Good introduction to the work of the Wyre-born poet.

Walking and guides

Fergusson, John *Orkney: 40 Coast & Country Walks* Pocket Mountains, 2016.

Martin, Felicity *Walks Orkney* Hallewell 2016.

Tait, Charles *The Orkney Guidebook* Charles Tait, 2012. Covers the main and lesser-visited archaeological and historical sites of the islands.

Wartime

Konstam, Angus *Scapa Flow: The Defences of Britain's Great Fleet Anchorage 1914–1915* Osprey, 2009. The best generalist guide to the wartime role and events of Scapa Flow.

McCutcheon, Campbell *The Ships of Scapa Flow* Amberley, 2013. Tales of the sinking and salvage of battleships and cruisers.

Paris, Philip *Orkney's Italian Chapel, The True Story of an Icon* Black and White, 2013. Engaging, intensely human account of the Italian POWs who built the chapel.

Sarkar, Dilip *The Sinking of HMS Royal Oak* Amberley, 2012. Moving account of the great wartime tragedy, focussing on accounts of survivors.

Stell, Geoffrey *Orkney at War: Defending Scapa Flow* Orcadian Ltd, 2011. Detailed narrative (in two volumes) with previously unpublished material on how and why Orkney became a wartime fortress.

Van der Vat, Dan *The Grand Scuttle* Birlinn, 2016. The remarkable story of the scuttling of the German fleet in 1919.

Wood, Lawson *The Bull and The Barrier: The Wrecks of Scapa Flow* The History Press, 2000. Comprehensive and illustrated historical guide to the wrecks from both world wars.

Index

Page numbers in **bold** indicate the main entries; those in *italics* indicate maps.

INDEX OF ADVERTISERS